Applying Turbo Pascal® Library Units

Related Titles of Interest

Turbo Pascal® DOS Utilities, *Alonso*

Programming with Macintosh Turbo Pascal®, *Swan*

Turbo C® Survival Guide, *Miller and Quilici*

Advanced Turbo C® Programmer's Guide, *Mosich and Shammas*

Turbo C® DOS Utilities, *Alonso*

Turbo C® and Quick C® Functions: Building Bocks
  for Efficient Code, *Barden*

The Turbo Programmer's Reference: Language Essentials, *Weiskamp*

Quick C® DOS Utilities, *Alonso*

C Programming Reference. An Applied Perspective, *Miller and Quilici*

C Wizard's Programming Reference, *Schwaderer*

Introducing C to Pascal Programmers, *Shammas*

DOS Productivity Tips and Tricks, *Held*

Applying Turbo Pascal®
Library Units

NAMIR CLEMENT SHAMMAS

WILEY

John Wiley & Sons, Inc.
New York • Chichester • Brisbane • Toronto • Singapore

Publisher: Stephen Kippur
Editor: Therese A. Zak
Managing Editor: Andrew Hoffer
Electronic Book Production: Publishers Network, Morrisville, PA

This publication is designed to provide accurate and authoritative information in regard to the subject matter covered. It is sold with the understanding that the publisher is not engaged in rendering legal, accounting, or other professional service. If legal advice or other expert assistance is required, the services of a competent professional person should be sought. FROM A DECLARATION OF PRINCIPLES JOINTLY ADOPTED BY A COMMITTEE OF THE AMERICAN BAR ASSOCIATION AND A COMMITTEE OF PUBLISHERS.

Library of Congress Cataloging in Publication Data:

Shammas, Namir Clement, 1954-
    Applying Turbo Pascal library units / Namir Clement Shammas.
      p. cm.
    Bibliography: p.
    ISBN 0-471-60616-2 (pbk.)
    1. Pascal (Computer program language) 2. Turbo Pascal (Computer
program) I. Title.
QA76.73P2S5 1988
005.26—dc19

Printed in the United States of America
88 89 10 9 8 7 6 5 4 3 2 1

*To Bobbi,
my wife and best friend, with whom I share many dreams*

CONTENTS

I N T R O D U C T I O N

This book focuses on applying the Turbo Pascal library units to popular data structures and algorithms. The book is aimed at the average to advanced Turbo Pascal programmer in all disciplines. It demonstrates building interrelated software toolkits. It also presents a number of techniques in the areas of software documentation and mapping the use of various components of different libraries involved in a software application.

The library units presented serve two main purposes. First, they are used as study cases and for practicing program design techniques. Second, they provide readers with either templates or nuclei libraries for their own software toolboxes. These libraries can be modified and expanded to fit the readers' applications.

I suggest and promote a style for coding programs that enhances their documentation and their readability. Chapter 2 discusses these coding styles and how using a few simple rules achieves these purposes.

This book is made up mostly of independent chapters. You should read the first two chapters to familiarize yourself with the concept of library units and the general presentation style. Other than that, you can read the other chapters in any sequence that you prefer.

CHAPTER

1

Library Units in Turbo Pascal 4.0

The first three versions of Turbo Pascal enabled a software developer to write large programs by using the chain and overlay features. Small and medium Turbo Pascal programs were able to use included files for importing various data objects and routines developed separately. However, these methods lacked much of the data and routine hiding, since you may access all of the data types, variables, and routines in an included file or overlay.

The advent of Turbo Pascal 4.0 brought with it the library unit feature. The same feature was first available on microcomputers as the UCSD Pascal implementation for the Apple II computer. If you are already familiar with the UCSD Pascal library units, then it is easier for you to learn how the library feature works in Turbo Pascal 4.0. This book revolves around applying the library units to popular algorithms and data structures.

A library unit is a separate programming unit composed of two parts: the interface and the implementation sections. The interface section essentially declares the exported constants, data types, variables, and routines. Only the complete routine headings need to be declared. The implementation section declares the local constants (that is, those not exported), data types, and variables. It also contains the full listings for both the exported and local routines, and may embody an optional module initialization code. Since the exported data objects are declared in the interface section, they need not (and should not) be redeclared in the implementation section. As for the declaration of routines in the interface section, it has an effect somewhat similar to a FORWARD declaration. You have the choice of restating the complete routine heading (for better readability) in the implementation section or simply inserting the routine type and its name.

Figure 1.1 shows a general outline for a library unit. The open and close brackets indicate optional items in a library unit. The same figure shows how flexible a library unit can be. For example, you can create special library units that export nothing but constants, data types, and variables. Listing 1.1 shows

1

Figure 1.1. General outline of a library unit.

```
UNIT <name>;
INTERFACE
[Uses <list of library units used>]
[CONST <list of exported constants>]
[TYPE <list of exported types>]
[VAR <list of exported variables>]
[<sequence of exported routine headings>]
IMPLEMENTATION
[CONST <list of local constants>]
[TYPE <list of local types>]
[VAR <list of local variables>]
[<sequence of exported and local routine code>]
[BEGIN
  <statement for unit initialization>]
END.
```

---

the source code for just such a library, DATALIB0.DAT. This library unit is used by other libraries in the rest of the book, since it provides various string-based types. I highly recommend the use of such special libraries to export general data types and constants.

To use a library unit, you must first compile it. Items may be imported from a compiled library unit in another library or program by simply utilizing the USES <library unit name> declaration. The smart Turbo Pascal linker only extracts those library routines that are used by other libraries and/or the main program. This valuable feature of the linker prevents the emitted EXE files from being unnecessarily huge. The source code of a library unit is compiled into a file with a TPU name extension. The Turbo Pascal package contains a librarian utility that can move compiled TPU libraries in and out of bigger TPL files that contain multiple libraries.

In the previous paragraphs I have praised the power and features of the library units. To be objective, I will discuss some of their shortcomings and weaknesses. These shortcomings have their roots in the standard Pascal language itself. In Turbo Pascal 4.0, Borland implements a Pascal that is closer to the ANSI than its previous versions. Other Pascal vendors have chosen to deviate greatly from the essential language features, while still regarding (and marketing) their packages as superset Pascal implementations.

The first weakness of Pascal is that it does not formally support generic routines. Generic routines are available in Ada (an offshoot of Pascal) that provide formal routine templates. This means, for example, that you write a generic library in Ada to implement a few of your favorite sorting routines. By nature, generic routines do not require you to specify the exact genre of data sorted. That process is left up to the instantiation of the generic routine (that is, ordering the compiler to create a tailored version to accommodate a particular data type) which occurs in the client application programs. Thus, generic routines minimize the code versions of the same routine that is customized to tackle various data types. Unfortunately, Pascal (and Turbo Pascal) lacks the support for generic coding. This has a major influence on how we view and use Turbo Pascal library units. Many of the libraries that I present in other chapters are regarded as templates for you to customize. This is true for libraries that handle sorting, searching, stacks, lists, trees, and virtual arrays. The fact that the above operations and data structures need to work on, or with, your particular data types makes the lack of generic coding a need yet to be tackled. There are a number of programming tricks in Turbo Pascal that use untyped parameters to implement a limited version of generic coding. This is definitely a welcome method, but not a satisfying replacement for formal generic coding of library routines.

The second feature not available in Turbo Pascal units is the formal mechanism for exporting opaque data types (that is, data types whose detailed declarations are kept hidden from the client programs). This feature is available in Modula-2, the successor of Pascal. Its absence in Pascal has less of an impact than that of generic coding. In brief, opaque types enable the library author to limit their use by client programmers. The latter cannot write their own routines to further manipulate opaque types. This means that the library author must plan and develop such libraries with greater care and provide every routine needed to manipulate the opaque types. The library author can implement the opaque type again later on, using a more efficient structure and pass the update to the client programmers. Since the client programmers were not able to write their own tools for the opaque types, no time is wasted in reprogramming. Opaque types are very useful in large software projects involving teams of programmers. They minimize the domino effect of recoding and the consequent cost overrun and project delays.

LIBRARY COMNLIB0.PAS

Listing 1.2 shows the source code for a sample library, COMNLIB0.PAS. As the name suggests, this library contains a few frequently used general routines. Normally, you create a library with related data objects and routines. However, you invariably end up using at least one library that deviates from this; COMNLIB0.PAS is such a library. Your own versions are most likely to vary in contents depending on the type of routines you develop. You can employ this library as a nucleus for your own customized general-purpose repertoire.

The routines are as follows:

```
PROCEDURE Write_Blanks(Num_Blanks : INTEGER { input   });
```

writes a Num_Blanks of WRITELNs.

```
PROCEDURE Center(Message    : STRING80; { input }
                 Line       : INTEGER;  { input }
                 Underline  : BOOLEAN;  { input }
                 Blank_Lines : INTEGER  { input });
```

centers a message on the specified line. If the line argument is negative, the routine first clears the screen. Other options include the ability to underline the displayed message and to emit a number of carriage returns after displaying the message.

```
FUNCTION File_Exists(Filename : STRING80 { input }) : BOOLEAN;
```

verifies if a text file exists.

```
FUNCTION RealPower(Base,              { input }
                   Exponent : REAL  { input }) : REAL;
```

is a version of the power function where the base and exponent are REAL-typed.

```
FUNCTION IntPower87(Base     : EXTENDED; { input }
                    Exponent : INTEGER   { input }) : EXTENDED;
```

is a version of the power function that uses the 80x87 chip. The base and returned value are both EXTENDED, and the exponent is an INTEGER.

```
FUNCTION IntgrPower(Base     : REAL;   { input }
                    Exponent : INTEGER { input }) : REAL;
```

is a version of the power function with a REAL base and an INTEGER exponent.

```
FUNCTION Factorial(N : BYTE { input }) : REAL;
```

This function returns the factorial of its BYTE-typed argument. Using a BYTE type ensures that you can calculate the factorial for all arguments. If the BYTE type is replaced with WORD, for instance, then the coding of the function should check for the valid upper limit of the argument values.

```
FUNCTION IsLower(Ch : CHAR { input }) : BOOLEAN;
FUNCTION IsUpper(Ch : CHAR { input }) : BOOLEAN;
FUNCTION IsLetter(Ch : CHAR { input }) : BOOLEAN;
FUNCTION IsDigit(Ch : CHAR { input }) : BOOLEAN;
FUNCTION IsCtrl(Ch : CHAR { input }) : BOOLEAN;
FUNCTION IsAlphanum(Ch : CHAR { input }) : BOOLEAN;
FUNCTION IsPunct(Ch : CHAR { input }) : BOOLEAN;
```

The above set of functions test whether a character is a lower-case letter, an upper-case letter, a letter (either lower-case or upper-case), a digit, a control character, a digit or a letter, or a punctuation character. If the character does not fall into any of the above categories, it is an extended ASCII character.

Listing 1.1. Source code for the DATALIB0.PAS library unit that exports only constants and data types.

```
UNIT DataLib0;
{=========================================================================


           Copyright (c) 1987, 1988   Namir Clement Shammas
     LIBRARY NAME: DataLib0
     VERSION: 1.0                                    DATE 09/23/1987
     PURPOSE: Provides commonly used data types.


  ======================================================================}

{**************************************************************************}
{************************} INTERFACE {***********************************}
{**************************************************************************}

CONST MAX_STRING = 255;
      LINE_LONG = 80;
TYPE STRING255 = STRING[MAX_STRING];
     STRING128 = STRING[128];
     STRING90 = STRING[90];
     STRING80 = STRING[LINE_LONG];
     STRING64 = STRING[64];
     STRING40 = STRING[40];
     STRING20 = STRING[20];
     STRING10 = STRING[10];
     { complex number record type }
     Complex = RECORD
             Treal,
             Timag : REAL;
     END;

{**************************************************************************}
{***********************} IMPLEMENTATION {*****************************}
{**************************************************************************}

     { no code needed }
END.
```

Listing 1.2 Source code for the COMNLIB0.PAS.

```
UNIT ComnLib0;
{=================================================================

            Copyright (c) 1987, 1988   Namir Clement Shammas
        LIBRARY NAME: ComnLib0
        VERSION: 1.0                                DATE 8/30/1987
        PURPOSE: Library of commonly used miscellaneous routines.
        UPDATE HISTORY:


    =============================================================}

{*****************************************************************}
{**************************} INTERFACE {*************************}
{*****************************************************************}

Uses CRT, DOS, DataLib0;
PROCEDURE Write_Blanks(Num_Blanks : BYTE { input  });
{- - - - - - - - - - - - - - - - - - - - - - - - - - - - - - -
ROUTINE PURPOSE: issues a number of WRITELNs.
PARAMETERS:
  INPUT: Num_Blanks - the number of WRITELNs issues.
HANDLING BAD ARGUMENTS: if the number of blanks is zero, no
carriage returns are issued. If the number of blanks exceeds
25, a ClrScr is issued instead.

                        ROUTINE DEPENDENCIES
                        --------------------


        Identifier Name          Identifier Type      Source Library
        ---------------          ---------------      ---------------

            ClrScr                  procedure             CRT

- - - - - - - - - - - - - - - - - - - - - - - - - - - - - - - }
PROCEDURE Center(Message    : STRING80; { input  }
                 Line       : INTEGER;  { input  }
                 Underline  : BOOLEAN;  { input  }
                 Blank_Lines : BYTE     { input  });
{- - - - - - - - - - - - - - - - - - - - - - - - - - - - - -

ROUTINE PURPOSE: displays a centered message. Options include
specifying the line where the message appears, clearing the
screen underlining the message, and issuing a number of blank
lines after the message.
PARAMETERS:
  INPUT: Message - the displayed heading.
         Line - the specified line number. If it is negative
            the screen is first cleared.
```

Under_Line - the boolean used to flag the need to underline
the heading.
Blank_Lines - the number of blank lines to follow the
heading.
HANDLING BAD ARGUMENTS: if the heading is a null string, the routine
exits without performing any task. If the line number is zero, the
program assigns a one to it.

ROUTINE DEPENDENCIES

Identifier Name	Identifier Type	Source Library
ClrScr	procedure	CRT
GotoXY	procedure	CRT
STRING80	string	DataLib0
Write_Blanks	procedure	local

- }
FUNCTION File_Exists(Filename : STRING80 { input }) : BOOLEAN;
{- -

ROUTINE PURPOSE: verifies if a text file exists.
PARAMETERS:
  INPUT: Filename - the name of the file checked for existence.
FUNCTION VALUE: if the file exists, a TRUE value is returned, else
a FALSE value is emitted.

ROUTINE DEPENDENCIES

Identifier Name	Identifier Type	Source Library
STRING80	string	DataLib0

- }
FUNCTION RealPower(Base,   { input }
            Exponent : REAL { input }) : REAL;
{- -

ROUTINE PURPOSE: implements a power function in Pascal for
real-typed arguments.
PARAMETERS:
  INPUT: Base - the base number.
         Exponent - the power to which the base number is raised.
FUNCTION VALUE: returns Base^Exponent.
HANDLING BAD ARGUMENTS: if the base is zero or negative, a zero is
returned by this function.

- }

```
FUNCTION IntPower87(Base     : EXTENDED; { input  }
                    Exponent : INTEGER   { input  }) : EXTENDED;
{- - - - - - - - - - - - - - - - - - - - - - - - - - - - - - -
```

ROUTINE PURPOSE: implements a power function in Pascal for
a real-typed base and an integer-typed exponent. This is the
version that works faster when an 80x87 chip is used.
PARAMETERS:
   INPUT: Base - the base number.
          Exponent - the power to which the base number is raised.
FUNCTION VALUE: returns Base^Exponent.
HANDLING BAD ARGUMENTS: if the base is zero or negative, a zero is
returned by this function.

```
- - - - - - - - - - - - - - - - - - - - - - - - - - - - - - - }
FUNCTION IntgrPower(Base     : REAL;    { input  }
                    Exponent : INTEGER { input  }) : REAL;
{- - - - - - - - - - - - - - - - - - - - - - - - - - - - - - -
```

ROUTINE PURPOSE: implements a power function in Pascal for
a real-typed base and an integer-typed exponent. This is the
version that works faster when an 80x87 chip is NOT used.
PARAMETERS:
   INPUT: Base - the base number.
          Exponent - the power to which the base number is raised.
FUNCTION VALUE: returns Base^Exponent.
HANDLING BAD ARGUMENTS: if the base is zero or negative, a zero is
returned by this function.

```
- - - - - - - - - - - - - - - - - - - - - - - - - - - - - - }
FUNCTION Factorial(N : BYTE { input  }) : REAL;
{- - - - - - - - - - - - - - - - - - - - - - - - - - - - - - -
```

ROUTINE PURPOSE: calculates a factorial.
PARAMETERS:
   INPUT: N - the number whose factorial is sought.
FUNCTION VALUE: function returns the factorial number of the
argument.

```
- - - - - - - - - - - - - - - - - - - - - - - - - - - - - - - }
FUNCTION IsLower(Ch : CHAR { input  }) : BOOLEAN;
{- - - - - - - - - - - - - - - - - - - - - - - - - - - - - - -
```

ROUTINE PURPOSE: verifies if a given character is a lower-case letter.
PARAMETERS:
   INPUT: Ch - the tested character.
FUNCTION VALUE: returns TRUE if the argument is a lower-case letter,
otherwise returns FALSE.

```
- - - - - - - - - - - - - - - - - - - - - - - - - - - - - - - }
```

```
FUNCTION IsUpper(Ch : CHAR { input  }) : BOOLEAN;
{- - - - - - - - - - - - - - - - - - - - - - - - - - - - - - - -

ROUTINE PURPOSE: verifies if a given character is a upper-case letter.
PARAMETERS:
   INPUT: Ch - the tested character.
FUNCTION VALUE: returns TRUE if the argument is a upper-case letter,
otherwise returns FALSE.


- - - - - - - - - - - - - - - - - - - - - - - - - - - - - - - - }
FUNCTION IsLetter(Ch : CHAR { input  }) : BOOLEAN;
{- - - - - - - - - - - - - - - - - - - - - - - - - - - - - - - -

ROUTINE PURPOSE: verifies if a given character is a letter.
PARAMETERS:
   INPUT: Ch - the tested character.
FUNCTION VALUE: returns TRUE if the argument is a letter,
otherwise returns FALSE.


- - - - - - - - - - - - - - - - - - - - - - - - - - - - - - - - }
FUNCTION IsDigit(Ch : CHAR { input  }) : BOOLEAN;
{- - - - - - - - - - - - - - - - - - - - - - - - - - - - - - - -

ROUTINE PURPOSE: verifies if a given character is a digit (0 to 9).
PARAMETERS:
   INPUT: Ch - the tested character.
FUNCTION VALUE: returns TRUE if the argument is a digit,
otherwise returns FALSE.


- - - - - - - - - - - - - - - - - - - - - - - - - - - - - - - - }
FUNCTION IsCtrl(Ch : CHAR { input  }) : BOOLEAN;
{- - - - - - - - - - - - - - - - - - - - - - - - - - - - - - - -

ROUTINE PURPOSE: verifies if a given character is a control
character (ASCII range of 0 to 27).
PARAMETERS:
   INPUT: Ch - the tested character.
FUNCTION VALUE: returns TRUE if the argument is a control character,
otherwise returns FALSE.


- - - - - - - - - - - - - - - - - - - - - - - - - - - - - - - - }
FUNCTION IsAlphanum(Ch : CHAR { input  }) : BOOLEAN;
{- - - - - - - - - - - - - - - - - - - - - - - - - - - - - - - -

ROUTINE PURPOSE: verifies if a given character is either a letter
or a digit.
PARAMETERS:
   INPUT: Ch - the tested character.
FUNCTION VALUE: returns TRUE if the argument is alphanumeric,
otherwise returns FALSE.
```

```
- - - - - - - - - - - - - - - - - - - - - - - - - - - - - - - - - }
FUNCTION IsPunct(Ch : CHAR { input  }) : BOOLEAN;
{- - - - - - - - - - - - - - - - - - - - - - - - - - - - - - - - -

ROUTINE PURPOSE: verifies if a given character is a punctuation
character.
PARAMETERS:
   INPUT: Ch - the tested character.
FUNCTION VALUE: returns TRUE if the argument is a punctuation
character, otherwise returns FALSE.

- - - - - - - - - - - - - - - - - - - - - - - - - - - - - - - - - }


{*********************************************************************}
{***********************} IMPLEMENTATION {***************************}
{*********************************************************************}

{------------------------ Write_Blanks ------}

PROCEDURE Write_Blanks(Num_Blanks : BYTE { input  });
BEGIN
    IF Num_Blanks > 25 THEN BEGIN
        ClrScr;
        EXIT
    END; { IF }
    WHILE Num_Blanks > 0 DO BEGIN
        WRITELN;
        DEC(Num_Blanks)
    END; { WHILE }
END; { Write_Blanks }

{----------------------------------------------------------- Center ------}

PROCEDURE Center(Message     : STRING80; { input  }
                 Line        : INTEGER;  { input  }
                 Underline   : BOOLEAN;  { input  }
                 Blank_Lines : BYTE      { input  });
VAR i, xoffset : BYTE;
BEGIN
    IF Message = '' THEN EXIT;
    IF Line <= 0 THEN BEGIN
        ClrScr;
        Line := ABS(Line);
        IF Line = 0 THEN Line := 1;
    END; { IF }
    xoffset := 40 - Length(Message) div 2;
    GotoXY(xoffset,Line);
    WRITE(Message);
    IF Underline THEN BEGIN
        GotoXY(xoffset,Line+1);
        FOR i := 1 TO Length(Message) DO
            WRITE('_');
```

```
          WRITELN;
       END;
       IF Blank_Lines > 0 THEN Write_Blanks(Blank_Lines);
    END; { Center }

    {----------------------------------------------------- File_Exists ----}
    FUNCTION File_Exists(Filename : STRING80 { input  }) : BOOLEAN;
    VAR filevar : TEXT;
        ok : BOOLEAN;
    BEGIN
        Assign(filevar, Filename);
        {$I-} Reset(filevar); {$I+}
        ok := (IOResult = 0);
        IF ok THEN Close(filevar);
        File_Exists := ok;
    END; { File_Exists }

    {----------------------------------------------------------- RealPower ----}

    FUNCTION RealPower(Base,              { input  }
                    Exponent : REAL  { input  }) : REAL;
    BEGIN
        IF Base > 0.0 THEN
            RealPower := Exp(Exponent * Ln(Base))
        ELSE
            RealPower := 0.0;
    END; { RealPower }

    {----------------------------------------------------- IntPower87 ----}

    FUNCTION IntPower87(Base     : EXTENDED; { input  }
                    Exponent : INTEGER   { input  }) : EXTENDED;
    BEGIN
        IF Base > 0.0 THEN
            IntPower87 := Exp(Exponent * Ln(Base))
        ELSE
            IntPower87 := 0.0;
    END; { IntPower87 }

    {----------------------------------------------------- IntgrPower ----}

    FUNCTION IntgrPower(Base     : REAL;    { input  }
                    Exponent : INTEGER  { input  }) : REAL;
    VAR prod : REAL;
        j, two_j : INTEGER;
    BEGIN
        IF Base > 0.0 THEN BEGIN
            j := 1;
            two_j := 2;
            prod := Base;
            WHILE two_j <= Exponent DO BEGIN
                j := two_j;
                two_j := 2 * two_j;
```

```
            prod := prod * prod;
        END;
        IF j < Exponent THEN
            WHILE j < Exponent DO BEGIN
                INC(j);
                prod := prod * Base;
            END;
        IntgrPower := prod;
    END
    ELSE
        IntgrPower := 0.0;
END;


{------------------------------------------------------ Factorial ------}

FUNCTION Factorial(N : BYTE { input  }) : REAL;
VAR product : REAL;
BEGIN
    product := 1.0;
    WHILE N > 1 DO BEGIN
        product := product * N;
        DEC(N)
    END; { WHILE }
    Factorial := product { return function result }
END; { Factorial }


{------------------------------------------------------ IsLower ------}

FUNCTION IsLower(Ch : CHAR { input  }) : BOOLEAN;
BEGIN
    IsLower := (Ch >= 'a') AND (Ch <= 'z')
END; { IsLower }


{------------------------------------------------------ IsUpper ------}

FUNCTION IsUpper(Ch : CHAR { input  }) : BOOLEAN;
BEGIN
    IsUpper := (Ch >= 'A') AND (Ch <= 'Z')
END; { IsUpper }


{------------------------------------------------------ IsLetter ------}

FUNCTION IsLetter(Ch : CHAR { input  }) : BOOLEAN;
BEGIN
    IsLetter := (Ch >= 'A') AND (Ch <= 'z')
```

```
END; { IsLetter }

{--------------------------------------------------------------- IsDigit ----}

FUNCTION IsDigit(Ch : CHAR { input }) : BOOLEAN;
BEGIN
    IsDigit := (Ch >= '0') AND (Ch <= '9')
END; { IsDigit }

{----------------------------------------------------------------- IsCtrl ----}

FUNCTION IsCtrl(Ch : CHAR { input }) : BOOLEAN;
BEGIN
    IsCtrl := (Ch >= CHR(0)) AND (Ch <= CHR(27))
END; { IsCtrl }

{------------------------------------------------------------ IsAlphanum ----}

FUNCTION IsAlphanum(Ch : CHAR { input }) : BOOLEAN;
BEGIN
    IsAlphanum := Ch IN ['0'..'9','A'..'z']
END; { IsAlphanum }

{-------------------------------------------------------------- IsPunct ----}

FUNCTION IsPunct(Ch : CHAR { input }) : BOOLEAN;
BEGIN
    IsPunct := (NOT IsAlphanum(Ch)) AND (NOT IsCtrl(Ch))
              AND (Ch < CHR(127))
END; { IsPunct }
END.
```

CHAPTER

2

Program Design and Documentation Techniques

Program design has evolved and matured in the past few decades. The principles of program design had been concerned mostly with programming large projects on very expensive mainframes and minicomputers. The evolution of program design has been driven by the need to meet deadlines for large projects tackled by teams of programmers. The interactions among the programmer team resulted in many problems related to updates and alterations. These were carried out by a particular team and caused a domino-effect of revisions by other teams. This gave more support to increasingly modular programming techniques. In addition, it caused the advent of highly modular languages spawned from Pascal, such as Ada and Modula-2.

Practicing sound program design is not monopolized by any particular language. For example, there is nothing to prevent you from writing good programs in BASIC, Pascal, and C. It is true that you may be limited or influenced by the features of the language or implementation, but that is a relative point. By contrast, you can also write bad BASIC, Pascal, and C programs, a temptation that most of us fall into.

In the rest of this chapter I will focus on some methods in Pascal that can enhance the code layout and documentation.

DEVELOPING LIBRARY UNITS

There are two main and interrelated guidelines that you should employ in planning and writing software building blocks using library units. The first is divide-and-conquer, and the other is extendibility.

Applying the first guideline means that you resist the temptation of lumping various data objects (that is, constants, data types, and variables) and routines in a few library units. In the previous chapter, I presented the libraries DATALIB0.PAS. This very small library has its distinct task to perform, and its contents are not swallowed or scattered within other

14

libraries. Also, notice that I am including the number zero with the name. This enables me to create other versions of data-exporting that suit future projects. The COMNLIB0.PAS library unit is another case, though somewhat special. While its routines are not so closely related as the one presented in the next chapters, the library as a whole still serves a purpose: to be the repertoire for general routines.

The proliferation of library units is accompanied by a number of rules to watch. They are as follows:

1. Avoid very general identifier names. For example, constants declared to size an array type in a sorting library should be **MAX_SIZE_SORT_ARRAY**, as opposed to **MAX_SIZE** or **MAX_ARRAY**. Likewise, avoid declaring two-dimensional matrices using **Matrix** as the identifier name. The name neither indicates the basic type associated with it, nor gives any idea of the matrix size. Rather, if you are declaring what you consider a small REAL-typed matrix, use **Small_Real_Matrix**. Make the identifier name indicative of the main parameters that affect the data structure you declare.

2. Avoid multiple copies of the same routine in different libraries. Instead, import these routines from one library. This pays off extremely well when you update the routine, since you tackle one version only. The update is effective once you recompile the libraries.

3. Minimize multiple copies of similar routines, especially those scattered in different libraries. Collect the similar routines in the same library to facilitate the update process, ensuring that all of the similar routines have been updated.

4. Avoid nested routines as much as possible. While the idea of deeply nested functions and procedures may be appealing, the overhead during runtime influences the programs' speed. Pascal programmers should learn from their C programming cousins to make all routines at the same level (in C you cannot write nested routines).

SOURCE CODE DOCUMENTATION STYLE

It is important to plan strategically the division of your reusable data objects and routines among several libraries. Moreover, you should pay close attention to the source code documentation style. Since Pascal is a case-insensitive language, there is a wide variation on writing reserved keywords, intrinsics, and user-defined identifiers. By applying a few rules, you can enhance the readability of your source code. I suggest the following coding rules that I also use in this book. Some of them are widely used, while others are my own additions:

1. Constants are written in upper-case letters and may use the underscore character.

2.   The names of global variables, exported routines, and the arguments in routines have the first letter in upper case. The remaining characters are written in lower case and upper case depending on the number of words forming the identifier. For example, **Interest, LowCost, FirstLocation,** and **Last_Array_Member** are identifier names that are in this category.

3.   The names of local variables, and both nested and unexported routines, are in lower case. Thus, **get_cursor, strlen,** and **char_pos** are identifiers in this category.

Using the above letter cases enables you to identify better the type of variable or routine. Concerning the names of the standard data types and keywords, I will be using them in upper case.

Another style rule for declaring procedures or functions is to arrange their parameters as follows:

1.   Each parameter is placed on a separate line.

2.   The VAR keywords associated with the parameters are aligned in one column.

3.   The first letter of the parameters' names are aligned in one column.

4.   The colons are aligned in one column.

5.   The first letter of the parameters' types are aligned in one column.

6.   Each parameter has a comment that indicates the data flow direction using { input } for input only, { output } for output only, and { in/out } for data I/O. These comments indicate the actual data flow. In Pascal the VAR declaration passes a parameter by reference, but it is not known whether the parameter will bring in data to be altered or will simply return data. Moreover, it is recommended that array-typed parameters should be passed by reference even if they only supply data to the routine. This minimizes stack space requirement but adds more confusion to the motive behind using the VAR declaration. Using the comments to indicate the data flow, you state exactly the intent of using the VAR.

An example for applying the above rules is the following procedure declaration:

```
PROCEDURE Sort_Array (VAR Data : StringArray; Size : WORD;
                 FirstChar, LastChar : BYTE;
                 Ascending : BOOLEAN; VAR OK : BOOLEAN);
```

is to rewrite it as shown below:

```
PROCEDURE Sort_Array    (VAR Data    : StringArray; { in/out }
                         Size        : WORD         { input }
                         FirstChar,                 { input }
                         LastChar    : BYTE;        { input }
                         Ascending   : BOOLEAN;     { input }
                         VAR OK      : BOOLEAN       { output });
```

Notice the difference in readability! The above fictitious routine sorts an array of strings. Thus, the **Data** parameter is passed by reference using the VAR declaration. Since the array brings in unordered data and returns them sorted, I put an {in/out} comment to indicate the flow of information. The **Size** parameter is an input parameter that specifies the actual number of elements to be sorted (in the common case of a partially filled array). The **FirstChar** and **LastChar** parameters indicate the portion of each string used in the sorting. Notice that the two parameters are placed on separate lines with the {input} comment after each. Another input parameter is the boolean **Ascending** which specifies the sort order. The last parameter is **OK** that is passed back to the calling routine. It informs the caller of the status of the sort. The accompanying {output} comment indicates the exact data flow direction.

To complement the style rule for declaring a routine, I also use and recommend organized comments to follow the routine's declaration. We often see routines in books and magazines that are followed by simple comments. I suggest the following form, applied to the above procedure declaration:

```
PROCEDURE Sort_Array   (VAR Data    : StringArray;  { in/out }
                        Size        : WORD;         { input }
                        FirstChar,                  { input }
                        LastChar    : BYTE;         { input }
                        Ascending   : BOOLEAN;      { input }
                        VAR OK      : BOOLEAN       { output });
{- - - - - - - - - - - - - - - - - - - - - - - - - - - - - - -
ROUTINE PURPOSE: sorts an array of strings in either ascending or
descending order, using the Shell-Metzner method.
PARAMETERS:
  INPUT: Size - the actual number of array elements.
         FirstChar - the first string character location used in
             the sorting comparisons.
         LastChar - the last string character location used in
             the sorting comparisons.
         Ascending - specifies the sort order.
  OUTPUT: OK - the boolean flag to signal that sorting occurred
             without any errors.
  IN/OUT: Data - the array of strings to be sorted.
FUNCTION VALUE: <none>.
HANDLING BAD ARGUMENTS: the routine exits (and assigns FALSE to
parameter OK) when:
1) The number of elements is less than two.
2) The parameters FirstChar and LastChar supply bad values.
COMMENTS: <none>
                       ROUTINE DEPENDENCIES
                       --------------------

     Identifier Name        Identifier Type      Source Library
     ---------------        ---------------      --------------

       CompareStr              function             Strings
       SwapString              procedure            Strings
- - - - - - - - - - - - - - - - - - - - - - - - - - - - - - - }
```

The above comment form documents various aspects of the declared procedure. This also includes error handling and routine dependencies. I feel the latter is very important in listing the other routines on which the fictitious procedure **Sort-Array** depends. This kind of information is vital in transplanting the above procedure into another library. The information mentioned also helps in debugging. The style I follow in the routine dependencies is to mention all imported data objects and routines, as well as local routines. Local data types are not mentioned, but that should not stop you from developing your own documentation style to handle local identifiers.

THE SOFTWARE BUS SCHEDULE TABLE

With the above documentation style and the routine dependencies mentioned, one may go another step. Consider the case where you have written a program and would like to document the interconnectivity between the main program and the libraries it uses. Figure 2.1 shows the basic form for the software bus schedule. This was inspired by Dr. Richard Wiener, who used the software bus diagrams to document interconnected calls in Modula-2 libraries. The software bus schedule is a modified text-based mapping of the interlibrary connection. Software bus lines are optionally named using single letters. The bus lines outline the library output, interface input, and implementation input. The latter indicates the items imported for the sole use of the implementation section. The items listed in the software bus should be sorted for easy retrieval.

Figure 2.2 shows an example for using the software bus schedule in a fictitious application BUSICALL.PAS. Three libraries are involved in the project. They are CRT.PAS, DATALIB0.PAS, XMODEM.PAS. The first two libraries only export data objects and routines. The third library, XMODEM.PAS, imports and exports items on the software bus lines. It imports various string types for both the interface and implementation sections and exports communication-related items. The main program (also dubbed MODULE main) shows the software bus lines it taps into and the imported items. This example gives you an idea of the scope and level of interaction between the various library units. The software bus schedule form is used to accompany the documentation of application programs in this book.

Figure 2.1. Basic form for the Software Bus Schedule.

```
                      SOFTWARE BUS SCHEDULE
PROJECT: <project name>
MODULE  <module name>
                                  Software Bus Schedule
                   A   B   C   D   E   F   G   H   I   J   K   L   M
OUTPUT
INTERFACE INPUT
IMPLEMENTATION INPUT
```

Figure 2.2.   Example for using the Software Bus Schedule.

```
                       SOFTWARE BUS SCHEDULE
PROJECT: BUSICALL.PAS
MODULE  CRT
                               Software Bus Schedule
               A  B  C  D  E  F  G  H  I  J  K  L  M
OUTPUT
proc ClrEol    X
proc ClrScr    X
proc GotoXY    X
func ReadKey   X
MODULE DataLib0
                               Software Bus Schedule
               A  B  C  D  E  F  G  H  I  J  K  L  M
OUTPUT
string STRING20      X
string STRING40      X
string STRING60      X
string STRING80      X
MODULE XModem


                               Software Bus Schedule
               A  B  C  D  E  F  G  H  I  J  K  L  M
OUTPUT
var Baud          X
proc GetBlock     X
proc InitSend     X
proc InitGet      X
var Parity        X
proc SendBlock    X
var StopBit       X
proc StopGet      X
proc StopSend     X
INTERFACE INPUT
string STRING20      X
string STRING80      X
IMPLEMENTATION INPUT
string STRING40      X
string STRING60      X
MODULE main
```

				Software Bus Schedule								
	A	B	C	D	E	F	G	H	I	J	K	L	M
INPUT													
var Baud				X									
proc ClrEol	X												
proc ClrScr	X												
proc GetBlock				X									
proc GotoXY	X												
proc InitSend				X									
proc InitGet				X									
var Parity				X									
func ReadKey	X												
proc SendBlock				X									
var StopBit				X									
proc StopGet				X									
proc StopSend				X									
string STRING80			X										

DOCUMENTING COMPILED FILES

The source code of a Turbo Pascal library unit contains both the interface and implementation parts. While the interface part is required by the client programmer, the implementation part is the more private part of your code. Therefore, if you plan to distribute your libraries in compiled form, I suggest that you manually store the interface part in a separate file, using, say, DEF extension names. It is interesting to note that Modula-2 libraries (also known as modules) require that the interface (called definition module) be stored in a file separate from the implementation module. Third-party libraries in Modula-2 come with the source code definition module and the compiled implementation module.

3

Basic Console I/O

This chapter looks at various libraries that provide you with basic console input/output tools. They include the following:

1. Library PCSCREEN.PAS that exports data structures and routines enabling you to access the address of the physical screen. The library also imports routines that enable you to store, recall, and swap screen pages in a Color Graphics Adapter video.

2. Library EDITLINE.PAS that exports a single routine to implement a one-line editor.

3. Library NUMINPUT.PAS that provides routines for error-proof and controlled numeric input.

4. Library SCREEN0.PAS that offers routines for fast output of basic types with display attribute control. The routines in this library write directly to the video screen.

5. Library SCREEN1.PAS is similar to SCREEN0.PAS, but uses the new features of Turbo Pascal 4.0 that enables you to write to the screen without explicitly addressing the video screen addresses.

BASIC SCREEN MANAGEMENT

Building a software toolbox for screen management and I/O involves a number of library units that access the screen directly. The first three versions of Turbo Pascal implemented **WRITELN** and **WRITE,** which use the slow (but safe) BIOS calls. Programmers using these earlier versions invariably resorted to direct access to the screen memory in order to develop programs that flashed text on the screen. I will call this technique the **explicit video access method.** Turbo Pascal 4.0 offers the programmer a much needed way out of the above dilemma, using the boolean variable **DirectVideo** exported by the **CRT** library unit. When **DirectVideo** is set to TRUE by a program, the **WRITE** and **WRITELN** statements write directly to the screen. I will name this second method the **implicit video access method.** Conversely, when the variable **DirectVideo** is set to FALSE, the slower BIOS routines are used for screen output. This important improvement probably serves both the novice and average programmers, who shy away from writing routines that directly access the screen. Nevertheless, I will present Turbo Pascal routines that use both **explicit** and **implicit** methods.

The essential ingredients in tackling explicit direct video access are the following:

1. Defining the data structures that represent the screen

2. Assigning memory addresses to the above structures

The above points state that we first design a **template** data structure before mapping it to a hardware address. It is worthwhile to mention that we can also use the data structure with variables in the RAM memory. This enables us to create, store, and retrieve memory-based screen images (or screen image, for short).

The data structures that are used in the PCSCREEN.PAS library are as follows:

1. A basic record that contains the displayed character and its attribute, as shown:

```
CharRec = RECORD
          Kar,            { displayed character }
          Attr : CHAR; { display attribute }
          END;
```

2. A matrix of screen rows and columns. The basic element of the matrix is the **CharRec** record:

```
TextScreenMatrix = ARRAY [1..MAX_ROW,1..MAX_COL] OF CharRec;
```

3. A text screen record that contains one field, namely, the matrix of screen characters. The choice for using a record structure is related to Pascal's ability to assign one record to another (of the same type). This assignment enables screen images to be easily copied.

```
TextScreen = RECORD
             Scr : TextScreenMatrix;
             END;
```

4. A pointer to the screen record. The pointer is a data handle that is assigned the physical screen address, making it possible to write the characters directly to the video.

```
Screen_Ptr = ^TextScreen;
```

Table 3.1. Addresses for screens with 80 columns and 25 rows.

Video Mode Number	Display Type	Address	Page number
7	Monochrome	$B000:$0000	N/A
2 or 3	Color	$B800:$0000	0 (CGA)
2 or 3	Color	$B800:$1000	1 (CGA)
2 or 3	Color	$B800:$2000	2 (CGA)
2 or 3	Color	$B800:$3000	3 (CGA)

Table 3.1 shows the screen addresses for the monochrome and the Color/ Graphics Adapter (CGA). Note that the CGA supports four 80x25 text screen pages, numbered zero through three. The CGA page addresses have the same segment value $B800 and an offset value calculated using the simple formula:

```
Offset address = page_number * $1000
```

The set of data types presented above are by no means the unique combination of structures that are used in accessing the screen. Another alternative is as follows:

```
TextScreenMatrix2 = ARRAY [1..MAX_ROW,1..MAX_COL,1..2] OF Char;
VAR
  MonoScreen  = TextScreenMatrix2 absolute $B000:$0000;
  ColorScreen = TextScreenMatrix2 absolute $B800:$0000;
```

Notice that the **TextScreenMatrix2** is a three-dimensional matrix. The third dimension stores the values for the character (at index 1) and its display attribute (at index 2). The memory layout of the third dimension is identical to that of **TextScreenMatrix** and the **CharRec** record presented. This shorter form might be tempting to employ. However, it is more awkward to manipulate a character and its attribute and requires nested loops to copy screen images. The two declared variables illustrate a popular method of defining **absolute** variables that are mapped onto the physical screen. This approach suffers from having to duplicate the screen output code: one for the monochrome screen and one for the color screen. Using a pointer to the screen is a better alternative, since we can simply assign an address to the pointer, using the **Ptr()** function, and avoid having to code two versions of the screen output statements.

Using a hierarchy of data types to arrive at the data type representing the screen enables us to easily manipulate the structure at various levels

The PCSCREEN.PAS library, shown in listing (3.1), unit performs the following types of tasks:

1. Displays text directly to the video screen and screen images.
2. Saves, restores, and clears the video screen and screen images.

3. Moves screen images (or parts of screen images). This may involve the physical screen and a screen image, or two screen images.

4. Copies and swaps CGA display pages.

The list of PCSCREEN library routines is as follows:

```
PROCEDURE DisplayString(VAR Screen : TextScreen;  { in/out }
                            Row    : RowRange;     { input  }
                            Col    : ColRange;     { input  }
                            Strng  : STRING80;     { input  }
                            Mode   : CHAR          { input  });
```

places a string at the given screen coordinates and uses the specified attributes. The output screen may be the physical screen or a screen image. A program may gradually and intermittently write to different screen images and select any one to display when appropriate.

```
PROCEDURE ClrScrn(VAR Screen : TextScreen { in/out };
                      Attrib : CHAR         { input  });
```

clears a screen using a specified attribute. This routine is primarily designed to clear screen images, but can also be used to clear the video using a special color.

```
PROCEDURE MoveScr(VAR SourceScrn,                    { in/out }
                      TargetScrn : TextScreen;       { in/out }
                      FirstRow,                       { input  }
                      LastRow    : RowRange;          { input  }
                      FirstCol,                       { input  }
                      LastCol    : ColRange;          { input  }
                      SaveFlag   : BOOLEAN            { input  });
```

moves all or parts of a screen. The source and target screens may be either the physical video or screen image. The copied portion of a screen is pasted on the parallel location of the target screen.

```
PROCEDURE Copy_CGA_Screen_Pages(Source_Page,          { input  }
                                Target_Page : BYTE  { input  });
```

copies one of the four screen pages of the CGA to another.

```
PROCEDURE Store_CGA_Screen_Pages(
                CGA_Page   : BYTE;        { input  }
                Mem_Screen : TextScreen { output });
```

stores one of the four screen pages of the CGA to memory.

```
PROCEDURE Recall_CGA_Screen_Pages(
                CGA_Page   : BYTE;        { input  }
                Mem_Screen : TextScreen { output });
```

pecalls one of the four screen pages of the CGA from memory.

```
PROCEDURE Swap_CGA_Screen_Pages(Page1,        { input  }
                            Page2  : BYTE { input  });
```

swaps two of the four screen pages of the CGA, using the memory for a temporary buffer.

```
PROCEDURE Swap_CGA_Screen_Pages2(Page1,            { input  }
                            Page2,                  { input  }
                            Buffer_Page : BYTE { input  });
```

swaps two of the four screen pages of the CGA, using a third CGA screen page as a temporary buffer.

Using the additional CGA screen pages enables you to move quickly among several screens. This is very advantageous when writing software that frequently swaps screens to provide on-line help.

THE EXPLICIT VIDEO ACCESS METHOD

I will present two versions of a library unit for screen output routines. Both versions provide you with routines to output strings, characters, 2-byte integers, and REAL-typed data. In each library, the routines come in two flavors: one that enables you to specify the display attribute, while the other uses the current attribute values. Since Turbo Pascal supports a number of derived types for integer and floating-point numbers, you may easily expand on the number of routines to cover all of these numeric data types. Using your text editor, you copy and paste the routines you want, and then modify the identifiers for the data types.

The first library version, SCREEN0.PAS (see Listing 3.2), employs the method of directly writing to the physical screen. Data structures from the general-purpose library, DATALIB0.PAS, and the PCSCREEN.PAS library unit are imported. The PCSCREEN.PAS library provides the pointer-type **Screen_Ptr** for the screen data structure. Each routine defines the local variable **video_ptr** that has the type **Screen_Ptr**. The address of the screen is supplied to the **video_ptr** using the predefined **Ptr()** function. The address depends on the type of display. This information is obtained by peeking at memory location $0040:$0049 using a local variable (call it **mode**) in one of several ways:

1. Declaring **mode** as a byte-typed absolute variable with the address $0040:$0049, as is the case in the library code. Using this method you simply read the value of **mode**. Keep in mind that you should never assign a value to the variable **mode** VAR mode : BYTE absolute $0040:$0049;

2. Declaring **mode** as a byte-typed variable and assign it the value of the memory location in question. The predefined **Mem[]** array is used, as shown below:

```
VAR mode : BYTE;


BEGIN
    mode := Mem[$0040:$0049];
```

3. Declaring **mode** as a pointer to a byte and assigning it the value of the memory location in question. The predefined **Ptr()** function is used, as shown below:

```
VAR mode : ^BYTE;


BEGIN
    mode^ := Ptr($0040,$0049);
```

Once the numeric code for the display type is available, a simple IF statement is employed to assign the physical screen address to the **video_ptr** pointer, as shown below:

```
IF mode IN [2..3] THEN
    video_ptr := Ptr($B800,$0000)
ELSE IF mode = 7 THEN
    video_ptr := Ptr($B000,$0000)
ELSE EXIT;
```

The above code fragment shows that when the numeric code for the display mode is 2 or 3, a color display with 80 columns and 25 rows is available. When the same code is 7, the display is monochrome with 80 columns and 25 rows. Table 3.2 shows the numeric codes for the display attributes.

It is worth pointing out that since the video pointers are mapped to existing hardware addresses, we do not need to use the **NEW()** used in allocating dynamic memory to pointers.

Accessing the elements of the physical screen is performed through using two levels of field references associated with the **TextScreen** record structure.

Table 3.2. Numeric code for display attributes.

Numeric code for display attribute	Display type
0	Black
1	Blue
2	Green
3	Cyan
4	Red
5	Magenta
6	Brown
7	Light Gray
8	Dark Gray
9	Light Blue
10	Light Green
11	Light Cyan
12	Light Red
13	Light Magenta
14	Yellow
15	White
128	Blinking

The SCREEN0.PAS library also exports enumerated data types and related routines that manage and calculate the display attributes. The library has three enumerated data types to tackle the character attributes for a color display. These attributes are used to specify the foreground and background colors, as well as whether or not the characters are displayed blinking. Concerning the monochrome display, one enumerated data type adequately handles the various attribute options. The SCREEN0.PAS library contains two functions that return the display attribute value as a byte-typed result. The arguments for these functions are of the enumerated type. Using English words as the enumerated values is much better than numeric codes that are easily forgotten by the casual library user.

The SCREEN0.PAS library performs the following general tasks:

1. Writes strings, characters, integers, and reals directly to the screen
2. Calculates the display attributes for the color and monochrome displays

The list of library routines is as follows:

```
PROCEDURE Disp_Str(Strng : STRING80; { input  }
                   Row,             { input  }
                   Col   : INTEGER   { input  });
```

displays a string at a specified screen coordinate.

```
PROCEDURE Disp_Chr(Ch  : CHAR;      { input  }
                   Row,             { input  }
                   Col : INTEGER { input  });
```

displays a single character at a specified screen coordinate.

```
PROCEDURE Disp_Real(X      : REAL;    { input  }
                    Width,            { input  }
                    Row,              { input  }
                    Col    : INTEGER { input  });
```

displays a REAL-typed number at a specified screen coordinate. The width of the displayed number is also supplied.

```
PROCEDURE Disp_Integer(K,            { input  }
                       Width,        { input  }
                       Row,          { input  }
                       Col    : INTEGER { input  });
```

displays an INTEGER-typed number at a specified screen coordinate. The width of the displayed number is also supplied.

```
FUNCTION Color_Attr(Foreground : ForeColorEnum; { input  }
                    Background : BackColorEnum; { input  }
                    Blinking   : BlinkEnum      { input  }):BYTE;
```

This function returns the byte-value of the color display attribute as designated by the values of the attribute-related enumerated types.

```
FUNCTION Mono_Attr(Display_Spec : MonoAttrEnum; { input  }
                   Blinking     : BlinkEnum      { input  }):BYTE;
```

This function returns the byte-value of the monochrome display attribute as specified by the values of the attribute-related enumerated types.

```
PROCEDURE Disp_StrA(Strng    : STRING80; { input  }
                    Row,                  { input  }
                    Col      : INTEGER;   { input  }
                    ByteAttr : BYTE       { input  });
```

displays a string at a specified screen coordinate using a selected display attribute.

```
PROCEDURE Disp_ChrA(Ch        : CHAR;     { input }
                    Row,                  { input }
                    Col       : INTEGER; { input }
                    ByteAttr : BYTE      { input });
```

displays a single character at a specified screen coordinate using a designated display attribute.

```
PROCEDURE Disp_RealA(X         : REAL;     { input }
                     Width,                { input }
                     Row,                  { input }
                     Col       : INTEGER; { input }
                     ByteAttr : BYTE      { input });
```

displays a REAL-typed number at a specified screen coordinate using a selected display attribute. The width of the displayed number is also supplied.

```
PROCEDURE Disp_IntegerA(K,                   { input }
                        Width,               { input }
                        Row,                 { input }
                        Col       : INTEGER; { input }
                        ByteAttr : BYTE      { input });
```

displays an INTEGER-typed number at a specified screen coordinate using a designated display attribute. The width of the displayed number is also supplied.

I have included commented code in each routine to provide one way for checking the supplied values of the row and column. The method uses the MOD function to ensure that the values are within a valid range. Uncommenting these lines adds more code and would slow down the routines' speed a little.

Regarding the fate of the display attributes, you should note the following:

1. The first set of screen output routines will place characters on the screen that inherit the current display attribute values. Thus, clearing the screen is highly recommended to prevent a poor-looking display.

2. The second set of screen output routines controls the display attribute for only the characters they placed on the screen.

THE IMPLICIT VIDEO ACCESS METHOD

The second library version, SCREEN1.PAS (see Listing 3.3), employs a new feature of Turbo Pascal 4.0 that enables the **WRITE** and **WRITELN** to write directly to the physical screen. The two screen output library versions differ in the following aspects:

1. The code in library SCREEN1.PAS is more on the high-level end than that of SCREEN0.PAS. This enhances the portability of the SCREEN1.PAS across a variety of hardware and operating systems. At the same time, you have no guarantee that the code of SCREEN1.PAS will always give the same fast performance under MS-DOS. On the other hand, SCREEN1.PAS may be regarded as a prototype of customized lower-level library code versions.

2. Library SCREEN1.PAS does not import data types from the library unit PCSCREEN.PAS.

3. The routines in SCREEN1.PAS use the **TextAttr** variable exported by the **CRT** library. They also use a local variable, **old_attr**, to save and restore the display attribute value stored by **TextAttr** prior to the routines' action.

CONSOLE INPUT

Having tackled console output, I now turn to look at console input. I present here two libraries to support controlled input from the keyboard. The first is EDITLINE.PAS which implements a one-line editor for string input. The NUMINPUT.PAS library offers routines for special numeric input. They enforce error checking and permit you to specify an optional range of valid numbers. These routines can be incorporated in your applications that do not tolerate bad numeric input or out-of-range values.

LIBRARY EDITLINE.PAS

This library, shown in Listing 3.4, exports one function that implements a one-line editor. The function is declared as follows:

```
FUNCTION Get_Input (Max_Len : BYTE { input  }) : STRING255;
```

The sole function parameter specifies the maximum input string length. The function initially displays that many background characters to let you know how many characters you may still enter. The one-line editor supports the insert and overwrite modes. You may also use the Delete, Backspace, Left, Right, Ctrl-Left, Ctrl-Right, End, and Home keys in editing your input. The function code also translates other cursor/page movement keys into a key in the above list. Pressing the [Enter] key terminates the string input/editing.

The library contains local routines to handle keyboard input and to alter the cursor size for the insert and overwrite modes.

LIBRARY NUMINPUT.PAS

This library, shown in Listing 3.5, exports routines to support error-proof and controlled numeric input for the INTEGER and REAL types. You can very easily modify the code to accommodate other integer or floating point types. The process involves a simple find/replace operation using a text editor to replace the names of the numeric types with those of your choice.

Using routines for error-proof numeric input guards against the user's input that does not constitute a correct number. Consequently, these routines reprompt the user for an input without causing the program to halt. Such routines are a real life-saver when entering large numerical matrices: imagine the frustration resulting from typing a bad number after entering 40 or 50 numbers when no input verification is implemented!

The second set of routines ensures that you enter a correct number and that it lies within a certain range of values.

The routines of this library are as follows:

```
PROCEDURE Read_Int(VAR I : INTEGER { output });
```

reads a user-typed integer. If a bad number is entered, the routine beeps, clears the user's input, and restores the cursor to its original position. This process is repeated until a valid INTEGER number is entered.

```
PROCEDURE Read_Int_Limit(VAR I    : INTEGER { output };
                         Low,              { input  }
                         High : INTEGER { input  });
```

reads a user-typed integer that lies in the interval [Low,High]. If a bad or out-of-range number is entered, the routine beeps, clears the user's input, and restores the cursor to its original position. This process is repeated until a valid INTEGER number is entered.

```
PROCEDURE Read_Real(VAR X : REAL { output });
```

reads a user-typed real number. If a bad number is entered, the routine beeps, clears the user's input, and restores the cursor to its original position. This process is repeated until a valid REAL number is entered.

```
PROCEDURE Read_Real_Limit(VAR X    : REAL; { output }
                          Low,             { input  }
                          High : REAL { input  });
```

reads a user-typed real that lies in the interval [Low,High]. If a bad or out-of-range number is entered, the routine beeps, clears the user's input, and restores the cursor to its original position. This process is repeated until a valid REAL number is entered.

Listing 3.1. Source code for library PCSCREEN.PAS.

```
UNIT PCScreen;
{======================================================================
Copyright (c) 1987, 1988    Namir Clement Shammas
    LIBRARY NAME: PCScreen
    VERSION: 1.0                                    DATE 09/24/1987
    PURPOSE: provides a library of basic screen management routines.
UPDATEHISTORY
:====================================================================}

{**********************************************************************}
{************************} INTERFACE {*********************************}
{**********************************************************************}

Uses CRT, DataLib0;
CONST MAX_ROW = 25;
    MAX_COL = 80;
TYPE RowRange = 1..MAX_ROW;
    ColRange = 1..MAX_COL;
    CharRec = RECORD
                Kar,              { displayed character }
                Attr : CHAR;  { display attribute }
              END;
    TextScreenMatrix = ARRAY [1..MAX_ROW,1..MAX_COL] OF CharRec;
    TextScreen = RECORD
                Scr : TextScreenMatrix;
              END;


    Screen_Ptr = ^TextScreen;
PROCEDURE DisplayString(VAR Screen : TextScreen; { in/out }
                        Row    : RowRange;    { input  }
                        Col    : ColRange;    { input  }
                        Strng  : STRING80;    { input  }
                        Mode   : CHAR         { input  });

{- - - - - - - - - - - - - - - - - - - - - - - - - - - - - - - - - -

ROUTINE PURPOSE: displays string Strng at Row,Col of screen 'Screen'.
The characters appear with attribute Mode.
PARAMETERS:
 INPUT: Row, Col - define the screen coordinate where the string is
          sent.
        Strng - the displayed string.
        Mode - the attribute used in the display.
```

IN/OUT: Screen - is the video or memory mapped screen that receives
          the output string.
HANDLING BAD ARGUMENTS: The row/column coordinates are not verified to
enable faster execution.
COMMENTS: This routine is able to write directly to the video screen
only when the Screen variable is declared as follows:
 VAR Screen : TextScreen Absolute $B000:0000;

```
- - - - - - - - - - - - - - - - - - - - - - - - - - - - - - - - - - - }
PROCEDURE ClrScrn(VAR Screen : TextScreen { in/out };
                     Attrib : CHAR        { input });
{- - - - - - - - - - - - - - - - - - - - - - - - - - - - - - - - - -
```

ROUTINE PURPOSE: clears a video or memory screen. Used mostly to
clear the latter.
PARAMETERS:
 IN/OUT: Screen - the screen being cleared.
          Attrib - the attribute used in clearing the screen.

```
- - - - - - - - - - - - - - - - - - - - - - - - - - - - - - - - - - - }
PROCEDURE MoveScr(VAR SourceScrn,                { in/out }
                     TargetScrn : TextScreen; { in/out }
                     FirstRow,                 { input  }
                     LastRow    : RowRange;    { input  }
                     FirstCol,                 { input  }
                     LastCol    : ColRange;    { input  }
                     SaveFlag   : BOOLEAN      { input });
{- - - - - - - - - - - - - - - - - - - - - - - - - - - - - - - - - -
```

ROUTINE PURPOSE: two-way copy of characters between the video
screen and the memory screen. This procedure may be used for partial
copying and restoring of screens. The Row/Col cardinal indices are
used to define the top left and bottom right corner of the copied
"window". SaveFlag indicates the direction of transfer.
PARAMETERS:
 INPUT: FirstRow, Last Row, FirstCol, LastCol - define the coordinates
          of the screen portion being moved.
        SaveFlag - when true, stores the screen image from the source
          to the target screen. Otherwise, characters are copied in
          the reverse direction.
 IN/OUT: SourceScrn, TargetScrn - the two screens (video or memory)
          that exchange characters.
HANDLING BAD ARGUMENTS: The supplied coordinates are checked and
their values adjusted, if necessary.

```
- - - - - - - - - - - - - - - - - - - - - - - - - - - - - - - - - - - - - }
PROCEDURE Copy_CGA_Screen_Pages(Source_Page,          { input   }

                                Target_Page  : BYTE { input  });
{- - - - - - - - - - - - - - - - - - - - - - - - - - - - - - - - - - - - -
```

ROUTINE PURPOSE: copies one 80-column CGA screen page to another.
PARAMETERS:
 INPUT: Source_Page - the source screen page number [0..3].
        Target_Page - the target screen page number [0..3].
HANDLING BAD ARGUMENTS: The routine aborts if out-of-range screen page
numbers are supplied. The routines ASSUMES that YOU DO HAVE A CGA
display.

```
- - - - - - - - - - - - - - - - - - - - - - - - - - - - - - - - - - - - }
PROCEDURE Store_CGA_Screen_Pages(
                        CGA_Page   : BYTE;      { input   }
                        Mem_Screen : TextScreen { output });
{- - - - - - - - - - - - - - - - - - - - - - - - - - - - - - - - - - - -
```

ROUTINE PURPOSE: stores an 80-column CGA screen page to memory.
PARAMETERS:
 INPUT: CGA_Page - the CGA page number stored in memory.
        Mem_Screen - the memory location storing the screen image.
HANDLING BAD ARGUMENTS: The routine aborts if an out-of-range value
is assigned to the CGA page parameter.

```
- - - - - - - - - - - - - - - - - - - - - - - - - - - - - - - - - - - - }
PROCEDURE Recall_CGA_Screen_Pages(
                        CGA_Page   : BYTE;      { input   }
                        Mem_Screen : TextScreen { output });
{- - - - - - - - - - - - - - - - - - - - - - - - - - - - - - - - - - - -
```

ROUTINE PURPOSE: recalls an 80-column CGA screen page from memory.
PARAMETERS:
 INPUT: CGA_Page - the CGA page number recalled in memory.
        Mem_Screen - the memory location containing a previously
              stored screen image.
HANDLING BAD ARGUMENTS: The routine aborts if an out-of-range value
is assigned to the CGA page parameter. The routine ASSUMES that the
memory location contains a correct screen image.

```
- - - - - - - - - - - - - - - - - - - - - - - - - - - - - - - - - - - - }
PROCEDURE Swap_CGA_Screen_Pages(Page1,          { input   }

                                Page2  : BYTE { input  });
{- - - - - - - - - - - - - - - - - - - - - - - - - - - - - - - - - - - -
```

ROUTINE PURPOSE: swaps two 80-column CGA pages. A temporary local
memory buffer is used in the operation.
PARAMETERS:
  INPUT: Page1 - the first CGA screen page number.
         Page2 - the second CGA screen page number.
HANDLING BAD ARGUMENTS: The routine aborts if either or both CGA
pages numbers are out-of-range. In addition, no action is taken if
the page numbers are equal.

- }
PROCEDURE Swap_CGA_Screen_Pages2(Page1,   { input }

                                 Page2,   { input }

                                 Buffer_Page : BYTE { input });
{- -

ROUTINE PURPOSE: swaps two 80-column CGA pages. A third vacant screen
page is used as a swapping buffer.
PARAMETERS:

  INPUT: Page1 - the first CGA screen page number.
         Page2 - the second CGA screen page number.
         Buffer_Page - the CGA screen page number for the buffer page.
HANDLING BAD ARGUMENTS: The routine aborts if any CGA page number
is out-of-range. In addition, no action is taken if any two pages
are equal.

- }

{***}
{***********************} IMPLEMENTATION {*************************}
{***}

{-- DisplayString ------}
PROCEDURE DisplayString(VAR Screen : TextScreen; { in/out }
                            Row   : RowRange;   { input }
                            Col   : ColRange;   { input }
                            Strng : STRING80;   { input }
                            Mode   : CHAR   { input });
VAR i : BYTE;
BEGIN
   FOR i := 1 TO Length(Strng) DO BEGIN
       Screen.Scr[Row,Col+i].Kar := Strng[i];
       Screen.Scr[Row,Col+i].Attr := Mode;
   END;
END; { DisplayString }

```
{------------------------------------------------------------ ClrScrn ----}

PROCEDURE ClrScrn(VAR Screen : TextScreen { in/out };
                      Attrib : CHAR       { input  });
VAR i : RowRange;
    j : ColRange;
BEGIN
 FOR i := 1 TO MAX_ROW DO
    FOR j := 1 TO MAX_COL DO BEGIN
      Screen.Scr[i,j].Kar := ' ';
      Screen.Scr[i,j].Attr := Attrib
    END; { FOR j }
END; { ClrScrn }

{-------------------------------------------------------- MoveScr --------}

PROCEDURE MoveScr(VAR SourceScrn,                { in/out }
                      TargetScrn : TextScreen; { in/out }
                      FirstRow,                 { input  }
                      LastRow    : RowRange;    { input  }
                      FirstCol,                 { input  }
                      LastCol    : ColRange;    { input  }
                      SaveFlag   : BOOLEAN      { input  });
VAR i : RowRange;
    j : ColRange;
BEGIN
 { Check Row/Col limits }
 IF FirstRow < 1 THEN FirstRow := 1;
 IF LastRow > MAX_ROW THEN LastRow := MAX_ROW;
 IF FirstCol < 1 THEN FirstCol := 1;
 IF LastCol > MAX_COL THEN LastCol := MAX_COL;
 IF SaveFlag THEN BEGIN
    FOR i := FirstRow TO LastRow DO
      FOR j := FirstCol TO LastCol DO BEGIN
        TargetScrn.Scr[i,j].Kar := SourceScrn.Scr[i,j].Kar;
        TargetScrn.Scr[i,j].Attr := SourceScrn.Scr[i,j].Attr;
      END
 END
 ELSE BEGIN
    FOR i := FirstRow TO LastRow DO
      FOR j := FirstCol TO LastCol DO BEGIN
        SourceScrn.Scr[i,j].Kar := TargetScrn.Scr[i,j].Kar;
        SourceScrn.Scr[i,j].Attr := TargetScrn.Scr[i,j].Attr;
      END;
 END; { IF }

END; { MoveScr }
```

```
{--------------------------------------- Copy_CGA_Screen_Pages ———}


PROCEDURE Copy_CGA_Screen_Pages(Source_Page,          { input  }
                                Target_Page : BYTE  { input  });
var source_screen, target_screen : Screen_Ptr;
BEGIN
   IF (Source_Page IN [0..3]) AND
      (Target_Page IN [0..3]) AND
      (Source_Page <> Target_Page) THEN BEGIN
       { obtain screen addresses }
       source_screen := Ptr($B800, Source_Page * $1000);
       target_screen := Ptr($B800, Target_Page * $1000);
       { copy screens by assigning pointers to record structures }
       target_screen^ := source_screen^
   END; { IF }
END; { Copy_CGA_Screen_Pages }


{--------------------------------------- Store_CGA_Screen_Pages ———}


PROCEDURE Store_CGA_Screen_Pages(
                      CGA_Page   : BYTE;        { input  }
                      Mem_Screen : TextScreen { output });
var cga_screen : Screen_Ptr;
BEGIN
   IF NOT (CGA_Page IN [0..3]) THEN EXIT;
   { obtain screen addresses }
   cga_screen := Ptr($B800, CGA_Page * $1000);
   { copy screens by assigning pointers to record structures }
   Mem_Screen := cga_screen^
END; { Store_CGA_Screen_Pages }


{--------------------------------------- Recall_CGA_Screen_Pages ———}


PROCEDURE Recall_CGA_Screen_Pages(
                      CGA_Page   : BYTE;        { input  }
                      Mem_Screen : TextScreen { output });
var cga_screen : Screen_Ptr;
BEGIN
   IF NOT (CGA_Page IN [0..3]) THEN EXIT;
   { obtain screen addresses }
   cga_screen := Ptr($B800, CGA_Page * $1000);
   { copy screens by assigning pointers to record structures }
   cga_screen^ := Mem_Screen
END; { Recall_CGA_Screen_Pages }
```

```
{---------------------------------------- Swap_CGA_Screen_Pages ------}

PROCEDURE Swap_CGA_Screen_Pages(Page1,           { input  }
                                Page2 : BYTE   { input  });
var screen1, screen2 : Screen_Ptr;
    mem_screen : TextScreen;
BEGIN
    IF (Page1 IN [0..3]) AND
       (Page2 IN [0..3]) AND
       (Page1 <> Page2) THEN BEGIN
        { obtain screen addresses }
        screen1 := Ptr($B800, Page1 * $1000);
        screen2 := Ptr($B800, Page2 * $1000);
        { copy screens by assigning pointers to record structures }
        mem_screen := screen1^;
        screen1^ := screen2^;
        screen2^ := mem_screen;
    END; { IF }
END; { Swap_CGA_Screen_Pages }


{---------------------------------------- Swap_CGA_Screen_Pages2 ------}

PROCEDURE Swap_CGA_Screen_Pages2(Page1,                { input  }
                                 Page2,                 { input  }
                                 Buffer_Page : BYTE   { input  });
var screen1, screen2, buffer_screen : Screen_Ptr;
BEGIN
    IF (Page1 IN [0..3])        AND
       (Page2 IN [0..3])        AND
       (Buffer_Page IN [0..3]) AND
       (Page1 <> Page2)         AND
       (Page1 <> Buffer_Page)  AND
       (Page2 <> Buffer_Page) THEN BEGIN
        { obtain screen addresses }
        screen1 := Ptr($B800, Page1 * $1000);
        screen2 := Ptr($B800, Page2 * $1000);
        buffer_screen := Ptr($B800, Buffer_Page * $1000);
        { copy screens by assigning pointers to record structures }
        buffer_screen^ := screen1^;
        screen1^ := screen2^;
        screen2^ := buffer_screen^;
    END; { IF }
END; { Swap_CGA_Screen_Pages2 }
END.
```

Listing 3.2. Source code for library SCREEN0.PAS.

```
UNIT Screen0;

{===============================================================


           Copyright (c) 1987, 1988   Namir Clement Shammas
     LIBRARY NAME: Screen0
     VERSION: 1.0                           DATE 09/24/1987
     PURPOSE: provides a library of routines to directly access the
              video screen.
     UPDATE HISTORY:


===============================================================}

{******************************************************************}
{************************} INTERFACE {****************************}
{******************************************************************}

Uses CRT, DataLib0, PCScreen;

    ForeColorEnum = (black, blue, green, cyan, red, magenta,
                     brown, white, gray, light_blue, light_green,
                     light_cyan, light_red, light_magenta, yellow,
                     bright_white);
    BackColorEnum = (black_, blue_, green_, cyan_, red_, magenta_,
                     brown_, white_);
    BlinkEnum     = (noblink, blink);
    MonoAttrEnum = (normal, highlight, underline, reverse);

PROCEDURE Disp_Str(Strng : STRING80; { input  }
                   Row,              { input  }
                   Col   : INTEGER   { input  });

{- - - - - - - - - - - - - - - - - - - - - - - - - - - - - - - - -

ROUTINE PURPOSE: writes a string directly to the screen memory.
PARAMETERS:
 INPUT: Strng - the string to be displayed.
        Row, Col - the screen row/column coordinates where the string
           characters are displayed.
HANDLING BAD ARGUMENTS: The routine is exited if the string argument
is a null string. Also, if the video mode is not 2, 3, or 7, the
routine exits.
```

```
                    ROUTINE DEPENDENCIES
                    --------------------


      Identifier Name           Identifier Type        Source Library
      ---------------           ---------------        --------------

         STRING80                   string                DataLib0
         Screen_Ptr                 pointer               PCScreen


- - - - - - - - - - - - - - - - - - - - - - - - - - - - - - - - - - - }
PROCEDURE Disp_Chr(Ch  : CHAR;    { input  }
                   Row,           { input  }
                   Col : INTEGER { input  });
{- - - - - - - - - - - - - - - - - - - - - - - - - - - - - - - - - - -
```

ROUTINE PURPOSE: writes a single character directly to the screen
memory.
PARAMETERS:
 INPUT: Ch - the character to be displayed.
        Row, Col - the screen row/column coordinates where the
           character is displayed.
HANDLING BAD ARGUMENTS: The routine is exited if the character argument
is null. Also, if the video mode is not 2, 3, or 7, the routine exits.

```
                    ROUTINE DEPENDENCIES
                    --------------------


      Identifier Name           Identifier Type        Source Library
      ---------------           ---------------        --------------

         Screen_Ptr                 pointer               PCScreen


- - - - - - - - - - - - - - - - - - - - - - - - - - - - - - - - - - - }
PROCEDURE Disp_Real(X     : REAL;    { input  }
                    Width,           { input  }
                    Row,             { input  }
                    Col   : INTEGER { input  });
{- - - - - - - - - - - - - - - - - - - - - - - - - - - - - - - - - - -
```

ROUTINE PURPOSE: writes a REAL number directly to the screen memory.
PARAMETERS:
 INPUT: X - the REAL number to be displayed.
        Width - specifies the size of the string image of the REAL
           number.
        Row, Col - the screen row/column coordinates where the
           number is displayed.
HANDLING BAD ARGUMENTS: If the video mode is not 2, 3, or 7, the
routine exits.

ROUTINE DEPENDENCIES

Identifier Name	Identifier Type	Source Library
STRING80	string	DataLib0
Screen_Ptr	pointer	PCScreen

```
- - - - - - - - - - - - - - - - - - - - - - - - - - - - - - - - - - }
PROCEDURE Disp_Integer(K,             { input  }
                       Width,         { input  }
                       Row,           { input  }
                       Col  : INTEGER { input  });
{- - - - - - - - - - - - - - - - - - - - - - - - - - - - - - - - - -
```

ROUTINE PURPOSE: writes an INTEGER number directly to the screen
memory.
PARAMETERS:
 INPUT: X - the INTEGER number to be displayed.
        Width - specifies the size of the string image of the INTEGER
          number.
        Row, Col - the screen row/column coordinates where the
          number is displayed.
HANDLING BAD ARGUMENTS: If the video mode is not 2, 3, or 7, the
routine exits.

ROUTINE DEPENDENCIES

Identifier Name	Identifier Type	Source Library
STRING80	string	DataLib0
Screen_Ptr	pointer	PCScreen

```
- - - - - - - - - - - - - - - - - - - - - - - - - - - - - - - - - }
FUNCTION Color_Attr(Foreground : ForeColorEnum; { input  }
                    Background : BackColorEnum;  { input  }
                    Blinking   : BlinkEnum     { input  }) : BYTE;
{- - - - - - - - - - - - - - - - - - - - - - - - - - - - - - - - - -
```

ROUTINE PURPOSE: returns the attribute for a color display.

PARAMETERS:
 INPUT: Foreground - the enumerated value for the foreground color.
        Background - the enumerated value for the background color.
        Blinking   - the enumerated value for blinking status.
FUNCTION VALUE: returns the ASCII code number that represents
the combined numeric code for foreground and background colors, as
well as the blinking status (see expression used below).

```
- - - - - - - - - - - - - - - - - - - - - - - - - - - - - - - - }
FUNCTION Mono_Attr(Display_Spec : MonoAttrEnum; { input  }
                   Blinking      : BlinkEnum    { input  }) : BYTE;
{- - - - - - - - - - - - - - - - - - - - - - - - - - - - - - - - -
```

ROUTINE PURPOSE: returns the attribute for a monochrome display.
PARAMETERS:
 INPUT: Display_Spec - the enumerated value for specifying the type
        of monochrome character to be displayed.
        Blinking   - the enumerated value for blinking status.
FUNCTION VALUE: returns the ASCII code number that represents
the combined numeric code for the display specification and the
blinking status (see expression used below).

```
- - - - - - - - - - - - - - - - - - - - - - - - - - - - - - - - }
PROCEDURE Disp_StrA(Strng    : STRING80; { input  }
                    Row,                 { input  }
                    Col      : INTEGER;  { input  }
                    ByteAttr : BYTE      { input  });
{- - - - - - - - - - - - - - - - - - - - - - - - - - - - - - - - -
```

ROUTINE PURPOSE: writes a string directly to the screen memory.
PARAMETERS:
 INPUT: Strng - the string to be displayed.
        Row, Col - the screen row/column coordinates where the string
        characters are displayed.
        ByteAttr - specifies the display attributes.
HANDLING BAD ARGUMENTS: The routine is exited if the string argument
is a null string. Also, if the video mode is not 2, 3, or 7, the
routine exits.

ROUTINE DEPENDENCIES

Identifier Name	Identifier Type	Source Library
STRING80	string	DataLib0
Screen_Ptr	pointer	PCScreen

```
- - - - - - - - - - - - - - - - - - - - - - - - - - - - - - - - - - }
PROCEDURE Disp_ChrA(Ch        : CHAR;      { input  }
                    Row,                   { input  }
                    Col       : INTEGER;   { input  }
                    ByteAttr  : BYTE       { input  });
{- - - - - - - - - - - - - - - - - - - - - - - - - - - - - - - - - -
```

ROUTINE PURPOSE: writes a single character directly to the screen memory.
PARAMETERS:
 INPUT: Ch - the character to be displayed.
       Row, Col - the screen row/column coordinates where the
         character is displayed.
       ByteAttr - the display attributes.
HANDLING BAD ARGUMENTS: The routine is exited if the character argument
is null. Also, if the video mode is not 2, 3, or 7, the routine exits.

ROUTINE DEPENDENCIES

Identifier Name	Identifier Type	Source Library
Screen_Ptr	pointer	PCScreen

```
- - - - - - - - - - - - - - - - - - - - - - - - - - - - - - - - - }
PROCEDURE Disp_RealA(X        : REAL;      { input  }
                    Width,                 { input  }
                    Row,                   { input  }
                    Col       : INTEGER;   { input  }
                    ByteAttr  : BYTE       { input  });
{- - - - - - - - - - - - - - - - - - - - - - - - - - - - - - - - - -
```

ROUTINE PURPOSE: writes a REAL number directly to the screen memory.
PARAMETERS:
 INPUT: X - the REAL number to be displayed.
       Width - specifies the size of the string image of the REAL
         number.
       Row, Col - the screen row/column coordinates where the
         number is displayed.
       ByteAttr - specifies the display attributes.
HANDLING BAD ARGUMENTS: If the video mode is not 2, 3, or 7, the
routine exits.

```
                    ROUTINE DEPENDENCIES
                    --------------------


        Identifier Name          Identifier Type       Source Library
        ---------------          ---------------       --------------

         STRING80                    string               DataLib0
         Screen_Ptr                  pointer              PCScreen


- - - - - - - - - - - - - - - - - - - - - - - - - - - - - - - - }
PROCEDURE Disp_IntegerA(K,                      { input  }
                    Width,                      { input  }
                    Row,                        { input  }
                    Col       : INTEGER; { input  }
                    ByteAttr : BYTE     { input  });
{- - - - - - - - - - - - - - - - - - - - - - - - - - - - - - - - -
```

ROUTINE PURPOSE: writes a INTEGER number directly to the screen memory.
PARAMETERS:
 INPUT: X - the INTEGER number to be displayed.
        Width - specifies the size of the string image of the INTEGER
           number.
        Row, Col - the screen row/column coordinates where the
           number is displayed.
        ByteAttr - specifies the display attributes.

HANDLING BAD ARGUMENTS: If the video mode is not 2, 3, or 7, the
routine exits.

```
                    ROUTINE DEPENDENCIES
                    --------------------


        Identifier Name          Identifier Type       Source Library
        ---------------          ---------------       --------------

         STRING80                    string               DataLib0
         Screen_Ptr                  pointer              PCScreen


- - - - - - - - - - - - - - - - - - - - - - - - - - - - - - - - }


{*********************************************************************}
{**********************} IMPLEMENTATION {**************************}
{*********************************************************************}


{$V-}
```

```
{---------------------------------------------------- Disp_Str ---------}

PROCEDURE Disp_Str(Strng : STRING80; { input  }
                   Row,              { input  }
                   Col    : INTEGER  { input  });
VAR video_ptr : Screen_Ptr;
    i : BYTE;
    mode : BYTE absolute $0040:$0049;
BEGIN
    IF Strng = '' THEN EXIT;
{-+-+-+-+-+-+-+-+-+-+-+-+-+-+-+-+-+-+-+-+-+-+-+-+-+-+-+-+-
The following two lines provide some protection against bad
row/column values. Including the code adds a bit of overhead.
    Row := Row MOD 24;
    Col := Col MOD 80;
-+-+-+-+-+-+-+-+-+-+-+-+-+-+-+-+-+-+-+-+-+-+-+-+-+-+-+-+-}

    IF mode IN [2..3] THEN
        video_ptr := Ptr($B800,$0000)
    ELSE IF mode = 7 THEN
        video_ptr := Ptr($B000,$0000)
    ELSE EXIT;
    FOR i := 1 TO Length(Strng) DO
        video_ptr^.Scr[Row,Col + i - 1].Kar := Strng[i];

{---------------------------------------------------- Disp_Chr ---------}

PROCEDURE Disp_Chr(Ch  : CHAR;    { input  }
                   Row,           { input  }
                   Col : INTEGER  { input  });
VAR video_ptr : Screen_Ptr;
    mode : BYTE absolute $0040:$0049;
BEGIN
    IF Ch = '' THEN EXIT;
{-+-+-+-+-+-+-+-+-+-+-+-+-+-+-+-+-+-+-+-+-+-+-+-+-+-+-+-+-
The following two lines provide some protection against bad
row/column values. Including the code adds a bit of overhead.
    Row := Row MOD 24;
    Col := Col MOD 80;
-+-+-+-+-+-+-+-+-+-+-+-+-+-+-+-+-+-+-+-+-+-+-+-+-+-+-+-+-}

    IF mode IN [2..3] THEN
        video_ptr := Ptr($B800,$0000)
    ELSE IF mode = 7 THEN
        video_ptr := Ptr($B000,$0000)
    ELSE EXIT;
    video_ptr^.Scr[Row,Col].Kar := Ch;
END; { Disp_Chr }
```

```
{------------------------------------------------- Disp_Real ———}

PROCEDURE Disp_Real(X       : REAL;     { input  }
                    Width,              { input  }
                    Row,                { input  }
                    Col     : INTEGER { input  });
VAR video_ptr : Screen_Ptr;
    i : BYTE;
    mode : BYTE absolute $0040:$0049;
    strng : STRING80;
BEGIN
{-+-+-+-+-+-+-+-+-+-+-+-+-+-+-+-+-+-+-+-+-+-+-+-+-+-+-
The following two lines provide some protection against bad
row/column values. Including the code adds a bit of overhead.
    Row := Row MOD 24;
    Col := Col MOD 80;
-+-+-+-+-+-+-+-+-+-+-+-+-+-+-+-+-+-+-+-+-+-+-+-+-+-+-}

    Str(X:Width,strng);
    IF mode IN [2..3] THEN
        video_ptr := Ptr($B800,$0000)
    ELSE IF mode = 7 THEN
        video_ptr := Ptr($B000,$0000)
    ELSE EXIT;
    FOR i := 1 TO Length(strng) DO
        video_ptr^.Scr[Row,Col + i -1].Kar := strng[i];
END; { Disp_Real }

{--------------------------------------------- Disp_Integer ———}

PROCEDURE Disp_Integer(K,                   { input  }
                       Width,               { input  }
                       Row,                 { input  }
                       Col     : INTEGER { input  });
VAR video_ptr : Screen_Ptr;
    mode : BYTE absolute $0040:$0049;
    i : BYTE;
    strng : STRING80;
BEGIN
{-+-+-+-+-+-+-+-+-+-+-+-+-+-+-+-+-+-+-+-+-+-+-+-+-+-+-
The following two lines provide some protection against bad
row/column values. Including the code adds a bit of overhead.
    Row := Row MOD 24;
    Col := Col MOD 80;
-+-+-+-+-+-+-+-+-+-+-+-+-+-+-+-+-+-+-+-+-+-+-+-+-+-+-}
```

```
   Str(K:Width,strng);
   IF mode IN [2..3] THEN
       video_ptr := Ptr($B800,$0000)
   ELSE IF mode = 7 THEN
       video_ptr := Ptr($B000,$0000)
   ELSE EXIT;
   FOR i := 1 TO Length(strng) DO
       video_ptr^.Scr[Row,Col + i - 1].Kar := strng[i];
END; { Disp_Integer }


{-------------------------------------------------- Color_Attr ———}


FUNCTION Color_Attr(Foreground : ForeColorEnum; { input  }
                    Background : BackColorEnum; { input  }
                    Blinking   : BlinkEnum     { input  }) : BYTE;
BEGIN
   { return the function value }
   Color_Attr :=         Ord(Foreground) +
                   16 * Ord(Background) +
                   128 * Ord(Blinking)
END; { Color_Attr }


{------------------------------------------------- Mono_Attr ———}


FUNCTION Mono_Attr(Display_Spec : MonoAttrEnum; { input  }
                   Blinking     : BlinkEnum     { input  }) : BYTE;
VAR attr : BYTE;
BEGIN
   CASE Display_Spec OF
       normal    : attr := 7;
       highlight : attr := 15;
       underline : attr := 65;
       reverse   : attr := 122;
       { set everything else to normal }
       ELSE        attr := 7;
   END; { CASE }
   { return the function value }
   Mono_Attr := attr + 128 * Ord(Blinking)
END; { Mono_Attr }


{-------------------------------------------------- Disp_StrA ———}


PROCEDURE Disp_StrA(Strng    : STRING80; { input  }
                    Row,                 { input  }
                    Col      : INTEGER;  { input  }
                    ByteAttr : BYTE      { input  });
```

```
VAR video_ptr : Screen_Ptr;
    attrib : CHAR;
    mode : BYTE absolute $0040:$0049;
    i : BYTE;
BEGIN
    IF Strng = '' THEN EXIT;
{-+-+-+-+-+-+-+-+-+-+-+-+-+-+-+-+-+-+-+-+-+-+-+-+-+-+-+-
The following two lines provide some protection against bad
row/column values. Including the code adds a bit of overhead.
    Row := Row MOD 24;
    Col := Col MOD 80;
-+-+-+-+-+-+-+-+-+-+-+-+-+-+-+-+-+-+-+-+-+-+-+-+-+-+-+-}

    attrib := CHR(ByteAttr);
    IF' mode IN [2..3] THEN
        video_ptr := Ptr($B800,$0000)
    ELSE IF mode = 7 THEN
        video_ptr := Ptr($B000,$0000)
    ELSE EXIT;
     FOR i := 1 TO Length(Strng) DO BEGIN
        video_ptr^.Scr[Row,Col + i - 1].Kar := Strng[i];
        video_ptr^.Scr[Row,Col + i - 1].Attr := attrib;
    END; { FOR }
END;


{------------------------------------------------------- Disp_ChrA ---------}


PROCEDURE Disp_ChrA(Ch          : CHAR;      { input  }
                    Row,                     { input  }
                    Col         : INTEGER;   { input  }
                    ByteAttr : BYTE          { input  });
VAR video_ptr : Screen_Ptr;
    attrib : CHAR;
    mode : BYTE absolute $0040:$0049;
BEGIN
    IF Ch = '' THEN EXIT;
{-+-+-+-+-+-+-+-+-+-+-+-+-+-+-+-+-+-+-+-+-+-+-+-+-+-+-+-
The following two lines provide some protection against bad
row/column values. Including the code adds a bit of overhead.
    Row := Row MOD 24;
    Col := Col MOD 80;
-+-+-+-+-+-+-+-+-+-+-+-+-+-+-+-+-+-+-+-+-+-+-+-+-+-+-+-}

    attrib := CHR(ByteAttr);
    IF mode IN [2..3] THEN
        video_ptr := Ptr($B800,$0000)
```

```
    ELSE IF mode = 7 THEN
        video_ptr := Ptr($B000,$0000)
    ELSE EXIT;
    video_ptr^.Scr[Row,Col].Kar := Ch;
    video_ptr^.Scr[Row,Col].Attr := attrib;
END; { Disp_ChrA }


{----------------------------------------------- Disp_RealA ———}


PROCEDURE Disp_RealA(X         : REAL;     { input  }
                     Width,                { input  }
                     Row,                  { input  }
                     Col     : INTEGER; { input  }
                     ByteAttr : BYTE       { input  });
VAR video_ptr : Screen_Ptr;
    i : BYTE;
    mode : BYTE absolute $0040:$0049;
    attrib : CHAR;
    strng : STRING80;
BEGIN
{-+-+-+-+-+-+-+-+-+-+-+-+-+-+-+-+-+-+-+-+-+-+-+-+-+-+-+-+-+-
The following two lines provide some protection against bad
row/column values. Including the code adds a bit of overhead.
    Row := Row MOD 24;
    Col := Col MOD 80;
-+-+-+-+-+-+-+-+-+-+-+-+-+-+-+-+-+-+-+-+-+-+-+-+-+-+-+-+-+-}

    Str(X:Width,strng);
    attrib := CHR(ByteAttr);
    IF mode IN [2..3] THEN
        video_ptr := Ptr($B800,$0000)
    ELSE IF mode = 7 THEN
        video_ptr := Ptr($B000,$0000)
    ELSE EXIT;
    FOR i := 1 TO Length(strng) DO BEGIN
        video_ptr^.Scr[Row,Col + i - 1].Kar := strng[i];
        video_ptr^.Scr[Row,Col + i - 1].Attr := attrib;
    END; { FOR }
END; { Disp_RealA }


{--------------------------------------------- Disp_IntegerA ———}


PROCEDURE Disp_IntegerA(K,                     { input  }
                        Width,                 { input  }
                        Row,                   { input  }
                        Col     : INTEGER; { input  }
```

```
                             ByteAttr : BYTE    { input  });
VAR video_ptr : Screen_Ptr;
    i : BYTE;
    mode : BYTE absolute $0040:$0049;
    attrib : CHAR;
    strng : STRING80;
BEGIN
{-+-+-+-+-+-+-+-+-+-+-+-+-+-+-+-+-+-+-+-+-+-+-+-+-+-+-+-+-
The following two lines provide some protection against bad
row/column values. Including the code adds a bit of overhead.
    Row := Row MOD 24;
    Col := Col MOD 80;
-+-+-+-+-+-+-+-+-+-+-+-+-+-+-+-+-+-+-+-+-+-+-+-+-+-+-+-+-}

    Str(K:Width,strng);
    attrib := CHR(ByteAttr);
    IF mode IN [2..3] THEN
        video_ptr := Ptr($B800,$0000)
    ELSE IF mode = 7 THEN
        video_ptr := Ptr($B000,$0000)
    ELSE EXIT;
    FOR i := 1 TO Length(strng) DO BEGIN
        video_ptr^.Scr[Row,Col + i - 1].Kar := strng[i];
        video_ptr^.Scr[Row,Col + i - 1].Attr := attrib;
    END; { FOR }
END; { Disp_IntegerA }
END.
```

Listing 3.3. Source code for library SCREEN1.PAS.

```
UNIT Screen1;


{================================================================


        Copyright (c) 1987, 1988   Namir Clement Shammas
    LIBRARY NAME: Screen1
    VERSION: 1.0                                 DATE 09/24/1987
    PURPOSE: provides routines to write directly to the screen.
    UPDATE HISTORY:


================================================================}
```

```
{*****************************************************************}
{**************************} INTERFACE {**************************}
{*****************************************************************}
```

```
Uses CRT, DataLib0;
TYPE
    ForeColorEnum = (black, blue, green, cyan, red, magenta,
                     brown, white, gray, light_blue, light_green,
                     light_cyan, light_red, light_magenta, yellow,
                     bright_white);
    BackColorEnum = (black_, blue_, green_, cyan_, red_, magenta_,
                     brown_, white_);
    BlinkEnum      = (noblink, blink);
    MonoAttrEnum = (normal, highlight, underline, reverse);
PROCEDURE Disp_Str(Strng : STRING80; { input  }
                   Row,               { input  }
                   Col   : INTEGER    { input  });
{- - - - - - - - - - - - - - - - - - - - - - - - - - - - - - - -
```

ROUTINE PURPOSE: writes a string directly to the screen memory.
PARAMETERS:
 INPUT: Strng - the string to be displayed.
        Row, Col - the screen row/column coordinates where the string
           characters are displayed.
HANDLING BAD ARGUMENTS: The routine is exited if the string argument
is a null string.

                        ROUTINE DEPENDENCIES

Identifier Name	Identifier Type	Source Library
DirectVideo	boolean	CRT
GotoXY	procedure	CRT
STRING80	string	DataLib0

```
- - - - - - - - - - - - - - - - - - - - - - - - - - - - - - - - }
PROCEDURE Disp_Chr(Ch  : CHAR;    { input  }
                   Row,            { input  }
                   Col : INTEGER { input  });
{- - - - - - - - - - - - - - - - - - - - - - - - - - - - - - - -
```

ROUTINE PURPOSE: writes a single character directly to the screen
memory.

PARAMETERS:
  INPUT: Ch — the character to be displayed.
         Row, Col — the screen row/column coordinates where the
           character is displayed.
HANDLING BAD ARGUMENTS: The routine is exited if the character argument
is null.

ROUTINE DEPENDENCIES

Identifier Name	Identifier Type	Source Library
DirectVideo	boolean	CRT
GotoXY	procedure	CRT

```
- - - - - - - - - - - - - - - - - - - - - - - - - - - - - - - - - - }
PROCEDURE Disp_Real(X      : REAL;   { input }
                 Width,              { input }
                 Row,                { input }
                 Col     : INTEGER { input });
{- - - - - - - - - - - - - - - - - - - - - - - - - - - - - - - - - -
```

ROUTINE PURPOSE: writes a REAL number directly to the screen memory.
PARAMETERS:
  INPUT: X — the REAL number to be displayed.
         Width — specifies the size of the string image of the REAL
           number.
         Row, Col — the screen row/column coordinates where the
           number is displayed.

ROUTINE DEPENDENCIES

Identifier Name	Identifier Type	Source Library
DirectVideo	boolean	CRT
GotoXY	procedure	CRT

```
- - - - - - - - - - - - - - - - - - - - - - - - - - - - - - - - - }
PROCEDURE Disp_Integer(K,                { input }
                 Width,                   { input }
                 Row,                     { input }
                 Col     : INTEGER { input });
{- - - - - - - - - - - - - - - - - - - - - - - - - - - - - - - - - -
```

ROUTINE PURPOSE: writes an INTEGER number directly to the screen
memory.
PARAMETERS:
  INPUT: X - the INTEGER number to be displayed.
         Width - specifies the size of the string image of the INTEGER
             number.
         Row, Col - the screen row/column coordinates where the
             number is displayed.

ROUTINE DEPENDENCIES

Identifier Name	Identifier Type	Source Library
DirectVideo	boolean	CRT
GotoXY	procedure	CRT

```
- - - - - - - - - - - - - - - - - - - - - - - - - - - - - - - - - }
FUNCTION Color_Attr(Foreground : ForeColorEnum; { input }
                    Background : BackColorEnum; { input }
                    Blinking   : BlinkEnum      { input }) : BYTE;
{- - - - - - - - - - - - - - - - - - - - - - - - - - - - - - - -
```

ROUTINE PURPOSE: returns the attribute 'character' for a color display.
PARAMETERS:
  INPUT: Foreground - the enumerated value for the foreground color.
         Background - the enumerated value for the background color.
         Blinking   - the enumerated value for blinking status.
FUNCTION VALUE: returns the ASCII code number representing
the combined numeric code for foreground and background colors, as
well as the blinking status (see expression used below).

```
- - - - - - - - - - - - - - - - - - - - - - - - - - - - - - - - - }
FUNCTION Mono_Attr(Display_Spec : MonoAttrEnum; { input }
                   Blinking     : BlinkEnum      { input }) : BYTE;
{- - - - - - - - - - - - - - - - - - - - - - - - - - - - - - - -
```

ROUTINE PURPOSE: returns the attribute 'character' for a monochrome
display.
PARAMETERS:
  INPUT: Display_Spec - the enumerated value for specifying the type
             of monochrome character to be displayed.
         Blinking   - the enumerated value for blinking status.
FUNCTION VALUE: returns the ASCII code number representing the
combined numeric code for the display specification the blinking
status (see expression used below).

```
- - - - - - - - - - - - - - - - - - - - - - - - - - - - - - - - - - - }
PROCEDURE Disp_StrA(Strng      : STRING80;  { input  }
                    Row,                    { input  }
                    Col        : INTEGER;   { input  }
                    ByteAttr   : BYTE       { input  });
{- - - - - - - - - - - - - - - - - - - - - - - - - - - - - - - - - -
```

ROUTINE PURPOSE: writes a string directly to the screen memory.
PARAMETERS:
 INPUT: Strng - the string to be displayed.
        Row, Col - the screen row/column coordinates where the string
          characters are displayed.
        ByteAttr - specifies the display attributes.
HANDLING BAD ARGUMENTS: The routine is exited if the string argument
is a null string.

ROUTINE DEPENDENCIES

Identifier Name	Identifier Type	Source Library
DirectVideo	boolean	CRT
TextAttr	byte	CRT
GotoXY	procedure	CRT
STRING80	string	DataLib0

```
- - - - - - - - - - - - - - - - - - - - - - - - - - - - - - - - - - - }
PROCEDURE Disp_ChrA(Ch        : CHAR;      { input  }
                    Row,                    { input  }
                    Col        : INTEGER;   { input  }
                    ByteAttr   : BYTE       { input  });
{- - - - - - - - - - - - - - - - - - - - - - - - - - - - - - - - - -
```

ROUTINE PURPOSE: writes a single character directly to the screen
memory.
PARAMETERS:
 INPUT: Ch - the character to be displayed.
        Row, Col - the screen row/column coordinates where the
          character is displayed.
        ByteAttr - the display attributes.
HANDLING BAD ARGUMENTS: The routine is exited if the character argument
is null.

ROUTINE DEPENDENCIES

Identifier Name	Identifier Type	Source Library
DirectVideo	boolean	CRT
TextAttr	byte	CRT
GotoXY	procedure	CRT

```
- - - - - - - - - - - - - - - - - - - - - - - - - - - - - - - - - }
PROCEDURE Disp_RealA(X        : REAL;    { input }
                     Width,              { input }
                     Row,                { input }
                     Col      : INTEGER; { input }
                     ByteAttr : BYTE     { input });
{- - - - - - - - - - - - - - - - - - - - - - - - - - - - - - - - -
```

ROUTINE PURPOSE: writes a REAL number directly to the screen memory.
PARAMETERS:
 INPUT: X - the REAL number to be displayed.
        Width - specifies the size of the string image of the REAL
          number.
        Row, Col - the screen row/column coordinates where the
          number is displayed.
        ByteAttr - specifies the display attributes.

ROUTINE DEPENDENCIES

Identifier Name	Identifier Type	Source Library
DirectVideo	boolean	CRT
TextAttr	byte	CRT
GotoXY	procedure	CRT

```
- - - - - - - - - - - - - - - - - - - - - - - - - - - - - - - - - }
PROCEDURE Disp_IntegerA(K,                  { input }
                        Width,              { input }
                        Row,                { input }
                        Col      : INTEGER; { input }
                        ByteAttr : BYTE     { input });
{- - - - - - - - - - - - - - - - - - - - - - - - - - - - - - - - -
```

ROUTINE PURPOSE: writes an INTEGER number directly to the screen
memory.

```
PARAMETERS:
  INPUT: X - the INTEGER number to be displayed.
         Width - specifies the size of the string image of the INTEGER
            number.
         Row, Col - the screen row/column coordinates where the
            number is displayed.
         ByteAttr - specifies the display attributes.
                        ROUTINE DEPENDENCIES
                        --------------------


         Identifier Name          Identifier Type      Source Library
         ---------------          ---------------      --------------

         DirectVideo                  boolean               CRT
         TextAttr                     byte                  CRT
         GotoXY                       procedure             CRT
- - - - - - - - - - - - - - - - - - - - - - - - - - - - - - - - - }

{***************************************************************}
{***********************} IMPLEMENTATION {***********************}
{***************************************************************}
{$V-}


{-------------------------------------------------- Disp_Str ---------}

PROCEDURE Disp_Str;
BEGIN
   IF Strng = '' THEN EXIT;
   DirectVideo := TRUE;
{-+-+-+-+-+-+-+-+-+-+-+-+-+-+-+-+-+-+-+-+-+-+-+-+-+-+-+-+-
The following two lines provide some protection against bad
row/column values. Including the code adds a bit of overhead.
   Row := Row MOD 24;
   Col := Col MOD 80;
-+-+-+-+-+-+-+-+-+-+-+-+-+-+-+-+-+-+-+-+-+-+-+-+-+-+-+-+-}


   GotoXY(Col, Row);
   WRITE(Strng);
END; { Disp_Str }


{-------------------------------------------------- Disp_Chr ---------}

PROCEDURE Disp_Chr(Ch  : CHAR;      { input }
                   Row,             { input }
                   Col : INTEGER { input });
BEGIN
   IF Ch = '' THEN EXIT;
   DirectVideo := TRUE;
```

```
{-+-+-+-+-+-+-+-+-+-+-+-+-+-+-+-+-+-+-+-+-+-+-+-+-+-+-+-+-+-
The following two lines provide some protection against bad
row/column values. Including the code adds a bit of overhead.
    Row := Row MOD 24;
    Col := Col MOD 80;
-+-+-+-+-+-+-+-+-+-+-+-+-+-+-+-+-+-+-+-+-+-+-+-+-+-+-+-+-+-}

    GotoXY(Col, Row);
    WRITE(Ch);
END; { Disp_Chr }


{------------------------------------------------- Disp_Real ———}

PROCEDURE Disp_Real(X        : REAL;    { input  }
                    Width,               { input  }
                    Row,                 { input  }
                    Col    : INTEGER { input  });
BEGIN
    DirectVideo := TRUE;
{-+-+-+-+-+-+-+-+-+-+-+-+-+-+-+-+-+-+-+-+-+-+-+-+-+-+-+-+-+-
The following two lines provide some protection against bad
row/column values. Including the code adds a bit of overhead.
    Row := Row MOD 24;
    Col := Col MOD 80;
-+-+-+-+-+-+-+-+-+-+-+-+-+-+-+-+-+-+-+-+-+-+-+-+-+-+-+-+-+-}

    GotoXY(Col,Row);
    WRITE(X:Width);
END; { Disp_Real }


{------------------------------------------------- Disp_Integer ———}

PROCEDURE Disp_Integer(K,                  { input  }
                       Width,               { input  }
                       Row,                 { input  }
                       Col    : INTEGER { input  });
BEGIN
    DirectVideo := TRUE;
{-+-+-+-+-+-+-+-+-+-+-+-+-+-+-+-+-+-+-+-+-+-+-+-+-+-+-+-+-+-
The following two lines provide some protection against bad
row/column values. Including the code adds a bit of overhead.
    Row := Row MOD 24;
    Col := Col MOD 80;
-+-+-+-+-+-+-+-+-+-+-+-+-+-+-+-+-+-+-+-+-+-+-+-+-+-+-+-+-+-}
```

```
      GotoXY(Col,Row);
      WRITE(K:Width);
END;


{------------------------------------------------------ Color_Attr ------}


FUNCTION Color_Attr(Foreground : ForeColorEnum; { input  }
                    Background : BackColorEnum; { input  }
                    Blinking   : BlinkEnum      { input  }) : BYTE;
BEGIN
    { return the function value }
    Color_Attr :=        Ord(Foreground) +
                  16 * Ord(Background) +
                  128 * Ord(Blinking)
END; { Color_Attr }


{------------------------------------------------------ Mono_Attr ------}


FUNCTION Mono_Attr(Display_Spec : MonoAttrEnum; { input  }
                   Blinking     : BlinkEnum      { input  }) : BYTE;
VAR attr : BYTE;
BEGIN
    CASE Display_Spec OF
        normal    : attr := 7;
        highlight : attr := 15;
        underline : attr := 65;
        reverse   : attr := 122;
        { set everything else to normal }
        ELSE          attr := 7;
    END; { CASE }
    { return the function value }
    Mono_Attr := attr + 128 * Ord(Blinking)
END; { Mono_Attr }


{------------------------------------------------------ Disp_StrA ------}


PROCEDURE Disp_StrA(Strng    : STRING80; { input  }
                    Row,                 { input  }
                    Col      : INTEGER;  { input  }
                    ByteAttr : BYTE      { input  });
VAR old_attr : BYTE;
BEGIN
    IF Strng = '' THEN EXIT;
    DirectVideo := TRUE;
    old_attr := TextAttr;
    TextAttr := ByteAttr;
```

```
{-+-+-+-+-+-+-+-+-+-+-+-+-+-+-+-+-+-+-+-+-+-+-+-+-+-+-+-+-
The following two lines provide some protection against bad
row/column values. Including the code adds a bit of overhead.
   Row := Row MOD 24;
   Col := Col MOD 80;
-+-+-+-+-+-+-+-+-+-+-+-+-+-+-+-+-+-+-+-+-+-+-+-+-+-+-+-+-+-}

   GotoXY(Col,Row);
   WRITE(Strng);
   TextAttr := old_attr;
END;

{------------------------------------------------ Disp_ChrA ————————}

PROCEDURE Disp_ChrA(Ch       : CHAR;     { input }
                    Row,                 { input }
                    Col     : INTEGER; { input }
                    ByteAttr : BYTE      { input });
VAR old_attr : BYTE;
BEGIN
   IF Ch = '' THEN EXIT;
   DirectVideo := TRUE;
   old_attr := TextAttr;
   TextAttr := ByteAttr;

{-+-+-+-+-+-+-+-+-+-+-+-+-+-+-+-+-+-+-+-+-+-+-+-+-+-+-+-+-
The following two lines provide some protection against bad
row/column values. Including the code adds a bit of overhead.
   Row := Row MOD 24;
   Col := Col MOD 80;
-+-+-+-+-+-+-+-+-+-+-+-+-+-+-+-+-+-+-+-+-+-+-+-+-+-+-+-+-+-}

   GotoXY(Col, Row);
   WRITE(Ch);
   TextAttr := old_attr;
END; { Disp_CharA }

{------------------------------------------------ Disp_RealA ————————}

PROCEDURE Disp_RealA(X       : REAL;     { input }
                    Width,               { input }
                    Row,                 { input }
                    Col     : INTEGER; { input }
                    ByteAttr : BYTE      { input });
```

```
VAR old_attr : BYTE;
BEGIN
    DirectVideo := TRUE;
    old_attr := TextAttr;
    TextAttr := ByteAttr;

{-+-+-+-+-+-+-+-+-+-+-+-+-+-+-+-+-+-+-+-+-+-+-+-+-+-+-+-+-
The following two lines provide some protection against bad
row/column values. Including the code adds a bit of overhead.
    Row := Row MOD 24;
    Col := Col MOD 80;
-+-+-+-+-+-+-+-+-+-+-+-+-+-+-+-+-+-+-+-+-+-+-+-+-+-+-+-+-+-}


    GotoXY(Col, Row);
    WRITE(X:Width);
    TextAttr := old_attr;
END;


{----------------------------------------------- Disp_IntegerA ------}

PROCEDURE Disp_IntegerA(K,                      { input  }
                        Width,                  { input  }
                        Row,                    { input  }
                        Col     : INTEGER; { input  }
                        ByteAttr : BYTE    { input  });
VAR old_attr : BYTE;
BEGIN
    DirectVideo := TRUE;
    old_attr := TextAttr;
    TextAttr := ByteAttr;

{-+-+-+-+-+-+-+-+-+-+-+-+-+-+-+-+-+-+-+-+-+-+-+-+-+-+-+-+-
The following two lines provide some protection against bad
row/column values. Including the code adds a bit of overhead.
    Row := Row MOD 24;
    Col := Col MOD 80;
-+-+-+-+-+-+-+-+-+-+-+-+-+-+-+-+-+-+-+-+-+-+-+-+-+-+-+-+-+-}


    GotoXY(Col, Row);
    WRITE(K:Width);
    TextAttr := old_attr;
END; { Disp_IntegerA }
END.
```

Listing 3.4. Source code for library EDITLINE.PAS.

```
UNIT EditLine;

{=====================================================================

             Copyright (c) 1987, 1988   Namir Clement Shammas
      LIBRARY NAME: EditLine
      VERSION: 1.0                                  DATE 09/23/1987
      PURPOSE: Provides one-line editor for string input.
      UPDATE HISTORY:


      =================================================================}

{*********************************************************************}
{************************} INTERFACE {*******************************}
{*********************************************************************}

Uses CRT, DOS, DataLib0;
FUNCTION Get_Input(Max_Len : BYTE { input  }) : STRING255;

{- - - - - - - - - - - - - - - - - - - - - - - - - - - - - - - - - -


ROUTINE PURPOSE: one-line editor routine that returns a string of up to
Max_Len characters. Routine support insert/overwrite mode, character
deletion, and cursor control keys.
PARAMETERS:
 INPUT: Max_Len - maximum number of characters to be inserted.
FUNCTION VALUE: the string typed by the end-user.
HANDLING BAD ARGUMENTS: If Max_Len is passed with a value of zero, the
routine assigns one to it.
                         ROUTINE DEPENDENCIES
                         --------------------
```

Identifier Name	Identifier Type	Source Library
STRING255	string	DataLib0
define_cursor	procedure	local
getchar	procedure	local
max	function	local
GotoXY	procedure	CRT
WhereX	function	CRT
WhereY	function	CRT

```
- - - - - - - - - - - - - - - - - - - - - - - - - - - - - - - - - - - - }

{*****************************************************************}
{***********************} IMPLEMENTATION {************************}
{*****************************************************************}

{$V-}

{------------------------------------------------- define_cursor -------}

PROCEDURE define_cursor(Low,         { input }
                        High : BYTE { input });
{- - - - - - - - - - - - - - - - - - - - - - - - - - - - - - - - -
```

ROUTINE PURPOSE: defines the cursor shape. Used to display normal
cursor (to indicate overwrite mode) and full-block cursor to indicate
insert mode.
PARAMETERS:
 INPUT: Low, High - the values that define the cursor height and
        exact location.

ROUTINE DEPENDENCIES

Identifier Name	Identifier Type	Source Library
Intr	procedure	DOS
Registers	record	DOS

```
- - - - - - - - - - - - - - - - - - - - - - - - - - - - - - - - - - - }
CONST INTERRUPT_NUM = $10;
VAR reg : Registers;
    ch, cl : BYTE;
BEGIN
    WITH reg DO BEGIN
        AX := $0100;
        ch := High;
        cl := Low;
        CX := 256 * ch + cl;
        Intr(INTERRUPT_NUM, reg)
    END; { WITH }
END; { define_cursor }

{------------------------------------------------------- get_char -------}

PROCEDURE getchar(VAR Ch1        : CHAR; { output }
                  VAR NumKeyCode : BYTE  { output });
```

```
{- - - - - - - - - - - - - - - - - - - - - - - - - - - - - - - - - - - -
```

ROUTINE PURPOSE: get character from the keyboard. If extended code
is detected, obtain the numeric code for the 'second' keystroke.
PARAMETERS:
 OUTPUT: Ch1 – the character for first (normal) keystroke.
         NumKeyCode – the ASCII code for extended key code.
COMMENTS: If an extended key code is detected, Ch1 is assigned ASCII
code zero, otherwise NumKeyCode is assigned a zero.

ROUTINE DEPENDENCIES

Identifier Name	Identifier Type	Source Library
KeyPressed	function	CRT
ReadKey	function	CRT

```
- - - - - - - - - - - - - - - - - - - - - - - - - - - - - - - - - - }
```

```
VAR ch2 : CHAR;
BEGIN
   NumKeyCode := 0;    { assign default }
   Ch1 := ReadKey;
   IF Ch1 = #0 THEN BEGIN
       ch2 := ReadKey;
       NumKeyCode := ORD(ch2)
   END;
END; { getchar }
```

```
{-------------------------------------------------------- max -------}
```

```
FUNCTION max(A, B : INTEGER { input  }) : INTEGER;
```

```
{- - - - - - - - - - - - - - - - - - - - - - - - - - - - - - - - - - - -
```

ROUTINE PURPOSE: returns the maximum of two integers.
PARAMETERS:
 INPUT: A – the first integer.
        B – the second integer.
FUNCTION VALUE: the largest value of parameters A or B.

```
- - - - - - - - - - - - - - - - - - - - - - - - - - - - - - - - - - }
```

```
BEGIN
   IF A > B THEN max := A ELSE max := B
END; { max }
```

```
{-------------------------------------------------------- Get_Input --------}

FUNCTION Get_Input(Max_Len : BYTE { input }) : STRING255;

{- - - - - - - - - - - - - - - - - - - - - - - - - - - - - - - - - - - - -
```

ROUTINE PURPOSE: one-line editor routine that returns a string of up to
Max_Len characters. Routine support insert/overwrite mode, character
deletion, and cursor control keys.
PARAMETERS:
 INPUT: Max_Len – the maximum number of characters to be inserted.
FUNCTION VALUE: the string typed by the end-user.
HANDLING BAD ARGUMENTS: If Max_Len is passed with a value of zero, the
routine assigns one to it.

ROUTINE DEPENDENCIES

Identifier Name	Identifier Type	Source Library
STRING255	string	DataLib0
define_cursor	procedure	local
getchar	procedure	local
max	function	local
GotoXY	procedure	CRT
WhereX	function	CRT
WhereY	function	CRT

```
- - - - - - - - - - - - - - - - - - - - - - - - - - - - - - - - - - - - - }

CONST BELL = #7; { bell character }
     BCHAR = #177; { background character }
     INSCHAR = #219; { Insert indicator }
     LARR = 75; { left arrow }
     RARR = 77; { right arrow }
     CLARR = 115; { Ctrl-Left arrow}
     CRARR = 116; { Ctrl-Right arrow }
     HOME_KEY = 71; { [Home] key }
     END_KEY = 79; { [End] key }
     INS_KEY = 82; { [Ins] key }
     DEL_KEY = 83; { [Del] key }
     BACKSP  = 8; { backspace }
```

```
VAR insertmode  : BOOLEAN;
    ch : CHAR;
    char_index, i, j, high, key_code, ord_ch, xpos, ypos : BYTE;
    strng   : STRING255;
BEGIN
    { Get cursor position }
    xpos := WhereX;
    ypos := WhereY;
    { test the value of Max_Len }
    IF Max_Len = 0 THEN Max_Len := 1;
    { fill with background character }
    FOR i := 1 TO Max_Len DO
        WRITE(BCHAR);
    GotoXY(xpos,ypos); { return to original cursor position }
    strng := ''; { initialize string }
    char_index := 1; { initialize character position index }
    insertmode := FALSE; { set to overwrite mode }
    getchar(ch, key_code);
    WHILE ch <> #13 DO BEGIN
        j := Length(strng);
        ord_ch := ORD(ch);
        { trap the backspace character }
        IF ord_ch = 8 THEN key_code := BACKSP;
        { translate the tab into a Ctrl-right arrow }
        IF ord_ch = 9 THEN key_code := CRARR;
        { trap [Esc] key to make it simply beep }
        IF (ord_ch = 27) AND (key_code = 0) THEN key_code := 1;
        IF key_code > 0 THEN BEGIN
            { translate the Shift-tab into a Ctrl-left arrow }
            IF key_code = 15 THEN key_code := CLARR;
            { translate the Up-arrow into a left arrow }
            IF key_code = 72 THEN key_code := LARR;
            { translate the Down-arrow into a right arrow }
            IF key_code = 80 THEN key_code := RARR;
            { translate the Page Up into Home key }
            IF key_code = 73 THEN key_code := HOME_KEY;
            { translate the Page Down into End key }
            IF key_code = 81 THEN key_code := END_KEY;
            CASE key_code OF
                BACKSP : BEGIN
                            IF char_index > 1 THEN
                                char_index := char_index - 1;
                            IF (char_index <= j) AND
                               (char_index > 0) THEN BEGIN
                                Delete(strng,char_index,1);
                                GotoXY(xpos,ypos);
```

```
                        WRITE(strng + BCHAR);
                END; { IF }
              END;
    LARR  : BEGIN
                IF char_index > 1 THEN DEC(char_index)
              END;
    RARR  : BEGIN
                IF (char_index < j) OR ((char_index = j) AND
                    (j < Max_Len))
                  THEN INC(char_index)
              END;
    CLARR : BEGIN
                IF char_index > 1 THEN DEC(char_index,2);
                WHILE (char_index > 1) AND
                      (strng[char_index] <> ` `) DO
                    DEC(char_index);
                IF char_index > 1 THEN INC(char_index);
              END;
    CRARR : BEGIN
                IF char_index < j THEN INC(char_index,2);
                WHILE (char_index < j) AND
                      (strng[char_index] <> ` `) DO
                    INC(char_index);
                IF char_index < j THEN INC(char_index);
              END;
HOME_KEY :  char_index := 1;
END_KEY  :  char_index := max(j,1);
INS_KEY  :  BEGIN
                    insertmode := NOT insertmode;
                  IF insertmode
                    { for Monochrome }
                    THEN define_cursor(12,0)
                    ELSE define_cursor(12,11);
                    { for CGA use
                      THEN define_cursor(7,0)
                      ELSE define_cursor(7,6); }
              END;
DEL_KEY :   IF (char_index <= j) AND
                (char_index > 0) THEN BEGIN
                Delete(strng,char_index,1);
                GotoXY(xpos+j-1,ypos);
                WRITE(BCHAR);
                GotoXY(xpos,ypos);
                WRITE(strng);
              END; { IF }
ELSE WRITELN(BELL);
```

```
                  END; { CASE }
                  GotoXY(xpos+char_index-1,ypos); { update cursor position }
            END
            ELSE BEGIN
                  IF insertmode THEN BEGIN
                        IF (char_index > j) AND (char_index < Max_Len) THEN
                              strng := strng + ch
                        ELSE IF (char_index <= j) THEN BEGIN
                              IF char_index > 1 THEN Insert(ch, strng, char_index)
                                          ELSE strng := ch + strng;
                        END; { IF }
                        { redisplay string }
                        GotoXY(xpos,ypos); WRITE(strng);
                        IF char_index < Max_Len THEN INC(char_index);
                        { reposition the cursor }
                        GotoXY(xpos+char_index-1,ypos);
                  END
                  ELSE BEGIN
                        GotoXY(xpos+char_index-1,ypos);
                        WRITE(ch);
                        IF char_index < Max_Len THEN INC(char_index);
                        IF (char_index >= j) AND (char_index < Max_Len) THEN
                              strng := strng + ch { concatenate }
                        ELSE IF (char_index < j) THEN BEGIN
                              Delete(strng, char_index-1, 1);
                              Insert(ch, strng, char_index-1);
                        END
                        ELSE IF (char_index - Max_Len) THEN BEGIN
                              Delete(strng, char_index, 1);
                              Insert(ch, strng, char_index);
                        END { IF }
                  END; { IF }
            END; { IF }
         getchar(ch, key_code);
   END; { WHILE ch <> #13 }
   define_cursor(12,11); { for monochrome }
   { define_cursor(7,6); for CGA }
   Get_Input := strng { return function value }
END; { Get_Input }
END.
```

Listing 3.5. Source code for library NUMINPUT.PAS.

```
UNIT NumInput;

{==================================================================
```

```
        Copyright (c) 1987, 1988    Namir Clement Shammas
    LIBRARY NAME: NumInput
    VERSION: 1.0                                    DATE 09/23/1987
    PURPOSE: Provides keyboard input routines for integer and reals
             that:
                1) Support error-proof input.
                2) Return values within specified ranges.
    COMMENTS:  This library can be easily expanded to include other
    integer and floating data types supported by Turbo Pascal 4.0 and
    later.
    UPDATE HISTORY:
```

```
==================================================================}
```

```
{******************************************************************}
{***************************} INTERFACE {**************************}
{******************************************************************}
```

```
Uses CRT, DataLib0;
PROCEDURE Read_Int(VAR I : INTEGER { output });
{- - - - - - - - - - - - - - - - - - - - - - - - - - - - - - - - -
```

```
ROUTINE PURPOSE: correctly inputs an integer from the keyboard.
PARAMETERS:
 OUTPUT: I - the sought integer.
HANDLING BAD ARGUMENTS: The routine performs internal checking to
validate the typed integer. Bad input causes the routine to beep,
clear the input, position the cursor to the original position, and
wait for new input.
```

                          ROUTINE DEPENDENCIES

Identifier Name	Identifier Type	Source Library
STRING80	string	DataLib0
ClrEol	procedure	CRT
GotoXY	procedure	CRT
WhereX	function	CRT
WhereY	function	CRT

```
- - - - - - - - - - - - - - - - - - - - - - - - - - - - - - - }
PROCEDURE Read_Int_Limit(VAR I    : INTEGER { output };
                             Low,           { input  }
                             High : INTEGER { input  });
{- - - - - - - - - - - - - - - - - - - - - - - - - - - - - - -
```

ROUTINE PURPOSE: Correctly inputs an integer (lying in a specified range) from the keyboard.

PARAMETERS:
  INPUT: Low - the lower range of accepted values.
         High - the upper range of accepted values.
  OUTPUT: I - the sought integer.
HANDLING BAD ARGUMENTS:

1) The routine performs internal checking to validate the typed integer. Bad input causes the routine to beep, clear the input, position the cursor to the original position, and wait for new input.

2) If parameter Low has a value greater than High, the values of the two parameters are swapped.

ROUTINE DEPENDENCIES

Identifier Name	Identifier Type	Source Library
STRING80	string	DataLib0
ClrEol	procedure	CRT
GotoXY	procedure	CRT
WhereX	function	CRT
WhereY	function	CRT

```
- - - - - - - - - - - - - - - - - - - - - - - - - - - - - - - }
PROCEDURE Read_Real(VAR X : REAL { output });
{- - - - - - - - - - - - - - - - - - - - - - - - - - - - - - -
```

ROUTINE PURPOSE: correctly inputs a real number from the keyboard.
PARAMETERS:
  OUTPUT: X - the sought real.
HANDLING BAD ARGUMENTS: The routine performs internal checking to validate the typed real. Bad input causes the routine to beep, clear the input, position the cursor to the original position, and wait for new input.

```
                    ROUTINE DEPENDENCIES
                    --------------------


        Identifier Name            Identifier Type        Source Library
        ---------------            ---------------        --------------

          STRING80                     string               DataLib0
          ClrEol                       procedure            CRT
          GotoXY                       procedure            CRT
          WhereX                       function             CRT
          WhereY                       function             CRT


- - - - - - - - - - - - - - - - - - - - - - - - - - - - - - - - - - }
PROCEDURE Read_Real_Limit(VAR X    : REAL; { output }
                              Low,          { input  }
                              High : REAL { input  });
{- - - - - - - - - - - - - - - - - - - - - - - - - - - - - - - - -
```

ROUTINE PURPOSE: correctly inputs a real number (lying in a specified
range) from the keyboard.
PARAMETERS:
  INPUT: Low - the lower range of accepted values.
         High - the upper range of accepted values.
  OUTPUT: X - the sought real number.
HANDLING BAD ARGUMENTS:
1) The routine performs internal checking to validate the typed real.
Bad input causes the routine to beep, clear the input, position the
cursor to the original position, and wait for new input.

2) If parameter Low has a value greater than High, the values of the
two parameters are swapped.

```
                    ROUTINE DEPENDENCIES
                    --------------------


        Identifier Name            Identifier Type        Source Library
        ---------------            ---------------        --------------

          STRING80                     string               DataLib0
          ClrEol                       procedure            CRT
          GotoXY                       procedure            CRT
          WhereX                       function             CRT
          WhereY                       function             CRT


- - - - - - - - - - - - - - - - - - - - - - - - - - - - - - - - - - }

{*****************************************************************}
{***********************} IMPLEMENTATION {***********************}
{*****************************************************************}

{-------------------------------------------------- Read_Int ----}

PROCEDURE Read_Int(VAR I : INTEGER { output });
CONST BEEP = ^G;
VAR error_code, xpos, ypos : INTEGER;
    strng : STRING80;
```

```
BEGIN
    { get cursor position }
    xpos := WhereX;
    ypos := WhereY;
    READLN(strng); { read string from keyboard }
    VAL(strng, I, error_code); { convert to integer }
    { is conversion OK? }
    WHILE error_code > 0 DO BEGIN
        WRITE(BEEP);
        { reposition cursor & clear to end-of-line }
        GotoXY(xpos, ypos); ClrEol;
        READLN(strng); { read another string }
        VAL(strng, I, error_code) { convert to integer }
    END;
END; { Read_Int }

{--------------------------------------------------- Read_Int_Limit ———}

PROCEDURE Read_Int_Limit(VAR I    : INTEGER { output };
                             Low,          { input  }
                             High : INTEGER { input  });
CONST BEEP = ^G;
VAR error_code, temp, xpos, ypos : INTEGER;
    strng : STRING80;
BEGIN
    IF Low > High THEN BEGIN { swap values }
        temp := Low;
        Low  := High;
        High := temp
    END;
    xpos := WhereX;
    ypos := WhereY;
    READLN(strng);
    VAL(strng, I, error_code);
    WHILE (error_code > 0) OR
          (I < Low) OR (I > High) DO BEGIN
        WRITE(BEEP);
        GotoXY(xpos, ypos); ClrEol;
        READLN(strng);
        VAL(strng, I, error_code)
    END;
END; { Read_Int_Limit }

{--------------------------------------------------- Read_Real ———}

PROCEDURE Read_Real(VAR X : REAL { output });
CONST BEEP = ^G;
VAR error_code, xpos, ypos : INTEGER;
    strng : STRING80;
BEGIN
    xpos := WhereX;
    ypos := WhereY;
```

```
     READLN(strng);
     VAL(strng, X, error_code);
     WHILE error_code > 0 DO BEGIN
         WRITE(BEEP);
         GotoXY(xpos, ypos); ClrEol;
         READLN(strng);
         VAL(strng, X, error_code)
     END;
END; { Read_Real }

{--------------------------------------- Read_Real_Limit ——}

PROCEDURE Read_Real_Limit(VAR X      : REAL; { output }
                              Low,        { input  }
                              High : REAL  { input  });
CONST BEEP = ^G;
VAR error_code, xpos, ypos : INTEGER;
    temp : REAL;
    strng : STRING80;
BEGIN
    IF Low > High THEN BEGIN { swap values }
        temp := Low;
        Low  := High;
        High := temp
    END;
    xpos := WhereX;
    ypos := WhereY;
    READLN(strng);
    VAL(strng, X, error_code);
    WHILE (error_code > 0) OR
          (X < Low) OR (X > High) DO BEGIN
        WRITE(BEEP);
        GotoXY(xpos, ypos); ClrEol;
        READLN(strng);
        VAL(strng, X, error_code)
    END;
END; { Read_Real_Limit }
END.
```

C H A P T E R

4

Strings

This chapter discusses four major string libraries. Each library specializes in one particular aspect of string manipulation. The libraries are as follows:

1. COMNSTR0.PAS – that contains a library of routines that implement rather common string operations.

2. SUPRSTR0.PAS – that offers a library of long strings, with a length capacity running in the few thousand characters. The routines perform basic operations on these long strings.

3. WORDSTR0.PAS – that supplies you with routines that enable you to parse strings into character-based words (not related to the predefined integer type WORD).

4. MINIGREP.PAS – that presents you with a library of text pattern matching routines.

LIBRARY COMNSTR0.PAS

This library, shown in Listing 4.1, presents a collection of string manipulation routines that complement those of Turbo Pascal. The routines are as follows:

```
FUNCTION UpperCaseStr(Strng : STRING255 { input  }) : STRING255;
```

converts its string-type argument into an upper-case string. For example, Uppercase('**Hello**') returns the string "HELLO".

```
FUNCTION LowerCaseStr(Strng : STRING255 { input  }) : STRING255;
```

converts its string-type argument into a lower-case string. For example,

Uppercase('**HELLO**') returns the string "hello".

```
FUNCTION IPos (SubStr,              { input }
              Strng     : STRING255; { input }
              StartIndex : BYTE      { input }) : BYTE;
```

works in a similar fashion as the predefined function **Pos()**. The difference is that **IPos()** permits you to include an offset that indicates where the string matching begins. For example, IPos(**ai,'The Rain in Spain'**,10) returns 15, obtained by scanning the substring **ai** starting at the 10th character. This enables you to bypass the **ai** in **Rain**, located at the 6th character.

```
FUNCTION CPos (SubStr,              { input }
              Strng     : STRING255; { input }
              CharMarker : CHAR      { input }) : BYTE;
```

is similar to function **IPos()**. The difference is that a character marker is used to locate where the string matching starts, instead of a numeric index. For example, CPos(**ai,The Rain in Spain,S**) returns 15, since scanning commences after the first occurrence of the letter **S**. The latter is used as the character marker.

```
FUNCTION RCPos (SubStr,             { input }
               Strng     : STRING255; { input }
               CharMarker : CHAR;    { input }
               Occurs    : BYTE      { input }) : BYTE;
```

is a modified version of function **CPos()**. The added feature is the function's ability to start string matching after the character marker has been encountered for a specified number of times. For example, RCPos(**ai,'The Rain in Spain'**,i,2) returns 15. This result is obtained in two stages: first, scanning the phase string and looking for two occurrences of the letter **i**; and second, by matching **ai** starting at the letter **n** found in the word **in**.

```
FUNCTION SPos (SubStr,              { input }
              Strng,                { input }
              StrMarker : STRING255 { input }) : BYTE;
```

is a version of function **CPos()** that uses a string marker instead of a character marker. For example, SPos(**ai,'The Rain in Spain', in**) returns 15. The result is obtained because the substring matching starts at the location of the substring **in**.

```
FUNCTION LastPos (SubStr,           { input }
                 Strng     : STRING255 { input }) : BYTE;
```

retur e location for the last occurrence of a substring in a string. Thus,

LastPos(**ai**,'**The Rain in Spain**') returns 15 because the rightmost substring pattern, **ai**, is located at the 15th character.

```
FUNCTION LeftStr(Strng    : STRING255; { in/out }
                 NumChars : BYTE        { input  }) : STRING255;
```

resembles the **LEFT$()** function in BASIC. It returns a specified number of leftmost characters. For example, LeftStr(**Hello There**,5) returns the string "Hello".

```
FUNCTION RightStr(Strng    : STRING255; { in/out }
                  NumChars : BYTE        { input  }) : STRING255;
```

resembles the **RIGHT$()** function in BASIC. It returns a specified number of rightmost characters. For example, RightStr(**Hello There**,5) returns the string "There".

```
FUNCTION PosMidStr(Strng : STRING255; { input }
                   First,             { input }
                   Last  : BYTE       { input }) : STRING255;
```

extracts a substring from a string by specifying the location of the first and last characters that define the substring. For example, PosMidStr('**Parisian**',4,6) returns the smaller string **"isi"**.

```
FUNCTION CountMidStr(Strng : STRING255; { input }
                     First,             { input }
                     Count : BYTE       { input }) : STRING255;
```

is similar to the **MID$()** function in BASIC. It extracts a substring from a string by specifying (1) the location of the first character to be copied, and (2) the number of characters that make up the substring. For example, PosMidStr(**Parisian**, 4, 3) returns the smaller string **"isi"**.

```
PROCEDURE DeleteMarker(VAR Strng      : STRING255; { in/out }
                           CharMarker : CHAR;      { input  }
                           CharCount  : BYTE;      { input  }
                           DelMarker  : BOOLEAN    { input  });
```

deletes a portion of a string by using a character marker. The marker determines where the string deletion begins. The length of the deleted substring is also specified, along with a flag that indicates whether or not the character marker itself is deleted. An example for using this procedure is as follows:

```
Strng := 'Hello @There';
DeleteMarker(Strng,'@',5,TRUE);
WRITELN(Strng); { writes "Hello " }
```

```
PROCEDURE OverWrite(     SubStr      : STRING255; { input  }
                     VAR Strng       : STRING255; { in/out }
                         StartIndex : BYTE        { input  });
```

overwrites parts of a string with a substring, starting at a specified character index. An example for calling this procedure is:

```
Strng := 'I love Pascal';
OverWrite('like', Strng, 3)
WRITELN(Strng); { writes "I like Pascal" }
```

```
PROCEDURE ReplaceString(     FindStr,                  { input  }
                             ReplaceStr  : STRING255; { input  }
                         VAR Strng       : STRING255; { in/out }
                             StartIndex  : BYTE;       { input  }
                             Frequency   : BYTE        { input  });
```

replaces one substring with another. The procedure also enables you to specify the starting location of the string translation. In addition, you can specify the maximum number of translated substrings. An example for utilizing this routine is as follows:

```
Strng := 'Ada is better than BASIC';
FindStr := 'Ada';
ReplaceStr := 'Pascal';
ReplaceString(FindStr, ReplaceStr, Strng, 1, 1);
WRITELN(Strng); { writes "Pascal is better than BASIC" }
```

```
PROCEDURE ReplaceRangeChar(FirstASCII,                 { input  }
                           LastASCII,                  { input  }
                           NewCharASCII,               { input  }
                           StartIndex   : BYTE;        { input  }
                       VAR Strng        : STRING255    { in/out });
```

replaces a range of characters found in a string with a new character. The routine enables you to specify the starting location where the character translation begins. An example for using this routine is as follows:

```
First := ORD('0');
Last  := ORD('9');
NewChar = ORD('+');
Strng := 'D2 H6 F2 H8 D2';
ReplaceRangeChar(First, Last, NewChar, 4, Strng);
WRITELN(Strng); { writes 'D2 H+ F+ H+ D+' }
```

```
FUNCTION RepeatStr(RptStr : STRING255; { input  }
                   Count   : BYTE       { input }) : STRING255;
```

creates a string by appending copies of a substring pattern. The number of replicated copies is also specified. For example, RepeatStr('+-',10) returns the string '+-+-+-+-+-+-+-+-+-+-'.

```
PROCEDURE PadLeft(VAR Strng   : STRING255; { in/out }
                      PadChar : CHAR;       { input  }
                      Count   : BYTE        { input });
```

pads a specified number of the same character to the left of a string. An example of using this routine is as follows:

```
    Strng := 'My name is Jack';
    PadLeft(Strng,'^',3);
    WRITELN(Strng); { writes "^^^My name is Jack" }
```

```
PROCEDURE PadRight(VAR Strng   : STRING255; { in/out }
                       PadChar : CHAR;       { input  }
                       Count   : BYTE        { input });
```

pads a specified number of the same character to the right of a string. An example of using this routine is as follows:

```
    Strng := 'My name is Jack';
    PadRight(Strng,'!',3);
    WRITELN(Strng); { writes "My name is Jack!!!" }
```

```
PROCEDURE PadEnds(VAR Strng    : STRING255; { in/out }
                      PadChar  : CHAR;       { input  }
                      AtEachEnd : BYTE        { input });
```

pads a specified number of any given character to both ends of a string. An example of using this routine is as follows:

```
    Strng := 'My name is Jack';
    PadEnds(Strng,'=',3);
    WRITELN(Strng); { writes "===My name is Jack===" }
```

```
FUNCTION ReverseStr(Strng : STRING255 { input }) : STRING255;
```

returns the reversed characters of an input string. For example,

```
ReverseStr('Pascal') returns the string 'lacsaP'.
```

```
FUNCTION Trim_Left(Strng    : STRING255; { input  }
                   TrimChar : CHAR        { input }):STRING255;
```

trims the left end of a string from a user-specified character. Normally, this is the space character. However, the routine is written to avoid limiting the trimmed character to just the space character. For example,

```
Trim_Left('   Hi there!',' ')
```

returns the string "Hi there!".

```
FUNCTION Trim_Right(Strng    : STRING255; { input  }
                    TrimChar : CHAR       { input  }):STRING255;
```

trims the right end of a string from a user-specified character. Normally, this is the space character. However, the routine is written to avoid limiting the trimmed character to just the space character. For example, Trim_Right(**'Hi there!','!'**) returns the string "Hi there".

```
FUNCTION Trim_Ends(Strng    : STRING255; { input  }
                   TrimChar : CHAR       { input  }):STRING255;
```

trims both ends of a string from a user-specified character. Normally, this is the space character. However, the routine is written to avoid limiting the trimmed character to just the space character. For example, Trim_Ends(**—'Hi there—','-'**) returns the string "Hi there".

LIBRARY SUPRSTR0.PAS

The **super** strings library, shown in Listing 4.2, offers routines to manage large strings. The sizes of these super strings go well beyond the 255-character limit of normal strings in Turbo Pascal. The constants and data structures used in defining super strings are presented below:

```
CONST MAX_SUPER_STRING = 3000;

TYPE
    SuperString = RECORD
        SSize : 0..MAX_SUPER_STRING;
        SStr  : ARRAY [1..MAX_SUPER_STRING] OF CHAR;
    END;
```

The MAX_SUPER_STRING constant specifies the maximum length of the super strings. The **SuperString** record structure consists of a string size counter and an array of characters. Using arrays of characters (as opposed to arrays of Turbo Pascal strings) results in going back to the basic string manipulation algorithms. Many of the routines use the predefined **Move()** routine to copy characters quickly from one string to another.

The routines of this library are as follows:

```
PROCEDURE Init_SuperStr(VAR SuperStr : SuperString { output });
Initializes a super string by setting its size field to zero.
```

```
PROCEDURE Str_to_SuperStr(VAR SuperStr : SuperString;{ output }
                              Strng    : STRING255   { input });
```

assigns a string to a super string. This procedure plays an important role in storing the first characters in a super string.

```
PROCEDURE SuperStr_to_Str(VAR SuperStr : SuperString;{ input }
                          VAR Strng    : STRING255   { output });
```

assigns a super string to a string, truncating the extra characters, if necessary.

```
PROCEDURE Copy_SuperStr(VAR OutSuperStr,              { output }
                            InSuperStr   : SuperString{ input });
```

copies the contents of one super string to another.

```
FUNCTION Length_SuperStr(SuperStr : SuperString { input }):WORD;
```

is the equivalent of the **Length()** function in Turbo Pascal. This function simply returns the value of the **SSize** field of a super string.

```
PROCEDURE LeftConcat_Str(VAR SuperStr : SuperString; { in/out }
                             Strng    : STRING255    { input });
```

concatenates a string to the left of a super string.

```
PROCEDURE LeftConcat_SuperStr(
         VAR LeftStr,                { input }
             RightStr : SuperString { in/out });
```

concatenates the **LeftStr** super string to the left of the **RightStr** super string.

```
PROCEDURE RightConcat_Str(
         VAR SuperStr : SuperString; { in/out }
             Strng    : STRING255    { input });
```

concatenates a string to the right of a super string.

```
PROCEDURE RightConcat_SuperStr(
         VAR LeftStr,                { in/out }
             RightStr : SuperString { input });
```

concatenates the **RightStr** super string to the right of the **LeftStr** super string.

```
PROCEDURE Insert_SuperStr(
          VAR SuperStr,                    { in/out }
              InStr       : SuperString;   { input  }
              StartIndex  : WORD           { input  });
```

inserts one super string inside another super string.

```
PROCEDURE Insert_Str(    Strng      : STRING255;   { input  }
                     VAR SuperStr   : SuperString; { in/out }
                         StartIndex : WORD          { input  });
```

inserts one string inside a super string. A character index is also supplied to indicate where the insertion begins.

```
PROCEDURE Delete_SuperStr(
          VAR SuperStr   : SuperString;{ in/out }
              StartIndex              { input  }
              CharCount  : WORD        { input  });
```

deletes portions of a super string. The index of the first deleted character and the number of removed characters are also specified.

```
FUNCTION PosStr(     SubStr     : STRING255;   { input  }
                 VAR SuperStr   : SuperString; { input  }
                     StartIndex : WORD         { input  })
                                                  : WORD;
```

locates a string inside a super string. An offset index is used to bypass a number of characters. This functions resembles **IPos()** in library COMNSTR0.PAS.

```
FUNCTION Pos_SuperStr(VAR SubStr,                  { input  }
                          SuperStr   : SuperString; { input  }
                          StartIndex : WORD         { input  })
                                                       : WORD;
```

locates a super string inside a bigger super string. An offset index is used to bypass a number of characters. This function is similar to the **IPos()** function in the COMNSTR0.PAS library.

```
PROCEDURE Mid_SuperStr(VAR SuperStr,                 { input  }
                           SubStr      : SuperString;{ output }
                           StartIndex,               { input  }
                           Count       : WORD        { input  });
```

extracts a portion of a super string. Starts at character location **StartIndex** and returns **Count** characters.

```
PROCEDURE Left_SuperStr(VAR SuperStr,                    { input  }
                            SubStr   : SuperString;{ output }
                            Count    : WORD          { input  });
```

extracts the left portion of a super string, returning **Count** characters.

```
PROCEDURE Right_SuperStr(VAR SuperStr,                   { input  }
                             SubStr   : SuperString;{ output }
                             Count    : WORD          { input  });
```

extracts the right portion of a super string, returning **Count** characters.

```
FUNCTION Compare_SuperStr(VAR SuperStr1,                 { input  }
                              SuperStr2 : SuperString { input  })
                                        : INTEGER;
```

compares two super strings and returns an integer-coded result. The possible
returned values are as follows:

```
+1 : SuperStr1 > SuperStr2
 0 : SuperStr1 = SuperStr2
-1 : SuperStr1 < SuperStr2
```

```
FUNCTION Compare_Str(
        VAR SuperStr : SuperString; { input  }
            Strng    : STRING255    { input  }) : INTEGER;
```

compares a super string and a string, returning an integer-coded result. The
possible returned values are as follows:

```
+1 : SuperStr > Strng
 0 : SuperStr = Strng
-1 : SuperStr < Strng
```

```
PROCEDURE Write_SuperStr(VAR SuperStr : SuperString { input });
```

displays a super string on the screen with page breaks.

```
PROCEDURE Print_SuperStr(VAR SuperStr : SuperString { input });
```

sends a copy of a super string to the line printer.

```
PROCEDURE Save_SuperStr(VAR SuperStr : SuperString; { input }
                            Filename : STRING255;    { input  }
                        VAR Done     : BOOLEAN       { output });
```

writes a super string to a sequential text file. Only one super string per file is allowed. This is not a limitation, since a single super string is even able to store short programs. The parameter **Done** is used to signal the success of the output process.

```
PROCEDURE Load_SuperStr(VAR SuperStr : SuperString; { output }
                            Filename : STRING255;   { input  }
                        VAR Done     : BOOLEAN      { output });
```

loads a single super string from a sequential text file. The parameter **Done** is used to signal the success of the input process. If the text file contains more characters than the capacity of the super string, the extra characters are ignored. This situation may arise when writing a super string to a file and then attempting to read it after the constant MAX_SUPER_STRING has been made smaller.

APPLICATION FOR SUPER STRINGS

Instead of writing a demonstration or application program for super strings, I will present the following application library: LONGSETS.PAS, shown in Listing 4.3, is a library that implements sets using super strings. The advantage of such a library is twofold. First, you can go beyond the current limitations of membership size in Turbo Pascal (assuming you have a large enough super string and small enough member names). Second, the names of the long set members can be reserved words, a feature not allowed in Turbo Pascal. The LONGSETS.PAS library contains a number of fundamental routines for set manipulation. For the sake of brevity, I have not made it extensive in functionality. Thus, I have not implemented set operations such as union, intersection, and difference.

The routines in the application library LONGSETS.PAS are as follows:

```
PROCEDURE Clear_Set(VAR StrSet : SuperString { output });
```

clears and initializes a super-string based set.

```
FUNCTION In_Set(    Member : STRING80;   { input  }
                VAR StrSet : SuperString { input  }) : BOOLEAN;
```

This function tests set membership and is similar to Turbo Pascal's IN <set variable or constant>.

```
PROCEDURE Add_Member(    Member : STRING80;   { input  }
                     VAR StrSet : SuperString; { in/out }
                     VAR Done   : BOOLEAN      { output });
```

adds a new member to the set. Duplicate members are not allowed. The routine is case sensitive, allowing you to store members with the same spelling but having different letter cases. You may store your set members in a uniform case (either upper case or lower case) to impose effectively case insensitivity.

```
PROCEDURE Del_Member(     Member : STRING80;      { input  }
                      VAR StrSet : SuperString; { in/out }
                      VAR Done   : BOOLEAN      { output });
```

deletes a member from the set. The routine is case sensitive. If you control the case of the members' name, then you have tighter control over membership deletion.

```
FUNCTION Get_Set_Size(VAR StrSet : SuperString { input  }) : WORD;
```

counts the number of members in a set.

```
FUNCTION LS_Ordl(     Member : STRING80;      { input  }
                  VAR StrSet : SuperString { input  }) : WORD;
```

determines the ordinal value of a member in a set. The first member has an ordinal value of one and not zero, as is the case with Turbo Pascal enumeration types.

```
FUNCTION LS_Val(     OrdVal : WORD;           { input  }
                 VAR StrSet : SuperString { input  }) : STRING80;
```

returns the set member with the supplied ordinal number. This function has no equivalent in Turbo Pascal and should prove to be very versatile.

```
FUNCTION LS_Succ(     Member : STRING80;      { input  }
                  VAR StrSet : SuperString { input  }) : STRING80;
```

returns the successor of the parameter-supplied set member. The successor of the last member is a null string.

```
FUNCTION LS_Pred(     Member : STRING80;      { input  }
                  VAR StrSet : SuperString { input  }) : STRING80;
```

returns the predecessor of the parameter-supplied set member. The predecessor of the first set member is a null string.

LIBRARY WORDTR0.PAS

This special library, shown in Listing 4.4, offers a special collection of routines. Rather than manipulating characters, text-based words are tackled. The library routines enable you to talk in terms of word position (instead of character position) and word count (instead of a number of characters). The routines are responsible for detecting the delimiters between words. To add flexibility to these routines, the word delimiters are not fixed. Instead, each routine accepts a string that contains the various delimiter characters. This enables you to utilize different punctuation characters, which adds more flexibility to the word manipulation.

The routines are written to handle properly leading and trailing delimiters. Placing a sequence of delimiters between words is also managed properly and does not confuse the scanning algorithms.

```
FUNCTION Count_Words (Words,                      { input  }
                      WordDelimStr : STRING255{ input  }) : BYTE;
```

counts the number of delimited words in string Words. For example,

```
Count_Words ('I like Pascal',' ')
```

returns 3, the number of space-delimited words in the string **I like Pascal**.

```
FUNCTION WordPos (WordStr,                        { input  }
                  Words,                          { input  }
                  WordDelimStr : STRING255; { input  }
                  WordIndex    : BYTE      { input  }) : BYTE;
```

returns the position of a word in a collection of words, starting at a specified word position. For example,

```
WordPos ('love','I love Pascal',' ',1)
```

returns 2, since **love** is the second word in the string containing the words.

```
PROCEDURE InsertWord(    WordStr,                      { input  }
                         WordDelimStr : STRING255; { input  }
                     VAR Words        : STRING255; { in/out }
                         AfterWord    : BYTE       { input  });
```

inserts a new word in a collection of words after a specific word number. An example of using this routine is as follows:

```
Words := 'I use Pascal';
InsertWord('Turbo',' ',Words,2);
WRITELN(Words); { writes "I use Turbo Pascal" }
```

```
PROCEDURE GetWord(     Words,                       { input  }
                       WordDelimStr : STRING255; { input  }
                   VAR WordSought   : STRING255; { output }
                       WordIndex    : BYTE       { input  });
```

returns the word at a specified word-based position. An example of utilizing this procedure is as follows:

```
GetWord('I use Turbo Pascal',' ',W,3);
WRITELN(W); { writes "Turbo" }
```

```
PROCEDURE DeleteWord(VAR Words        : STRING255;{ in/out }
                         WordDelimStr : STRING255;{ input  }
                         WordIndex,              { input  }
                         Wordcount    : BYTE     { input  });
```

deletes a specified number of words, starting with a particular word position number. An example for employing this routine is as follows:

```
Words := 'Good morning sunshine';
DeleteWord(Words,' ',2,2);
WRITELN(Words); { writes "Good" }
```

```
PROCEDURE TranslateWord(    FindWord,                  { input  }
                            ReplaceWord,               { input  }
                            WordDelimStr : STRING255;  { input  }
                        VAR Words        : STRING255;  { in/out }
                            WordIndex,                 { input  }
                            Frequency    : BYTE        { input  });
```

translates words in a string of words. You also specify the starting word position for the translation and the maximum number of translated words. An example of translating words is as follows:

```
Words := 'This software uses a mouse';
Translate('mouse','key',' ',Words,1,100);
WRITELN(Words); { writes "This software uses a key" }
```

LIBRARY MINIGREP.PAS

This library, shown in Listing 4.5, presents a set of Turbo Pascal routines for text matching included in an application program. Text pattern matching may be as basic as locating a specific text or as advanced as UNIX's GREP (Global Regular Expression Parser). Because of this variation, the first order of business is to define the features, capabilities, and limitations of the text-matching routines. The processed pattern may contain the following:

1. Fixed text: represents the basic text sought. Consider the following sentence: "The rain in Spain stays mainly in the plain." Text patterns such as "rain", "Spain" and "ain" find a match in the given sentence.

2. Wildcards: this includes the **?** and the ***** symbols used in a manner similar to that of MS-DOS. Thus, the following example patterns match with the above sentence:

```
rain*Spain*mainly
r??n*ma??ly*plain
```

3. Alternate text or subpatterns: are enclosed in braces and use the bar symbol as the delimiter character. For example, the following pattern matches the above sentence:

```
{rain|storm}*{Spain|France|Russia}*mainly*{plain|lab}
```

A pattern may not consist of only wildcards, since such a pattern would obviously match with every character! The limitations of the implemented version are as follows:

1. The pattern matcher is case sensitive.
2. The characters {} | *? may not be part of a normal text pattern.
3. No nested alternate subpatterns are allowed. There can be only one level of alternate subpatterns. Thus, a nested alternate pattern such as {Th{is | at | ese | ose}} must be rewritten as {This | That | These | Those}.
4. No text translation (that is, find/replace) is included.

What is the method involved in processing the patterns specified above? The answer is found in the good old divide-and-conquer strategy. First, the pattern processing revolves around the fact that it is parsed and converted into a list of subpatterns. This enables the pattern to be easily reused with multiple text lines, as is the case when processing a text file. The pattern parsing and conversion occurs in two main steps:

1. Handling alternate subpatterns. This takes place by building a set of strings that represents all of the possible combinations generated from the alternate subpatterns. For example, consider that the following pattern:

```
The {rain|storm}*{Spain|France}*plain
```

yields the four following string patterns:

```
The rain*Spain*plain
The storm*Spain*plain
The rain*France*plain
The storm*France*plain
```

Notice two things: first, the above patterns inherit any wildcard characters from the parent pattern; and secondly, neighboring fixed and alternate subpatterns are concatenated ("The" is concatenated with "rain" and "storm"). This leads to simplifying the emitted patterns.

2. Handling wildcards. Each of the pattern strings obtained in the first
    step is converted into a list of subpatterns. The wildcards act as a
    subpattern delimiter. When the list is created, an accompanying char-
    acter offset is also calculated and stored along with each subpattern.
    The offset value indicates the distance (in characters) between two
    neighboring subpatterns. If the **?** wildcard is encountered, the routine
    counts the total number of **?**s in sequence. The result is assigned to the
    character offset associated with the next subpattern. By contrast, if an
    * wildcard is scanned, the offset is set equal to zero. This signals that
    there is no specific character offset required to fulfill a pattern match.

The library routines that perform pattern matching are as follows:

```
PROCEDURE Prepare_Pattern(VAR Input_Pattern : STRING255;{in/out}
                          VAR Error_Message : STRING80  {output});
```

This procedure is used to preprocess the pattern as follows:

```
- Delete leading and trailing wildcards.

- Remove clusters of '*' wildcards.

- Verify that the number of open and close braces are equal
  and properly used.

- Verify that each alternate pattern contains at least two
  subpatterns.
```

The above preparation simplifies pattern processing in the other routines.
In the case of error detection in the pattern string, the **Error_Message** returns
a diagnostic message from the procedure.

```
PROCEDURE Make_Strings(
          Input_Pattern       : STRING255;       { input  }
          VAR Patterns        : Patterns_Array;  { output }
          VAR Total_SubPattern : BYTE            { output });
```

converts the input pattern (as returned by **Prepare_Pattern**) into an array of
string patterns. This routine tackles alternate subpatterns and yields an array
of one or more string patterns. The procedure first tests whether or not there are
any alternate subpatterns by scanning for the open-brace character. If none is
found, then a single element array is returned. Otherwise, character-by-
character scanning is employed. The routine keeps track of any **pending** text
originated by fixed subpatterns and wildcards. As subpatterns are extracted,
they are concatenated with the pending text. The procedure also builds the
array of string patterns. The first set of alternate subpatterns is used to create
a new array of strings. When subsequent alternate subpatterns are extracted,

two things occur: first, the copies of the current pattern strings are replicated as needed; secondly, the new subpatterns are concatenated with the new array of string patterns.

```
PROCEDURE Make_Lists (
         VAR Patterns        : Patterns_Array;       { input  }
             Total_SubPattern : BYTE;                 { input  }
         VAR Pattern_Lists   : Pattern_List_Array;  { output }
         VAR Num_Alt         : Integer_Array        { output });
```

converts the array of string patterns into a two-dimensional array of subpattern lists. This procedure breaks down the string patterns where wildcards are located. The character offset is also calculated and stored with each subpattern, as discussed earlier.

```
FUNCTION Has_Pattern (
             Line            : STRING255;          { input  }
             Total_SubPattern : BYTE;               { input  }
         VAR Pattern_Lists   : Pattern_List_Array; { input  }
         VAR Num_Alt,                               { input  }
             PatternPos      : Integer_Array       { output })
                                                   : BOOLEAN;
```

This is a double-purpose logical function. First, the boolean result of the function itself signals whether or not the pattern matching was successful. What about the matching character position? Since alternate subpatterns may generate several matching children patterns, I decided to use an array of integers to return the location where each child pattern matches. Array **PatternPos** returns the above result. The array should be scanned for positive values reflecting the sought results. It is important to point out that the current version of the pattern matching does not handle the tab characters. Thus, you should convert the tab characters into spaces in your text file before performing pattern matching. Otherwise, the tab character may cause lower values for the character locations. .

APPLICATION MINIGREP

The application program USE_GREP.PAS, shown in Listing 4.6, enables you to perform the following:

1.   Enter a text pattern. The program assigns its own default pattern. The current pattern is always displayed.

2.   Enter a line of text to test the pattern. Pressing return assigns a null string to the variable **Line**. This, in turn, causes the program to assign

a default string: a famous quote from a popular musical! This option enables you to experiment with pattern matching. A message is displayed to comment on the outcome of the pattern matching. A successful match leads to the display of the text line and the carat character on the screen line below it pointing to the matching location.

3. Enter a text filename to be scanned. The program inquires whether or not you want to echo the output to a printer and/or a text file.

Figure 4.1 shows a screen image for a sample session with USE_GREP.PAS. Text lines that match are shown with the carat character on the subsequent line pointing to the matching location. The text lines are numbered for your convenience.

Figure 4.2 shows a sample output generated by scanning the library MINIGREP.PAS with the pattern {FOR|WHILE|REPEAT|UNTIL}. The pattern seeks to display the lines that contain the beginning and end of the FOR, WHILE, and REPEAT loops.

There is a programmer's proverb that says "A program is never really finished." This is certainly true for the collection of pattern-matching routines presented here. You may ask, "Where do we go from here?" The routines and the application program may be enhanced to carry out the following:

1. Offer case sensitivity options.

2. Allow the {|*?} characters to be part of a pattern. Following the footsteps of GREP, this would involve the use of the backslash character. This character signals that the one following it is to be treated as part of a text. Thus, the following pattern "Balance*Interest" seeks the text "Balance*Interest".

3. Adapt the program to find the multiple occurrences of the same pattern on a text line. This is carried out by reprocessing the appropriate right portion of the text line.

4. Handle nested alternate subpatterns.

Incorporating a text translation feature brings forth many choices for the programmer. The basic question is, "How do you handle text with wildcards and alternate subpatterns?" Do you simply replace a matching pattern with a string, or consider translating specific subpatterns? While the answer is beyond the scope of this article, the topic of translating text patterns is important and cannot be totally ignored. With the pattern matching routines at your fingertips, you can perhaps proceed to design your custom translation routines.

The software bus schedule for program USE_GREP.PAS is shown in Figure 4.3.

Figure 4.1. Screen image for a sample session with USE_GREP.PAS.

```
                    Pattern Matching Utility
                    _____


0) Exit
1) Type a pattern (current pattern is "{FOR|WHILE|REPEAT|UNTIL}")
2) Type a text line
3) Scan a text file

Enter choice by number : 3

Enter filename ? minigrep.pas

Echo to printer? (Y/N) n
Echo to text file? (Y/N) y
Enter output filename ? grep.dmp
```

Figure 4.2. Output file, GREP.DMP, created during a sample session with USE_GREP.PAS.

```
223:    WHILE (strlen > 0) AND (Input_Pattern[1] IN ['?', '*']) DO BEGIN
        ^

234:    WHILE (strlen > 0) AND
        ^

238:    END; { WHILE }
             ^

247:    WHILE i > 0 DO BEGIN
        ^

250:    END; { WHILE }
             ^

258:    FOR i := 1 TO strlen DO BEGIN
        ^

285:    END; { FOR i }
             ^

305:    FOR i := 1 TO MAX_STRING_ARRAY DO
        ^

320:        FOR char_ptr2 := 1 TO ORD(lestr[0]) DO BEGIN
            ^

356:                    FOR i := 1 TO Total_SubPattern DO BEGIN
                        ^
```

```
359:                        END; { FOR }
                              ^
364:                        FOR i := Total_SubPattern+1 TO
                            ^
368:                        END; { FOR }
                              ^
371:                        FOR j := 1 TO num_subpattern DO
                            ^
373:                          FOR i := 1 TO Total_SubPattern DO BEGIN
                              ^
377:                            END; { FOR }
                                ^
394:          END; { FOR }
                ^
402:            FOR i := 1 TO Total_SubPattern DO
                ^
426:    FOR i := 1 TO MAX_STRING_ARRAY DO BEGIN
        ^
428:          FOR j := 1 TO MAX_ALTERNATIVES DO
              ^
430:    END; { FOR }
          ^
432:    FOR j := 1 TO Total_SubPattern DO BEGIN
        ^
439:          FOR char_ptr2 := 1 TO ORD(lestr[0]) DO BEGIN
              ^
459:                WHILE lestr[char_ptr2] = '?' DO BEGIN
                    ^
462:                END; { WHILE }
                      ^
469:          END; { FOR char_ptr2 }
                ^
482:      END; { FOR j }
            ^
510:    FOR i := 1 TO Total_SubPattern DO BEGIN
        ^
516:          WHILE (match OR redo) AND (NOT found) DO BEGIN
              ^
530:            WHILE (j <= Num_Alt[i]) AND match DO BEGIN
                ^
551:            END; { WHILE }
                  ^
555:          END; { WHILE }
                ^
563:        END; { FOR i }
              ^
```

Figure 4.3. Software Bus Schedule for USE_GREP.PAS.

SOFTWARE BUS SCHEDULE

PROJECT: USE_GREP.PAS
MODULE CRT

	Software Bus Schedule					
	A	B	C	D	E	F
OUTPUT						
proc ClrEol	X					
proc ClrScr	X					
proc GotoXY	X					
func ReadKey	X					
func WhereX	X					
func WhereY	X					

MODULE DataLib0

	Software Bus Schedule					
	A	B	C	D	E	F
OUTPUT						
string STRING80		X				
string STRING255		X				

MODULE PRINTER

	Software Bus Schedule					
	A	B	C	D	E	F
OUTPUT						
device LST			X			

MODULE ComnLib0

	Software Bus Schedule					
	A	B	C	D	E	F
OUTPUT						
proc Center				X		
func YesNo				X		
INTERFACE INPUT						
string STRING80		X				

```
IMPLEMENTATION INPUT
proc ClrEol             X
proc ClrScr             X
proc GotoXY             X
func ReadKey            X
func WhereX             X
func WhereY             X
```

MODULE   ComnStr0

	Software Bus Schedule					
	A	B	C	D	E	F

OUTPUT

	A	B	C	D	E	F
func PosMidStr					X	
func IPos					X	

INTERFACE INPUT

	A	B	C	D	E	F
string STRING255		X				

MODULE   MiniGrep

	Software Bus Schedule					
	A	B	C	D	E	F

OUTPUT

	A	B	C	D	E	F
func Has_Pattern						X
proc Make_Lists						X
proc Make_Strings						X
array Patterns_Array						X
array Patterns_List_Array						X
proc Prepare_Pattern						X

INTERFACE INPUT

	A	B	C	D	E	F
string STRING80		X				
string STRING255		X				

IMPLEMENTATION INPUT

	A	B	C	D	E	F
func PosMidStr					X	
func IPos					X	

MODULE   main

	Software Bus Schedule					
	A	B	C	D	E	F

ROUTINEINPUT

	A	B	C	D	E	F
string STRING255		X				

```
INPUT
proc Center                                            X
proc GotoXY              X
func Has_Pattern                                              X
array Integer_Array
device LST                          X
proc Make_Lists                                              X
proc Make_Strings                                            X
array Patterns_Array                                        X
array Patterns_List_Array                                   X
proc Prepare_Pattern                                        X
func ReadKey             X
string STRING255                    X
func YesNo                                      X
```

Listing 4.1. Source code for library COMNSTR0.PAS.

```
UNIT ComnStr0;

{=================================================================

        Copyright (c) 1987, 1988   Namir Clement Shammas
    LIBRARY NAME: ComnStr0
    VERSION: 1.0                                DATE 09/23/1987
    PURPOSE: Library for additional common string operations.
    UPDATE HISTORY:

    =================================================================}

{****************** :********************************************}
{**************************} INTERFACE {************************}
{****************************************************************}

Uses DataLib0;
{ STRING255 is imported from DataLib0 and used by all routines }

{----------------------------------------------- UpperCaseStr ------}

FUNCTION UpperCaseStr(Strng : STRING255 { input  }) : STRING255;
{- - - - - - - - - - - - - - - - - - - - - - - - - - - - - - -

ROUTINE PURPOSE: returns the upper-case version of an input string.
PARAMETERS:
 INPUT: Strng - the input string.
FUNCTION VALUE: returns the upper-case characters of string Strng.
HANDLING BAD ARGUMENTS: If the input string is null, a null string
is returned.
```

- }
```
FUNCTION LowerCaseStr(Strng : STRING255 { input  }) : STRING255;
{- - - - - - - - - - - - - - - - - - - - - - - - - - - - - - - - -
```
ROUTINE PURPOSE: returns the lower-case version of an input string.
PARAMETERS:
 INPUT: Strng - the input string.
FUNCTION VALUE: returns the lower-case characters of string Strng.
HANDLING BAD ARGUMENTS: If the input string is null, a null string
is returned.

- }
```
FUNCTION IPos(SubStr,                    { input }
             Strng      : STRING255; { input }
             StartIndex : BYTE        { input }) : BYTE;
{- - - - - - - - - - - - - - - - - - - - - - - - - - - - - - - - -
```

ROUTINE PURPOSE: returns the position of a substring in a string,
given an offset value that specifies where the search begins.
PARAMETERS:
 INPUT: SubStr - the string for the search pattern.
         Strng - the main string.
         StartIndex - the offset for the search.
FUNCTION VALUE: returns the location of the first match, or zero if no
match occurs.
HANDLING BAD ARGUMENTS: A zero value is returned by the function when:
    1) Either Strng or SubStr is a null string.
    2) The value of StartIndex exceeds the length of Strng.
    3) The value of StartIndex is less than one.

- }
```
FUNCTION CPos(SubStr,                    { input }
             Strng      : STRING255; { input }
             CharMarker : CHAR        { input }) : BYTE;
{- - - - - - - - - - - - - - - - - - - - - - - - - - - - - - - - -
```

ROUTINE PURPOSE: returns the position of a substring in a string.
The search begins after the location of the character marker.
PARAMETERS:
 INPUT: SubStr - the string for the search pattern.
         Strng - the main string.
         CharMarker - the character marker used to determine the
            starting search location.
FUNCTION VALUE: returns the location of the first match, or zero if no match
occurs.
HANDLING BAD ARGUMENTS: A zero value is returned by the function when:
    1) Either Strng or SubStr is a null string.
    2) The character marker is null.

- }
```
FUNCTION RCPos(SubStr,                    { input }
              Strng      : STRING255; { input }
              CharMarker : CHAR;       { input }
              Occurs     : BYTE        { input }) : BYTE;
{- - - - - - - - - - - - - - - - - - - - - - - - - - - - - - - - -
```

ROUTINE PURPOSE: scans a string for a substring. The search begins only after a specified number of character markers has been encountered.
PARAMETERS:
  INPUT: SubStr - the string for the search pattern.
            Strng - the main string.
            CharMarker - the character marker used to determine the
                starting search location.
            Occurs - the specified frequency of string matching.
FUNCTION VALUE: returns the location of the specified match occurrence, or zero if not enough matches occur.
HANDLING BAD ARGUMENTS:
A) A zero value is returned by the function when:
    1) Either Strng or SubStr is a null string.
    2) The character marker is null.
B) If the value of Occurs is less than one, Occurs is set equal to 1.

```
- - - - - - - - - - - - - - - - - - - - - - - - - - - - - - - - - }
FUNCTION SPos(SubStr,                 { input }
             Strng,                   { input }
             StrMarker   : STRING255 { input }) : BYTE;
{- - - - - - - - - - - - - - - - - - - - - - - - - - - - - - - - -
```

ROUTINE PURPOSE: returns the position of substring SubStr in string Strng. The search begins after the location of the string marker StrMarker. If the character marker is not found the search is aborted.
PARAMETERS:
  INPUT: SubStr - the pattern substring used in the search.
        Strng - the string searched.
        StrMarker - the string that contains the marker that specifies
           where the search begins.
FUNCTION VALUE: returns the position of the matching string, or zero if no match is found.
HANDLING BAD ARGUMENTS: If any of the three string-typed parameters passes a null value, the function is exited returning a zero value.

```
- - - - - - - - - - - - - - - - - - - - - - - - - - - - - - - - - }
FUNCTION LastPos(SubStr,                 { input }
                 Strng       : STRING255 { input }) : BYTE;
{- - - - - - - - - - - - - - - - - - - - - - - - - - - - - - - - -
```

ROUTINE PURPOSE: returns the position of the last occurrence of a substring in a string.
PARAMETERS:
  INPUT: SubStr - the substring used in the matching.
        Strng - the main string.

FUNCTION VALUE: the character index value of the matched substring is returned. If no match is found, a zero value is returned.

HANDLING BAD ARGUMENTS: If either string-typed arguments passes a null string, the function exits returning a zero value.

- }

```
FUNCTION LeftStr(Strng    : STRING255; { in/out }
                 NumChars : BYTE        { input  }) : STRING255;
```

{- -

ROUTINE PURPOSE: returns the NumChars leftmost characters of a string.
PARAMETERS:
 INPUT: Strng - the source string.
        NumChars - the number of characters to extract.
FUNCTION VALUE: the leftmost NumChars characters of string Strng.
HANDLING BAD ARGUMENTS: If NumChars is less than one, only the first character of the original string is returned as the new string.
If Numchars exceeds the length of the original string, the entire string is returned (i.e., a NOP).

- }
```
FUNCTION RightStr(Strng    : STRING255; { in/out }
                  NumChars : BYTE        { input  }) : STRING255;
```
{- -

ROUTINE PURPOSE: returns the NumChars rightmost characters of a string.
PARAMETERS:
 INPUT: Strng - the source string.
        NumChars - the number of characters to extract.
FUNCTION VALUE: the rightmost NumChars characters of string Strng.
HANDLING BAD ARGUMENTS: If NumChars is less than one, only the last character of the original string is returned as the new string.
If Numchars exceeds the length of the original string, the entire string is return (i.e. a NOP).

- }
```
FUNCTION PosMidStr(Strng : STRING255; { input  }
                   First,             { input  }
                   Last  : BYTE       { input  }) : STRING255;
```
{- -

ROUTINE PURPOSE: extracts the middle portion of a string by specifying the position of the first and last characters.
PARAMETERS:
 INPUT: Strng - the source string.
        First - the first character to be extracted.
        Last - the last character extracted.
FUNCTION VALUE: the extracted string.

HANDLING BAD ARGUMENTS: The function aborts, returning a null
string when:
1) The source string is a null string.
2) Bad argument values have been assigned to the parameters
   Last and/or First.

```
- - - - - - - - - - - - - - - - - - - - - - - - - - - - - - - - - }
FUNCTION CountMidStr(Strng : STRING255; { input  }
                     First,             { input  }
                     Count : BYTE       { input  }) : STRING255;
{- - - - - - - - - - - - - - - - - - - - - - - - - - - - - - - - -
```

ROUTINE PURPOSE: extracts the middle portion of a string by specifying
the position of the first character and the number of characters
extracted.
PARAMETERS:
 INPUT: Strng - the source string.
        First - the first character to be extracted.
        Count - the number of characters extracted.
FUNCTION VALUE: the extracted string.
HANDLING BAD ARGUMENTS: The function aborts, returning a null
string if the source is a null string.

```
- - - - - - - - - - - - - - - - - - - - - - - - - - - - - - - - - }
PROCEDURE DeleteMarker(VAR Strng     : STRING255; { in/out }
                           CharMarker : CHAR;      { input  }
                           CharCount  : BYTE;      { input  }
                           DelMarker  : BOOLEAN    { input  });
{- - - - - - - - - - - - - - - - - - - - - - - - - - - - - - - - -
```

ROUTINE PURPOSE: deletes CharCount characters of a string using a
character marker. The logical parameter DelMarker is used to decide
whether or not the marker character itself is also removed. The
number of characters specified in CharCount EXCLUDES the character
marker.
PARAMETERS:
 INPUT: CharMarker - the character marker used in specifying where
        the deletion process begins.
        CharCount - the number of characters to be deleted.
        DelMarker - the flag that signals whether or not the marker
        character itself is also deleted.
 IN/OUT: the modified string.
HANDLING BAD ARGUMENTS: The procedure exits if either the source string
or the character marker is null.

```
- - - - - - - - - - - - - - - - - - - - - - - - - - - - - - - - - }
PROCEDURE OverWrite(    SubStr     : STRING255; { input  }
                    VAR Strng      : STRING255; { in/out }
                        StartIndex : BYTE       { input  });
{- - - - - - - - - - - - - - - - - - - - - - - - - - - - - - - - -
```

ROUTINE PURPOSE: overwrites the parts of string Strng with SubStr,
starting at the StartIndex position. If the resulting string tends
to grow, the substring is truncated.
PARAMETERS:
  INPUT: SubStr - the substring containing the overwriting text.
         StartIndex - the character index where previous text
              is overwritten.
  IN/OUT: Strng - the modified string.
HANDLING BAD ARGUMENTS: The procedure exits if either the source string
or the substring is a null string.

```
- - - - - - - - - - - - - - - - - - - - - - - - - - - - - - - - - }
PROCEDURE ReplaceString(    FindStr,                   { input  }
                            ReplaceStr  : STRING255; { input  }
                        VAR Strng       : STRING255; { in/out }
                            StartIndex  : BYTE;      { input  }
                            Frequency   : BYTE       { input  });
{- - - - - - - - - - - - - - - - - - - - - - - - - - - - - - - - -
```

ROUTINE PURPOSE: replaces substring FindStr with ReplaceStr in string
Strng. The StartIndex specifies where the substring scanning begins,
and the Frequency parameter provides the maximum number of substring
translations. If that count is too high, the extra is ignored.
PARAMETERS:
  INPUT: FindStr - the substring sought for replacement.
         ReplaceStr - the replacement substring.
         StartIndex - the location where text translation begins.
         Frequency - the maximum number of translations to conduct.
  IN/OUT: Strng - the modified string.
HANDLING BAD ARGUMENTS: The procedure exits if either the source string
or FindStr is null. In addition, if the value of StartIndex exceeds
the length of the source string, the routine exits.

```
- - - - - - - - - - - - - - - - - - - - - - - - - - - - - - - - - }
PROCEDURE ReplaceRangeChar(    FirstASCII,              { input }
                               LastASCII,               { input }
                               NewCharASCII,            { input }
                               StartIndex   : BYTE;     { input }
                           VAR Strng        : STRING255 { in/out });
{- - - - - - - - - - - - - - - - - - - - - - - - - - - - - - - - -
```

ROUTINE PURPOSE: replaces all occurrences of any character with an
ASCII code value in the range [FirstASCII,LastASCII] with a character
whose ASCII code is NewCharASCII. The StartIndex specifies where
the character translation is to occur.
PARAMETERS:
  INPUT: FirstASCII - the ASCII code for the lower range of
              translatable characters.
         LastASCII - the ASCII code for the upper range of translatable
              characters.
         NewCharASCII - the ASCII code for the replacement character.
         StartIndex - the string location where the character
              translation begins.

IN/OUT: Strng - the source/destination string to be examined.
HANDLING BAD ARGUMENTS:
(A) The routine is exited without performing any character translation
when:
    1) The source string is a null string.
    2) Any of the arguments FirstASCII, LastASCII, and NewCharASCII
       are outside the range 1..255.
    3) The argument FirstASCII is greater than LastASCII.
    4) The argument StartIndex is greater than the length of the
       source string.
(B) If the value of argument StartIndex is less than one, it is set
equal to one.

```
- - - - - - - - - - - - - - - - - - - - - - - - - - - - - - - - - - }
FUNCTION RepeatStr(RptStr : STRING255; { input  }
                   Count  : BYTE        { input }) : STRING255;
{- - - - - - - - - - - - - - - - - - - - - - - - - - - - - - - - - -
```

ROUTINE PURPOSE: creates a large string by repeatedly concatenating
a substring.
FUNCTION VALUE: a string that contains Count number of string RptStr.
PARAMETERS:
 INPUT: RptStr - the small string used in building the large string.
        Count - the number of RptStr to be concatenated.
HANDLING BAD ARGUMENTS:
(A) The function returns a null if the building string is null.
(B) If the argument Count is less than one, it is set equal to one.
(C) If the argument Count tends to produce a string beyond the capacity
of string type STRING255, its value is adjusted accordingly.

                    ROUTINE DEPENDENCIES

Identifier Name	Identifier Type	Source Library
MAX_STRING	constant	DataLib0

```
- - - - - - - - - - - - - - - - - - - - - - - - - - - - - - - - - - }
PROCEDURE PadLeft(VAR Strng   : STRING255; { in/out }
                      PadChar : CHAR;       { input  }
                      Count   : BYTE        { input }) ;
{- - - - - - - - - - - - - - - - - - - - - - - - - - - - - - - - - -
```

ROUTINE PURPOSE: pads characters to the left end of a string.
PARAMETERS:
 INPUT: PadChar - the padding character.
         AtEachEnd - the number of characters to be padded at the left
            end.
 IN/OUT: Strng - the padded string.

HANDLING BAD ARGUMENTS:
(A) The routine is exited without padding the string when either the source string or the padding character is null.
(B) If the argument AtEachEnd is less than one, its value is set equal to one.
(C) If the number of padded characters exceeds the constant MAX_STRING, the number in question is adjusted.

ROUTINE DEPENDENCIES

Identifier Name	Identifier Type	Source Library
MAX_STRING	constant	DataLib0
RepeatStr	function	local

```
- - - - - - - - - - - - - - - - - - - - - - - - - - - - - - - - - }
PROCEDURE PadRight(VAR Strng   : STRING255; { in/out }
                       PadChar : CHAR;      { input  }
                       Count   : BYTE       { input  });
{- - - - - - - - - - - - - - - - - - - - - - - - - - - - - - - - -
```

ROUTINE PURPOSE: pads characters to the right end of a string.
PARAMETERS:
  INPUT: PadChar - the padding character.
          AtEachEnd - the number of characters to be padded at the
            right end.
  IN/OUT: Strng - the padded string.
HANDLING BAD ARGUMENTS:
(A) The routine is exited without padding the string when the source string or the padding character is null.
(B) If the argument AtEachEnd is less than one, its value is set equal to one.
(C) If the number of padded characters exceeds the constant MAX_STRING, the number in question is adjusted.

ROUTINE DEPENDENCIES

Identifier Name	Identifier Type	Source Library
MAX_STRING	constant	DataLib0
RepeatStr	function	local

```
- - - - - - - - - - - - - - - - - - - - - - - - - - - - - - - - - }
PROCEDURE PadEnds(VAR Strng     : STRING255; { in/out }
                      PadChar   : CHAR;      { input  }
                      AtEachEnd : BYTE       { input  });
{- - - - - - - - - - - - - - - - - - - - - - - - - - - - - - - - -
```

ROUTINE PURPOSE: pads characters to both ends of a string.
PARAMETERS:
  INPUT: PadChar – the padding character.
           AtEachEnd – the number of characters to be padded at each
             end.
  IN/OUT: Strng – the padded string.
HANDLING BAD ARGUMENTS:
(A) The routine is exited without padding the string when the source
string or the padding character is null.
(B) If the argument AtEachEnd is less than one, its value is set equal
to one.
(C) If the number of padded characters exceeds the constant MAX_STRING,
the number in question is adjusted.

ROUTINE DEPENDENCIES

Identifier Name	Identifier Type	Source Library
MAX_STRING	constant	DataLib0
RepeatStr	function	local

- }
FUNCTION ReverseStr(Strng : STRING255 { input }) : STRING255;
{- -

ROUTINE PURPOSE: returns the reversed characters of a given string.
PARAMETERS:
  INPUT: Strng – the source string to be reversed.
FUNCTION VALUE: the function returns a reversed string.
HANDLING BAD ARGUMENTS: The function returns a null string when
the source string is a null string.

- }
FUNCTION Trim_Left(Strng   : STRING255; { input }
                   TrimChar : CHAR   { input }) : STRING255;
{- -

ROUTINE PURPOSE: trims trailing characters from a string.
PARAMETERS:
  INPUT: Strng – the source string to be trimmed.
           TrimChar – the character to be removed from the left end of
             the source string.
FUNCTION VALUE: the function returns a left-trimmed string.
HANDLING BAD ARGUMENTS: The function returns a null string when:
    1) The source string or trimming character is null.
    2) The source string contains only a sequence of the
       trimming character.

- }

```
FUNCTION Trim_Right(Strng    : STRING255; { input  }
                    TrimChar : CHAR       { input  }) : STRING255;
{- - - - - - - - - - - - - - - - - - - - - - - - - - - - - - - - -
```

ROUTINE PURPOSE: trims leading characters from a string.
PARAMETERS:
 INPUT: Strng - the source string to be trimmed.
         TrimChar - the character to be removed from the left end of
             the source string.
FUNCTION VALUE: the function returns a right-trimmed string.
HANDLING BAD ARGUMENTS: The function returns a null string when:
    1) The source string or trimming character is null.
    2) The source string contains only a sequence of the
       trimming character.

```
- - - - - - - - - - - - - - - - - - - - - - - - - - - - - - - - - }
FUNCTION Trim_Ends(Strng    : STRING255; { input  }
                   TrimChar : CHAR       { input  }) : STRING255;
{- - - - - - - - - - - - - - - - - - - - - - - - - - - - - - - - -
```

ROUTINE PURPOSE: trims leading and trailing characters from a string.
PARAMETERS:
 INPUT: Strng - the source string to be trimmed.
         TrimChar - the character to be removed from the head and
             tail of the source string.
FUNCTION VALUE: the function returns a trimmed string.
HANDLING BAD ARGUMENTS: The function returns a null string when:
    1) The source string or trimming character is null.
    2) The source string contains only a sequence of the
       trimming character.

ROUTINE DEPENDENCIES

Identifier Name	Identifier Type	Source Library
Trim_Left	function	local
Trim_Right	function	local

```
- - - - - - - - - - - - - - - - - - - - - - - - - - - - - - - - - }


{*****************************************************************}
{***********************} IMPLEMENTATION {************************}
{*****************************************************************}

{$V-}
```

```pascal
{---------------------------------------------- UpperCaseStr ————}

FUNCTION UpperCaseStr(Strng : STRING255 { input  }) : STRING255;
VAR i, strlen : BYTE;
BEGIN
    strlen := Length(Strng);
    IF strlen = 0 THEN BEGIN
        UpperCaseStr := '';
        EXIT;
    END; { IF }
    FOR i := 1 TO strlen DO
        Strng[i] := UpCase(Strng[i]);
    UpperCaseStr := Strng;
END; { UpperCaseStr }


{---------------------------------------------- LowerCaseStr ————}

FUNCTION LowerCaseStr(Strng : STRING255 { input  }) : STRING255;
VAR i, strlen, ascii_shift : BYTE;
BEGIN
    strlen := Length(Strng);
    IF strlen = 0 THEN BEGIN
        LowerCaseStr := '';
        EXIT;
    END; { IF }
    ascii_shift := ORD('a') - ORD('A');
    FOR i := 1 TO strlen DO
        IF (Strng[i] >= 'A') AND (Strng[i] <= 'Z') THEN
            Strng[i] := CHR(ORD(Strng[i]) + ascii_shift);
    LowerCaseStr := Strng;
END; { LowerCaseStr }


{---------------------------------------------- IPos ————}

FUNCTION IPos(SubStr,                  { input }
              Strng       : STRING255; { input }
              StartIndex  : BYTE       { input }) : BYTE;
VAR strpos : BYTE;
BEGIN
    {- - - - - - - - Argument checking  - - - - - - - -}
    IF (Strng = '') OR (SubStr = '') THEN BEGIN
        IPos := 0;
        EXIT;
    END; { IF }
    {- - - - - - - Main body of the procedure - - - - - - - - - -}
    strpos := 0; { initialize with default function value }
    IF (StartIndex > 0) AND (StartIndex <= Length(Strng)) THEN BEGIN
        { clip leading part of the string Strng? }
        IF StartIndex > 1 THEN Delete(Strng, 1, StartIndex);
        strpos := POS(SubStr, Strng);
```

```
        IF (strpos > 0) AND (StartIndex > 1) THEN
            INC(strpos, StartIndex);
    END; { IF }
    IPos := strpos { return function value }
END; { IPos }


{---------------------------------------------------- CPos --------}

FUNCTION CPos(SubStr,                    { input }
              Strng       : STRING255; { input }
              CharMarker  : CHAR        { input }) : BYTE;
VAR markerpos, strpos : BYTE;
BEGIN
    {- - - - - - - - Argument checking  - - - - - - - -}
    IF (Strng = '') OR (SubStr = '') OR (CharMarker = '') THEN BEGIN
        CPos := 0;
        EXIT;
    END; { IF }
    {- - - - - - - - Main body of the procedure - - - - - - - - - -}
    markerpos := Pos(CharMarker, Strng); { locate marker }
    strpos := 0;
    IF markerpos > 0 THEN BEGIN
        IF markerpos > 1 THEN Delete(Strng, 1, markerpos);
        strpos := POS(SubStr, Strng);
        IF (strpos > 0) AND (markerpos > 1) THEN
            INC(strpos, markerpos);
    END; { IF }
    CPos := strpos { return function value }
END; { CPos }


{-------------------- ------------------------------- RCPos --------}

FUNCTION RCPos(SubStr,                    { input }
               Strng       : STRING255; { input }
               CharMarker  : CHAR;       { input }
               Occurs      : BYTE        { input }) : BYTE;
VAR markerpos, strpos, total_offset : BYTE;
BEGIN
    {- - - - - - - - Argument checking  - - - - - - - -}
    IF (Strng = '') OR (SubStr = '') OR (CharMarker = '') THEN BEGIN
        RCPos := 0;
        EXIT;
    END; { IF }
    {- - - - - - - - Main body of the procedure - - - - - - - - - -}
    IF Occurs < 1 THEN Occurs := 1; { check & adjust occurrence value }
    total_offset := 0; { initialize total offset }
    markerpos := Pos(CharMarker, Strng); { locate first marker }
```

```pascal
    WHILE (markerpos > 0) AND (Occurs > 0) DO BEGIN
        Delete(Strng, 1, markerpos);
        { update character offset }
        INC(total_offset, markerpos);
        { find next marker position }
        markerpos := Pos(CharMarker, Strng);
        DEC(Occurs); { decrement occurrence count }
    END; { WHILE }
    strpos := 0;
    IF Occurs = 0 THEN BEGIN
        strpos := POS(SubStr, Strng);
        IF strpos > 0  THEN INC(strpos, total_offset);
    END; { IF }
    RCPos := strpos { return function value }
END; { RCPos }


{--------------------------------------------------------- SPos ———}

FUNCTION SPos(SubStr,                    { input }
              Strng,                     { input }
              StrMarker   : STRING255 { input }) : BYTE;
VAR markerpos, strpos : BYTE;
BEGIN
    {- - - - - - - - Argument checking  - - - - - - - -}
    IF (Strng = '') OR (SubStr = '') OR (StrMarker = '') THEN BEGIN
        SPos := 0;
        EXIT;
    END; { IF }
    {- - - - - - - - Main body of the procedure - - - - - - - - - -}
    markerpos := Pos(StrMarker, Strng); { locate marker }
    strpos := 0;
    IF markerpos > 0 THEN BEGIN
        IF markerpos > 1 THEN Delete(Strng, 1, markerpos);
        strpos := POS(SubStr, Strng);
        IF (strpos > 0) AND (markerpos > 1) THEN
            INC(strpos, markerpos);
    END; { IF }
    SPos := strpos { return function value }
END; { SPos }


{--------------------------------------------------------- LastPos ———}

FUNCTION LastPos(SubStr,                    { input }
                 Strng        : STRING255 { input }) : BYTE;
VAR lastloc, index : BYTE;
BEGIN
    {- - - - - - - - Argument checking  - - - - - - - -}
    IF (Strng = '') OR (SubStr = '') THEN BEGIN
        LastPos := 0;
        EXIT;
    END; { IF }
```

```
{- - - - - - - - Main body of the procedure - - - - - - - - - -}
lastloc := 0; { initialize index }
index := POS(SubStr, Strng); { locate first substring occurrence }
WHILE index > 0 DO BEGIN
    { save the location of the last match }
    lastloc := lastloc + index;
    Delete(Strng, 1, index); { truncate string }
    index := POS(SubStr, Strng); { find location of next match }
END; { WHILE }
LastPos := lastloc { return function value }
END; { LastPos }


{-------------------------------------------------- LeftStr ------}

FUNCTION LeftStr(Strng    : STRING255; { in/out }
                 NumChars : BYTE       { input  }) : STRING255;
BEGIN
   IF Length(Strng) > 0 THEN
       IF NumChars < 1 THEN
           Strng := Strng[1] { i.e. make NumChars = 1 }
       ELSE IF NumChars > Length(Strng) THEN
           Strng := Strng { return the same string }
       ELSE
           Delete(Strng, NumChars+1, (Length(Strng)-NumChars));
   LeftStr := Strng { return function value }
END; { LeftStr }


{-------------------------------------------------- RightStr ------}

FUNCTION RightStr(Strng    : STRING255; { in/out }
                  NumChars : BYTE       { input  }) : STRING255;
VAR strlen : BYTE;
BEGIN
   strlen := Length(Strng);
   IF strlen > 0 THEN
       IF NumChars < 1 THEN
           Strng := Strng[strlen] { i.e. make NumChars = 1 }
       ELSE IF NumChars > strlen THEN
           Strng := Strng { return the same string }
       ELSE
           Delete(Strng, 1, (strlen-NumChars));
   RightStr := Strng { return function value }
END; { RightStr }


{-------------------------------------------- PosMidStr ------}

FUNCTION PosMidStr(Strng : STRING255; { input }
                   First,            { input }
                   Last  : BYTE      { input }) : STRING255;
VAR strlen, count : BYTE;
```

```
BEGIN
    {- - - - - - - - Argument checking  - - - - - - - -}
    IF (Strng = '') OR (Last < First) THEN BEGIN { bad arguments }
        PosMidStr := '';
        EXIT
    END; { IF }
    strlen := Length(Strng);
    IF First < 0 THEN First := 1
    ELSE IF First > strlen THEN First := strlen;
    IF Last < 0 THEN Last := 1
    ELSE IF Last > strlen THEN Last := strlen;
    { second comparison of First and Last values }
    IF First > Last THEN EXIT;
    {- - - - - - - - Main body of the procedure - - - - - - - - - -}
    count := Last - First + 1;
    IF First > 1 THEN BEGIN
        Delete(Strng, 1, First-1);
        DEC(Last, First - 1); { adjust value of Last }
        { update strlen with new string length }
        strlen := Length(Strng);
    END; { IF }
    IF Last < strlen THEN Delete(Strng, (Last+1), (strlen-Last));
    PosMidStr := Strng { return function value }
END; { PosMidStr }


{---------------------------------------------------- CountMidStr ------}


FUNCTION CountMidStr(Strng : STRING255; { input  }
                     First,                { input  }
                     Count : BYTE       { input  }) : STRING255;
VAR strlen  : BYTE;
BEGIN
    {- - - - - - - - Argument checking  - - - - - - - -}
    IF Strng = '' THEN BEGIN
        CountMidStr := '';
        EXIT
    END; { IF }
    strlen := Length(Strng);
    IF First < 0 THEN First := 1
    ELSE IF First > strlen THEN First := strlen;
    IF Count < 0 THEN Count := 1
    ELSE IF (First + Count) > strlen THEN
            Count := strlen - First + 1;
    {- - - - - - - - Main body of the procedure - - - - - - - - - -}
    IF First > 1 THEN BEGIN
        Delete(Strng, 1, First-1);
        { update strlen with new string length }
        DEC(strlen,(First-1))
    END; { IF }
    IF Count < strlen THEN Delete(Strng, (Count+1), (strlen-Count));
    CountMidStr := Strng { return function value }
END; { CountMidStr }
```

```
{-------------------------------------------------- DeleteMarker --------}

PROCEDURE DeleteMarker(VAR Strng      : STRING255; { in/out }
                           CharMarker : CHAR;       { input  }
                           CharCount  : BYTE;    { input  }
                           DelMarker  : BOOLEAN     { input  });
VAR strlen, markerpos : BYTE;
BEGIN
    {- - - - - - - - Argument checking - - - - - - - -}
    IF (Strng = '') OR (CharMarker = '') THEN EXIT;
    strlen := Length(Strng);
    IF CharCount < 0 THEN CharCount := 1
    ELSE IF CharCount > strlen THEN CharCount := strlen;
    {- - - - - - - - Main body of the procedure - - - - - - - - - -}
    markerpos := POS(CharMarker, Strng);
    IF markerpos > 0 THEN BEGIN
        Delete(Strng, markerpos+1, CharCount);
        IF DelMarker THEN Delete(Strng, markerpos, 1);
    END; { IF }
END; { DeleteMarker }

{-------------------------------------------------- OverWrite --------}

PROCEDURE OverWrite(    SubStr     : STRING255; { input  }
                   VAR Strng      : STRING255; { in/out }
                        StartIndex : BYTE       { input  });
VAR i, strlen, substrlen : BYTE;
BEGIN
    {- - - - - - - - Argument checking - - - - - - - -}
    IF (Strng = '') OR (SubStr = '') THEN EXIT;
    strlen := Length(Strng);
    substrlen := Length(SubStr);
    IF StartIndex < 0 THEN StartIndex := 1
    ELSE IF StartIndex > strlen THEN EXIT
    ELSE IF (StartIndex + substrlen) > strlen THEN
            StartIndex := strlen - substrlen;
    {- - - - - - - - Main body of the procedure - - - - - - - - - -}
    { overwrite portions of the string Strng }
    FOR i := 1 TO Substrlen DO
        Strng[i+StartIndex-1] := SubStr[i];
END; { OverWrite }

{-------------------------------------------------- ReplaceString --------}

PROCEDURE ReplaceString(    FindStr,                   { input  }
                        ReplaceStr : STRING255; { input  }
                   VAR Strng      : STRING255; { in/out }
                        StartIndex : BYTE;       { input  }
                        Frequency  : BYTE        { input  });
VAR find_strlen, repl_strlen,
    strlen, match_pos : BYTE;
BEGIN
```

```
    {- - - - - - - - Argument checking  - - - - - - - -}
    IF (FindStr = '') OR (Strng = '') THEN EXIT;
    strlen := Length(Strng);
    find_strlen := Length(FindStr);
    repl_strlen := Length(ReplaceStr);
    IF StartIndex < 0 THEN StartIndex := 1
    ELSE IF StartIndex > strlen THEN EXIT;
    IF Frequency < 0 THEN Frequency := 1;
    {- - - - - - - - Main body of the procedure - - - - - - - - - - -}
    match_pos := POS(FindStr, Strng);
    WHILE (match_pos > 0) AND (Frequency > 0) DO  BEGIN
        Frequency := Frequency - 1;
        { remove string found }
        Delete(Strng, match_pos, find_strlen);
        { replace it with new ReplaceStr }
        IF repl_strlen > 0 THEN Insert(ReplaceStr, Strng, match_pos);
        { find next matching strings }
        match_pos := POS(FindStr, Strng);
    END; { WHILE }
END; { ReplaceString }


{-------------------------------------------------- ReplaceRangeChar ———}

PROCEDURE ReplaceRangeChar(    FirstASCII,                  { input  }
                               LastASCII,                   { input  }
                               NewCharASCII,                { input  }
                               StartIndex     : BYTE;       { input  }
                        VAR Strng             : STRING255 { in/out });
VAR charascii, i, strlen : BYTE;
BEGIN
    {- - - - - - - - Argument checking  - - - - - - - -}
    IF (Strng = '') OR (FirstASCII > LastASCII) OR
        (NOT ((FirstASCII IN [1..255])    AND
              (LastASCII IN [1..255])     AND
              (Newcharascii IN [1..255]))) THEN
        EXIT;
     strlen := Length(Strng);
     IF StartIndex < 1 THEN StartIndex := 1
     ELSE IF StartIndex > strlen THEN EXIT;
    {- - - - - - - - Main body of the procedure - - - - - - - - - - -}
    FOR i := StartIndex TO strlen DO BEGIN
        charascii := ORD(Strng[i]);
        IF (charascii >= FirstASCII) AND (charascii <= LastASCII) THEN
            Strng[I] := CHR(NewCharASCII);
    END; { FOR }
END; { ReplaceRangeChar }
```

```
{------------------------------------------------- RepeatStr ---------}

FUNCTION RepeatStr(RptStr : STRING255;  { input  }
                   Count  : BYTE        { input  }) : STRING255;
VAR i, strlen : BYTE;
    strng : STRING255;
BEGIN
    strng := '';
    IF RptStr = '' THEN BEGIN
        RepeatStr := '';
        EXIT
    END; { IF }
    strlen := Length(RptStr);
    IF Count < 1 THEN Count := 1
    ELSE IF (Count * strlen) > MAX_STRING THEN
        Count := MAX_STRING div strlen; { adjust Count }
    FOR i := 1 TO Count DO
        strng := strng + RptStr;
    RepeatStr := strng;
END; { RepeatStr }


{------------------------------------------------- PadLeft ---------}

PROCEDURE PadLeft(VAR Strng   : STRING255;  { in/out }
                      PadChar : CHAR;        { input  }
                      Count   : BYTE         { input  });
VAR strlen : BYTE;
BEGIN
    {- - - - - - - - Argument checking - - - - - - - -}
    IF (Strng = '') OR (PadChar = '') THEN EXIT;
    strlen := Length(Strng);
    IF Count < 1 THEN Count := 1
    ELSE IF Count > (MAX_STRING - strlen) THEN
        Count := MAX_STRING - strlen;
    {- - - - - - - - Main body of the procedure - - - - - - - - - -}
    { concatenate the two strings }
    Strng := RepeatStr(PadChar, Count) + Strng;
END; { PadLeft }


{------------------------------------------------- PadRight ---------}

PROCEDURE PadRight(VAR Strng   : STRING255;  { in/out }
                       PadChar : CHAR;        { input  }
                       Count   : BYTE         { input  });
VAR strlen : BYTE;
BEGIN
    {- - - - - - - - Argument checking - - - - - - - -}
    IF (Strng = '') OR (PadChar = '') THEN EXIT;
    strlen := Length(Strng);
    IF Count < 1 THEN Count := 1
    ELSE IF Count > (MAX_STRING - strlen) THEN
        Count := MAX_STRING - strlen;
```

```
{- - - - - - - - Main body of the procedure - - - - - - - - - -}
{ concatenate the two strings }
Strng := Strng + RepeatStr(PadChar, Count);
END; { PadRight }


{--------------------------------------------------- PadEnds ————}

PROCEDURE PadEnds(VAR Strng     : STRING255; { in/out }
                      PadChar   : CHAR;      { input  }
                      AtEachEnd : BYTE       { input  });
VAR strlen : BYTE;
    padstr : STRING255;
BEGIN
    {- - - - - - - - Argument checking - - - - - - - -}
    IF (Strng = '') OR (PadChar = '') THEN EXIT;
    strlen := Length(Strng);
    IF AtEachEnd < 1 THEN AtEachEnd := 1
    ELSE IF AtEachEnd > ((MAX_STRING - strlen) div 2) THEN
        AtEachEnd := (MAX_STRING - strlen) div 2;
    {- - - - - - - - Main body of the procedure - - - - - - - - - -}
    padstr := RepeatStr(PadChar, AtEachEnd); { created padded string }
    Strng := padstr + Strng + padstr; { concatenate the three strings }
END; { PadEnds }


{--------------------------------------------------- ReverseStr ————}

FUNCTION ReverseStr(Strng : STRING255 { input }) : STRING255;
VAR ch : CHAR;
    i, n, strlen : BYTE;
BEGIN
    strlen := Length(Strng);
    n := strlen div 2;
    FOR i := 1 TO n DO BEGIN
        ch := Strng[i];
        Strng[I] := Strng[strlen-i+1];
        Strng[strlen-i+1] := ch;
    END; { FOR }
    ReverseStr := Strng { return function value }
END; { ReverseStr }


{--------------------------------------------------- Trim_Left ————}

FUNCTION Trim_Left(Strng    : STRING255; { input }
                   TrimChar : CHAR       { input }) : STRING255;
VAR i, strlen : BYTE;
BEGIN
    IF Strng = '' THEN BEGIN
        Trim_Left := '';
        EXIT
```

```
      END; { IF }
      strlen := Length(Strng);
      i := 1;
      WHILE (i <= strlen) AND (Strng[i] = TrimChar) DO
          INC(i);
      Delete(Strng, 1, i-1);
      Trim_Left := Strng { return function value }
  END; { Trim_Left }


  {--------------------------------------------------- Trim_Right ------}

  FUNCTION Trim_Right(Strng    : STRING255; { input  }
                      TrimChar : CHAR       { input  }) : STRING255;
  VAR i, strlen : BYTE;
  BEGIN
      IF Strng = '' THEN BEGIN
          Trim_Right := '';
          EXIT
      END; { IF }
      strlen := Length(Strng);
      i := strlen;
      WHILE (i > 0) AND (Strng[i] = TrimChar) DO
          DEC(i);
      Delete(Strng, i + 1, strlen - i);
      Trim_Right := Strng { return function value }
  END; { Trim_Right }


  {--------------------------------------------------- Trim_Ends ------}

  FUNCTION Trim_Ends(Strng    : STRING255; { input  }
                     TrimChar : CHAR       { input  }) : STRING255;
  BEGIN
      Strng := Trim_Left(Strng, TrimChar);
      IF Strng <> '' THEN Strng := Trim_Right(Strng, TrimChar);
      Trim_Ends := Strng { return function value }
  END; { Trim_Ends }
  END.
```

Listing 4.2. Source code for library SUPRSTR0.PAS.

```
UNIT SuprStr0;

{======================================================================

        Copyright (c) 1987, 1988    Namir Clement Shammas
    LIBRARY NAME: SuprStr0
    VERSION: 1.0                                  DATE 09/23/1987
    PURPOSE: Support of strings exceeding 255 characters.
    UPDATE HISTORY:

======================================================================}

{**********************************************************************}
{************************} INTERFACE {*********************************}
{**********************************************************************}

Uses CRT, PRINTER, DataLib0;
{$V-}
CONST MAX_SUPER_STRING = 3000;
TYPE
    SuperString = RECORD
        SSize : WORD;
        SStr  : ARRAY [1..MAX_SUPER_STRING] OF CHAR;
    END;

PROCEDURE Init_SuperStr(VAR SuperStr : SuperString { output });
{- - - - - - - - - - - - - - - - - - - - - - - - - - - - - -

ROUTINE PURPOSE: initializes a Super String.
PARAMETERS:
 IN/OUT: SuperStr - the initialized super string.

- - - - - - - - - - - - - - - - - - - - - - - - - - - - - - - - }
PROCEDURE Str_to_SuperStr(VAR SuperStr : SuperString; { output }
                              Strng    : STRING255    { input });
{- - - - - - - - - - - - - - - - - - - - - - - - - - - - - -

ROUTINE PURPOSE: assigns a string to a Super String.
PARAMETERS:
 INPUT: Strng - the normal string used to assign a super string.
 OUTPUT: SuperStr - the assigned super string.

- - - - - - - - - - - - - - - - - - - - - - - - - - - - - - - - }
PROCEDURE SuperStr_to_Str(VAR SuperStr : SuperString; { input }
                              VAR Strng : STRING255    { output });
{- - - - - - - - - - - - - - - - - - - - - - - - - - - - - -

ROUTINE PURPOSE: assigns a Super String to a string. Truncate if
necessary.
```

PARAMETERS:
  INPUT: SuperStr - the source 'super' string.
  OUTPUT: Strng - the destination string.

- }
PROCEDURE Copy_SuperStr (VAR OutSuperStr,   { output }
                            InSuperStr   : SuperString { input });
{- -

ROUTINE PURPOSE: assigns one Super String to another.
PARAMETERS:
  INPUT: InSuperStr - the input string.
  OUTPUT: OutSuperStr - the output string.

- }
FUNCTION Length_SuperStr (VAR SuperStr : SuperString { input }) : WORD;
{- -

ROUTINE PURPOSE: returns the length of a super string.
PARAMETERS:
  INPUT: SuperStr - the super string whose length is sought.
FUNCTION VALUE: the length of the super string argument.

- }
PROCEDURE LeftConcat_Str (VAR SuperStr : SuperString; { in/out }
                            Strng   : STRING255   { input });
{- -

ROUTINE PURPOSE: concatenates a string to the left of a super string.
PARAMETERS:
  INPUT: Strng - the string concatenated to a super string.
  IN/OUT: SuperStr - the modified super string.
COMMENTS: The size of the concatenated string is truncated if the
resulting string tends to exceed the capacity of the super string.

                      ROUTINE DEPENDENCIES

Identifier Name	Identifier Type	Source Library
MAX_SUPER_STRING	constant	local

- }
PROCEDURE LeftConcat_SuperStr (VAR LeftStr,   { input }
                                RightStr : SuperString { in/out });
{- -

ROUTINE PURPOSE: concatenates one super string to the left of another
super string.

PARAMETERS:
 INPUT: LeftStr – the super string concatenated to the left of
        another.
 IN/OUT: RightStr – the modified super string.
COMMENTS: The size of the concatenated string is truncated if the
resulting string tends to exceed the capacity of the super string.

```
                    ROUTINE DEPENDENCIES
                    --------------------

        Identifier Name         Identifier Type        Source Library
        ---------------         ---------------        --------------

        MAX_SUPER_STRING           constant                local

- - - - - - - - - - - - - - - - - - - - - - - - - - - - - - - - - }
PROCEDURE RightConcat_Str(VAR SuperStr : SuperString; { in/out }
                              Strng    : STRING255    { input  });
{- - - - - - - - - - - - - - - - - - - - - - - - - - - - - - - - -
```

ROUTINE PURPOSE: concatenates a string to the left of a super string.
PARAMETERS:
 INPUT: Strng – the string concatenated to the left of a super string.
 IN/OUT: Super-Str – the modified super string.
COMMENTS: The size of the concatenated string is truncated if the
resulting string tends to exceed the capacity of the super string.

```
                    ROUTINE DEPENDENCIES
                    --------------------

        Identifier Name         Identifier Type        Source Library
        ---------------         ---------------        --------------

        MAX_SUPER_STRING           constant                local

- - - - - - - - - - - - - - - - - - - - - - - - - - - - - - - - }
PROCEDURE RightConcat_SuperStr(VAR LeftStr,              { in/out }
                                   RightStr : SuperString { input  });
{- - - - - - - - - - - - - - - - - - - - - - - - - - - - - - - - -
```

ROUTINE PURPOSE: concatenates one super string to the right of another
super string.
PARAMETERS:
 INPUT: LeftStr – the super string concatenated to the right of
        another.
 IN/OUT: RightStr – the modified super string.
COMMENTS: The size of the concatenated string is truncated if the
resulting string tends to exceed the capacity of the super string.

```
                    ROUTINE DEPENDENCIES
                    --------------------

        Identifier Name         Identifier Type        Source Library
        ---------------         ---------------        --------------

        MAX_SUPER_STRING           constant                local
```

```
- - - - - - - - - - - - - - - - - - - - - - - - - - - - - - - - }
PROCEDURE Insert_SuperStr(VAR SuperStr,                 { in/out }
                             InStr      : SuperString; { input  }
                             StartIndex : WORD          { input  });
{- - - - - - - - - - - - - - - - - - - - - - - - - - - - - - - -
```

ROUTINE PURPOSE: inserts a super string inside another super string.
PARAMETERS:
 INPUT: InStr - the inserted super string.
        StartIndex - the location where InStr is inserted.
 IN/OUT: SuperStr - the modified super string.
HANDLING BAD ARGUMENTS: The procedure aborts when:
1) The modified superstring is a null string.
2) The StartIndex exceeds the length of the modified super string.

ROUTINE DEPENDENCIES

Identifier Name	Identifier Type	Source Library
MAX_SUPER_STRING	constant	local

```
- - - - - - - - - - - - - - - - - - - - - - - - - - - - - - - }
PROCEDURE Insert_Str(    Strng      : STRING255;  { input  }
                     VAR SuperStr   : SuperString; { in/out }
                         StartIndex : WORD          { input  });
{- - - - - - - - - - - - - - - - - - - - - - - - - - - - - - -
```

ROUTINE PURPOSE: inserts a string inside a super string.
PARAMETERS:
 INPUT: Strng - the inserted string.
        StartIndex - the location where InStr is inserted.
 IN/OUT: SuperStr - the modified super string.
HANDLING BAD ARGUMENTS: The procedure aborts when:
1) The inserted string is a null string.
2) The StartIndex exceeds the length of the modified super string.

ROUTINE DEPENDENCIES

Identifier Name	Identifier Type	Source Library
MAX_SUPER_STRING	constant	local

```
- - - - - - - - - - - - - - - - - - - - - - - - - - - - - - - }
PROCEDURE Delete_SuperStr(VAR SuperStr   : SuperString; { in/out }
                              StartIndex,                { input  }
                              CharCount    : WORD        { input  });
{- - - - - - - - - - - - - - - - - - - - - - - - - - - - - - -
```

ROUTINE PURPOSE: deletes portions of a super string.

PARAMETERS:
 INPUT: StartIndex - the location where the character deletion begins.
       CharCount - the number of characters to be deleted.
 IN/OUT: SuperStr - the modified super string.
HANDLING BAD ARGUMENTS: The routine aborts when the parameter
StartIndex is greater than the length of the super string.

```
- - - - - - - - - - - - - - - - - - - - - - - - - - - - - - - - - - }
FUNCTION PosStr(    SubStr     : STRING255;   { input  }
               VAR SuperStr    : SuperString; { input  }
                   StartIndex : WORD         { input  }) : WORD;
{- - - - - - - - - - - - - - - - - - - - - - - - - - - - - - - - - -
```

ROUTINE PURPOSE: locates a string inside a super string.
PARAMETERS:
 INPUT: SubStr - the string-typed pattern used in the text search.
       SuperStr - the scanned super string.
       StartIndex - the location where the matching begins.
FUNCTION VALUE: the location where the pattern finds a match, or zero
if none is found.
HANDLING BAD ARGUMENTS: The function aborts, returning a zero value
when:
1) The supplied substring is a null string.
2) The starting search location is greater than the string length.

```
- - - - - - - - - - - - - - - - - - - - - - - - - - - - - - - - - - }
FUNCTION Pos_SuperStr(VAR SubStr,                  { input  }
                     SuperStr   : SuperString; { input  }
                     StartIndex : WORD         { input  }) : WORD;
{- - - - - - - - - - - - - - - - - - - - - - - - - - - - - - - - - -
```

ROUTINE PURPOSE: locates a super string inside a bigger super string.
PARAMETERS:
 INPUT: SubStr - the smaller super string.
       SuperStr - the large super string.
       StartIndex - the starting search character location.
FUNCTION VALUE: the character location where the substring matches the
string. A zero is returned if no match is found at the specified
character offset.
HANDLING BAD ARGUMENTS: The function aborts, returning a zero value
when:
1) The supplied substring is a null string.
2) The starting search location is greater than the string length.

```
- - - - - - - - - - - - - - - - - - - - - - - - - - - - - - - - - - }
PROCEDURE Mid_SuperStr(VAR SuperStr,                { input  }
                      SubStr     : SuperString; { output }
                      StartIndex,               { input  }
                      Count      : WORD         { input  });
{- - - - - - - - - - - - - - - - - - - - - - - - - - - - - - - - - -
```

ROUTINE PURPOSE: extracts a portion of a super string. Starts at
character location StartIndex and returns Count characters.
PARAMETERS:
  INPUT: SuperStr – the source super string.
         StartIndex – the starting character location.
         Count – the size of the extracted super string.
  OUTPUT: SubStr – the extracted substring.
HANDLING BAD ARGUMENTS: The routine returns a null string if the
length of the main string is zero, or if the starting character
location is greater than the length of the main string.

                      ROUTINE DEPENDENCIES

        Identifier Name   Identifier Type   Source Library
        ---------------   ---------------   --------------
        MAX_SUPER_STRING   constant   local

- }
PROCEDURE Left_SuperStr(VAR SuperStr,   { input }
                            SubStr   : SuperString; { output }
                            Count   : WORD   { input });
{- -

ROUTINE PURPOSE: extracts the left portion of a super string,
returning Count characters.
PARAMETERS:
  INPUT: SuperStr – the source super string.
         Count – the size of the extracted substring.
  OUTPUT: SubStr – the extracted substring.
HANDLING BAD ARGUMENTS: The routine aborts, returning a null substring
when:
1) The main super string has a length of zero.
2) The size of the extracted substring is zero.
If the size of the extracted substring is greater than the constant
MAX_SUPER_STRING, the size is adjusted to equal the value of that
constant.

                      ROUTINE DEPENDENCIES

        Identifier Name   Identifier Type   Source Library
        ---------------   ---------------   --------------
        MAX_SUPER_STRING   constant   local

- }
PROCEDURE Right_SuperStr(VAR SuperStr,   { input }
                             SubStr   : SuperString; { output }
                             Count   : WORD   { input });
{- -

ROUTINE PURPOSE: extracts the right portion of a super string,
returning Count characters.

PARAMETERS:
 INPUT: SuperStr - the source super string.
        Count - the size of the extracted substring.
 OUTPUT: SubStr - the extracted substring.
HANDLING BAD ARGUMENTS: The routine aborts, returning a null substring
when:
1) The main super string has a length of zero.
2) The size of the extracted substring is zero.
If the size of the extracted substring is greater than the constant
MAX_SUPER_STRING, the size is adjusted to equal the value of that
constant.

ROUTINE DEPENDENCIES

Identifier Name	Identifier Type	Source Library
MAX_SUPER_STRING	constant	local

```
- - - - - - - - - - - - - - - - - - - - - - - - - - - - - - - - - }
FUNCTION Compare_SuperStr(VAR SuperStr1,              { input  }
                          SuperStr2 : SuperString { input  })
                                                : INTEGER;
{- - - - - - - - - - - - - - - - - - - - - - - - - - - - - - - -
```

ROUTINE PURPOSE: compares two super strings and returns an
integer-coded result.
PARAMETERS:
 INPUT: SuperStr1 - the first super string.
        SuperStr2 - the second super string.
FUNCTION VALUE: The possible returned values are:
   +1 : SuperStr1 > SuperStr2
    0 : SuperStr1 = SuperStr2
   -1 : SuperStr1 < SuperStr2

```
- - - - - - - - - - - - - - - - - - - - - - - - - - - - - - - - }
FUNCTION Compare_Str(VAR SuperStr : SuperString; { input  }
                     Strng    : STRING255    { input  }) : INTEGER;
{- - - - - - - - - - - - - - - - - - - - - - - - - - - - - - -
```

ROUTINE PURPOSE: compares a super string and a string, returning
an integer-coded result.
PARAMETERS:
 INPUT: SuperStr - the first super string.
        Strng - the second string.
FUNCTION VALUE: The possible returned values are:
   +1 : SuperStr > Strng
    0 : SuperStr = Strng
   -1 : SuperStr < Strng

```
- - - - - - - - - - - - - - - - - - - - - - - - - - - - - - - - - }
PROCEDURE Write_SuperStr(VAR SuperStr : SuperString { input });
{- - - - - - - - - - - - - - - - - - - - - - - - - - - - - - - - -
```

ROUTINE PURPOSE: displays a super string on the screen with page
brakes.
PARAMETERS:
 INPUT: SuperStr - the displayed super string.
HANDLING BAD ARGUMENTS: The routine exits if a zero-length super string
is supplied as an argument.

```
- - - - - - - - - - - - - - - - - - - - - - - - - - - - - - - - - }
PROCEDURE Print_SuperStr(VAR SuperStr : SuperString { input });
{- - - - - - - - - - - - - - - - - - - - - - - - - - - - - - - - -
```

ROUTINE PURPOSE: prints a super string.
PARAMETERS:
 INPUT: SuperStr - the printed super string.
HANDLING BAD ARGUMENTS: The routine exits if a zero-length super string
is supplied as an argument.

```
- - - - - - - - - - - - - - - - - - - - - - - - - - - - - - - - - }
PROCEDURE Save_SuperStr(VAR SuperStr : SuperString; { input  }
                            Filename : STRING255;   { input  }
                        VAR Done     : BOOLEAN      { output });
{- - - - - - - - - - - - - - - - - - - - - - - - - - - - - - - - -
```

ROUTINE PURPOSE: writes a super string to a text file.
PARAMETERS:
 INPUT: SuperStr - the super string to be written to the text file.
        Filename - the destination text filename.
 OUTPUT: Done - the logical flag used to signal whether or not the
               write was successful.
HANDLING BAD ARGUMENTS: The routine exits if a zero-length super string
is supplied as an argument.

```
- - - - - - - - - - - - - - - - - - - - - - - - - - - - - - - - - }
PROCEDURE Load_SuperStr(VAR SuperStr : SuperString; { output }
                            Filename : STRING255;   { input  }
                        VAR Done     : BOOLEAN      { output });
{- - - - - - - - - - - - - - - - - - - - - - - - - - - - - - - - -
```

ROUTINE PURPOSE: loads a super string from a text file.
PARAMETERS:
 INPUT: SuperStr - the super string to be read from the text file.
        Filename - the source text filename.
 OUTPUT: Done - the logical flag used to signal whether or not the
               read operation was successful.
HANDLING BAD ARGUMENTS: The routine exits if a zero-length super string
is supplied as an argument.

```
- - - - - - - - - - - - - - - - - - - - - - - - - - - - - - - - - - - - - }

{********************************************************************}
{***********************} IMPLEMENTATION {**************************}
{********************************************************************}

{-------------------------------------------------- Init_SuperStr -------}

PROCEDURE Init_SuperStr(VAR SuperStr : SuperString { output });
BEGIN
   SuperStr.SSize := 0;
END; { Init_SuperStr }

{-------------------------------------------------- Str_to_SuperStr -------}

PROCEDURE Str_to_SuperStr(VAR SuperStr : SuperString; { output }
                              Strng     : STRING255    { input  });
VAR i : WORD;
BEGIN
   WITH SuperStr DO BEGIN
       { assign string length to that of the super String }
       SSize := Length(Strng);
       IF SSize > 0 THEN { copy contents of a non-null string }
           { use }
                   { FOR i := 1 TO SSize DO SStr[i] := Strng[i]; }
           { or }
                   Move(Strng[1], SStr, SSize);
   END; { WITH }
END; { Str_to_SuperStr }

{-------------------------------------------------- SuperStr_to_Str -------}

PROCEDURE SuperStr_to_Str(VAR SuperStr : SuperString; { input  }
                              VAR Strng     : STRING255    { output });
VAR i, strlen : WORD;
BEGIN
   WITH SuperStr DO BEGIN
       strlen := SSize; { get the size of the super String }
       { is super String too large ?}
       IF strlen > MAX_STRING THEN
           strlen := MAX_STRING; { truncate copied length }
       Strng := ''; { initialize string }
       IF strlen = 0 THEN EXIT;
       { copy characters to string }
       { use }
           { FOR i := 1 TO strlen DO Strng := Strng + SStr[i]; }
       { or }
           Move(SStr, Strng[1], SSize);
       { assign length of string by accessing the special 0th index }
       Strng[0] := CHR(strlen);
   END; { WITH }
END; { SuperStr_to_Str }
```

```
{------------------------------------------------- Copy_SuperStr  ———}

PROCEDURE Copy_SuperStr(VAR OutSuperStr,                    { output }
                            InSuperStr  : SuperString { input  });
BEGIN
   { copy record structures }
   OutSuperStr := InSuperStr
END; { Copy_SuperStr }

{----------------------------------------------- Length_SuperStr  ———}

FUNCTION Length_SuperStr(VAR SuperStr : SuperString { input  }) : WORD;
BEGIN
   Length_SuperStr := SuperStr.SSize
END; { Length_SuperStr }

{------------------------------------------------- LeftConcat_Str ———}

PROCEDURE LeftConcat_Str(VAR SuperStr : SuperString; { in/out }
                            Strng    : STRING255    { input  });
VAR i, k, strlen : WORD;
BEGIN
   IF Strng = '' THEN EXIT; { do nothing }
   WITH SuperStr DO BEGIN
      strlen := Length(Strng); { get size of the left string }
      k := SSize;
      IF (strlen + SSize) > MAX_SUPER_STRING THEN
         strlen := MAX_SUPER_STRING - SSize;
      { shift current string contents by strlen characters }
      { use }
         { FOR i := k DOWNTO 1 DO SStr[i+strlen] := SStr[i]; }
      { or }
         Move(SStr, SStr[strlen+1], k);
      { copy left string on the 'old' portion of right string }
      { use }
         { FOR i := 1 TO strlen DO SStr[i] := Strng[i]; }
      { or }
         Move(Strng[1], SStr, strlen);
      { update the length of the right super string }
      INC(SSize, strlen);
   END; { WITH }
END; { LeftConcat_Str }

{--------------------------------------------- LeftConcat_SuperStr ———}

PROCEDURE LeftConcat_SuperStr(VAR LeftStr,                  { input  }
                                 RightStr : SuperString { in/out });
VAR i, left_strlen, right_strlen : WORD;
```

```
BEGIN
    left_strlen := LeftStr.SSize; { get size of left string }
    IF left_strlen = 0 THEN EXIT; { do nothing }
    right_strlen := RightStr.SSize;
    IF (left_strlen + RightStr.SSize) > MAX_SUPER_STRING THEN
        left_strlen := MAX_SUPER_STRING - right_strlen;
    { shift current string contents by 'right_strlen' characters }
    { use }
        { FOR i := right_strlen DOWNTO 1 DO
            RightStr.SStr[i+left_strlen] := RightStr.SStr[i]; }
    { or }
        Move(RightStr.SStr, RightStr.SStr[left_strlen+1],
                            right_strlen);
    { copy left string on the 'old' portion of right string }
    { use }
        { FOR i := 1 TO left_strlen DO
            RightStr.SStr[i] := LeftStr.SStr[i]; }
    { or }
        Move(LeftStr.SStr, RightStr.SStr, left_strlen);
    { update the length of the right super string }
    INC(RightStr.SSize, left_strlen);
END; { LeftConcat_SuperStr }

{---------------------------------------------- RightConcat_Str ----------}

PROCEDURE RightConcat_Str(VAR SuperStr : SuperString; { in/out }
                              Strng     : STRING255    { input });
VAR i, strlen : WORD;
BEGIN
    IF Strng = '' THEN EXIT;
    WITH SuperStr DO BEGIN
        strlen := Length(Strng);
        IF (strlen + SSize) > MAX_SUPER_STRING THEN
            strlen := MAX_SUPER_STRING - SSize;
        IF strlen > 0 THEN
            { use }
                { FOR i := 1 TO strlen DO
                    SStr[SSize + i] := Strng[i]; }
            { or }
                Move(Strng[1],SuperStr.SStr[SSize+1],strlen);
        INC(SSize,strlen);
    END; { WITH }
END; { RightConcat_Str }

{------------------------------------------ RightConcat_SuperStr ----------}

PROCEDURE RightConcat_SuperStr(VAR LeftStr,                 { in/out }
                                   RightStr  : SuperString { input });
VAR i, strlen : WORD;
```

```
BEGIN
   strlen := RightStr.SSize;
   IF strlen = 0 THEN EXIT; { do nothing }
   IF (strlen + LeftStr.SSize) > MAX_SUPER_STRING THEN
           strlen := MAX_SUPER_STRING - LeftStr.SSize;
   IF strlen > 0 THEN
       { use }
         { FOR i := 1 TO strlen DO
             LeftStr.SStr[LeftStr.SSize + i] := RightStr.SStr[i]; }
       { or }
         Move(RightStr.SStr[1], LeftStr.SStr[LeftStr.SSize + 1],
                                                       strlen);
   INC(LeftStr.SSize, strlen);
END; { RightConcat_SuperStr }

{------------------------------------------------ Insert_SuperStr ------}

PROCEDURE Insert_SuperStr(VAR SuperStr,                   { in/out }
                              InStr      : SuperString; { input  }
                              StartIndex : WORD          { input  });
VAR i, j, k : WORD;
BEGIN
   j := InStr.SSize;
   k := SuperStr.SSize;
   IF j < 1 THEN EXIT;
   IF StartIndex < 1 THEN StartIndex := 1
   ELSE IF StartIndex >= k THEN EXIT;
   IF (j + k) > MAX_SUPER_STRING THEN
       j := MAX_SUPER_STRING - k;
   { shift current string contents by
     'k - StartIndex + 1' characters }
   { use }
     { FOR i := k DOWNTO StartIndex DO
         SuperStr.SStr[i+j] := SuperStr.SStr[i]; }
   { or }
     Move(SuperStr.SStr[StartIndex], SuperStr.SStr[StartIndex+j],
         (k - StartIndex + 1));
   { copy left string on the 'old' portion of right string }
   { use }
     { FOR i := 1 TO j DO
         SuperStr.SStr[i+StartIndex-1] := InStr.SStr[i]; }
   { or }
     Move(InStr.SStr[1], SuperStr.SStr[StartIndex], j);
   { update the length of the right super string }
   INC(SuperStr.SSize, j);
END; { Insert_SuperStr }

{------------------------------------------------ Insert_Str ------}

PROCEDURE Insert_Str(    Strng      : STRING255;  { input  }
                     VAR SuperStr   : SuperString; { in/out }
                         StartIndex : WORD          { input  });
VAR i, j : WORD;
```

```
BEGIN
   IF Strng = '' THEN EXIT; { do nothing }
   IF StartIndex < 1 THEN StartIndex := 1
   ELSE IF StartIndex >= SuperStr.SSize THEN EXIT;
   WITH SuperStr DO  BEGIN
       j := Length(Strng);
       IF (j + SSize) > MAX_SUPER_STRING THEN
           j := MAX_SUPER_STRING - SSize;
       { shift current string contents by 'j' characters }
       { use }
          { FOR i := SSize DOWNTO StartIndex DO
               SStr[i+j] := SStr[i]; }
       { or }
          Move(SStr[StartIndex], SStr[StartIndex+j],
                   (SSize - StartIndex + 1));
       { copy left string on the 'old' portion of right string }
       { use }
          { FOR i := 1 TO j DO
               SStr[i+StartIndex-1] := Strng[i]; }
       { or }
          Move(Strng[1], SStr[StartIndex], j);
       { update the length of the right super string }
       INC(SSize, j);
   END; { WITH }
END; { Insert_Str }


{-------------------------------------------------- Delete_SuperStr ———}


PROCEDURE Delete_SuperStr(VAR SuperStr     : SuperString; { in/out }
                              StartIndex,                 { input  }
                              CharCount   : WORD          { input  });
VAR i, j : WORD;
BEGIN
   IF StartIndex < 1 THEN StartIndex := 1
   ELSE IF StartIndex >= SuperStr.SSize THEN EXIT;
   IF CharCount < 1 THEN CharCount := 1
   ELSE IF CharCount >= SuperStr.SSize THEN BEGIN
       SuperStr.SSize := 0; { delete entire string }
       EXIT
   END; { IF }
   WITH SuperStr DO BEGIN
       j := StartIndex + CharCount;
       IF j < MAX_SUPER_STRING THEN BEGIN
           FOR i := StartIndex TO (SSize - CharCount) DO
               SStr[i] := SStr[i + CharCount];
           DEC(SSize, CharCount);
       END
       ELSE SSize := StartIndex - 1;
   END; { WITH }
END; { Delete_SuperStr }
```

```
{----------------------------------------------- PosStr -------}

FUNCTION PosStr(     SubStr      : STRING255;   { input  }
                 VAR SuperStr    : SuperString; { input  }
                     StartIndex : WORD          { input  }) : WORD;
VAR i, j, k, last, strlen, substrlen : WORD;
    nomatch : BOOLEAN;
BEGIN
    strlen := SuperStr.SSize;
    substrlen := Length(SubStr);
    IF (substrlen = 0) OR (StartIndex > strlen) THEN BEGIN
        PosStr := 0;
        EXIT
    END;
    IF StartIndex < 1 THEN StartIndex := 1;
    k := 0;
    IF strlen > substrlen THEN BEGIN
        i := StartIndex - 1;
        last := strlen - substrlen;
        nomatch := TRUE;
        WHILE (i <= last) AND nomatch DO BEGIN
            INC(i);
            IF SubStr[1] = SuperStr.SStr[i] THEN BEGIN
                k := i;
                j := 2;
                INC(i);
                nomatch := FALSE;
                WHILE (j <= substrlen) AND (NOT nomatch) DO
                    IF SubStr[j] = SuperStr.SStr[i] THEN BEGIN
                        INC(i);
                        INC(j)
                    END
                    ELSE nomatch := TRUE;
                { restore index before complete matching was attempted }
                IF nomatch THEN BEGIN
                    i := k + 1;
                    k := 0
                END;
            END; { IF SubStr[1] = SuperStr.SStr[i] }
        END; { WHILE (i <= last) AND nomatch }
    END; { IF strlen > substrlen }
    PosStr := k
END; { PosStr }

{------------------------------------------- Pos_SuperStr -------}

FUNCTION Pos_SuperStr(VAR SubStr,                   { input  }
                          SuperStr   : SuperString; { input  }
                          StartIndex : WORD         { input  }) : WORD;
VAR i, j, k, last, strlen, substrlen : WORD;
    nomatch : BOOLEAN;
```

```
BEGIN
    strlen := SuperStr.SSize;
    substrlen := SubStr.SSize;
    IF (substrlen = 0) OR (StartIndex > strlen) THEN BEGIN
        Pos_SuperStr := 0;
        EXIT
    END;
    IF StartIndex < 1 THEN StartIndex := 1;
     k := 0;
    IF strlen > substrlen THEN BEGIN
        i := StartIndex - 1;
        last := strlen - substrlen;
        nomatch := TRUE;
        WHILE (i <= last) AND nomatch DO BEGIN
            INC(i);
            IF SubStr.SStr[1] = SuperStr.SStr[i] THEN BEGIN
                k := i;
                j := 2;
                INC(i);
                nomatch := FALSE;
                WHILE (j <= substrlen) AND NOT nomatch DO
                    IF SubStr.SStr[j] = SuperStr.SStr[i] THEN BEGIN
                        INC(i);
                        INC(j);
                    END
                    ELSE nomatch := TRUE;
                { restore index before complete matching was attempted }
                IF nomatch THEN BEGIN
                    i := k + 1;
                    k := 0
                END;
            END; { IF SubStr.SStr[1] = SuperStr.SStr[i] }
        END; { WHILE (i <= last) AND nomatch }
    END; { IF strlen > substrlen }
    Pos_SuperStr := k;
END; { Pos_SuperStr }

{------------------------------------------------ Mid_SuperStr ------}

PROCEDURE Mid_SuperStr(VAR SuperStr,                     { input  }
                           SubStr        : SuperString;  { output }
                           StartIndex,                    { input  }
                           Count         : WORD           { input  });
VAR i : WORD;
BEGIN
    SubStr.SSize := 0;
    IF (SuperStr.SSize = 0) OR (StartIndex > SuperStr.SSize) THEN
        EXIT;
    IF (StartIndex > 0) AND (Count > 0) THEN BEGIN
        IF (StartIndex + Count) > MAX_SUPER_STRING THEN
```

```
              Count := MAX_SUPER_STRING - StartIndex;
        SubStr.SSize := Count;
        { use }
          { FOR i := 1 TO Count DO
              SubStr.SStr[i] := SuperStr.SStr[i+StartIndex-1]; }
        { or }
          Move(SuperStr.SStr[StartIndex], SubStr.SStr[1], Count);
        END; { IF }
END; { Mid_SuperStr }


{------------------------------------------------ Left_SuperStr ————}

PROCEDURE Left_SuperStr(VAR SuperStr,                    { input  }
                            SubStr    : SuperString; { output }
                            Count     : WORD          { input  });
VAR i : WORD;
BEGIN
   SubStr.SSize := 0; { set default value }
   IF SuperStr.SSize = 0 THEN EXIT;
   IF Count > 0 THEN BEGIN
      { is count larger than super String limit ? }
      IF Count > MAX_SUPER_STRING THEN Count := MAX_SUPER_STRING;
      SubStr.SSize := Count;
      { use }
        { FOR i := 1 TO Count DO
            SubStr.SStr[i] := SuperStr.SStr[i]; }
      { or }
        Move(SuperStr.SStr[1], SubStr.SStr[1], Count);
   END; { IF }
END; { Left_SuperStr }


{------------------------------------------------ Right_SuperStr ————}

PROCEDURE Right_SuperStr(VAR SuperStr,                   { input  }
                             SubStr   : SuperString; { output }
                             Count    : WORD          { input  });
VAR i, j, k : WORD;
BEGIN
   SubStr.SSize := 0; { set default value }
   IF SuperStr.SSize = 0 THEN EXIT;
   IF Count > 0 THEN BEGIN
      { is count larger than super String limit ? }
      IF Count > MAX_SUPER_STRING THEN Count := MAX_SUPER_STRING;
      j := SuperStr.SSize;
      SubStr.SSize := Count;
      k := j - Count;
      { use }
        { FOR i := 1 TO Count DO
            SubStr.SStr[i] := SuperStr.SStr[k+i]; }
      { or }
        Move(SuperStr.SStr[k+1], SubStr.SStr[1], Count);
```

```
    END; { IF }
END; { Right_SuperStr }


{---------------------------------------------- Compare_SuperStr ----------}

FUNCTION Compare_SuperStr(VAR SuperStr1,               { input  }
                              SuperStr2 : SuperString { input  })
                                                         : INTEGER;
VAR i, min_length : WORD;
    diff, result : LONGINT;
BEGIN
    { handle null super Strings }
    IF (SuperStr1.SSize = 0) AND (SuperStr2.SSize = 0) THEN
        result := 0 { both strings are nulls }
    ELSE IF SuperStr2.SSize = 0 THEN
        result := 1
    ELSE IF SuperStr1.SSize = 0 THEN
        result := -1
    ELSE BEGIN { neither super string is a null }
        min_length := SuperStr1.SSize;
        IF min_length > SuperStr2.SSize THEN
            min_length := SuperStr2.SSize;
        i := 1;
        WHILE (i <= min_length) AND
              (SuperStr1.SStr[i] = SuperStr2.SStr[i]) DO
            INC(i);
        IF i > min_length THEN DEC(i);
        IF SuperStr1.SStr[i] <> SuperStr2.SStr[i] THEN
            IF SuperStr1.SStr[i] > SuperStr2.SStr[i] THEN
                result := 1
            ELSE
                result := -1
        ELSE BEGIN
            diff := LONGINT(SuperStr1.SSize) -
                    LONGINT(SuperStr2.SSize);
            IF diff <> 0 THEN diff := ABS(diff) div diff;
            result := INTEGER(diff)
        END; { IF }
    END; { IF }
    Compare_SuperStr := result { return function value }
END; { Compare_SuperStr }


{---------------------------------------------- Compare_Str ----------}

FUNCTION Compare_Str(VAR SuperStr : SuperString; { input  }
                         Strng    : STRING255    { input  }) : INTEGER;
VAR i, minlen, strlen : WORD;
    diff, result : LONGINT;
BEGIN
    WITH SuperStr DO BEGIN
```

```
        strlen := Length(Strng);
        minlen := strlen;
        { handle null strings }
        IF (SSize = 0) AND (minlen = 0) THEN
            result := 0 { both strings are nulls }
        ELSE IF minlen = 0 THEN
            result := 1
        ELSE IF SSize = 0 THEN
            result := -1
        ELSE BEGIN { neither super String is null }
            IF minlen > SSize THEN minlen := SSize;
            i := 1;
            WHILE (i <= minlen) AND (SStr[i] = Strng[i]) DO
                INC(i);
            IF i > minlen THEN i := minlen;
            IF SStr[i] <> Strng[i] THEN
                IF SStr[i] > Strng[i] THEN
                    result := 1
                ELSE
                    result := -1
            ELSE BEGIN
                diff := LONGINT(SSize) - LONGINT(strlen);
                IF diff <> 0 THEN diff := ABS(diff) div diff;
                result := INTEGER(diff)
            END; { IF }
        END; { IF }
    END; { WITH }
    Compare_Str := result { return function value }
END; { Compare_Str }

{------------------------------------------------ Write_SuperStr ------}

PROCEDURE Write_SuperStr(VAR SuperStr : SuperString { input });
CONST LOWER_LIMIT = 1920;
      UPPER_LIMIT = 1999;
VAR count, i, delta : WORD;
    ch : CHAR;
BEGIN
    WITH SuperStr DO BEGIN
        IF SSize = 0 THEN EXIT;
        count := 1;
        FOR i := 1 TO SSize DO BEGIN
            CASE SStr[i] OF
                #13 : delta := 80;
                ^i  : delta := 8;
                ELSE  delta := 1;
            END; { CASE }
            INC(count, delta);
            IF count >= UPPER_LIMIT THEN BEGIN
                count := 0;
```

```
                    WRITE(^G);
                    ch := ReadKey;
                    IF ch in ['Q','q'] THEN EXIT;
                END; { IF }
                WRITE(SStr[i]);
            END; { FOR }
            WRITELN;
        END; { WITH }
    END; { Write_SuperStr }


{--------------------------------------------- Print_SuperStr ------}

PROCEDURE Print_SuperStr(VAR SuperStr : SuperString { input });
VAR i : WORD;
BEGIN
    WITH SuperStr DO BEGIN
        IF SSize = 0 THEN EXIT;
        FOR i := 1 TO SSize DO
            WRITE(LST,SStr[i]);
        WRITELN(LST);
    END; { WITH }
END; { Print_SuperStr }

{----------------------------------------- Save_SuperStr ------}

PROCEDURE Save_SuperStr(VAR SuperStr : SuperString; { input }
                            Filename : STRING255;   { input  }
                        VAR Done     : BOOLEAN      { output });
VAR i : WORD;
    filevar : TEXT;
BEGIN
    Done := FALSE;
    WITH SuperStr DO BEGIN
        IF SSize = 0 THEN EXIT;
        Assign(filevar, Filename);
        { set I/O error trapping }
        {$I-} Rewrite(filevar); {$I+}
        IF IOResult <> 0 THEN { file not found }
            EXIT;
        FOR i := 1 TO SSize DO
            WRITE(filevar,SStr[i]);
        Close(filevar);
        Done := TRUE;
    END; { WITH }
END; { Save_SuperStr }
```

```
{------------------------------------------------ Load_SuperStr ------}

PROCEDURE Load_SuperStr(VAR SuperStr : SuperString; { output }
                            Filename : STRING255;   { input  }
                        VAR Done     : BOOLEAN      { output });
VAR i : WORD;
    filevar : TEXT;
BEGIN
    Done := FALSE;
    WITH SuperStr DO BEGIN
        IF SSize = 0 THEN EXIT;
        Assign(filevar, Filename);
        { set I/O error trapping }
        {$I-} Reset(filevar); {$I+}
        IF IOResult > 0 THEN { File not found }
            EXIT;
        i := 0;
        WHILE (NOT Eof(filevar)) AND (i < MAX_SUPER_STRING) DO BEGIN
            INC(i);
            READ(filevar,SStr[i])
        END; { WHILE }
        Close(filevar);
    END; { WITH }
END; { Save_SuperStr }
END.
```

Listing 4.3. Source code for application library LONGSETS.PAS.

```
UNIT LongSets;

{=======================================================================


            Copyright (c) 1987, 1988    Namir Clement Shammas
    LIBRARY NAME: LongSets
    VERSION: 1.0                                  DATE 10/26/1987
    PURPOSE: uses the routines in library SuprStr0 to implement a
             small library for string-based sets.
    UPDATE HISTORY:


=======================================================================}
```

```
{***************************************************************}
{************************} INTERFACE {**************************}
{***************************************************************}

Uses CRT, PRINTER, DataLib0, SuprStr0;
CONST SET_DELIM = ','; { delimiter for set members }

PROCEDURE Clear_Set(VAR StrSet : SuperString { output });
{- - - - - - - - - - - - - - - - - - - - - - - - - - - - - - -
```

ROUTINE PURPOSE: clears and initializes a string-based set.
PARAMETERS:
 OUTPUT: StrSet - the initialized set.

ROUTINE DEPENDENCIES

Identifier Name	Identifier Type	Source Library
SET_DELIM	constant	local
SuperString	record	SuprStr0

```
- - - - - - - - - - - - - - - - - - - - - - - - - - - - - - - }
FUNCTION In_Set(    Member : STRING80;   { input  }
                VAR StrSet : SuperString { input  }) : BOOLEAN;
{- - - - - - - - - - - - - - - - - - - - - - - - - - - - - - -
```

ROUTINE PURPOSE: tests set membership.
PARAMETERS:
  INPUT: Member - the tested member.
         StrSet - the tested set.
FUNCTION VALUE: returns TRUE if Member IS in set StrSet.
HANDLING BAD ARGUMENTS: If Member is a null string or the string set
has less than two characters, the function exits.

ROUTINE DEPENDENCIES

Identifier Name	Identifier Type	Source Library
SET_DELIM	constant	local
STRING80	string	DataLib0
SuperString	record	SuprStr0
PosStr	function	SuprStr0

```
- - - - - - - - - - - - - - - - - - - - - - - - - - - - - - - }
PROCEDURE Add_Member(    Member : STRING80;      { input  }
                     VAR StrSet : SuperString;   { in/out }
                     VAR Done   : BOOLEAN        { output });
{- - - - - - - - - - - - - - - - - - - - - - - - - - - - - - -
```

ROUTINE PURPOSE: adds a new member to the set. Duplicate members are not allowed. The routine is case-sensitive.
PARAMETERS:
  INPUT: Member - the new 'candidate' member.
  OUTPUT: Done - a flag that indicates whether or not the new member was actually added.
  IN/OUT: StrSet - the expanding set.
HANDLING BAD ARGUMENTS: The routine exits if Member is either a null string or represents an existing set member.

ROUTINE DEPENDENCIES

Identifier Name	Identifier Type	Source Library
SET_DELIM	constant	local
STRING80	string	DataLib0
SuperString	record	SuprStr0
PosStr	function	SuprStr0
RightConcat_Str	procedure	SuprStr0

- }
PROCEDURE Del_Member(Member : STRING80;   { input }
                     VAR StrSet : SuperString; { in/out }
                     VAR Done   : BOOLEAN   { output });
{- -

ROUTINE PURPOSE: deletes a member from the set. The routine is case-sensitive.
PARAMETERS:
  INPUT: Member - the deleted member.
  OUTPUT: Done - a flag that indicates whether or not the new member was actually deleted.
  IN/OUT: StrSet - the shrunk set.
HANDLING BAD ARGUMENTS: The routine exits if Member is either a null string or represents an nonexisting set member.

ROUTINE DEPENDENCIES

Identifier Name	Identifier Type	Source Library
SET_DELIM	constant	local
STRING80	string	DataLib0
SuperString	record	SuprStr0
PosStr	function	SuprStr0
Delete_SuperStr	procedure	SuprStr0

- }
FUNCTION Get_Set_Size(VAR StrSet : SuperString { input }) : WORD;
{- -

ROUTINE PURPOSE: counts the number of members in a set.
PARAMETERS:
  INPUT: Str Set - the set whose members are counted.
FUNCTION VALUE: returns the sought count.

ROUTINE DEPENDENCIES

Identifier Name	Identifier Type	Source Library
SET_DELIM	constant	local
SuperString	record	SuprStr0

- }

```
FUNCTION LS_Ord(    Member : STRING80;   { input  }
               VAR StrSet : SuperString { input  }) : WORD;
{- - - - - - - - - - - - - - - - - - - - - - - - - - - - - - - -
```

ROUTINE PURPOSE: determines the ordinal value of a member in a set.
The first member has an ordinal value of one.
PARAMETERS:
  INPUT: Member - the member whose ordinal value is sought.
         StrSet - the set containing Member.
FUNCTION VALUE: returns the ordinal number of a valid set member.
HANDLING BAD ARGUMENTS: If the tested member is not in the set, a
value of zero is returned.
COMMENTS:

ROUTINE DEPENDENCIES

Identifier Name	Identifier Type	Source Library
SET_DELIM	constant	local
STRING80	string	DataLib0
SuperString	record	SuprStr0
PosStr	function	SuprStr0

- }

```
FUNCTION LS_Val(    OrdVal : WORD;       { input  }
               VAR StrSet : SuperString { input  }) : STRING80;
{- - - - - - - - - - - - - - - - - - - - - - - - - - - - - - - -
```

ROUTINE PURPOSE: returns the set member with the supplied ordinal
number.
PARAMETERS:
  INPUT: OrdVal - the ordinal value of the sought member.
         StrSet - the searched set.
FUNCTION VALUE: returns the string containing the member requested by
ordinal value.
HANDLING BAD ARGUMENTS: If an ordinal value of zero is supplied, a
null string is returned by the function. A high ordinal value that
exceeds the membership size also causes a null string to be returned.

```
                        ROUTINE DEPENDENCIES
                        --------------------

        Identifier Name           Identifier Type      Source Library
        ---------------           ---------------      --------------

            SET_DELIM                 constant             local
            STRING80                  string               DataLib0
            SuperString               record               SuprStr0


- - - - - - - - - - - - - - - - - - - - - - - - - - - - - - - - - }
FUNCTION LS_Succ(    Member : STRING80;    { input  }
                 VAR StrSet : SuperString { input  }) : STRING80;
{- - - - - - - - - - - - - - - - - - - - - - - - - - - - - - - -
```

ROUTINE PURPOSE: returns the successor of the parameter-supplied
set member.
PARAMETERS:
  INPUT: Member — the predecessor of the sought member.
         StrSet — the set involved in the operation.
FUNCTION VALUE: returns the string representing the successor of
Member.
HANDLING BAD ARGUMENTS: A null string is returned if:
1) String Member is null.
2) The set super string has less than two characters.
3) The supplied Member is the last set member.

```
                        ROUTINE DEPENDENCIES
                        --------------------

        Identifier Name           Identifier Type      Source Library
        ---------------           ---------------      --------------

            SET_DELIM                 constant             local
            STRING80                  string               DataLib0
            SuperString               record               SuprStr0
            PosStr                    function             SuprStr0


- - - - - - - - - - - - - - - - - - - - - - - - - - - - - - - - - }
FUNCTION LS_Pred(    Member : STRING80;    { input  }
                 VAR StrSet : SuperString { input  }) : STRING80;
{- - - - - - - - - - - - - - - - - - - - - - - - - - - - - - - -
```

ROUTINE PURPOSE: returns the predecessor of the parameter-supplied
set member.
PARAMETERS:
  INPUT: Member — the successor of the sought member.
         StrSet — the set involved in the operation.
FUNCTION VALUE: returns the string representing the predecessor of
Member.
HANDLING BAD ARGUMENTS: A null string is returned if:
1) String Member is null.
2) The set super string has less than two characters.
3) The supplied Member is the first set member.

```
                    ROUTINE DEPENDENCIES
                    --------------------

        Identifier Name          Identifier Type      Source Library
        ---------------          ---------------      --------------
        SET_DELIM                   constant          local
        STRING80                    string            DataLib0
        SuperString                 record            SuprStr0
        PosStr                      function          SuprStr0


- - - - - - - - - - - - - - - - - - - - - - - - - - - - - - - - - - - }


{*****************************************************************}
{***********************} IMPLEMENTATION {***********************}
{*****************************************************************}

{$V-}

{---------------------------------------------- Clear_Set ------}

PROCEDURE Clear_Set(VAR StrSet : SuperString { output });
BEGIN
    WITH StrSet DO BEGIN
        SStr[1] := SET_DELIM;
        SSize := 1
    END; { WITH }
END; { Clear_Set }

{---------------------------------------------- In_Set ------}

FUNCTION In_Set(    Member : STRING80;   { input  }
               VAR StrSet : SuperString { input  }) : BOOLEAN;
BEGIN
    IF (Member = '') OR (StrSet.SSize < 2) THEN BEGIN
        In_Set := FALSE;
        EXIT
    END; { IF }
    Member := SET_DELIM + Member + SET_DELIM;
    { does member already exist ? }
    IF PosStr(Member, StrSet, 1) > 0 THEN In_Set := TRUE
                                ELSE In_Set := FALSE;
END; { In_Set }

{---------------------------------------------- Add_Member ------}

PROCEDURE Add_Member(    Member : STRING80;     { input  }
                    VAR StrSet : SuperString; { in/out }
                    VAR Done   : BOOLEAN      { output });
```

```
BEGIN
    Done := FALSE;
    IF Member = '' THEN EXIT;
    Member := Member + SET_DELIM;
    { does member already exist ? }
    IF PosStr(SET_DELIM + Member, StrSet, 1) > 0 THEN EXIT;
    RightConcat_Str(StrSet, Member);
    Done := TRUE;
END; { Add_Member }

{------------------------------------------------ Del_Member ------}

PROCEDURE Del_Member(     Member : STRING80;     { input  }
                      VAR StrSet : SuperString; { in/out }
                      VAR Done   : BOOLEAN       { output }); 
VAR location : WORD;
BEGIN
    Done := FALSE;
    IF Member = '' THEN EXIT;
    Member := Member + SET_DELIM;
    { does member already exist ? }
    location :=  PosStr(SET_DELIM + Member, StrSet, 1);
    IF location = 0 THEN EXIT; { Member is not in the set }
    { delete the substring characters }
    Delete_SuperStr(StrSet, location, Length(Member));
    Done := TRUE;
END; { Del_Member }

{------------------------------------------------ Get_Set_Size --}

FUNCTION Get_Set_Size(VAR StrSet : SuperString { input  }) : WORD;
VAR i, count : WORD;
BEGIN
    WITH StrSet DO BEGIN
        count := 0;
        i := 2;
        WHILE (i <= SSize) DO BEGIN
            IF SStr[i] = SET_DELIM THEN INC(count);
            INC(i);
        END; { WHILE }
        Get_Set_Size := count { return function value }
    END; { WITH }
END; { Get_Set_Size }

{------------------------------------------------ LS_Ord ------}

FUNCTION LS_Ord(    Member : STRING80;    { input  }
                VAR StrSet : SuperString { input  }) : WORD;
VAR char_loc, i, count : WORD;
```

```
BEGIN
    char_loc := PosStr(SET_DELIM + Member + SET_DELIM, StrSet, 1);
    IF char_loc = 0 THEN BEGIN
        LS_Ord := 0;
        EXIT
    END; { IF }
    WITH StrSet DO BEGIN
        count := 0;
        i := 1;
        WHILE (i <= char_loc) DO BEGIN
            IF SStr[i] = SET_DELIM THEN INC(count);
            INC(i)
        END; { WHILE }
        LS_Ord := count { return function value }
    END; { WITH }
END; { LS_Ord }

{------------------------------------------------ LS_Val ———}

FUNCTION LS_Val(    OrdVal : WORD;        { input  }
                VAR StrSet : SuperString { input  }) : STRING80;
VAR strng : STRING80;
    first_char, i, j, count : WORD;
BEGIN
    IF OrdVal = 0 THEN BEGIN
        LS_Val := '';
        EXIT
    END; { IF }
    WITH StrSet DO BEGIN
        i := 1;
        WHILE (i < SSize) AND (OrdVal > 0) DO BEGIN
            IF SStr[i] = SET_DELIM THEN BEGIN
                DEC(OrdVal);
            END; { IF }
            INC(i)
        END; { WHILE }
        IF OrdVal > 0 THEN
            LS_Val := ''
        ELSE BEGIN
            first_char := i;
            WHILE (i <= SSize) AND (SStr[i] <> SET_DELIM) DO
                INC(i);
            strng := '';
            FOR j := first_char TO i-1 DO
                strng := strng + SStr[j];
            LS_Val := strng { return function value }
        END; { IF }
```

```
        END; { WITH }
END; { LS_Val }


{----------------------------------------------- LS_Succ ------}

FUNCTION LS_Succ(    Member : STRING80;    { input  }
                   VAR StrSet : SuperString { input  }) : STRING80;
VAR strng : STRING80;
    char_loc, first, i, j : WORD;
BEGIN
    IF (Member = '') OR (StrSet.SSize < 2) THEN BEGIN
        LS_Succ := '';
        EXIT
    END; { IF }
    char_loc := PosStr(SET_DELIM + Member + SET_DELIM, StrSet, 1);
    IF char_loc = 0 THEN BEGIN
        LS_Succ := '';
        EXIT
    END; { IF }
    WITH StrSet DO BEGIN
        { obtain index to next member }
        i := char_loc + Length(Member) + 2;
        IF i >= SSize THEN BEGIN { already at end of super string }
            LS_Succ := '';
            EXIT
        END; { IF }
        first := i;
        WHILE (i <= SSize) AND (SStr[i] <> SET_DELIM) DO
            INC(i);
        strng := '';
        FOR j := first  TO i-1 DO
            strng := strng + SStr[j];
        LS_Succ := strng { return function value }
    END; { WITH }
END; { LS_Succ }


{----------------------------------------------- LS_Pred ------}

FUNCTION LS_Pred(    Member : STRING80;    { input  }
                   VAR StrSet : SuperString { input  }) : STRING80;
VAR strng : STRING80;
    char_loc, i, j, last : WORD;
BEGIN
    IF (Member = '') OR (StrSet.SSize < 2) THEN BEGIN
        LS_Pred := '';
        EXIT
    END; { IF }
    char_loc := PosStr(SET_DELIM + Member + SET_DELIM, StrSet, 1);
    IF char_loc = 0 THEN BEGIN
```

```
            LS_Pred := '';
            EXIT
      END; { IF }
      WITH StrSet DO BEGIN
            last := char_loc - 1;
            { obtain index to last member }
            i := last;
            IF i <= 1 THEN BEGIN { already at start of super string }
                  LS_Pred := '';
                  EXIT
            END; { IF }
            WHILE (i > 0) AND (SStr[i] <> SET_DELIM) DO
                  DEC(i);
            strng := '';
            FOR j := i+1 TO last DO
                  strng := strng + SStr[j];
            LS_Pred := strng { return function value }
      END; { WITH }
END; { LS_Pred }
END.
```

Listing 4.4. Source code for library WORDSTR0.PAS.

```
UNIT WordStr0;

{=====================================================================


            Copyright (c) 1987, 1988   Namir Clement Shammas
      LIBRARY NAME: WordStr0
      VERSION: 1.0                                DATE 8/24/1987
      PURPOSE: provides a library of routines to manipulate string-based
            'words'.
      UPDATE HISTORY:


======================================================================}


{********************************************************************}
{***********************} INTERFACE {*******************************}
{********************************************************************}


Uses DataLib0, ComnStr0;
FUNCTION Count_Words(Words,                    { input  }
                  WordDelimStr : STRING255 { input  }) : BYTE;
{- - - - - - - - - - - - - - - - - - - - - - - - - - - - - - - - - -

ROUTINE PURPOSE: counts the number of delimited words in string Words.
```

PARAMETERS:
  INPUT: Words - the examined string.
         WordDelimStr - the string containing the set of delimiting
              characters.
FUNCTION VALUE: returns the number of delimited words in the Words
string.
HANDLING BAD ARGUMENTS: The function exits and returns a zero count if
string Words is a null string. If the WordDelimStr is supplied as a
null string, it is assigned a space character.
COMMENTS:

ROUTINE DEPENDENCIES

Identifier Name	Identifier Type	Source Library
found_delimiter	function	local
STRING255	string	DataLib0

- }

```
FUNCTION WordPos (WordStr,                    { input  }
                  Words,                       { input  }
                  WordDelimStr : STRING255;   { input  }
                  WordIndex    : BYTE          { input  }) : BYTE;
{- - - - - - - - - - - - - - - - - - - - - - - - - - - - - - - - - - -
```

ROUTINE PURPOSE: returns the position of WordStr in Words, starting
at the WordIndex'th word.
PARAMETERS:
  INPUT: WordStr - the sought word.
         Words - the string containing a collection of words.
         WordDelimStr - the string containing the set of delimiting
              characters.
         WordIndex - the number of the first word involved in the
              search.
FUNCTION VALUE: the word sequence number of the string WordStr in the
string Words.
HANDLING BAD ARGUMENTS: The function exits, returning a zero value,
when:
1) Either strings Words or WordStr is a null string.
2) The string WordStr is not found in string Words. This is a
quick check performed using the POS() Turbo Pascal function.
If the WordDelimStr is supplied as a null string, it is assigned
a space character. If the value of WordIndex is less than one, it
is set equal to one.

ROUTINE DEPENDENCIES

Identifier Name	Identifier Type	Source Library
found_delimiter	function	local
IPos	function	ComnStr0
STRING255	string	DataLib0

```
- - - - - - - - - - - - - - - - - - - - - - - - - - - - - - - - - }
PROCEDURE InsertWord(     WordStr,                  { input  }
                         WordDelimStr : STRING255; { input  }
                    VAR Words        : STRING255; { in/out }
                         AfterWord    : BYTE      { input  });
{- - - - - - - - - - - - - - - - - - - - - - - - - - - - - - - -
```

ROUTINE PURPOSE: inserts WordStr in Words after word number AfterWord.
PARAMETERS:
    INPUT: WordStr - the inserted word.
           WordDelimStr - the string containing the set of delimiting
              characters.
           AfterWord - the word-based location where insertion takes
              place.
    IN/OUT: Words - the main string containing the inserted word.
HANDLING BAD ARGUMENTS: If the WordDelimStr is supplied as a null
string, it is assigned a space character. If the value of AfterWord
is less than one, it is set equal to one.

ROUTINE DEPENDENCIES

Identifier Name	Identifier Type	Source Library
CountMidStr	function	ComnStr0
found_delimiter	function	local
LeftStr	function	ComnStr0
STRING255	string	DataLib0

```
- - - - - - - - - - - - - - - - - - - - - - - - - - - - - - - - - }
PROCEDURE GetWord(     Words,                  { input  }
                      WordDelimStr : STRING255; { input  }
                 VAR WordSought   : STRING255; { output }
                      WordIndex    : BYTE      { input  });
{- - - - - - - - - - - - - - - - - - - - - - - - - - - - - - - -
```

ROUTINE PURPOSE: returns the word at word-based position WordIndex.
PARAMETERS:
    INPUT: Words - the string containing a collection of words.
           WordDelimStr - the string containing the set of delimiting
              characters.
           WordIndex - the sought word number.
    OUTPUT: WordSought - the sought word.
HANDLING BAD ARGUMENTS: If the WordDelimStr is supplied as a null
string, it is assigned a space character. If the value of AfterWord
is less than one, it is set equal to one.

                         ROUTINE DEPENDENCIES

    Identifier Name   Identifier Type   Source Library
    ---------------   ---------------   --------------

     CountMidStr   function   ComnStr0
     found_delimiter   function   local
     STRING255   string   DataLib0

- }
PROCEDURE DeleteWord(VAR Words   : STRING255; { in/out }
                         WordDelimStr   : STRING255; { input }
                         WordIndex,   { input }
                         Wordcount   : BYTE   { input });
{- -

ROUTINE PURPOSE: deletes Wordcount words in Words, starting with
word number WordIndex.
PARAMETERS:
   INPUT: WordDelimStr – the string containing the set of delimiting
            characters.
          WordIndex – the number of the first deleted word.
          WordCount – the number of deleted words.
   IN/OUT: Words – the main string from which words are deleted.
HANDLING BAD ARGUMENTS: If the WordDelimStr is supplied as a null
string, it is assigned a space character. If the values of WordIndex
and/or WordCount are less than one, they are set equal to one.

                         ROUTINE DEPENDENCIES

    Identifier Name   Identifier Type   Source Library
    ---------------   ---------------   --------------

     found_delimiter   function   local
     LeftStr   function   ComnStr0
     PosMidStr   function   ComnStr0
     STRING255   string   DataLib0

- }
PROCEDURE TranslateWord(FindWord,   { input }
                            ReplaceWord,   { input }
                            WordDelimStr : STRING255; { input }
                        VAR Words   : STRING255; { in/out }
                            WordIndex,   { input }
                            Frequency   : BYTE   { input });
{- -

ROUTINE PURPOSE: replaces word FindWord with ReplaceWord in Words.
PARAMETERS:
   INPUT: FindWord – the sought word.
          ReplaceWord – the replacement for word FindWord.
          WordDelimStr – the string containing the set of delimiting
            characters.

WordIndex - the number of the first words examined for
translation.
Frequency - the maximum number allowed translations.
IN/OUT: Word - the string containing the translated words.
HANDLING BAD ARGUMENTS: The routine exits if either the strings Words
and/or FindWord are null strings. If the values of WordIndex and/or
Frequency are less than one, they are set equal to one. If the
WordDelimStr is supplied as a null string, it is assigned a
space character.

ROUTINE DEPENDENCIES

Identifier Name	Identifier Type	Source Library
DeleteWord	procedure	local
InsertWord	procedure	local
STRING255	string	DataLib0
WordPos	function	local

- }

```
{*****************************************************************}
{***********************} IMPLEMENTATION {***********************}
{*****************************************************************}
```

{————————————— Found_Delimiter ————}

```
FUNCTION found_delimiter(Strng,              { input  }
                         Delim : STRING255; { input  }
                         Index : BYTE       { input  }) : BOOLEAN;
```

{- -

SCOPE : Local.
ROUTINE PURPOSE: detects the boundary between a delimiter character
and one that is not.
PARAMETERS:
  INPUT: Strng - the string being examined.
         Delim - the string containing the set of delimiting
             characters.
         Index - character location tested.
FUNCTION VALUE: the function returns a TRUE value if the character at
the Index location is not a delimiter and that at (Index+1) is.

ROUTINE DEPENDENCIES

Identifier Name	Identifier Type	Source Library
STRING255	string	DataLib0

```
- - - - - - - - - - - - - - - - - - - - - - - - - - - - - - - - - - - - }
BEGIN
    IF Index > 1 THEN
      found_delimiter := (POS(Strng[Index-1], Delim) = 0) AND
                         (POS(Strng[Index],   Delim) > 0)
    ELSE
      found_delimiter := FALSE;
END; { found_delimiter }


{-------------------------------------------------- Count_Words ---------}

FUNCTION Count_Words(Words,                          { input  }
                     WordDelimStr : STRING255 { input  }) : BYTE;
VAR i, count, strlen : BYTE;
    not_found : BOOLEAN;
BEGIN
    IF Words = '' THEN BEGIN
        count_Words := 0;
        EXIT
    END;
    strlen := Length(Words);
    IF WordDelimStr = '' THEN WordDelimStr := ' ';
    count := 1; { initialize word count }
    FOR i := 1 TO strlen-1 DO
        IF found_delimiter(Words, WordDelimStr, i) THEN
            INC(count);
    IF count = 1 THEN BEGIN
    { suspected of having delimiter symbols only }
        not_found := TRUE;
        i := 1;
        WHILE (i <= strlen) and not_found DO
            IF Pos(Words[i], WordDelimStr) > 0
                THEN not_found := FALSE
                ELSE INC(i);
        IF not_found THEN count := 0;
    END; { IF }
    Count_Words := count { return function value }
END; { Count_Words }


{-------------------------------------------------- WordPos ---------}

FUNCTION WordPos(WordStr,                    { input }
                 Words,                      { input }
                 WordDelimStr : STRING255;   { input }
                 WordIndex    : BYTE         { input }) : BYTE;
VAR i, n, strlen, count, ptr : BYTE;
BEGIN
```

```
    IF (WordStr = '') OR (Words = '') THEN BEGIN
        WordPos := 0;
        EXIT
    END; { IF }
    IF (Pos(WordStr, Words) = 0) THEN BEGIN
        { sought word is not is string at all }
        WordPos := 0;
        EXIT
    END; { IF }
    IF WordDelimStr = '' THEN WordDelimStr := ' ';
    IF WordIndex < 1 THEN WordIndex := 1;
    { Search for the WordIndex'th word }
    strlen := Length(Words);
    n := WordIndex - 1;
    i := 1;
    { Loop until you find a non-WordDelimStr
      char or the end-of-string               }
    WHILE (i <= strlen) AND (POS(Words[i], WordDelimStr) > 0) DO
        INC(i);
    IF i > strlen THEN BEGIN
        WordPos := 0;
        EXIT;
    END; { IF }
    IF n > 0 THEN INC(i);
    WHILE (i <= strlen) AND (n > 0) DO BEGIN
        IF found_delimiter(Words, WordDelimStr, i) THEN DEC(n);
        INC(i);
    END; { WHILE }
    IF n > 0 THEN
        WordPos := 0
    ELSE BEGIN
        IF i > 1 THEN DEC(i);
        ptr := IPos(WordStr, Words, i);
        IF WordIndex = 1 THEN count := 1
                         ELSE count := 0;
        WHILE (i < ptr) DO BEGIN
            IF found_delimiter(Words, WordDelimStr, i) THEN
                INC(count);
            INC(i);
        END; { WHILE }
        IF count > 0 THEN WordPos := count + WordIndex - 1
                     ELSE WordPos := 0;
    END; { IF }
END; { WordPos }

{-------------------------------------------------- InsertWord -------}

PROCEDURE InsertWord(    WordStr,                    { input  }
                        WordDelimStr : STRING255; { input  }
                    VAR Words        : STRING255; { in/out }
                        AfterWord    : BYTE       { input  });
VAR i, n, strlen, ptr : BYTE;
```

```
BEGIN
    IF WordDelimStr = '' THEN WordDelimStr := ' ';
    IF AfterWord =0 THEN BEGIN { Concatenate to the left }
        Words := WordStr + WordDelimStr[1] + Words;
        EXIT;
    END;
    { Search for the AfterWord'th word }
    strlen := Length(Words);
    n := AfterWord;
    i := 1;
    { Loop until you find a non-WordDelimStr
      char or the end-of-string              }
    WHILE (i < strlen) AND (POS(Words[i],WordDelimStr) > 0) DO
        INC(i);
    IF n > 0 THEN INC(i);
    WHILE (i <= strlen) AND (n > 0) DO BEGIN
        IF found_delimiter(Words, WordDelimStr, i) THEN DEC(n);
        INC(i);
    END; { WHILE }
    IF n = 0 THEN BEGIN { found the AfterWord'th word }
        ptr := i - 1;
    { The same delimiter character at ptr is used in the insertion }
        Words := LeftStr(Words, ptr)          +
                 WordStr                       +
                 CountMidStr(Words, ptr, strlen)
    END
    ELSE IF n = 1 THEN   { append as the last word }
        Words := Words + WordDelimStr[1] + WordStr;
END; { InsertWord }

{---------------------------------------------- GetWord ------}

PROCEDURE GetWord(     Words,                     { input  }
                       WordDelimStr : STRING255;  { input  }
                   VAR WordSought   : STRING255;  { output }
                       WordIndex    : BYTE        { input  });
VAR i, n, strlen, ptr1 : BYTE;
BEGIN
    IF WordIndex < 1 THEN WordIndex := 1;
    IF WordDelimStr = '' THEN WordDelimStr := ' ';
    n := WordIndex - 1;
    i := 1;
    strlen := Length(Words);
    { Loop until you find a non-WordDelimStr char or the end-of-string }
    WHILE (i < strlen) AND (POS(Words[i],WordDelimStr) > 0) DO
        INC(i);
    IF i > strlen THEN BEGIN
        WordSought := '';
        EXIT;
    END; { IF }
```

```
      IF n > 0 THEN INC(i);
      WHILE (i <= strlen) AND (n > 0) DO BEGIN
          IF found_delimiter(Words, WordDelimStr, i) THEN DEC(n);
          INC(i);
      END; { WHILE }
      IF (n > 0) THEN
          WordSought := ''
      ELSE BEGIN
          { Loop until you find a non-WordDelimStr
            char or the end-of-string                }
          WHILE (i < strlen) AND (POS(Words[i],WordDelimStr) > 0) DO
              INC(i);
          ptr1 := i;
          n := 1;
          WHILE (i <= strlen) AND (n > 0) DO BEGIN
              IF found_delimiter(Words, WordDelimStr, i) THEN DEC(n);
              INC(i);
          END; { WHILE }
          WordSought := CountMidStr(Words,ptr1,i-ptr1)
      END; { IF }
END; { GetWord }

{------------------------------------------------ DeleteWord ------}

PROCEDURE DeleteWord(VAR Words          : STRING255; { in/out }
                         WordDelimStr   : STRING255; { input  }
                         WordIndex,                  { input  }
                         Wordcount      : BYTE       { input  });
VAR i, strlen, n, ptr1 : BYTE;
BEGIN
    IF WordDelimStr = '' THEN WordDelimStr := ' ';
    IF WordIndex < 0 THEN WordIndex := 1;
    IF WordCount < 1 THEN WordCount := 1;
    { Search for the WordIndex'th word }
    strlen := Length(Words);
    n := WordIndex - 1;
    i := 1;
    { Loop until you find a non-WordDelimStr char or the end-of-string }
    WHILE (i < strlen) AND (POS(Words[i],WordDelimStr) > 0) DO
        INC(i);
    IF n > 0 THEN INC(i);
    WHILE (i <= strlen) AND (n > 0) DO BEGIN
        IF found_delimiter(Words, WordDelimStr, i) THEN DEC(n);
        INC(i);
    END; { WHILE }
    IF n = 0 THEN { found the WordIndex'th word }
    { Loop until you find a non-WordDelimStr char or the end-of-string }
    WHILE (i < strlen) AND (POS(Words[i],WordDelimStr) > 0) DO
        INC(i);
```

```
    ptr1 := i - 1; { First character to delete }
    n := Wordcount;
    WHILE (i <= strlen) AND (n > 0) DO BEGIN
        IF found_delimiter(Words, WordDelimStr, i) THEN DEC(n);
        INC(i);
    END; { WHILE }
    IF (n > 0) OR (i > strlen) THEN  { Delete to the end of string }
        Words := LeftStr(Words,ptr1-1)
    ELSE IF ptr1 < 2 THEN
        Words := PosMidStr(Words, i, strlen)
    ELSE { Deletion ends before the end of string }
        Words := LeftStr(Words, ptr1) + PosMidStr(Words, i, strlen);
END; { DeleteWord }


{------------------------------------------------ TranslateWord ----}

PROCEDURE TranslateWord(    FindWord,                  { input  }
                           ReplaceWord,               { input  }
                           WordDelimStr : STRING255; { input  }
                       VAR Words        : STRING255; { in/out }
                           WordIndex,                 { input  }
                           Frequency    : BYTE       { input  });
VAR index : BYTE;
BEGIN
    IF (FindWord = '') OR  (Words = '') THEN  EXIT;
    IF WordIndex < 1 THEN WordIndex := 1;
    IF WordDelimStr = '' THEN WordDelimStr := ' ';
    IF Frequency < 1 THEN Frequency := 1;
    { get first location of first occurrence of FindWord }
    index := WordPos(FindWord, Words, WordDelimStr, WordIndex);
    { translation loop }
    WHILE (index > 0) AND (Frequency > 0) DO BEGIN
        DEC(Frequency);
        { remove found word }
        DeleteWord(Words, WordDelimStr, index, 1);
        IF ReplaceWord <> '' THEN { replace with non-null word }
            InsertWord(ReplaceWord, WordDelimStr, Words, index - 1);
        { get index for the next word }
        IF Frequency > 0 THEN
            index := WordPos(FindWord, Words, WordDelimStr, index);
    END; { WHILE }
END; { TranslateWord }
END.
```

Listing 4.5. Source code for library MINIGREP.PAS.

```pascal
UNIT MiniGrep;

{=================================================================

          Copyright (c) 1987, 1988    Namir Clement Shammas
     LIBRARY NAME: MiniGrep
     VERSION: 1.0                                 DATE 10/26/1987
     PURPOSE: performs text pattern matching that involve the
     '?' and '*' wildcards as well as "alternate" subpatterns.

     The '?' and '*' wildcards are used in a manner similar to the
     MS/PC-DOS wildcards. Each '?' symbol matches a single character,
     while the '*' symbol matches any number of characters.

     Alternate subpatterns are enclosed in braces with the bar symbol
     as the internal delimiter.

     UPDATE HISTORY:

=================================================================}

{*****************************************************************}
{***********************} INTERFACE {****************************}
{*****************************************************************}

{$V-}
Uses DataLib0, ComnStr0;
CONST
     { Size of array of pointers to pattern strings }
     MAX_STRING_ARRAY = 32;
     MAX_ALTERNATIVES = 5; { Maximum number of alternate subpattern }
                           { per group of subpatterns.             }
  TYPE
     PatternStrPtr = ^STRING255; { pointer to a pattern string type }
     Patterns_Array = ARRAY[1..MAX_STRING_ARRAY] OF PatternStrPtr;
     Pattern_List_Record = RECORD
                          SubPattern : STRING255;
                          Char_Offset : INTEGER;
                        END;
     Pattern_List_Ptr = ^Pattern_List_Record;
     Pattern_List_Array =
        ARRAY[1..MAX_STRING_ARRAY, 1..MAX_ALTERNATIVES] OF
          Pattern_List_Ptr;
     Integer_Array = ARRAY[1..MAX_STRING_ARRAY] OF BYTE;
PROCEDURE Prepare_Pattern(VAR Input_Pattern : STRING255; { in/out }
                          VAR Error_Message : STRING80    { output });
```

{- -

ROUTINE PURPOSE: performs the following preparations and checking:
1) Removes leading and trailing wildcards.
2) Removes clusters of the '*' wildcards.
3) Verifies that the number of open and close braces are
   balanced and in the correct order.
4) Verifies that any subpattern group contains at least two
   alternate subpatterns.
PARAMETERS:
  OUTPUT: Error_Message - any error message that indicates the problem
          with the examined pattern control string.
  IN/OUT: Input_Pattern - the pattern control string in question.
HANDLING BAD ARGUMENTS: The routine returns an error message for the
following reasons:
1) The Input_Pattern contains nothing but wildcards.
2) The number of open and close braces are not equal or are
   out of sequence or there are nested alternate subpatterns.
3) A subpattern group has no multiple alternate subpatterns.

ROUTINE DEPENDENCIES

Identifier Name	Identifier Type	Source Library
STRING80	string	DataLib0
STRING255	string	DataLib0

- }
PROCEDURE Make_Strings(
              Input_Pattern   : STRING255;   { input }
          VAR Patterns   : Patterns_Array; { output }
          VAR Total_SubPattern : BYTE   { output });
{- -

ROUTINE PURPOSE: creates an array of multiple strings if alternate
subpatterns are used. Otherwise, a single pattern string is returned.
PARAMETERS:
  INPUT: Input_Pattern - the preprocessed pattern control string.
  OUTPUT: Patterns - the array of subpatterns.
          Total_SubPattern - the total number of subpatterns.

ROUTINE DEPENDENCIES

Identifier Name	Identifier Type	Source Library
STRING80	string	DataLib0
PosMidStr	function	ComnStr0

```
- - - - - - - - - - - - - - - - - - - - - - - - - - - - - - - - - }
PROCEDURE Make_Lists(
              VAR Patterns           : Patterns_Array;      { input  }
                  Total_SubPattern : BYTE;                  { input  }
              VAR Pattern_Lists      : Pattern_List_Array; { output }
              VAR Num_Alt            : Integer_Array        { output });
{- - - - - - - - - - - - - - - - - - - - - - - - - - - - - - - - -
```

ROUTINE PURPOSE: converts the string patterns that may contain
wildcards. It breaks down the string patterns at the wildcard
location into smaller substrings.
PARAMETERS:
   INPUT: Patterns – the array of patterns.
          Total_SubPattern – the total number of subpatterns.
   OUTPUT: Pattern_Lists – the array of subpattern lists.
          Num_Alt – the array of subpattern counts.

ROUTINE DEPENDENCIES

Identifier Name	Identifier Type	Source Library
PosMidStr	function	ComnStr0

```
- - - - - - - - - - - - - - - - - - - - - - - - - - - - - - - - }
FUNCTION Has_Pattern(
              Line                   : STRING255;          { input  }
              Total_SubPattern     : BYTE;                  { input  }
          VAR Pattern_Lists          : Pattern_List_Array; { input  }
          VAR Num_Alt,                                      { input  }
              PatternPos             : Integer_Array        { output })
                                                            : BOOLEAN;
{- - - - - - - - - - - - - - - - - - - - - - - - - - - - - - - -
```

ROUTINE PURPOSE: scans the string 'Line' and returns two types of
results:
1) The boolean returned by the function signals whether or not there
   is any match with the supplied pattern(s).
2) The array PatternPos indicates the first character where each
   pattern found a match in string 'Line'.
PARAMETERS:
   INPUT: Line – the line of text examined for existing patterns.
          Total_SubPattern – the number of subpatterns.
          Pattern_Lists – the array of pattern lists.
          Num_Alt – the array of alternate subpatterns.
   OUTPUT: PatternPos – the first location for each subpattern.
FUNCTION VALUE: returns TRUE if any pattern matching has been found.
The logical value is a simple and fast indicator for the pattern
matching outcome.

```
                      ROUTINE DEPENDENCIES
                      --------------------

        Identifier Name          Identifier Type      Source Library
        ---------------          ---------------      --------------
          STRING255                  string             DataLib0
          IPos                       function           ComnStr0
          PosMidStr                  function           ComnStr0

  - - - - - - - - - - - - - - - - - - - - - - - - - - - - - - - - - - }

{*******************************************************************}
{***********************} IMPLEMENTATION {**************************}
{*******************************************************************}

{------------------------------------------------ Prepare_Pattern ------}
PROCEDURE Prepare_Pattern(VAR Input_Pattern : STRING255; { in/out }
                          VAR Error_Message : STRING80   { output });
  VAR i,
  brace_level,
      num_alternatives, strlen : BYTE;
BEGIN
    Error_Message := ''; { initialize error message }
    { Delete leading spaces and wildcards }
    strlen := Length(Input_Pattern);
    WHILE (strlen > 0) AND (Input_Pattern[1] IN ['?', '*']) DO BEGIN
        DELETE(Input_Pattern, 1, 1);
        DEC(strlen)
    END;
    IF strlen = 0 THEN BEGIN
        Error_Message := 'Pattern contains only spaces and wildcards';
        EXIT
    END; { IF }
    { Delete trailing spaces and wildcards }
    WHILE (strlen > 0) AND
          (Input_Pattern[strlen] IN ['?', '*']) DO BEGIN
        DELETE(Input_Pattern, strlen, 1);
        DEC(strlen);
    END; { WHILE }
    IF strlen = 0 THEN BEGIN
        Error_Message := 'Pattern contains only spaces and wildcards';
        EXIT
    END; { IF }
    { Remove clusters of '*' wildcards }
    i := Pos('**', Input_Pattern);
    WHILE i > 0 DO BEGIN
        DELETE(Input_Pattern, i, 1);
        i := Pos('**', Input_Pattern);
```

```
    END; { WHILE }
    { Verify number of open and closed braces, and correct usage }
    { initialize number of braces }
    brace_level := 0;
    { Scan the pattern string for braces }
    FOR i := 1 TO strlen DO BEGIN
      IF Input_Pattern[i] IN ['{', '|', '}'] THEN BEGIN
          CASE Input_Pattern[i] OF
             '{' : BEGIN
                      INC(brace_level);
                      num_alternatives := 0 {reset number of alternate}
                                            {subpattern counter         }
                   END;
             '|' : INC(num_alternatives);
             '}' : BEGIN
                      DEC(brace_level);
                      IF num_alternatives = 0 THEN BEGIN
                        Error_Message :=
                            'Subpattern with no alternate text';
                        EXIT
                      END; { IF }
                   END;
          END; { CASE }
          IF NOT (brace_level IN [0..1]) THEN BEGIN
            Error_Message := 'Bad usage of braces';
            EXIT
          END; { IF }
       END; { IF }
    END; { FOR i }
END; { Prepare_Pattern }

{-------------------------------------------------- Make_Strings ------}

PROCEDURE Make_Strings(
                Input_Pattern     : STRING255;     { input  }
            VAR Patterns          : Patterns_Array; { output }
            VAR Total_SubPattern : BYTE            { output });
VAR i, j, k,
    char_ptr1, char_ptr2,      { character indices }
    num_subpattern : BYTE;
    first_time : BOOLEAN;
    letext : ARRAY[1..MAX_ALTERNATIVES] OF STRING255;
    lestr, pending_text : STRING255;
BEGIN
    { Initialize array of pointers }
    FOR i := 1 TO MAX_STRING_ARRAY DO
        Patterns[i] := NIL;
    IF Pos('{', Input_Pattern) = 0 THEN BEGIN
    { Input_Pattern has no subpatterns. One pointer is used  }
        NEW(Patterns[1]);      { allocate dynamic space }
        Patterns[1]^ := Input_Pattern;
        Total_SubPattern := 1
```

```
END
ELSE BEGIN
    lestr := Input_Pattern;
    char_ptr1 := 1;
    first_time := TRUE;
    pending_text := '';    { initialize any leading pattern text }
    FOR char_ptr2 := 1 TO ORD(lestr[0]) DO BEGIN
      IF lestr[char_ptr2] IN ['{', '|', '}'] THEN
        CASE lestr[char_ptr2] OF
          '{' : BEGIN
                  IF char_ptr2 > char_ptr1 THEN
                    { extract pending fixed subpattern     }
                    { and store in Pending_Text identifier }
                    pending_text :=
                        PosMidStr(lestr, char_ptr1, char_ptr2-1);
                  num_subpattern := 0;
                  { update first char pointer }
                  char_ptr1 := char_ptr2 + 1;
                END;
          '|' : BEGIN
                  INC(num_subpattern);
                  { extract pending fixed subpattern }
                  letext[num_subpattern] :=
                        PosMidStr(lestr, char_ptr1, char_ptr2-1);

                  { update first char pointer }
                  char_ptr1 := char_ptr2 + 1;
                END;
          '}' : BEGIN
                  INC(num_subpattern);
                  { extract pending fixed subpattern }
                  letext[num_subpattern] :=
                        PosMidStr(lestr, char_ptr1, char_ptr2-1);
                  { update first char pointer }
                  char_ptr1 := char_ptr2 + 1;
                  IF first_time THEN BEGIN
                    { create the first set of pattern strings }
                    first_time := FALSE;
                    Total_SubPattern := num_subpattern;
                    FOR i := 1 TO Total_SubPattern DO BEGIN
                      NEW(Patterns[i]);
                      Patterns[i]^ := pending_text+letext[i]
                    END; { FOR }
                  END
                  ELSE BEGIN
                    { expand the number of pattern strings }
                    { duplicate latest subpatterns }
                    FOR i := Total_SubPattern+1 TO
                        Total_SubPattern*num_subpattern DO BEGIN
                      NEW(Patterns[i]);
```

```
                              Patterns[i]^ := Patterns[i-Total_SubPattern]^
                         END; { FOR }
                         { append new subpatterns }
                         FOR j := 1 TO num_subpattern DO
                           FOR i := 1 TO Total_SubPattern DO BEGIN
                             k := (j-1)*Total_SubPattern+i;
                             Patterns[k]^ := Patterns[k]^ +
                                             pending_text + letext[j]
                           END; { FOR }
                         { update total subpattern count }
                         Total_SubPattern := Total_SubPattern*
                         num_subpattern;
                         { re-initialize subpattern count }
                         num_subpattern := 0;
                         { reset the pending_text string }
                         pending_text := '';
                       END; { IF }
                   END;
              END; { CASE }
            {END IF }
        END; { FOR }
        { is there any trailing fixed subpattern ? }
        IF char_ptr1 < char_ptr2 THEN BEGIN
          { extract pending fixed subpattern }
          pending_text := PosMidStr(lestr, char_ptr1, char_ptr2-1);
          { update string patterns }
          FOR i := 1 TO Total_SubPattern DO
            Patterns[i]^ := Patterns[i]^+pending_text;
        END; { IF }
      END; { IF }
    END; { Make_Pattern_Strings }

{---------------------------------------------- Make_Lists --------}

PROCEDURE Make_Lists(
            VAR Patterns        : Patterns_Array;      { input  }
                Total_SubPattern : BYTE;               { input  }
            VAR Pattern_Lists    : Pattern_List_Array; { output }
            VAR Num_Alt          : Integer_Array       { output });
VAR i, j,
    char_ptr1, char_ptr2,
    curr_shift { Current character offset value } : BYTE;
    lestr : STRING255;       { a copy of a pattern string }

BEGIN
    { Initialize pattern list }
    FOR i := 1 TO MAX_STRING_ARRAY DO BEGIN
        Num_Alt[i] := 0;
        FOR j := 1 TO MAX_ALTERNATIVES DO
          Pattern_Lists[i, j] := NIL;
```

```
      END; { FOR }
      FOR j := 1 TO Total_SubPattern DO BEGIN
          { Assign string pattern to local string }
          lestr := Patterns[j]^;
          char_ptr1 := 1;       { reset first character pointer }
          curr_shift := 0;      { reset current character offset value }
          Num_Alt[j] := 0;      { initialize number of subpatterns }
          FOR char_ptr2 := 1 TO ORD(lestr[0]) DO BEGIN
            IF lestr[char_ptr2] IN ['?', '*'] THEN BEGIN
              INC(Num_Alt[j]);
              i := Num_Alt[j];  { copy to scalar }
              NEW(Pattern_Lists[j, i]);
              { assign subpattern string and offset to record }
              Pattern_Lists[j, i]^.SubPattern :=
                  PosMidStr(lestr, char_ptr1, char_ptr2-1);
              Pattern_Lists[j, i]^.Char_Offset := curr_shift;
              IF lestr[char_ptr2] = '*' THEN BEGIN
                { move first character pointer }
                char_ptr1 := char_ptr2+1;
                { assign zero to current shift value. This is a }
                { numeric code to signal that the last wildcard }
                { was a '*'                                     }
                curr_shift := 0;
              END
              ELSE BEGIN
                 curr_shift := 0; { reset shift value }
                 WHILE lestr[char_ptr2] = '?' DO BEGIN
                   INC(char_ptr2); { increment character pointer }
                   INC(curr_shift) { increment to count for '?' }
                 END; { WHILE }
                 char_ptr1 := char_ptr2;
                 char_ptr2 := char_ptr2-1; { reset to last '?' }
              END; { IF }
            END; { IF }
          END; { FOR char_ptr2 }
          { any pending characters }
          IF char_ptr1 < char_ptr2 THEN BEGIN
            INC(Num_Alt[j]);
            i := Num_Alt[j];    { copy to scalar }
            NEW(Pattern_Lists[j, i]);
            { assign subpattern string and offset to record }
            Pattern_Lists[j, i]^.SubPattern :=
              PosMidStr(lestr, char_ptr1, char_ptr2);
            Pattern_Lists[j, i]^.Char_Offset := curr_shift;
          END; { IF }
      END; { FOR j }
  END; { Make_Lists }
```

```
{--------------------------------------------------- Has_Pattern --------}

FUNCTION Has_Pattern(
                Line              : STRING255;          { input  }
                Total_SubPattern  : BYTE;               { input  }
            VAR Pattern_Lists     : Pattern_List_Array; { input  }
            VAR Num_Alt,                                { input  }
                PatternPos        : Integer_Array       { output })
                                                        : BOOLEAN;
VAR i, j, char_shift, charpos, first_match_location : BYTE;
    found_pattern,{ store intermediate values for function result }
    match, { flag matched substring }
    found, { flag to signal that a match was found }
    redo   { flag to retry the same set of pattern string at a }
           { different position } : BOOLEAN;
    lestr : STRING255;
    start : Integer_Array;  { array to track the starting position }
                            { for matching pattern }
BEGIN
    found_pattern := FALSE; { initialize function result }
    FOR i := 1 TO Total_SubPattern DO BEGIN
        match := TRUE;
        redo := FALSE;
        found := FALSE;
        start[1] := 1; { start at the beginning of the line }
        WHILE (match OR redo) AND (NOT found) DO BEGIN
            redo := FALSE;
            lestr := Pattern_Lists[i, 1]^.SubPattern;
            char_shift := 0; { always zero for the first subpattern }
            charpos := IPos(lestr, Line, start[1]);
            IF charpos > 0 THEN BEGIN
               start[1] := charpos + Length(lestr);
               first_match_location := charpos;
            END
            ELSE match := FALSE;
            j := 2;
            WHILE (j <= Num_Alt[i]) AND match DO BEGIN
                start[j] := start[j-1];
                lestr := Pattern_Lists[i, j]^.SubPattern;
                char_shift := Pattern_Lists[i, j]^.Char_Offset;
                charpos := IPos(lestr, Line, start[j]);
                IF charpos > 0 THEN BEGIN
                  IF char_shift > 0 THEN
                    IF charpos <> (start[j-1]+char_shift) THEN BEGIN
                      match := FALSE;
                      redo := TRUE;
                    END; { IF }
                  IF match THEN start[j] := charpos + Length(lestr);
                END
                ELSE match := FALSE;
                INC(j);
            END; { WHILE }
```

```
        found := match;
      END; { WHILE }
      IF match THEN PatternPos[i] := first_match_location
              ELSE PatternPos[i] := 0;
      { update pattern matching flag }
      found_pattern := found_pattern OR match;
    END; { FOR i }
    Has_Pattern := found_pattern
END; { Has_Pattern }
END.
```

Listing 4.6. Source code for library USE_GREP.PAS.

```
PROGRAM Text_Pattern_Matching;
{$V-,R+,S+}
{$M 8912, 8912, 20000}


{=====================================================================


                  Text Pattern Matching Program
              Copyright (c) 1988  Namir Clement Shammas.
This program demonstrates the use of library MiniGrep in scanning
for either single subpatterns typed from the keyboard or for
multiple patterns from a text file.


=====================================================================}

Uses CRT, PRINTER, DataLib0, ComnLib0,
     ComnStr0, MiniGrep;
CONST
    { default pattern }
    DEF_PATTERN = '{rain|storm}*{Spain|France}*plain';
    { default line }
    DEF_LINE = 'The rain in Spain stays mainly in the plain';
  VAR EchoPrint, { flag to echo output to printer }
    EchoText { flag to echo output to a text file } : BOOLEAN;
    Ch : CHAR;
    Choice, Total_SubPattern : BYTE;
    L, Line_Count : INTEGER;
    Error_Message, PatternString, Line : STRING255;
    Patterns : Patterns_Array;
    List : Pattern_List_Array;
    Num_Alt, PatPos : Integer_Array;
    FileVar, TextVar : TEXT;

{-------------------------------------------- SetFile ----}

PROCEDURE SetFile(    Message    : STRING255; { input  }
                      Input_Mode : BOOLEAN;   { input  }
                  VAR FVar       : TEXT       { output });
{- - - - - - - - - - - - - - - - - - - - - - - - - - - - - - - - - - -
```

```
ROUTINE PURPOSE: opens a text file for input or output.
PARAMETERS:
  INPUT: Message - the prompt string.
         Input_Mode - a flag used to indicate whether the file is
             opened for input or output.
             When FALSE, file input is carried out.
             When TRUE, file output is carried out.
  OUTPUT: FVar - a TEXT-type variable.
```

ROUTINE DEPENDENCIES

Identifier Name	Identifier Type	Source Library
STRING255	string	DataLib0

- }

```
VAR ok : BOOLEAN;
    fname : STRING255;
BEGIN
    REPEAT
        WRITE(Message);
        READLN(fname); WRITELN;
        ASSIGN(FVar, fname);
        IF Input_Mode THEN
            {$I-} RESET(FVar)    {$I+}
        ELSE
            {$I-} REWRITE(FVar); {$I+}
        ok := IOResult = 0;
        IF NOT ok THEN BEGIN
            WRITELN('Error: Cannot open file ', fname);
            WRITELN;
        END; { IF }
    UNTIL ok;
END; { SetFile }
```

{ -

ROUTINE DEPENDENCIES

Identifier Name	Identifier Type	Source Library
Center	procedure	ComnLib0
GotoXY	procedure	CRT
Has_Pattern	function	MiniGrep
Integer_Array	array	MiniGrep
LST	device	PRINTER
Make_Lists	procedure	MiniGrep
Make_Strings	procedure	MiniGrep
Patterns_Array	array	MiniGrep
Patterns_List_Array	array	MiniGrep
Prepare_Pattern	procedure	MiniGrep
ReadKey	function	CRT
SetFile	procedure	local
STRING255	string	DataLib0
YesNo	function	ComnLib0

- }

```
BEGIN { ——— M A I N ——— }
    PatternString := DEF_PATTERN; { set pattern to default pattern }
    REPEAT
      REPEAT
        Center('Pattern Matching Utility', -1, TRUE, 0);
        GotoXY(1, 5);
        WRITELN('0) Exit'); WRITELN;
        WRITE('1) Type a pattern (current pattern is "');
        WRITELN(PatternString, '")'); WRITELN;
        WRITELN('2) Type a text line'); WRITELN;
        WRITELN('3) Scan a text file '); WRITELN;
        WRITELN; WRITELN;
        WRITE('Enter choice by number : ');
        READLN(Choice); WRITELN;
      UNTIL Choice IN [0..3];
      CASE Choice OF
        0 : WRITELN('End of program');
        1 : BEGIN
              WRITE('Enter pattern ? ');
              READLN(PatternString); WRITELN;
              IF PatternString = '' THEN PatternString := DEF_PATTERN;
              { prepare string and create list of subpatterns }
              Prepare_Pattern(PatternString, Error_Message);
              IF Error_Message = '' THEN BEGIN
                 Make_Strings(PatternString, Patterns,
                                             Total_SubPattern);
                 Make_Lists(Patterns, Total_SubPattern,
                                             List, Num_Alt);
              END
              ELSE BEGIN
                 WRITELN(Error_Message);
                 HALT
              END;
            END;
        2 : BEGIN
              WRITE('Enter text line ? '); READLN(Line); WRITELN;
              IF Line = '' THEN Line := DEF_LINE;
              IF Has_Pattern(Line, Total_SubPattern,
                            List, Num_Alt, PatPos) THEN
              BEGIN
                 WRITELN('Pattern ', PatternString, ' matches string ');
                 WRITELN(Line);
                 FOR L := 1 TO Total_SubPattern DO
                   IF PatPos[L] > 0 THEN WRITELN('^' : PatPos[L]);
              END
              ELSE
                 WRITELN('Pattern does not match');
              WRITELN; WRITE('press any key to continue');
              Ch := ReadKey; WRITELN;
            END;
```

```
   3 : BEGIN
          SetFile('Enter filename ? ', TRUE, FileVar);
          EchoPrint := YesNo('Echo to printer');
          WRITELN;
          EchoText := YesNo('Echo to text file');
          WRITELN;
          IF EchoText THEN
             SetFile('Enter output filename ? ', FALSE, TextVar);
          Line_Count := 0; { initialize line counter }
          WHILE NOT EOF(FileVar) DO BEGIN
             READLN(FileVar, Line); { read a new line }
             INC(Line_Count); { update line count }
             IF Has_Pattern(Line, Total_SubPattern, List,
                            Num_Alt, PatPos) THEN BEGIN
               WRITELN(Line_Count:4,':',Line);
               IF EchoPrint THEN
                   WRITELN(LST,Line_Count:4,':',Line);
               IF EchoText THEN
                   WRITELN(TextVar,Line_Count:4,':',Line);
               FOR L := 1 TO Total_SubPattern DO
                  IF PatPos[L] > 0 THEN BEGIN
                    WRITELN('^':(PatPos[L]+5));
                    IF EchoPrint THEN
                        WRITELN(LST,'^':(PatPos[L]+5));
                    IF EchoText THEN
                        WRITELN(TextVar,'^':(PatPos[L]+5));
                  END; { IF }
             END; { IF }
          END; { WHILE }
          Close(FileVar);
          IF EchoText THEN Close(TextVar);
          WRITELN; WRITE('press any key to continue');
          Ch := ReadKey; WRITELN;
       END;
   END; { CASE }
 UNTIL Choice = 0;
END.
```

5

Virtual and Sparse Arrays

Arrays are very important data structures. They are noted for the flexibility of randomly accessing their members. Arrays normally employ integer-typed indices for access. Arrays may be created in one or more dimensions. In this chapter I will present libraries that tackle virtual and sparse matrices (two-dimensional arrays).

LIBRARY VM.PAS

Virtual matrices are very large matrices that require much memory, creating one of two problems: (1) their space requirement exceeds available memory space, or (2) while they do fit in the available space, no room is left for other arrays or variables.

The techniques of virtual memory have their roots in the days of 4K-memory computers! In those days, the limited memory dictated that most of the data and program actually reside on a disk. Only a small portion that is being executed or used is in memory. Thus, continuous swapping of program code and data was the method used to execute most programs. The idea is that virtual memory resembles living beyond one's financial means by taking out bank loans to compensate for the slack in cash. Implementing a virtual matrix begins by pretending that you have a wealth of memory space to store the large matrix. However, since this is not true, the virtual system resorts to storing the matrix in a random access file while keeping a smaller portion in memory. The latter is important to minimize disk access. As a rule of thumb, the bigger the memory space allotted to store portions of a matrix, the faster the virtual system.

In designing a virtual system to store and recall array elements, paying special attention to the memory-resident portion (I will call it the submatrix) is very important. Using a divide-and-conquer strategy, the memory dedicated for the submatrix is divided into several virtual pages. During a steady-state operation, the memory contains several equal-sized virtual pages read from various parts of the matrix. When a new page is read into memory, another one must be swapped back to disk. To optimize the performance, you need to have the right number of virtual pages and correct page size. An increased number of virtual pages provides you with high resolution for accessing the matrix (the highest resolution is the ideal case of having enough memory for the entire matrix). However, you must also pay attention to the size of the virtual page, since using bigger sizes does not mean better performance in this case. Having to write a large-sized page back to disk just because one element has been changed is also wasting time in writing numerous unaltered elements. The recommendation is to use a size that is closest to the file I/O buffer size employed by the operating system. This may be 128, 512, or 1024 bytes, depending on the buffer size of the operating system. Having virtual pages with these sizes is ideal, since they minimize the I/O effort and speed things up.

Library VM.PAS, shown in Listing 5.1, implements a virtual matrix design. I will continue discussing the implementation of a virtual matrix system using the VM.PAS library.

The first part in the design of a virtual system is to define the data structure of the memory page system. These pages are stored in a table (or catalog, if you want). I have chosen to divide the main matrix into a matrix of pages. This means that the single elements of the large matrix fall into a two-dimensional array of pages, with their own row and column numbers. This is shown as the **RRP** (short for Rows in a RAM Page) and **CRP** (short for Columns in a RAM page) constants shown below:

```
CONST MAX_VM_ROW = 100;   { maximum rows of VM pages }
      MAX_VM_TABLE = 10; { size of VM Table }
      RRP = 10; { Number of rows in a VM page }
      CRP = 10; { Number of columns in a VM page }
      VM_MISSING = 1.0E+37; { Numeric code for missing number }
```

The virtual system also specifies the maximum number of rows in the matrix of VM pages. The **MAX_VM_TABLE** constant declares the number of VM pages coresident in the memory at any time. Each virtual page is a matrix containing **RRP** and **CRP** elements, as shown below:

```
TYPE  VMtype = REAL;
      FName = STRING80;
      RAM_Page_Type = ARRAY [1..RRP,1..CRP] OF VMtype;
      Table_Rec = RECORD
                        Dirty_Bit : BOOLEAN;
                        Page_Num, Freq : WORD;
                        RAM_Page : RAM_Page_Type;
                  END;

      Table_Array = ARRAY [1..MAX_VM_TABLE] OF Table_Rec;
      VM_File_Type = FILE OF RAM_Page_Type;
```

The **Table_Rec** record contains the following fields:

1. Dirty bit field: used to indicate whether or not a page has been modified. This information is used while swapping a page. If the dirty bit is TRUE, the page is written to disk before another is read; otherwise, the current page is simply overwritten. This saves time through bypassing unnecessary disk write operations.

2. Page number field: stores the page identification number. This number is calculated using the following:

```
page_no = mat_row + (mat_col - 1) * MAX_VM_ROW;
```

The above number is used by the system to find out if a requested virtual page is already in memory. Keep in mind that this page number has nothing to do with the index of the table array (that is, page-table entry number).

3. Frequency field: used to count the number of times a memory-resident page has been retrieved. The frequency provides a basic statistical tool to decide which page to swap out. In general, there are many other criteria for selecting a page to be swapped to disk: some even contradict each other! The page with the least frequency is selected for swapping to disk.

4. Virtual page: contains a matrix that is a small part of the main matrix.

The array-type **Table_Array** stores the virtual page, while the file-type **VM_File_Type** stores pages in random access files.

The following routines are exported by the VM.PAS library:

```
PROCEDURE SetUpVM(VAR VM_File    : VM_File_Type; { in/out }
                      Max_Pages  : WORD;         { input  }
                      FileName   : FName;        { input  }
                  VAR Table      : Table_Array;  { output }
                  VAR ErrorMsg   : STRING80      { output });
```

initializes an instance of virtual data structure. The routine uses the parameter **ErrorMsg** to indicate the type of errors that may occur. This may be due to a bad filename or insufficient disk space.

```
PROCEDURE CloseVM(VAR VM_File : VM_File_Type { input });
```

terminates an instance of VM data by closing the VM data file. Data in the virtual page table is not written to file, assuming that the virtual matrix is no longer needed.

```
PROCEDURE VM_Store(    X        : VMtype;       { input  }
                       Row,                     { input  }
                       Col      : WORD;         { input  }
                   VAR VM_File  : VM_File_Type; { input  }
                   VAR Table    : Table_Array;  { in/out }
                   VAR Done     : BOOLEAN       { output });
```

stores **X** in the VM system at **Row, Col** location. The routine checks to see if the sought VM page is already in memory. If so, only memory storage is performed. On the other hand, if the sought VM page is not already in memory, one is swapped to read the VM page needed. The VM page written back to disk is the one least used.

```
FUNCTION VM_Recall(
          Row,                        { input  }
          Col     : WORD;             { input  }
     VAR VM_File : VM_File_Type;     { input  }
     VAR Table   : Table_Array;      { in/out }
     VAR Done    : BOOLEAN           { output }) : VMtype;
```

recalls an element from the VM system. The routine checks to see if the sought VM page is already in memory. If so, only a memory access operation is performed. On the other hand, if the sought VM page is not already in memory, one is swapped to read the VM page needed. The VM page written back to disk is the least used one.

A VM DEMONSTRATION PROGRAM

To demonstrate the use of the VM.PAS, I wrote a simple automatic demonstration program USE_VM.PAS, shown in Listing 5.2. It exercises storing and retrieving data from a virtual matrix. The program creates a virtual matrix with 1000 rows and 100 columns. Under the specifications of the VM.PAS library, this requires the creation of 1000 pages to store the virtual matrix. In my system I have drive **E:** as a 2 MByte RAM-drive. I used that drive to store the virtual matrix data file, VM.DAT.

The program stores 20 real-typed random numbers in random locations of the virtual matrix. The virtual rows and columns are stored in two arrays to enable the program to retrieve the data later. The program first lists the virtual matrix elements that are selected and the values assigned to each. It pauses, while waiting for you to strike any key. Next, it retrieves the virtual matrix elements previously stored and displays them near the input values. This enables you to verify the equality of both sets of numbers. Figure 5.1 shows a screen image for a sample session with program USE_VM.PAS. Figure 5.2 contains the software bus schedule for the USE_VM.PAS program project.

More ambitious projects dealing with virtual matrices would tackle implementing matrix operations. These include addition, subtraction, multiplication, and inversion, to name just a few. The first three operations are implemented as a straight-forward adaptation of the basic algorithms. However, the inversion of virtual matrices requires you to employ special algorithms tailored for large matrices. Using the standard routines may not be adequate to maintain any decent level of accuracy.

Figure 5.1. Screen image during a session with demonstration program.

```
USE_VM.PAS.

Creating virtual matrix ...
VM_Mat[  1,  7] = 350.11 ?=? 350.11
VM_Mat[406, 55] = 691.02 ?=? 691.02
VM_Mat[638, 33] = 770.03 ?=? 770.03
VM_Mat[852, 17] = 954.63 ?=? 954.63
VM_Mat[142, 32] = 207.50 ?=? 207.50
VM_Mat[587, 17] = 762.23 ?=? 762.23
VM_Mat[451, 66] = 644.19 ?=? 644.19
VM_Mat[312, 57] = 651.95 ?=? 651.95
VM_Mat[326, 66] = 938.84 ?=? 938.84
VM_Mat[494, 35] = 602.25 ?=? 602.25
VM_Mat[964, 30] = 326.20 ?=? 326.20
VM_Mat[575, 46] = 142.37 ?=? 142.37
VM_Mat[986, 23] = 410.90 ?=? 410.90
VM_Mat[ 41, 29] = 358.31 ?=? 358.31
VM_Mat[999,  5] = 832.72 ?=? 832.72
VM_Mat[ 20, 46] = 728.82 ?=? 728.82
VM_Mat[460, 59] = 896.49 ?=? 896.49
VM_Mat[413, 64] = 832.87 ?=? 832.87
VM_Mat[ 90, 72] = 102.93 ?=? 102.93
VM_Mat[488, 65] = 632.25 ?=? 632.25

press any key to continue
```

Figure 5.2. Software bus schedule for the USE_VM.PAS application.

```
                     SOFTWARE BUS SCHEDULE

PROJECT: USE_VM.PAS
MODULE CRT
                              Software Bus Schedule
                     A             B             C

OUTPUT
proc ClrEol          X
proc ClrScr          X
proc GotoXY          X
func ReadKey         X
```

MODULE DataLib0

	Software Bus Schedule		
	A	B	C
OUTPUT			
string STRING80		X	

MODULE VM

	Software Bus Schedule		
	A	B	C
OUTPUT			
const CRP			X
const MAX_VM_ROW			X
const RRP			X
proc SetUpVM			X
func VM_Recall			X
proc VM_Store			X
INTERFACE INPUT			
string STRING80			
	X		

MODULE   main

	Software Bus Schedule		
	A	B	C
INPUT			
proc ClrEol	X		
proc ClrScr	X		
const CRP			X
proc GotoXY	X		
const MAX_VM_ROW			X
func ReadKey	X		
const RRP			X
proc SetUpVM			X
string STRING80		X	
func VM_Recall			X
proc VM_Store			X

LIBRARY SPARSMAT.PAS

Sparse arrays suffer from a memory space problem that is, in a way, the opposite of that with virtual arrays. While sparse arrays and matrices normally have adequate space, many of their elements are zeros or nulls. In other words, significant data is dispersed in arrays and matrices that are rich with space-wasting zeros. The solution to this problem lies in storing the elements of sparse arrays and matrices in a more contiguous memory space. However, these elements must still be mapped to the original indices of the sparse array or matrix. In this chapter I will present two mechanisms to maintain sparse matrices in contiguous memory spaces. Both methods share the same matrix unwrapping scheme: the columns of the matrix are concatenated with each other to form one long array. Thus, the row and column indices of a matrix are used to calculate the index of an equivalent one-dimensional sparse array. I will call the calculated index the rank of a sparse matrix element. Remember that elements of the sparse matrix are randomly requested, thus mapping themselves on various parts of the large sparse array. This means that a well-designed sparse matrix system requires data structures that support fast insertions. Library SPARSMAT.PAS, shown in Listing 5.3, contains the data objects and routines for both flavors of sparse matrix implementations.

The first method uses dynamically allocated singly linked lists. Inserting new elements in such lists does not require shifting any elements, as is the case with arrays. However, accessing lists can be slow, since you must scan from the head of the list and scroll through the linked list elements. The solution to this problem is to utilize an array of pointers to linked lists. Since arrays may be accessed at random, the method inherits that flexible feature. Thus, the method is able to zoom in on a particular linked list and reduce list traversal time. Once the right linked list is accessed, new elements of a sparse matrix can be quickly inserted. The array of list pointers succeeds in providing fast searching and insertion of data. The constants and data types related to the list scheme are as follows:

```
CONST { constants for list-based sparse matrices }
      MAX_SMLIST_COL : WORD = 1000;
      WIDTH_SMLIST = 100;
      NUM_SMLIST_COL = 10; { MAX_SPARSE_LIST_COL / WIDTH_SMLIST }
      SMLIST_MISSING = -1.0E+20;
TYPE { basic data type for each matrix element }
      SMtype = REAL;
      { data types for list-based sparse matrices }
      SMList_Ptr= ^SMList_Matrix;
      SMList_Ptr_Array = ARRAY [1..NUM_SMLIST_COL] OF SMList_Ptr;
      SMList_Matrix = RECORD
                  Member : SMtype; { or any other type }
                  Rank   : WORD;
                  Next : SMList_Ptr
              END;
```

The **SMList_Matrix** record contains fields that store the value and rank of the sparse matrix elements. A third pointer-type field is used to maintain the links in the list. The array-type **SMList_Ptr_Array** is used to declare variables that store the array of lists.

Binary trees provide a more attractive alternate structure to efficiently manage sparse matrices. The binary tree structure single-handedly provides both swift searching and insertion of data. A sparse matrix is maintained using a single binary tree.

```
CONST   { constants for tree-based sparse matrices }
        MAX_SMTREE_COL = 1000;
        SMTREE_MISSING = -1.0E+30;


TYPE { data types for list-based sparse matrices }
     SMTree_Ptr = ^SMTree_Mat_Node;
     SMTree_Mat_Node = RECORD
                   Member : SMtype;
                   Rank : WORD;
                   Left, Right : SMTree_Ptr;
                   END;
```

The routines of library SPARSMAT.PAS are as follows:

```
PROCEDURE SetUp_SMList(VAR List : SMList_Ptr_Array { output });
```

initializes the heads of the linked list array.

```
PROCEDURE SetUp_SMTree(VAR Tree_Root : SMTree_Ptr { output });
```

initializes the root of the binary tree used in indexing the sparse matrix elements.

```
FUNCTION Search_SMList(VAR Head     : SMList_Ptr; { input  }
                           Match    : WORD;       { input  }
                       VAR Last,                  { in/out }
                           Current  : SMList_Ptr  { in/out })
                                                  : BOOLEAN;
```

searches a linked list for a matching index rank **Match**.

```
PROCEDURE Search_SMTree(
              VAR Tree_Root : SMTree_Ptr; { input  }
                  Match     : WORD        { input  });
```

searches the binary tree containing the matrix indices for an element with a given rank number.

```
PROCEDURE Store_SMList(
          VAR List_Head : SMList_Ptr_Array; { in/out }
              Element   : SMtype;       { input  }
              Row,                      { input  }
              Col       : WORD          { input  });
```

stores the value of **Element** at the specified row/column. The actual process involves calculating the rank index and then inserting the element in the appropriate list.

```
PROCEDURE Store_SMTree(
          VAR Tree_Root : SMTree_Ptr; { in/out }
              Element   : SMtype;     { input  }
              Row,                    { input  }
              Col       : WORD        { input  });
```

stores the value of **Element** at the specified row/column. The actual process involves calculating the rank index and then inserting the element in the tree location.

```
FUNCTION Recall_SMList(
          VAR List_Head : SMList_Ptr_Array; { input }
              Row,                      { input }
              Col       : WORD          { input }) : SMtype;
```

recalls a sparse matrix element from the specified row/column coordinates. If no element has been previously stored in the specified matrix coordinates, a zero is returned.

```
FUNCTION  Recall_SMTree(
          VAR Tree_Root : SMTree_Ptr; { input  }
              Row,                    { input  }
              Col       : WORD        { input  }) : SMtype;
```

recalls a sparse matrix element from the specified row/column coordinates. If no element has been previously stored in the specified matrix coordinates, a zero is returned.

SPARSE MATRIX DEMONSTRATION PROGRAM

I wrote a small automatic demonstration program for manipulating sparse matrices using the binary tree storage scheme. Listing 5.4 contains the demo program USE_SM.PAS. The program performs the following:

1. Initializes two sparse matrices with randomly distributed data. Each matrix has five rows and five columns.

2. Adds the above two matrices, storing the result in a third sparse matrix.

3. Displays all of the three sparse matrices involved.

The program contains three local routines: **Init_SM**, **Add_SM_Mat**, and **Display_SM_Mat**. The first routine initializes a sparse matrix and randomly stores **MAX_ELEMENTS** in it. The second routine, **Add_SM_Mat**, adds two sparse matrices and stores the result in a separate third matrix. The **Display_SM_Mat** displays an entire matrix.

The routines have been tailored for this particular demonstration program, which is why I have not created a separate general library for the sparse matrix operations. Figure 5.3 shows a screen image of a sample session with program USE_SM.PAS. The software bus schedule for the program is found in Figure 5.4.

Figure 5.3. Screen image of a sample session with program USE_SM.PAS.

```
Matrix A is
 2.78  1.19  0.00  0.00  0.00
 0.00  0.00  0.00  0.00  0.00
 7.36  0.00  6.57  6.05  0.00
 0.00  7.44  0.00  0.00  0.00
 9.50  0.00  0.00  0.00  0.00

Matrix B is
 0.00  2.87  0.00  0.00  0.00
 0.00  0.00  6.13  9.32  0.00
 0.00  5.58  0.47  0.00  0.00
 0.00  0.00  0.00  0.00  0.00
 0.00  3.45  0.00  0.00  0.00

Matrix C is
 2.78  4.06  0.00  0.00  0.00
 0.00  0.00  6.13  9.32  0.00
 7.36  5.58  7.04  6.05  0.00
 0.00  7.44  0.00  0.00  0.00
 9.50  3.45  0.00  0.00  0.00
```

Figure 5.4. The software bus schedules for USE_SM.PAS

SOFTWARE BUS SCHEDULE

PROJECT: USE_SM.PAS
MODULE SparsMat

	Software Bus Schedule	
	A	B
OUTPUT		
pointer SMTree_Ptr		X
proc SetUp_SMTree		X
proc Store_SMTree		X
func Recall_SMTree		X

MODULE CRT

	Software Bus Schedule	
	A	B
OUTPUT		
proc ClrScr	X	

MODULE main

	Software Bus Schedule	
	A	B
INPUT		
proc ClrScr	X	
func Recall_SMTree		X
proc SetUp_SMTree		X
pointer SMTree_Ptr		X
proc Store_SMTree		X

Listing 5.1. Source code for the library VM.PAS.

```
UNIT VM;
{=====================================================================


              Copyright (c) 1987, 1988    Namir Clement Shammas
       LIBRARY NAME: VM
       VERSION:  1.0                                 DATE 02/23/1987
       PURPOSE: library supports virtual memory system of arrays and
                matrices. Best used with RAM-disks.
       UPDATE HISTORY:


 ===================================================================}
{*********************************************************************}
{**************************} INTERFACE {*****************************}
{*********************************************************************}
Uses DataLib0;
CONST MAX_VM_ROW = 100;  { maximum rows of VM pages }
      MAX_VM_TABLE = 10; { size of VM Table }
      RRP = 10; { Number of rows in a VM page }
      CRP = 10; { Number of columns in a VM page }
      VM_MISSING = 0.0; { Numeric code for missing number }
TYPE  VMtype = REAL;
      FName = STRING80;
      RAM_Page_Type = ARRAY [1..RRP,1..CRP] OF VMtype;
      Table_Rec = RECORD
                        Dirty_Bit : BOOLEAN;
                        Page_Num, Freq : WORD;
                        RAM_Page : RAM_Page_Type;
                  END;
      Table_Array = ARRAY [1..MAX_VM_TABLE] OF Table_Rec;
      VM_File_Type = FILE OF RAM_Page_Type;

PROCEDURE SetUpVM(VAR VM_File   : VM_File_Type; { in/out }
                      Max_Pages : WORD;         { input  }
                      FileName  : FName;        { input  }
                  VAR Table     : Table_Array;  { output }
                  VAR ErrorMsg  : STRING80      { output });
{- - - - - - - - - - - - - - - - - - - - - - - - - - - - - - - - - -

ROUTINE PURPOSE: initializes an instance of virtual data.
PARAMETERS:
  INPUT: Max_Pages - maximum number of matrix pages.
         FileName - name of file used to store virtual matrix.
  OUTPUT: Table - memory-based table of VM data.
          ErrorMsg - string containing any error message.
  IN/OUT: VM_File - text-type file variable used to store VM data.
```

HANDLING BAD ARGUMENTS: the routine uses ErrorMsg to indicate the
types of errors that may occur. This could be one of either:
  1) The supplied filename is bad; or
  2) Insufficient storage space for the VM file.

```
                      ROUTINE DEPENDENCIES
                      --------------------

        Identifier Name          Identifier Type        Source Library
        ---------------          ---------------        --------------

           STRING80                  string                DataLib0

- - - - - - - - - - - - - - - - - - - - - - - - - - - - - - - - - - - }
PROCEDURE CloseVM(VAR VM_File : VM_File_Type { input });
{- - - - - - - - - - - - - - - - - - - - - - - - - - - - - - - - - - -
```

ROUTINE PURPOSE: terminates an instance of VM data by closing the
VM data file.
PARAMETERS:
  INPUT: VM_File - VM data file handle.

```
- - - - - - - - - - - - - - - - - - - - - - - - - - - - - - - - - - - }
PROCEDURE VM_Store(     X        : VMtype;         { input  }
                        Row,                        { input  }
                        Col      : WORD;           { input  }
                    VAR VM_File : VM_File_Type;    { input  }
                    VAR Table    : Table_Array;    { in/out }
                    VAR Done     : BOOLEAN         { output });
{- - - - - - - - - - - - - - - - - - - - - - - - - - - - - - - - - - -
```

ROUTINE PURPOSE: stores X in the VM system at Row, Col location. The
routine checks to see if the sought VM page is already in memory. If
so, only memory storage is performed. On the other hand, if the
sought VM page is not already in memory, one is swapped to read the
VM page needed. The VM page written back to disk is the one least
used.
PARAMETERS:
  INPUT: X - the stored value.
         Row, Col - the row/column of the virtual matrix.
         VM_File - the VM data file handle.
  OUTPUT: Done - the flag used to indicate success of operation.
  IN/OUT: Table - the memory-resident catalog for VM-pages in memory.
HANDLING BAD ARGUMENTS: if the column number specified is too big,
the routine does nothing.

```
                        ROUTINE DEPENDENCIES
                        --------------------

        Identifier Name          Identifier Type      Source Library
        ---------------          ---------------      --------------

          locate_page               function              local
          search_table              function              local

- - - - - - - - - - - - - - - - - - - - - - - - - - - - - - - - - }
FUNCTION VM_Recall(    Row,                    { input  }
                       Col     : WORD;         { input  }
                   VAR VM_File : VM_File_Type; { input  }
                   VAR Table   : Table_Array;  { in/out }
                   VAR Done    : BOOLEAN       { output }) : VMtype;
{- - - - - - - - - - - - - - - - - - - - - - - - - - - - - - - -
```

ROUTINE PURPOSE: recalls an element from the VM system. The
routine checks to see if the sought VM page is already in memory. If
so, only memory storage is performed. On the other hand, if the
sought VM page is not already in memory, one is swapped to read the
VM page needed. The VM page written back to disk is the least used
one.
PARAMETERS:
  INPUT: Row, Col – the virtual matrix row/column of the recalled
         element.
         VM_File – the VM data file handle.
  OUTPUT: Done – the flag used to signal success of the operation.
  IN/OUT: Table – memory-resident catalog for VM-pages in memory.
FUNCTION VALUE: returns the value of the sought element.
HANDLING BAD ARGUMENTS: if the column number specified is too big,
the routine does nothing.

```
                        ROUTINE DEPENDENCIES
                        --------------------

        Identifier Name          Identifier Type      Source Library
        ---------------          ---------------      --------------

          locate_page               function              local
          search_table              function              local

- - - - - - - - - - - - - - - - - - - - - - - - - - - - - - - - - }


{*********************************************************************}
{***********************} IMPLEMENTATION {***************************}
{*********************************************************************}
```

```
{------------------------------------------------------- SetUpVM -------}

PROCEDURE SetUpVM(VAR VM_File   : VM_File_Type; { in/out }
                      Max_Pages : WORD;          { input  }
                      FileName  : FName;         { input  }
                  VAR Table     : Table_Array;   { output }
                  VAR ErrorMsg  : STRING80       { output });
VAR i, j, K : WORD;
    io_status : BOOLEAN;
BEGIN
  { Open file }
  Assign(VM_File, FileName);
  {$i-} Rewrite(VM_File); {$i+}
  IF IOResult <> 0 THEN BEGIN
     ErrorMsg := 'Cannot open file';
     EXIT
  END;
  { Initialize VM Table }
  FOR K := 1 TO MAX_VM_TABLE DO BEGIN
      WITH Table[K] DO BEGIN
          Dirty_Bit := FALSE;
          Page_Num := 0;
          Freq := 0;
          FOR i := 1 TO RRP DO
              FOR j := 1 TO CRP DO
                  RAM_Page[i,j] := 0.0;
      END; { WITH }
  END; { FOR }
  { Initialize VM file records }
  SEEK(VM_FILE, 1);
  FOR k := 1 TO Max_Pages DO BEGIN
      {$i-} WRITE(VM_File, Table[1].RAM_Page); {$i-}
      IF IOResult <> 0 THEN BEGIN
         ErrorMsg := 'Error in creating a page';
         EXIT
      END;
  END; { FOR }
  ErrorMsg := '';
END; { SetUpVM }


{------------------------------------------------------- CloseVM -------}

PROCEDURE CloseVM(VAR VM_File : VM_File_Type { input });
BEGIN
  Close(VM_File)
END; { CloseVM }
```

```
{---------------------------------------------- search_table --------}

FUNCTION search_table(VAR Table : Table_Array { input }) : WORD;

{- - - - - - - - - - - - - - - - - - - - - - - - - - - - - - - - -
SCOPE: Local.
ROUTINE PURPOSE: searches for the VM page used with the least
frequency.
PARAMETERS:
  INPUT: Table - the memory-resident catalog for VM-pages in memory.
FUNCTION VALUE: returns the VM page number used with the least
frequency.
- - - - - - - - - - - - - - - - - - - - - - - - - - - - - - - - - - }

VAR i, min_freq, index : WORD;
BEGIN
    min_freq := Table[1].Freq;
    index := 1;
    FOR i := 2 TO MAX_VM_TABLE DO
        IF min_freq > Table[i].Freq THEN BEGIN
            index := i;
            min_freq := Table[i].Freq
        END; { IF }
    search_table := index { return function value }
END; { search_table }

{---------------------------------------------- locate_page --------}

FUNCTION locate_page(    Page_No : WORD;         { input }
                    VAR Table   : Table_Array { input }) : WORD;

{- - - - - - - - - - - - - - - - - - - - - - - - - - - - - - - - -
SCOPE : Local.
ROUTINE PURPOSE: locates a VM Page in the VM Table.
PARAMETERS:
  INPUT: Page_No - the sought VM page number.
         Table - the memory-resident catalog for VM-pages in memory.
FUNCTION VALUE: returns the catalog entry number of the sought VM
page number. If not present in the catalog, a zero is returned.
- - - - - - - - - - - - - - - - - - - - - - - - - - - - - - - - - - }

VAR i, index : WORD;
    found : BOOLEAN;
BEGIN
    i := 1;
    found := FALSE;
```

```
    WHILE (i <= MAX_VM_TABLE) AND (NOT found) DO BEGIN
        found := Table[i].Page_Num = Page_No;
        INC(i)
    END;
    DEC(i);
    IF found THEN index := i ELSE index := 0;
    locate_page := index
END; { locate_page }


{----------------------------------------------------- VM_Store -------}

PROCEDURE VM_Store(    X        : VMtype;        { input  }
                      Row,                       { input  }
                      Col      : WORD;           { input  }
                  VAR VM_File : VM_File_Type;    { input  }
                  VAR Table   : Table_Array;     { in/out }
                  VAR Done    : BOOLEAN          { output });

VAR mat_row, mat_col, page_no, index : WORD;
BEGIN
    Done := TRUE;
    mat_row := (Row - 1) DIV RRP + 1;
    mat_col := (Col - 1) DIV CRP + 1;
    IF mat_row <= MAX_VM_ROW
    THEN BEGIN
        page_no := mat_row + (mat_col - 1) * MAX_VM_ROW;
        index := locate_page(page_no, Table);
        IF index > 0
        THEN
            WITH Table[index] DO BEGIN
                RAM_Page[((Row-1) MOD RRP + 1),
                         ((Col-1) MOD CRP + 1)] := X;
                INC(Freq);
                Dirty_Bit := TRUE;
            END { WITH }
        ELSE BEGIN
            index := search_table(Table);
            WITH Table[index] DO BEGIN
                IF Dirty_Bit THEN BEGIN { Write RAM page? }
                    SEEK(VM_FILE, Page_Num);
                    WRITE(VM_FILE, RAM_Page);
                END; { IF }
                SEEK(VM_FILE, page_no);
                READ(VM_FILE, RAM_Page);
                RAM_Page[((Row-1) MOD RRP + 1),
                         ((Col-1) MOD CRP + 1)] := X;
```

```
                    Page_Num := page_no;
                    Dirty_Bit := TRUE;
                    Freq := 1;
                END; { WITH }
            END; { IF }
        END { THEN clause }
        ELSE
            Done := FALSE;


END; { VM_Store }


{-------------------------------------------------- VM_Recall ---------}


FUNCTION VM_Recall(     Row,                      { input  }
                        Col    : WORD;            { input  }
                    VAR VM_File : VM_File_Type;   { input  }
                    VAR Table   : Table_Array;    { in/out }
                    VAR Done    : BOOLEAN         { output }) : VMtype;

VAR mat_row, mat_col,
    page_no, index : WORD;
    x : VMtype;
BEGIN
    Done := TRUE;
    mat_row := (Row - 1) DIV RRP + 1;
    mat_col := (Col - 1) DIV CRP + 1;
    IF mat_row <= MAX_VM_ROW
    THEN BEGIN
        page_no := mat_row + (mat_col - 1) * MAx_VM_ROW;
        index := locate_page(page_no, Table);
        IF index > 0 THEN
            WITH Table[index] DO BEGIN
                x := RAM_Page[((Row-1) MOD RRP + 1),
                              ((Col-1) MOD CRP + 1)];
                INC(Freq);
            END { WITH }
        ELSE BEGIN
            index := search_table(Table);
            WITH Table[index] DO BEGIN
                IF Dirty_Bit THEN BEGIN { Write RAM page? }
                    SEEK(VM_FILE, Page_Num);
                    WRITE(VM_FILE, RAM_Page);
                END; { IF }
                SEEK(VM_FILE, page_no);
                READ(VM_FILE, RAM_Page);
                x := RAM_Page[((Row-1) MOD RRP + 1),
```

```
                          ((Col-1) MOD CRP + 1)];
                Page_Num := page_no;
                Dirty_Bit := FALSE;
                Freq := 1;
            END; { WITH }
        END; { IF }
    END { THEN clause }
    ELSE BEGIN
        Done := FALSE;
        x := VM_MISSING;
    END; { IF }
    VM_Recall := x;
END; { VM_Recall }
END.
```

Listing 5.2. Source code for the demonstration program USE_VM.PAS.

```
PROGRAM Use_VM;

{────────────────────────────────

  Program demonstrates a simple virtual matrix. The matrix
  is assigned random numbers, stored at random locations.
  The program also retrieves these stored numbers.
  ───────────────────────────────}

{$R+}
{$V-}
Uses CRT, DataLib0, VM;
     { drive E: is a 2 Meg RAM-drive of my system }
CONST VM_FILENAME = 'E:\VM.DAT';
      MAX_ITER = 20;
      MAX_PAGES = 1000;
VAR   VM_Table : Table_Array;
      VM_Fyle : VM_File_Type;
      ErrorMsg : STRING80;
      i, Rows, Cols : WORD;
      Row, Col : ARRAY [1..MAX_ITER] OF WORD;
      X : REAL;
      Ch : CHAR;
      Ok : BOOLEAN;

{- - - - - - - - - - - - - - - - - - - - - - - - - - - - - - - - - -
```

```
                    ROUTINE DEPENDENCIES
                    --------------------

       Identifier Name          Identifier Type       Source Library
       ----------------         ---------------       --------------

          ClrEol                  procedure               CRT
          ClrScr                  procedure               CRT
          CRP                     constant                VM
          GotoXY                  procedure               CRT
          MAX_VM_ROW              constant                VM
          ReadKey                 function                CRT
          RRP                     constant                VM
          SetUpVM                 procedure               VM
          STRING80                string                  DataLib0
          VM_Recall               function                VM
          VM_Store                procedure               VM
- - - - - - - - - - - - - - - - - - - - - - - - - - - - - - - - - }

BEGIN
 ClrScr;
 WRITELN('Creating virtual matrix ...');
 { creat virtual matrix }
 SetUpVM(VM_Fyle, MAX_PAGES, VM_FILENAME, VM_Table, ErrorMsg);
 Rows := RRP * MAX_VM_ROW;
 Cols := MAX_PAGES div CRP;
 Randomize;
 IF ErrorMsg = '' THEN BEGIN
    { store random data in random location }
    FOR i := 1 TO MAX_ITER DO BEGIN
        Row[i] := (Trunc(Random * Rows) + 1) MOD Rows;
        Col[i] := (Trunc(Random * Cols) + 1) MOD Cols;
        X := 100.0 + Random * 900.0;
        WRITELN('VM_Mat[',Row[i]:3,',',Col[i]:3,'] = ',X:5:2);
        VM_Store(X, Row[i], Col[i], VM_Fyle, VM_Table, Ok);
    END;
    GotoXY(1,23);
    WRITE(^G);
    WRITE('press any key to recall the same data from the VM matrix');
    Ch := ReadKey;
    GotoXY(1,23);
    ClrEol;
    { recall data in random order }
    FOR i := MAX_ITER DOWNTO 1 DO BEGIN
        X := VM_Recall(Row[i], Col[i], VM_Fyle, VM_Table, Ok);
        GotoXY(26,i+1);
        IF Ok THEN
            WRITELN('?=? ',X:5:2)
```

```
         ELSE
             WRITELN('Out of range');
      END;
      CloseVM(VM_Fyle);
      GotoXY(1,23);
      WRITE(^G'press any key to continue');
      Ch := ReadKey;
  END
  ELSE BEGIN
      WRITELN(ErrorMsg);
      WRITELN; WRITELN;
  END;
END.
```

Listing 5.3. Source code for the library SPARSMAT.PAS.

```
UNIT SparsMat;
{============================================================

          Copyright (c) 1987, 1988   Namir Clement Shammas
      LIBRARY NAME: SparsMat
      VERSION:  1.0                        DATE 2/22/1987
      PURPOSE: library provides two sets of routines to manipulate
              sparse matrices. The first uses an array of pointers
              to linked lists; the second uses a single binary tree
              to store/recall sparse matrix elements.
      UPDATE HISTORY:


================================================================}


{*******************************************************************}
{************************} INTERFACE {*****************************}
{*******************************************************************}


CONST { constants for list-based sparse matrices }
      MAX_SMLIST_COL : WORD = 1000;
      WIDTH_SMLIST = 100;
      NUM_SMLIST_COL = 10; { MAX_SMLIST_COL / WIDTH_SMLIST }
      SMLIST_MISSING = 0.0;
      { constants for tree-based sparse matrices }
      MAX_SMTREE_COL : WORD = 1000;
      SMTREE_MISSING = 0.0;
TYPE { basic data type for each matrix element }
```

```
      SMtype = REAL;
      { data types for list-based sparse matrices }
      SMList_Ptr= ^SMList_Matrix;
      SMList_Ptr_Array = ARRAY [1..NUM_SMLIST_COL] OF SMList_Ptr;
      SMList_Matrix = RECORD
                  Member : SMtype; { or any other type }
                  Rank   : WORD;
                  Next : SMList_Ptr
             END;
      { data types for tree-based sparse matrices }
      SMTree_Ptr = ^SMTree_Matrix_Node;
      SMTree_Matrix_Node = RECORD
                  Member : SMtype; { or any other type }
                  Rank   : INTEGER;
                  Left, Right : SMTree_Ptr;
             END;
PROCEDURE SetUp_SMList(VAR List : SMList_Ptr_Array { output });
{- - - - - - - - - - - - - - - - - - - - - - - - - - - - - - - -


ROUTINE PURPOSE: initializes the heads of the linked list array.
PARAMETERS:
  OUTPUT: List - the array of pointers to linked lists.


- - - - - - - - - - - - - - - - - - - - - - - - - - - - - - - - - }
PROCEDURE SetUp_SMTree(VAR Tree_Root : SMTree_Ptr { output });
{- - - - - - - - - - - - - - - - - - - - - - - - - - - - - - - -


ROUTINE PURPOSE: initializes the root of the binary tree used in
indexing the sparse matrix elements.
PARAMETERS:
  OUTPUT: Tree_Root - the root of the dynamic binary tree.


- - - - - - - - - - - - - - - - - - - - - - - - - - - - - - - - - }
FUNCTION Search_SMList(VAR Head    : SMList_Ptr; { input  }
                           Match   : WORD;       { input  }
                       VAR Last,                 { in/out }
                           Current : SMList_Ptr  { in/out })
                                             : BOOLEAN;
{- - - - - - - - - - - - - - - - - - - - - - - - - - - - - - - -


ROUTINE PURPOSE: searches a linked list for a matching index `rank'.
PARAMETERS:
  INPUT: Head - the head of linked list searched.
         Match - supplied rank whose match is sought.
  IN/OUT: Last, Current - the previous and current list pointers.
FUNCTION VALUE: returns TRUE is the sought index rank is found,
otherwise returns FALSE.
```

```
- - - - - - - - - - - - - - - - - - - - - - - - - - - - - - - - - - - }
PROCEDURE Search_SMTree(
          VAR Tree_Root : SMTree_Ptr; { input  }
              Match     : WORD        { input  });
{- - - - - - - - - - - - - - - - - - - - - - - - - - - - - - - - - - -
```

ROUTINE PURPOSE: searches the binary tree containing the matrix
indices for an element with given row/column numbers.
PARAMETERS:
  INPUT: Match - the rank of the sought element.
  IN/OUT - Tree_Root. Input is the root of a binary tree used in
           storing the indices of current sparse matrix elements.
           The output represents the pointer to the matched
           element, or NIL if no match occurs.

```
- - - - - - - - - - - - - - - - - - - - - - - - - - - - - - - - - - - }
PROCEDURE Store_SMList(
          VAR List_Head : SMList_Ptr_Array; { in/out }
              Element   : SMtype;           { input  }
              Row,                          { input  }
              Col       : WORD              { input  });
{- - - - - - - - - - - - - - - - - - - - - - - - - - - - - - - - - - -
```

ROUTINE PURPOSE: stores the value of Element at the specified
row/column. The actual process involves calculating the rank
index and then inserting the element in the appropriate list.
PARAMETERS:
  INPUT: Element - the input data.
         Row, Col - the row/column matrix coordinates.
  IN/OUT: List_Head - the array of pointers to linked lists.
HANDLING BAD ARGUMENTS: Bad matrix coordinates prevent storing the
value of Element in the sparse matrix.

ROUTINE DEPENDENCIES

Identifier Name	Identifier Type	Source Library
Search_SMList	function	local

```
- - - - - - - - - - - - - - - - - - - - - - - - - - - - - - - - - - - }
PROCEDURE Store_SMTree(
          VAR Tree_Root : SMTree_Ptr; { in/out }
              Element   : SMtype;     { input  }
              Row,                    { input  }
              Col       : WORD        { input  });
{- - - - - - - - - - - - - - - - - - - - - - - - - - - - - - - - - - -
```

ROUTINE PURPOSE: stores the value of Element at the specified
row/column. The actual process involves calculating the rank
index and then inserting the element in the tree location.
PARAMETERS:
  INPUT: Element - the input data.
        Row, Col - the row/column matrix coordinates.
  IN/OUT: Tree_Root - the root of binary tree used in storing the
          indices of current sparse matrix elements.
HANDLING BAD ARGUMENTS: Bad matrix coordinates prevent storing the
value of Element in the sparse matrix.

ROUTINE DEPENDENCIES

Identifier Name	Identifier Type	Source Library
Search_SMTree	function	local

```
- - - - - - - - - - - - - - - - - - - - - - - - - - - - - - - - - }
FUNCTION Recall_SMList(
          VAR List_Head : SMList_Ptr_Array; { input }
              Row,                           { input }
              Col       : WORD               { input }) : SMtype;
{- - - - - - - - - - - - - - - - - - - - - - - - - - - - - - - -
```

ROUTINE PURPOSE: recalls a sparse matrix element.
PARAMETERS:
  INPUT: List_Head - the array of list pointers.
       Row, Col - the row/column matrix coordinates of the
          recalled element.
FUNCTION VALUE: returns the value of the sought element.
HANDLING BAD ARGUMENTS: if the sought element has not been previously
stored in the sparse matrix, a numeric code for missing numbers is
returned.

ROUTINE DEPENDENCIES

Identifier Name	Identifier Type	Source Library
Search_SMList	function	local

```
- - - - - - - - - - - - - - - - - - - - - - - - - - - - - - - - - }
FUNCTION  Recall_SMTree(
          VAR Tree_Root : SMTree_Ptr; { input  }
              Row,                     { input  }
              Col       : WORD         { input  }) : SMtype;
{- - - - - - - - - - - - - - - - - - - - - - - - - - - - - - - -
```

ROUTINE PURPOSE: recalls a sparse matrix element.
PARAMETERS:
  INPUT: Tree_Root - the root of a binary tree used in storing the
           indices of current sparse matrix elements.
         Row, Col - the row/column matrix coordinates of the
           recalled element.
FUNCTION VALUE: returns the value of the sought element.
HANDLING BAD ARGUMENTS: if the sought element has not been previously
stored in the sparse matrix, a numeric code for missing numbers is
returned.

ROUTINE DEPENDENCIES

Identifier Name	Identifier Type	Source Library
Search_SMTree	function	local

- }

```
{*****************************************************************}
{***********************} IMPLEMENTATION {************************}
{*****************************************************************}

PROCEDURE SetUp_SMList (VAR List : SMList_Ptr_Array { output });
VAR index : WORD;
BEGIN
    FOR index := 1 TO NUM_SMLIST_COL DO
        List[index] := NIL;
END; { SetUp_SMList }


{----------------------------------------------- SetUp_SMTree -------}


PROCEDURE SetUp_SMTree (VAR Tree_Root : SMTree_Ptr { output });
BEGIN
    Tree_Root := NIL;
END; { SetUp_SMTree }


{----------------------------------------------- Search_SMList ------}


FUNCTION Search_SMList (VAR Head    : SMList_Ptr; { input  }
                            Match   : WORD;       { input  }
                        VAR Last,                 { in/out }
                            Current : SMList_Ptr  { in/out })
                                                  : BOOLEAN;
```

```
BEGIN
    Last := NIL;
    Current := Head;
    WHILE (Current^.Rank < Match) AND (Current <> NIL) DO BEGIN
        Last := Current;
        Current := Current^.Next
    END;
    Search_SMList := (Current^.Rank = Match)
END; { Search_SMList }


{------------------------------------------------- Search_SMTree ------}

PROCEDURE Search_SMTree(
          VAR Tree_Root : SMTree_Ptr; { input  }
              Match     : WORD        { input });
VAR done  : BOOLEAN;
BEGIN
    REPEAT
        IF Tree_Root = NIL
        THEN
            done := TRUE
        ELSE IF Tree_Root^.Rank = Match THEN
            done := TRUE
        ELSE BEGIN
            done := FALSE;
            IF Match < Tree_Root^.Rank
                THEN Tree_Root := Tree_Root^.Left
                ELSE Tree_Root := Tree_Root^.Right
        END; { IF }
    UNTIL done;
END; { Search_SMTree }


{------------------------------------------------- Store_SMList ---}

PROCEDURE Store_SMList(
          VAR List_Head : SMList_Ptr_Array; { in/out }
              Element   : SMtype;           { input  }
              Row,                          { input  }
              Col       : WORD              { input });

VAR bin_num, match : WORD;
    head, item, Last, current : SMList_Ptr;
    found : BOOLEAN;
```

```
BEGIN
     match := Row + (Col - 1) * MAX_SMLIST_COL;
     bin_num := (Col - 1) DIV WIDTH_SMLIST + 1;
     found := Search_SMList(List_Head[bin_num], match, Last, current);
     IF found
     THEN
         current^.Member := Element
     ELSE BEGIN
         NEW(item); { create new list element }
         WITH item^ DO BEGIN
            Member := Element;
            Rank := Row + (Col - 1) * MAX_SMLIST_COL;
            Next := NIL;
         END;
         head := List_Head[bin_num];
         IF head = NIL
         THEN
            List_Head[bin_num] := item
         ELSE BEGIN
            found := Search_SMList(head, item^.Rank, Last, current);
            IF Last = NIL
            THEN BEGIN { Insert as the new Head of the list }
               item^.Next := head;
               List_Head[bin_num] := item
            END
            ELSE BEGIN
               item^.Next := Last^.Next;
               Last^.Next := item
            END;
         END;
     END; { IF }
END; { Store_SMList }


{------------------------------------------------ Store_SMTree ------}


PROCEDURE Store_SMTree(
            VAR Tree_Root : SMTree_Ptr; { in/out }
                Element   : SMtype;     { input }
                Row,                    { input }
                Col       : WORD        { input });

VAR loc_ptr, item : SMTree_Ptr;
    match : WORD;
```

```
BEGIN
    match := Row + (Col - 1) * MAX_SMTREE_COL;
    loc_ptr := Tree_Root;
    Search_SMTree(loc_ptr, match);
    IF loc_ptr = NIL
    THEN BEGIN
        NEW(item);
        WITH item^ DO BEGIN
            Member := Element;
            Rank := Row + (Col - 1) * MAX_SMTREE_COL;
            Left := NIL;
            Right := NIL;
        END;
        loc_ptr := Tree_Root;
        WHILE loc_ptr <> NIL DO BEGIN
            WITH loc_ptr^ DO BEGIN
                IF item^.Rank < Rank
                THEN
                    IF Left <> NIL
                    THEN
                        loc_ptr := Left
                    ELSE BEGIN
                        Left := item;
                        loc_ptr := NIL
                    END
                ELSE
                    IF Right <> NIL
                    THEN
                        loc_ptr := Right
                    ELSE BEGIN
                        Right := item;
                        loc_ptr := NIL
                    END;
            END; { WITH }
        END; { WHILE }
        IF Tree_Root = NIL THEN Tree_Root := item;
    END { THEN clause }
    ELSE loc_ptr^.Member := Element;
END; { Store_SMTree }
```

```
{------------------------------------------------------ Recall_SMList ----}

FUNCTION Recall_SMList(
            VAR List_Head : SMList_Ptr_Array; { input }
                Row,                          { input }
                Col      : WORD               { input }) : SMtype;

VAR found : BOOLEAN;
    bin_num, match : WORD;
    last, current : SMList_Ptr;
    result : SMtype;
BEGIN
    match := Row + (Col - 1) * MAX_SMLIST_COL;
    bin_num := (Col - 1) DIV WIDTH_SMLIST + 1;
    found := Search_SMList(List_Head[bin_num], match, last, current);
    IF found THEN result := current^.Member
            ELSE result := SMLIST_MISSING;
    Recall_SMList := result { return function value }
END; { Recall_SMList }

{------------------------------------------------------ Recall_SMTree ----}

FUNCTION  Recall_SMTree(
            VAR Tree_Root : SMTree_Ptr; { input  }
                Row,                    { input  }
                Col       : WORD        { input  }) : SMtype;

VAR match : WORD;
    loc_ptr : SMTree_Ptr;
    result : SMtype;
BEGIN
    match := Row + (Col - 1) * MAX_SMTREE_COL;
    loc_ptr := Tree_Root;
    Search_SMTree(loc_ptr, match);
    IF loc_ptr = NIL
    THEN
        result := SMTREE_MISSING
    ELSE
        result := loc_ptr^.Member;
    Recall_SMTree := result;
END; { Recall_SMTree }

END.
```

Listing 5.4. Source code for the demonstration program USE_SM.PAS.

```
PROGRAM Use_SM;
{$M 8912, 8912, 200000}
Uses CRT, DataLib0, SparsMat;


{================================================================


Simple program that demonstrates the access of sparse matrices.
The program creates two sparse matrices by randomly selecting
a number of locations in each matrix and assigning random data
to them. The program proceeds to add the two sparse matrices,
creating a third one. All of the matrices are displayed.

   version 1.0                              Date 11/10/87


================================================================}


CONST MAX_SM_COL = 5; { columns in each matrix }
      MAX_SM_ROW = 5; { rows in each matrix }
      MAX_ELEMENTS = 7; { number of non-zero elements in a
                          sparse matrix }
{ declare the pointers to the three matrices }
VAR MatA, MatB, MatC : SMTree_Ptr;


{----------------------------------------------------- Init_SM ——}


PROCEDURE Init_SM(VAR Mat : SMTree_Ptr { in/out });
{- - - - - - - - - - - - - - - - - - - - - - - - - - - - - - - -


ROUTINE PURPOSE: initializes a sparse matrix by filling a few elements
(whose row/column coordinates are randomly chosen) with random data.
PARAMETERS:
   IN/OUT: Mat - the initialized sparse matrix.

                       ROUTINE DEPENDENCIES
                       --------------------

        Identifier Name         Identifier Type      Source Library
        ---------------         ---------------      --------------

        SetUp_SMTree            procedure            SparsMat
        SMTree_Ptr              pointer              SparsMat
        Store_SMTree            procedure            SparsMat
```

```
- - - - - - - - - - - - - - - - - - - - - - - - - - - - - - - - - - - - - - - - }

VAR i, row, col : WORD;
    data : REAL;
BEGIN
    SetUp_SMTree(Mat);
    { Randomize;  has a bug!! }
    FOR i := 1 TO MAX_ELEMENTS DO BEGIN
        row  := Trunc(Random * MAX_SM_ROW) + 1;
        col  := Trunc(Random * MAX_SM_COL) + 1;
        data := Random * 10.0;
        Store_SMTree(Mat, data, row, col)
    END;
END; { Init_SM }
```

```
{-------------------------------------------------------- Add_SM_Mat ——}

PROCEDURE Add_SM_Mat(VAR ResMat,              { output }
                    MatA,                     { input  }
                    MatB   : SMTree_Ptr { input });
{- - - - - - - - - - - - - - - - - - - - - - - - - - - - - - - - - - - -
```

ROUTINE PURPOSE: adds two sparse matrices and returns the result as a
third sparse matrix.
PARAMETERS:
  INPUT: MatA, MatB - the pointers to the added sparse matrices.
  OUTPUT: ResMat - the pointer to the resulting sparse matrix.

ROUTINE DEPENDENCIES

Identifier Name	Identifier Type	Source Library
Recall_SMTree	procedure	SparsMat
SMTree_Ptr	pointer	SparsMat
Store_SMTree	procedure	SparsMat

```
- - - - - - - - - - - - - - - - - - - - - - - - - - - - - - - - - - - - - - - }

VAR i, j : WORD;
    a, b : REAL;
BEGIN
    FOR i := 1 TO MAX_SM_ROW DO
        FOR j := 1 TO MAX_SM_COL DO BEGIN
            a := Recall_SMTree(MatA, i, j);
            b := Recall_SMTree(MatB, i, j);
            Store_SMTree(ResMat, a + b, i, j)
        END; { FOR }
END;
```

```
{----------------------------------------------- Display_SM_Mat ———}

PROCEDURE Display_SM_Mat(VAR Mat : SMTree_Ptr { input });
{- - - - - - - - - - - - - - - - - - - - - - - - - - - - - - - - -

ROUTINE PURPOSE: displays the entire contents of a sparse matrix.
PARAMETERS:
  INPUT: Mat - the pointer for the displayed sparse matrix.


                        ROUTINE DEPENDENCIES
                        --------------------

        Identifier Name         Identifier Type        Source Library
        ---------------         ---------------        --------------

        Recall_SMTree             procedure              SparsMat
        SMTree_Ptr                pointer                SparsMat

- - - - - - - - - - - - - - - - - - - - - - - - - - - - - - - - - - }

VAR i, j : WORD;
    a : REAL;
BEGIN
    FOR i := 1 TO MAX_SM_ROW DO BEGIN
        FOR j := 1 TO MAX_SM_COL DO BEGIN
            a := Recall_SMTree(Mat, i, j);
            WRITE(a:5:2,' ');
        END;
        WRITELN;
    END;
    WRITELN;
END; { Display_SM_Mat }

{- - - - - - - - - - - - - - - - - - - - - - - - - - - - - - - - -
                        ROUTINE DEPENDENCIES
                        --------------------

        Identifier Name         Identifier Type        Source Library
        ---------------         ---------------        --------------

        Add_SM_Mat                procedure              local
        Display_SM_Mat            procedure              local
        ClrScr                    procedure              CRT
        Init_SM                   procedure              local
        Recall_SMTree             procedure              SparsMat
        SetUp_SMTree              pointer                SparsMat
        SMTree_Ptr                pointer                SparsMat

- - - - - - - - - - - - - - - - - - - - - - - - - - - - - - - - - - }
```

```
BEGIN
    ClrScr;
    Randomize;
    WRITELN('Matrix A is'); WRITELN;
    Init_SM(MatA);
    Display_SM_Mat(MatA);
    WRITELN('Matrix B is'); WRITELN;
    Init_SM(MatB);
    Display_SM_Mat(MatB);
    WRITELN('Matrix C is'); WRITELN;
    SetUp_SMTree(MatC);
    Add_SM_Mat(MatC, MatA, MatB);
    Display_SM_Mat(MatC);
END.
```

C H A P T E R

6

Internal Sorting

Sorting is among the most important tasks in data processing, if not **the** most important. Through sorting, computers succeed in bringing order out of chaos. It makes searching for specific data items much easier. Sorting is divided into two classes: internal and external. Internal sorting works by having the entire data reside in memory while the sorting process is in progress. By contrast, external sorting resorts to saving a portion of the data on disk. Internal sorting is limited by the availability of memory, while external sorting is limited by the disk space. Since the amount of a computer's memory is typically smaller than the mass storage capacity of a disk, external sorting gains the upper hand in tackling large data files.

Rather than focusing heavily on the algorithms for popular sorting methods, I will concentrate more on the program design of internal-sorting libraries. I have elected to implement a selection of popular sorting algorithms: Shell, QuickSort (in both recursive and nonrecursive versions), and the Radix sort.

The various software design parameters facing the implementation of an internal sorting library are as follows:

1. The presence of nonkey fields in the array of data

2. The size of the data array being sorted

3. The data type of the sort key.

Writing routines that simply sort just arrays is very easy. However, real-world models often include more elaborate data structures, implemented using Pascal records. When handling simple arrays, the members of the array are simultaneously the keys used in the sorting. By contrast, complex data structures possess distinct key fields with values extracted from other fields in the record. This factor adds complexity to the task of writing sorting routines, especially since Pascal lacks the facilities to support generic routines. This means that the **general** sorting library developed is also a template for more customized versions.

The second design parameter poses the problem of handling arrays of various sizes. Since arrays are either static or dynamic, we have two major routes of handling the variation in size:

1. Static arrays. The simplest approach is to declare an array size that is acceptable by the compiler and is sufficiently large. This covers various array sizes (having the same sort-key data type). Occasionally, you will need to increase the size of the array. The advantage of static arrays is that their space is preallocated when the program starts running: no bad surprises!

2. Dynamic arrays. This kind of array is useful in creating tailor-fitted array sizes. Under Turbo Pascal, there are a few tricks that can be employed to utilize dynamic arrays. The first method declares a pointer to a one-member array. This is illustrated using the following code fragment:

```
TYPE One_Elem = ^ARRAY [1..1] OF WORD;
VAR  Dynam_Arr = One_Elem;
     NData, I : WORD;
BEGIN
   WRITE('Enter size of array : ');
   READLN(NData);
   { create the array }
   GetMem(Dynam_Arr, NData * SizeOf(WORD));
   FOR I := 1 TO NData DO
     Dynam_Arr^[I] := I DIV 2;
```

The **One_Elem** pointer type is the first ingredient used in building a dynamic array. The **Dynam_Arr** pointer is declared and employed in the dynamic allocation of the array, using the **GetMem** routine. The number of tailor-fitted elements is determined by **NData** at run-time. The space allocated to the array connected with **Dynam_Arr** pointer is equal to (NData * SizeOF(WORD)). The dynamic array elements are accessed by using a pointer reference coupled with an array indexing reference, as shown in the FOR loop.

Applying the above methods to writing sorting routines that tackle variable-size arrays involves placing pointer-typed parameters in the parameter list. Listing 6.1 shows a miniature sort library, DYNSORT1.PAS, that implements the Shell-Metzner sort method using the above dynamic array scheme.

The second method for using dynamic arrays involves untyped parameters. The technique is shown in the following bubble sort routine that sorts variable-size arrays of WORD-typed integers:

```
PROCEDURE BubbleSort(VAR Data; NData : WORD);
TYPE Super_Array = ARRAY [1..MaxInt] OF WORD;
```

```
VAR Super_Data : Super_Array ABSOLUTE Data;
    I, J : WORD;
BEGIN
   FOR I := 1 TO NData-1 DO
     FOR J := I+1 TO NData DO
       IF Super_Data[I] > Super_Data[J] THEN
           Swap_Data(I,J)
END;
```

The sorted array is passed via the untyped parameter **Data**. The bubble sort routine declares a large array type, **Super_Array**, with the same basic data type as that of the intended array. The next step is to create the array **Super_Data** using the **Super_Array** type and the absolute declaration to overlay **Super_Data** on **Data**. This opens the way for the procedure to access the elements of array **Data** by referring to those of **Super_Data**.

While this method seems to be attractive, it has its own drawbacks. The first is that declaring a huge array with **MaxInt** elements will be rejected by the compiler for many nonsimple data types and even basic floating types. The second disadvantage stems from the fact that the routine cannot be adapted to tackle multidimensional arrays of any data type. These limitations make the second programming trick work in rather limited cases. Listing 6.2 shows the listing of library DYNASORT2.PAS using the above technique. The listing is presented to give you an idea of what a version of Shell sort looks like. Unfortunately, the Turbo Pascal compiler refuses to compile the library, due to large memory space requirements of the local huge arrays in procedure **ShellSort**.

The third parameter in designing a library of sorting routines is the data type for the sort keys. Normally, the keys are integers, reals, or strings. Nevertheless, each distinct data type requires its own library version. If it were possible to construct generic versions in Pascal, you would be required to provide information regarding the size of the sort key data type and routines that perform the needed comparisons.

LIBRARY SORT.PAS

Listing 6.3 shows the SORT.PAS library that contains routines for the insertion sort, ShellSort, QuickSort, and radix sort methods. The library interface declares the constant MAX_SORT_ARRAY_SIZE that specifies the size of the static arrays. In turn, this defines a range of valid indices, **SortRange**. The **RadixDigit** subrange indicates that up to five-digit integers may be sorted by the radix sort routine. The library also defines a 20-character string type, **SortStr**, used for the sort keys. The **InfoRec** record contains a field for the sort key and may include other data fields inserted during the library customization. Three array types are also defined: an array of **InfoRec** records, and two arrays of integers. The **RadixArray** allows radix sorting of numbers between 0 and 65535. These types are utilized in defining the **SortRec** record structure which contains three fields: a data counter, an array of **InfoRec**-typed records, and an array of integer-based indices. These declarations are shown below:

```
CONST MAX_SORT_ARRAY_SIZE  = 500;
TYPE
     SortRange = 1..MAX_SORT_ARRAY_SIZE;
     RadixDigits = 1..5;
     SortStr = STRING[20];
     InfoRec = RECORD
        { Info : any data type }
        Key : SortStr;
     END;
     DataRecArray = ARRAY [SortRange] OF InfoRec;
     SortIndexArray = ARRAY [SortRange] OF SortRange;
     RadixArray = ARRAY [SortRange] OF WORD;
     SortRec = RECORD
        NumData    : WORD;
        DataArray  : DataRecArray;
        SortIndex  : SortIndexArray
     END;
```

The **SortRec** record structure reveals that sorting indices are utilized to store the sorted order of the array of keys. Thus, the physical data of the sort key (and any other field inserted in **InfoRec**) are not relocated. You may wish to avoid swapping data to save time, especially when dealing with large-sized and/ or numerous records.

Customizing the SORT.PAS library may involve one or more of the following alterations:

1. Constant MAX_SORT_ARRAY_SIZE may be increased or decreased to meet the requirement of your array sizes. Keep in mind that the high constant values accompanied by the large size of the customized **InfoRec** may be rejected by the Pascal compiler.

2. The **RadixDigits** subrange may be increased to accommodate the radix sorting of long integers.

3. The size of the **SortStr** may be conveniently adjusted to fit the needs of your custom versions.

4. The data type associated key can be altered to an integer or a floating point type. You may incorporate other fields in the **InfoRec** records.

5. The removal of unused routines. This makes the customized library version more compact.

Renaming the routines in the customized library is highly recommended to avoid conflicts created by simultaneously utilizing multiple versions of the same routine. Renaming the custom library unit, however, is mandatory.

The routines of the SORT.PAS library areas follows:

```
PROCEDURE InsertSort(VAR Data : SortRec { in/out });
```

performs an insertion sort using the array of sort keys and array of indices. The algorithm works by gradually creating an ordered subarray. It is created by inserting elements from the unsorted subarray portion. The algorithm is described using the following example. Consider the unordered array of chemical symbols with an initial sequence:

```
S  He  Zn  Cu  Fe  Cl  Br  Li  Na  Ca
```

The first member is assigned to its position until it is replaced by another element with higher precedence. The partially sorted array looks like (I will use the bar symbol to delimit the sorted subarray from the unsorted one):

```
S | He  Zn  Cu  Fe  Cl  Br  Li  Na  Ca
```

Next, the second element, **He**, is selected and compared with the members of the sorted subarray (in this case **S**). This results in moving element **He** to the first position and element **S** to second place. The array now looks like:

```
He  S | Zn  Cu  Fe  Cl  Br  Li  Na  Ca
```

The third element, **Zn**, is selected and the above process of comparison is repeated. It turns out that **Zn** should remain, at least for now, in third place. Repeating the process with element **Cu** results in placing it as the first element and moving the sorted subarray by one position to the right. The array becomes as follows:

```
Cu  He  S  Zn | Fe  Cl  Br  Li  Na  Ca
```

The above insertion process is repeated until all of the array elements are examined. The sorted array now becomes as follows:

```
Br  Ca  Cl  Cu  Fe  He  Li  Na  S  Zn
```

The implementation of the **InsertSort** routine differs from that of the other sort routines in that duplicate keys are not allowed. This feature enables you to ensure the uniqueness of the inserted key. Consequently, the array count may decrease after **InsertSort** is finished processing an array.

```
PROCEDURE ShellSort(VAR Data : SortRec { in/out });
```

implements the Shell-Metzner sorting algorithm. The Shell method has overcome the problem of the basic bubble sort by comparing distant neighbors. The workings of the algorithm are illustrated using the following example. Consider, once more, the same array of chemical symbols:

```
S  He  Zn  Cu  Fe  Cl  Br  Li  Na  Ca
```

Since the array has ten elements, the Shell sort method starts by comparing elements five elements apart. This divides the array into two subarrays:

```
S   He  Zn  Cu  Fe  Cl  Br  Li  Na  Ca
_____  _____
1   2   3   4   5    1   2   3   4   5
```

The elements having the same index number are compared and swapped, if necessary. Thus, elements **S** and **Cl** are compared and accordingly swapped, to give the following:

```
Cl  He  Zn  Cu  Fe  S   Br  Li  Na  Ca
_____  _____
1   2   3   4   5    1   2   3   4   5
```

Similarly **He** and **Br** are compared and swapped. The process is repeated for the other subarray members. The first pass yields the following:

```
Cl  Br  Li  Cu  Ca  S   He  Zn  Na  Fe
_____  _____
1   2   3   4   5    1   2   3   4   5
```

For a reason that will become clear later, the Shell sort method required another round of comparisons of the elements, since the last round resulted in swapping elements. The second round of comparison proceeds without any elements being swapped. This means that all array members that are five elements apart are in order. However, the array as a whole is far from being in perfect sorted order. The next step is to halve the distance of compared neighbors. Using integer division, that number is reduced to two. The new set of subarrays becomes as follows:

```
Cl  Br  Li  Cu  Ca  S   He  Zn  Na  Fe
__  __  __  __  __  __  __  __  __  __
1   2   1   2   1   2   1   2   1   2
```

Thus, the elements **Cl** and **Li** are compared but not swapped. The next elements compared are **Br** and **Cu**, resulting in each element maintaining its location. However, comparing elements **Li** and **Ca** results in their exchange of locations. The first round of comparison is carried out (with **Zn** and **Fe** being the last elements compared) resulting in the following:

```
Cl  Br  Ca  Cu  He  S   Li  Fe  Na  Zn
__  __  __  __  __  __  __  __  __  __
1   2   1   2   1   2   1   2   1   2
```

At the end of the first round of comparing neighbors two elements apart, you can see that they are NOT in order. Thus, a second round of comparison is very much justified. The first elements compared, **Cl** and **Ca**, require swapping. Likewise, the **S** and **Fe** elements are swapped. At the end of this round, the array looks like:

```
Ca Br  Cl  Cu  He  Fe  Li  S   Na  Zn
—  —   —   —   —   —   —   —   —   —
1  2   1   2   1   2   1   2   1   2
```

Since the last round resulted in elements being swapped, the Shell method carried out a third round of comparison. This time, members that are two elements apart are in order and no swapping takes place. Next, the algorithm resorts to reducing the distance between compared elements. The number decreases from two to one. This means that immediate neighboring elements are compared, just as with the normal operation of the bubble sort method. The previous rounds of comparisons and swapping have enabled the array elements to travel close to their final position. The rounds of comparisons begin by examining elements **Ca** and **Br**, and swapping them. The process is repeated for the rest of the array members. Additional rounds of comparisons occur until no elements are swapped. The sorted array is as follows:

```
Br  Ca  Cl Cu  Fe  He  Li  Na  S   Zn
```

```
PROCEDURE RecQuickSort(VAR Data : SortRec { in/out });
```

implements the powerful QuickSort method using recursive calls. The QuickSort algorithm works by cleverly implementing a divide-and-conquer strategy. The basic strategy of this algorithm is to select a median element from an array and divide the array into two subarrays: one with elements less than the median, the other with elements equal to or greater than the median. This task instills an increased order in the array as a whole. To attain a perfect order, the above task is repeated with each subarray, creating lower level medians and subarrays. The recursive nature of this algorithm becomes evident when the above is repeated on each sublist.

The basic strategy of QuickSort is illustrated by the following example. The initial array is as follows:

```
S  He  Zn  Cu  Fe  Cl  Br  Li  Na  Ca
```

The median is selected, say, as the middle element, **Fe**. The array is divided into two subarrays. The left subarray has its members less than **Fe**, while the right subarray has its members greater than **Fe**, as shown below:

```
He Cu  Cl  Br  Ca              <— left subarray
                Fe             <— median
             S  Zn  Li  Na     <— right subarray
```

The process is repeated recursively with each subarray. For example, the above left subarray is split by selecting **Cl** as the median. The nested left subarray has three elements, while the right one has only one element (that is, it is considered sorted!):

```
He  Br  Ca       <- left subarray
        Cl       <- median
            Cu   <- right subarray
```

The above process is continued until the deeply nested subarrays have either one or no elements. When this state is reached the algorithm rolls back to gradually build ordered subarrays and eventually produce a sorted array.

The procedure **RecQuickSort** contains a nested routine that performs the recursive calls. The overhead of that recursive routine is minimized by passing only the left and right indices of a subarray.

```
PROCEDURE QuickSort(VAR Data : SortRec { in/out });
```

implements a nonrecursive QuickSort version. This version dictates that an explicit stack be used to keep track of the subarrays created. Under the above recursive version, the stack is internally maintained by the compiled code.

```
PROCEDURE Reverse_Array_Order(VAR Data : SortRec { in/out });
```

is a simple routine that reverses the order of the array indices. All of the sorting routines arrange the indices to yield an ascending-order array. This routine enables you to toggle between the ascending and descending order of a sorted array.

```
PROCEDURE IntRadixSort(VAR Numbers : RadixArray;  { in/out }
                           NData   : WORD;        { input  }
                           Digits  : RadixDigits { input });
```

implements the radix sort algorithm for integers. The algorithm employs an interesting technique in arranging an array of numbers. I will explain by using the following example. Consider this array of three-digit numbers:

```
132  213  321  231  111  232  112  221  123
```

The first step is to create bins for the least-significant numbers. Normally there are ten bins, but I am limiting my example, for the sake of brevity, to three digits. The numbers are arranged in bins of ones, twos, and threes, as follow:

```
1s  ->  321 231 111 221
2s  ->  132 232 112
3s  ->  213 123
```

The above step commences to breathe some order into the data. The next step is to repeat the above operation using the next significant digit (that is, tens). The bins of tens, twenties, and thirties are shown below:

```
10s -> 111 112 213
20s -> 321 221 123
30s -> 231 132 232
```

Notice that in creating the new bin arrays, the elements from the previous ones were selected according to their position in the arrays. Next, the process of bin arrangement goes one step further to tackle the most significant digits, the hundreds. The new bin arrays created are as follows:

```
100s -> 111 112 123 132
200s -> 213 221 231 232
300s -> 321
```

By concatenating the latter bin arrays, we obtain the sorted array:

```
111    112    123    132    213    221    231    232    321
```

APPLICATION: TEXT FILE SORTING UTILITY

A simple application for the SORT.PAS library is program USE_SORT.PAS, which sorts a small text file. The program has the following features and limitations:

1. Up to MAX_SORT_ARRAY_SIZE lines in a user-specified file are sorted. The excess lines are ignored.

2. You can specify the portion of the text line to supply the sorting key. The sort key type, **SortStr**, in SORT.PAS has 20 characters. This was changed to 80 characters to accommodate reading lines that occupy the width of a screen. The text lines need not be of equal size and the program is instructed on how to resolve the problem arising with short lines. The length of these lines may be smaller than the specified starting and ending characters used in extracting the sort keys.

3. You can specify an output file where the sorted text lines are sent.

The USE_SORT.PAS program shown in Listing 6.4 includes the following routines:

1. Procedure **Warn**: used to display a warning message informing you that you have entered a bad filename or pathname.

2. Boolean function **Get_Lines**: is utilized to read the text lines from the user-specified text filename. If a bad pathname or filename is supplied, the routine returns a FALSE value. A successful read operation yields a TRUE value. The function will read text lines until it encounters the end-of-file marker or reaches the maximum capacity of the array of lines. In the latter case, the function abruptly stops reading more text lines.

3. Boolean function **Put_Lines**: performs the reverse action of function **Get_Lines**. The array of text lines in memory is written to a sequential text file. The output filename is an argument received by this function. If the function cannot open the file, it returns a FALSE value; otherwise, a TRUE logical value is emitted.

4. Procedure **Goodby**: is employed by the main program section to sign off and halt the Pascal program.

5. Procedure **Build_Keys**: is responsible for extracting the sorting keys from the lines of text. The routine code is able to tackle text lines that may fall short of the user-specified character positions used in extracting the keys.

The main code portion is assigned the task of displaying the screen form and invoking various local and library routines. The **Get_Input** routine is imported from library EDITLINE.PAS to provide a one-line editor for keying in the filenames. The **Get_Input** routines are contained in REPEAT-UNTIL loops. The UNTIL clauses use the logical value of functions **Get_Lines** and **Put_Lines**. The program exits if the name of the input file is a null string. Entering a null string for the output filename is interpreted as a bad pathname, and the corresponding warning message is displayed.

The **Read_Int_Limit** is employed to obtain the character locations. Using this routine ensures two things: error-proof integer input and that the input value falls within the desired range. The program also displays brief status messages to indicate that file I/O and sorting are in progress.

Figure 6.1 displays the table for the software bus schedule of program USE_SORT.PAS. The different schedules indicate the flow of different program constructs between the exporting and the importing libraries.

Figure 6.2 shows the screen image for a sample session with program USE_SORT.PAS. The screen image shows the prompts for the input and output filenames, as well as those for the substring limits for the sorting keys. Figure 6.3 discloses the contents of the sample input data file DIR.DOC. The data file contains the edited contents of a redirected DOS directory command. Figure 6.4 displays the ordered contents of the output file SORTDIR.DOC. By specifying the 16th to the 21st characters, the output file is sorted according to file sizes.

Figure 6.1. The table of the software bus schedule for program USE_SORT.PAS.

SOFTWARE BUS SCHEDULE TABLE PROJECT: USE_SORT.PAS

MODULE CRT	Software Bus Schedule												
	A	B	C	D	E	F	G	H	I	J	K	L	M
OUTPUT													
proc ClrScr		X											
proc GotoXY		X											
func WhereX		X											
func WhereY		X											

MODULE DataLib0	Software Bus Schedule												
	A	B	C	D	E	F	G	H	I	J	K	L	M
OUTPUT													
string STRING80	X												
string STRING90	X												
string STRING255	X												

MODULE EditLine	Software Bus Schedule												
	A	B	C	D	E	F	G	H	I	J	K	L	M
OUTPUT													
func Get_Input				X									
INTERFACE INPUT													
string STRING255	X												
proc GotoXY		X											
func WhereX		X											
func WhereY		X											

MODULE ComnLib0	Software Bus Schedule												
	A	B	C	D	E	F	G	H	I	J	K	L	M
OUTPUT													
proc Center			X										
proc Write_Blanks			X										
INTERFACE INPUT													
proc ClrScr			X										
proc GotoXY			X										

MODULE ComnStr0

	A	B	C	D	E	F	G	H	I	J	K	L	M
Software Bus Schedule													

OUTPUT

	A	B	C	D	E	F	G	H	I	J	K	L	M
func PosMidStr						X							

INTERFACE INPUT

	A	B	C	D	E	F	G	H	I	J	K	L	M
string STRING255	X												

MODULE NumInput

	A	B	C	D	E	F	G	H	I	J	K	L	M
Software Bus Schedule													

OUTPUT

	A	B	C	D	E	F	G	H	I	J	K	L	M
proc Read_Int_Limit					X								

INTERFACE INPUT

	A	B	C	D	E	F	G	H	I	J	K	L	M
proc ClrScr		X											
proc GotoXY		X											
func WhereX		X											
func WhereY		X											

MODULE Sort

	A	B	C	D	E	F	G	H	I	J	K	L	M
Software Bus Schedule													

OUTPUT

	A	B	C	D	E	F	G	H	I	J	K	L	M
const MAX_SORT_ARRAY_SIZE					X								
proc ShellSort					X								
record SortRec					X								

MODULE main program

	A	B	C	D	E	F	G	H	I	J	K	L	M
Software Bus Schedule													

INPUT

	A	B	C	D	E	F	G	H	I	J	K	L	M
proc Center			X										
proc ClrScr		X											
proc Get_Input				X									
proc GotoXY		X											
const MAX_SORT_ARRAY_SIZE					X								
func PosMidStr							X						
proc Read_Int_Limit				X									
proc ShellSort					X								
rec SortRec					X								
string STRING80	X												
string STRING90	X												
proc Write_Blanks			X										

Figure 6.2. Screen image of a sample session with program USE_SORT.PAS.

```
                              PROGRAM TO SORT A TEXT FILE


        INPUT FILENAME            : dir.doc
        LOCATION OF FIRST CHARACTER : 17
        LOCATION OF LAST  CHARACTER : 21
        OUTPUT FILENAME           : sortdir.doc

        Writing ....
```

Figure 6.3. Contents of sample data file DIR.DOC.

```
BASECONV PAS     6242    2-03-87    4:23p
CMPLXLIB PAS     5694    2-03-87    7:26p
COMNLIB0 PAS     2277    2-04-87    9:57p
DATALIB0 PAS     1286    2-04-87    9:05p
DYNSORT1 PAS     3302    2-05-87    4:38a
DYNSORT2 PAS     3284    2-05-87    4:39a
EDITLINE PAS    13228    2-04-87   11:56p
MENUITEM PAS     4510    1-31-87    2:53a
MENUPULL PAS    22914    2-04-87    2:55a
NUMINPUT PAS     8484    2-03-87    9:50p
PCINFO   PAS    11282    2-03-87   12:48a
PCSCREEN PAS    12271    2-04-87    5:53p
RPNCALC  PAS    17110    2-04-87    8:23a
SCREEN0  PAS    20124    2-04-87    5:54p
SCREEN1  PAS    17392    2-04-87    5:54p
SORT     PAS    16512    2-05-87    5:21p
STACKARR PAS     6020    2-04-87    5:51p
STACKLST PAS     5874    2-04-87    5:52p
SUPRSTR0 PAS    27776    1-30-87   11:36p
TSTSORT2 PAZ    11778    2-05-87    2:21a
WORDSTR0 PAS     9761    1-29-87    1:30a
COMNSTR0 PAS    38487    2-05-87    2:57p
TSTSORT1 PAS    11585    2-05-87    5:05p
```

Figure 6.4. Contents of output data file SORTDIR.DOC.

```
DATALIB0 PAS      1286    2-04-87     9:05p
COMNLIB0 PAS      2277    2-04-87     9:57p
DYNSORT2 PAS      3284    2-05-87     4:39a
DYNSORT1 PAS      3302    2-05-87     4:38a
MENUITEM PAS      4510    1-31-87     2:53a
CMPLXLIB PAS      5694    2-03-87     7:26p
STACKLST PAS      5874    2-04-87     5:52p
STACKARR PAS      6020    2-04-87     5:51p
BASECONV PAS      6242    2-03-87     4:23p
NUMINPUT PAS      8484    2-03-87     9:50p
WORDSTR0 PAS      9761    1-29-87     1:30a
PCINFO   PAS     11282    2-03-87    12:48a
TSTSORT1 PAS     11585    2-05-87     5:05p
TSTSORT2 PAZ     11778    2-05-87     2:21a
PCSCREEN PAS     12271    2-04-87     5:53p
EDITLINE PAS     13228    2-04-87    11:56p
SORT     PAS     16512    2-05-87     5:21p
RPNCALC  PAS     17110    2-04-87     8:23a
SCREEN1  PAS     17392    2-04-87     5:54p
SCREEN0  PAS     20124    2-04-87     5:54p
MENUPULL PAS     22914    2-04-87     2:55a
SUPRSTR0 PAS     27776    1-30-87    11:36p
COMNSTR0 PAS     38487    2-05-87     2:57p
```

Listing 6.1. Source code for the DYNSORT1.PAS library.

```
    UNIT DynSort1;
{===============================================================

        Copyright (c) 1987, 1988   Namir Clement Shammas
    LIBRARY NAME: DynSort1
    VERSION:  1.0                              DATE 8/20/1987
    PURPOSE: provides a routine to perform shell sort using dynamic
            arrays.
    UPDATE HISTORY:


===============================================================}

{*****************************************************************}
{***********************} INTERFACE {****************************}
{*****************************************************************}
```

```
TYPE
    SortStr = STRING[20];
    InfoRec = RECORD
        { Info : any data type }
        Key : SortStr;
    END;
    DataRecArray = ARRAY [1..1] OF InfoRec;
    SortIndexArray = ARRAY [1..1] OF WORD;
    SortRec = RECORD
        NumData   : WORD;
        DataArray : ^DataRecArray;
        SortIndex : ^SortIndexArray
    END;
```

{————————————————————————}

```
PROCEDURE ShellSort(VAR Data : SortRec { in/out });
```
{- -

```
ROUTINE PURPOSE: procedure that uses the Shell-Metzner sort method.
PARAMETERS:
  IN/OUT: Data - the record containing the data to be sorted,
               including the sort keys, sort indices, and the
               actual number of data.
```

- }

{***}
{***********************} IMPLEMENTATION {***************************}
{***}

{-- ShellSort ——}

```
PROCEDURE ShellSort(VAR Data : SortRec { in/out });
VAR i, j, n, m, skip : WORD;
    inorder : BOOLEAN;
BEGIN
    WITH Data DO BEGIN
        IF NumData > 1 THEN BEGIN
            { initialize indices }
            FOR i := 1 TO NumData DO
                SortIndex^[i] := i;
            skip := NumData;
            WHILE skip > 1 DO BEGIN
                skip := skip DIV 2;
                REPEAT
                    inorder := TRUE;
                    FOR j := 1 TO NumData - skip DO BEGIN
                        i := j + skip;
                        n := SortIndex^[i];
```

```
                              m := SortIndex^[j];
                              IF DataArray^[n].Key < DataArray^[m].Key THEN
                              BEGIN
                                   { swap indices }
                                   SortIndex^[i] := m;
                                   SortIndex^[j] := n;
                                   inorder := FALSE
                              END; { IF }
                        END; { FOR }
                  UNTIL inorder;
              END; { WHILE skip > 1 }
         END; { IF NumData > 1 }
     END; { WITH Data }
END; { ShellSort }
END.
```

Listing 6.2. Source code for the DYNSORT2.PAS library.

```
UNIT DynSort2;
{=====================================================================

          Copyright (c) 1987, 1988   Namir Clement Shammas
     LIBRARY NAME: DynSort2
     VERSION: 1.0                                 DATE 8/20/1987
     PURPOSE: provides a routine to perform shell sort using
              dynamic arrays.
     UPDATE HISTORY:


======================================================================}

{*********************************************************************
****** PROGRAM WILL NOT COMPILE DUE TO LARGE MEMORY REQUIREMENT ******
*********************************************************************}

{*********************************************************************}
{************************} INTERFACE {*******************************}
{*********************************************************************}

TYPE
     SortStr = STRING[20];
     InfoRec = RECORD
        { Info : any data type }
        Key : SortStr;
     END;

PROCEDURE ShellSort(VAR Data;              { input  }
                    VAR Index;             { output }
                    NumData : WORD { input  }));
```

```
{- - - - - - - - - - - - - - - - - - - - - - - - - - - - - - - - - - - -

ROUTINE PURPOSE: procedure that uses the Shell-Metzner sort method.
PARAMETERS:
   INPUT: Data - the untyped parameter passing the array of data.
          Num_Data - the actual number of data.
   OUTPUT: Index - the untyped parameter passing the array of indices.

- - - - - - - - - - - - - - - - - - - - - - - - - - - - - - - - - - - }

{******************************************************************}
{***********************} IMPLEMENTATION {*************************}
{******************************************************************}

{--------------------------------------------------- ShellSort ----}
PROCEDURE ShellSort(VAR Data;                { input  }
                    VAR Index;               { output }
                        NumData : WORD { input  });
TYPE Super_Data = ARRAY [1..MaxInt] OF InfoRec;
     Super_Index = ARRAY [1..MaxInt] OF WORD;
VAR i, j, n, m, skip  : WORD;
    inorder : BOOLEAN;
    DataArry : Super_Data ABSOLUTE Data;
    SortIndex : Super_Index ABSOLUTE Index;
BEGIN
    WITH Data DO BEGIN
        IF NumData > 1 THEN BEGIN
            { initialize indices }
            FOR i := 1 TO NumData DO
                SortIndex[i] := i;
            skip := NumData;
            WHILE skip > 1 DO BEGIN
                skip := skip DIV 2;
                REPEAT
                    inorder := TRUE;
                    FOR j := 1 TO NumData - skip DO BEGIN
                        i := j + skip;
                        n := SortIndex[i];
                        m := SortIndex[j];
                        IF DataArray[n].Key < DataArray[m].Key THEN BEGIN
                            { swap indices }
                            SortIndex[i] := m;
                            SortIndex[j] := n;
                            inorder := FALSE
                        END; { IF }
                    END; { FOR }
                UNTIL inorder;
            END; { WHILE skip > 1 }
        END; { IF NumData > 1 }
    END; { WITH Data }
END; { ShellSort }
END.
```

Listing 6.3. Source code for the SORT.PAS library.

```
UNIT Sort;
{=================================================================

          Copyright (c) 1987, 1988    Namir Clement Shammas
     LIBRARY NAME: Sort
     VERSION: 1.0                             DATE 8/20/1987
     PURPOSE: provides a routine to perform insertion sort, shell
              sort, QuickSort, and the radix sort methods.
     UPDATE HISTORY:     + 10/22/87 inserted RadixArray type and changed
the data type
     of the 'Numbers' parameter in routine 'IntRadixSort'.


=================================================================}

{*******************************************************************}
{**************************} INTERFACE {***************************}
{*******************************************************************}

CONST MAX_SORT_ARRAY_SIZE = 200;
TYPE
     SortRange = 1..MAX_SORT_ARRAY_SIZE;
     RadixDigits = 1..5;
     SortStr = STRING[20];
     InfoRec = RECORD
        { Info : any data type }
        Key : SortStr;
     END;
     DataRecArray = ARRAY [SortRange] OF InfoRec;
     SortIndexArray = ARRAY [SortRange] OF SortRange;
     RadixArray = ARRAY[SortRange] OF WORD;
     SortRec = RECORD
        NumData    : WORD;
        DataArray : DataRecArray;
        SortIndex : SortIndexArray
     END;


{────────────────────────────────────────────────}


PROCEDURE InsertSort(VAR Data : SortRec { in/out });
{- - - - - - - - - - - - - - - - - - - - - - - - - - - - - - - - -


ROUTINE PURPOSE: procedure that uses the insertion sort method. This
version is implemented such that data with duplicate keys are
eliminated.
PARAMETERS:
  IN/OUT: Data - the record containing the data to be sorted, including
               the sort keys, sort indices, and the actual number
               of data.
HANDLING BAD ARGUMENTS: if the array size is less than one, the routine
exits. If the array size is greater than the constant
```

MAX_SORT_ARRAY_SIZE, the size is set equal to that constant.

ROUTINE DEPENDENCIES

Identifier Name	Identifier Type	Source Library
MAX_SORT_ARRAY_SIZE	constant	local

- }

PROCEDURE ShellSort(VAR Data : SortRec { in/out });
{- -

ROUTINE PURPOSE: procedure that uses the Shell-Metzner sort method.
PARAMETERS:
  IN/OUT: Data - the record containing the data to be sorted, including
          the sort keys, sort indices, and the actual number
          of data.
HANDLING BAD ARGUMENTS: if the array size is less than one, the routine
exits. If the array size is greater than the constant
MAX_SORT_ARRAY_SIZE, the size is set equal to that constant.

ROUTINE DEPENDENCIES

Identifier Name	Identifier Type	Source Library
MAX_SORT_ARRAY_SIZE	constant	local

- }

PROCEDURE RecQuickSort(VAR Data : SortRec { in/out });
{- -

ROUTINE PURPOSE: procedure that uses a recursive QuickSort method.
PARAMETERS:
  IN/OUT: Data - the record containing the data to be sorted, including
          the sort keys, sort indices, and the actual number
          of data.
HANDLING BAD ARGUMENTS: if the array size is less than one, the routine
exits. If the array size is greater than the constant
MAX_SORT_ARRAY_SIZE, the size is set equal to that constant.

ROUTINE DEPENDENCIES

Identifier Name	Identifier Type	Source Library
MAX_SORT_ARRAY_SIZE	constant	local
Sort	procedure	internal

- }

PROCEDURE QuickSort(VAR Data : SortRec { in/out });
{- -

ROUTINE PURPOSE: procedure that uses a non-recursive QuickSort method.
PARAMETERS:
  IN/OUT: Data - the record containing the data to be sorted, including
          the sort keys, sort indices, and the actual number
          of data.
HANDLING BAD ARGUMENTS: if the array size is less than one, the routine
exits. If the array size is greater than the constant
MAX_SORT_ARRAY_SIZE the size is set equal to that constant.

                    ROUTINE DEPENDENCIES

        Identifier Name   Identifier Type   Source Library
        ---------------   ---------------   --------------

      MAX_SORT_ARRAY_SIZE   constant   local

- }
PROCEDURE IntRadixSort (VAR Numbers : RadixArray; { in/out }
                            NData   : WORD;   { input }
                            Digits   : RadixDigits { input   });
{- -

ROUTINE PURPOSE: procedure that implements the radix sort method.
PARAMETERS:
  INPUT: NData - the actual number of data.
         Digits - the number of significant digits.
  IN/OUT: Numbers - the numeric array to be sorted.
HANDLING BAD ARGUMENTS: if the array size is less than one, the routine
exits. If the array size is greater than the constant
MAX_SORT_ARRAY_SIZE, the size is set equal to that constant.

                    ROUTINE DEPENDENCIES

        Identifier Name   Identifier Type   Source Library
        ---------------   ---------------   --------------

      MAX_SORT_ARRAY_SIZE   constant   local

- }
PROCEDURE Reverse_Array_Order(VAR Data : SortRec { in/out });
{- -

ROUTINE PURPOSE: alters the indices to reverse the order of
a presumably sorted array within a record of type SortRec.
PARAMETERS:
  IN/OUT: Data - the record containing the sorted data.
HANDLING BAD ARGUMENTS: if the array size is less than one, the routine
exits. If the array size is greater than the constant
MAX_SORT_ARRAY_SIZE, the size is set equal to that constant.

```
                      ROUTINE DEPENDENCIES
                      --------------------

       Identifier Name          Identifier Type      Source Library
       ---------------          ---------------      --------------

    MAX_SORT_ARRAY_SIZE            constant              local

- - - - - - - - - - - - - - - - - - - - - - - - - - - - - - - - - }


{*******************************************************************}
{**********************} IMPLEMENTATION {**************************}
{*******************************************************************}


{------------------------------------------------------ InsertSort ------}
PROCEDURE InsertSort(VAR Data : SortRec { in/out });
VAR i, j, k, n, m : WORD;
    nomatch : BOOLEAN;
BEGIN
  WITH Data DO BEGIN
    IF NumData = 0 THEN EXIT
    ELSE IF NumData > MAX_SORT_ARRAY_SIZE THEN
        NumData := MAX_SORT_ARRAY_SIZE;
    { initialize the array of indices }
    FOR i := 1 TO NumData DO
        SortIndex[i] := i;
    i := 2; { start with the second array element }
    WHILE (i <= NumData) DO BEGIN
        { start with the first element of the current sorted sub-array }
        j := 1;
        nomatch := TRUE;
        WHILE (j < i) AND nomatch DO BEGIN
            n := SortIndex[i];
            m := SortIndex[j];
            IF DataArray[n].Key < DataArray[m].Key THEN BEGIN
                nomatch := FALSE;
                FOR k := i-1 DOWNTO j DO
                    SortIndex[k+1] := SortIndex[k];
                SortIndex[j] := i
            END
            ELSE IF DataArray[n].Key > DataArray[m].Key THEN
                INC(j)
            ELSE BEGIN { found duplicate entry }
                nomatch := FALSE;
                FOR k := i TO NumData-1 DO
                    DataArray[i] := DataArray[i+1];
                DEC(i);
                DEC(NumData);
            END; { IF }
        END; { WHILE   (j < i) AND nomatch }
        INC(i);
```

```
      END; { WHILE i <= NumData  }
   END; { WITH }
END; { InsertSort }

{-------------------------------------------------------- ShellSort ——}

PROCEDURE ShellSort(VAR Data : SortRec { in/out });
VAR i, j, n, m, skip  : WORD;
    inorder : BOOLEAN;
BEGIN
    WITH Data DO BEGIN
        IF NumData = 0 THEN EXIT
        ELSE IF NumData > MAX_SORT_ARRAY_SIZE THEN
              NumData := MAX_SORT_ARRAY_SIZE;
        { initialize indices }
        FOR i := 1 TO NumData DO
            SortIndex[i] := i;
        skip := NumData;
        WHILE skip > 1 DO BEGIN
            skip := skip DIV 2;
            REPEAT
                inorder := TRUE;
                FOR j := 1 TO NumData - skip DO BEGIN
                    i := j + skip;
                    n := SortIndex[i];
                    m := SortIndex[j];
                    IF DataArray[n].Key < DataArray[m].Key THEN BEGIN
                        { swap indices }
                        SortIndex[i] := m;
                        SortIndex[j] := n;
                        inorder := FALSE
                    END; { IF }
                END; { FOR }
            UNTIL inorder;
        END; { WHILE skip > 1 }
    END; { WITH Data }
END; { ShellSort }

{-------------------------------------------------------- RecQuickSort ——}

PROCEDURE RecQuickSort(VAR Data : SortRec { in/out });
VAR k : WORD;
    median, tempo : InfoRec;

{-------------------------------------------------- RecQuickSort : Sort ——}

PROCEDURE Sort(Left,          { input  }
               Right : WORD { input  });
{- - - - - - - - - - - - - - - - - - - - - - - - - - - - - - - - - - -
```

```
SCOPE: local to RecQuickSort
ROUTINE PURPOSE: work horse procedure for the recursive QuickSort
                 method.
PARAMETERS:
   INPUT - Left and Right - the indices for the left and right sub-
           array being sorted.

- - - - - - - - - - - - - - - - - - - - - - - - - - - - - - - - - - }

VAR i, j, tempo  : WORD;
    median : InfoRec;
BEGIN
    WITH Data DO BEGIN
        i := Left;
        j := Right;
        median := DataArray[ SortIndex[(Left + Right) div 2] ];
        REPEAT
            WHILE DataArray[ SortIndex[i] ].Key < median.Key DO
                INC(i);
            WHILE median.Key < DataArray[ SortIndex[j] ].Key DO
                DEC(j);
            IF i <= j THEN BEGIN
                tempo := SortIndex[i];
                SortIndex[i] := SortIndex[j];
                SortIndex[j] := tempo;
                INC(i);
                DEC(j);
            END; { IF }
        UNTIL  i > j;
        IF Left < j THEN Sort(Left,j);
        IF i < Right THEN Sort(i,Right);
    END; { WITH }
END; { Sort }
BEGIN
    IF Data.NumData = 0 THEN EXIT
    ELSE IF Data.NumData > MAX_SORT_ARRAY_SIZE THEN
              Data.NumData := MAX_SORT_ARRAY_SIZE;
    { initialize indices }
    FOR k := 1 TO Data.NumData DO
        Data.SortIndex[k] := k;
    Sort(1, Data.NumData)
END; { RecQuickSort }

{-------------------------------------------------- QuickSort ------}

PROCEDURE QuickSort(VAR Data : SortRec { in/out });
TYPE indexrec = RECORD
        left, right : WORD;
    END;
    loc_stack_array_type = ARRAY [1..1] OF indexrec;
    loc_stack_ptr = ^loc_stack_array_type;
```

```
VAR i, j, lt, rt, stack_height, tempo : WORD;
    median : InfoRec;
    stack : loc_stack_ptr;
BEGIN
    WITH Data DO BEGIN
        IF NumData = 0 THEN EXIT
        ELSE IF NumData > MAX_SORT_ARRAY_SIZE THEN
                NumData := MAX_SORT_ARRAY_SIZE;
        { initialize indices }
        FOR i := 1 TO NumData DO
            SortIndex[i] := i;
        { adjust size to match the run-time size of array }
        GetMem(stack, NumData * Sizeof(indexrec) );
        { initialize stack }
        stack_height := 1;
        stack^[1].left := 1;
        stack^[1].right := NumData;
        REPEAT
            lt := stack^[stack_height].left;
            rt := stack^[stack_height].right;
            DEC(stack_height);
            REPEAT
                i := lt;
                j := rt;
                median := DataArray[ SortIndex[(lt + rt) div 2] ];
                REPEAT
                    WHILE DataArray[ SortIndex[i] ].Key < median.Key DO
                        INC(i);
                    WHILE median.Key < DataArray[ SortIndex[j] ].Key DO
                        DEC(j);
                    IF i <= j THEN BEGIN
                        tempo := SortIndex[i];
                        SortIndex[i] := SortIndex[j];
                        SortIndex[j] := tempo;
                        INC(i);
                        DEC(j);
                    END; { IF }
                UNTIL  i > j;
                IF i < rt THEN BEGIN
                    INC(stack_height);
                    stack^[stack_height].left := i;
                    stack^[stack_height].right := rt
                END; { IF }
                rt := j;
            UNTIL lt >= rt;
        UNTIL stack_height = 0;
    END; { WITH Data }
END; { QuickSort }
```

```
{----------------------------------------------------------- IntRadixSort ------}

PROCEDURE IntRadixSort(VAR Numbers : RadixArray; { in/out }
                           NData   : WORD;        { input  }
                           Digits  : RadixDigits { input  });

TYPE bin_matrix = ARRAY [0..9,1..MAX_SORT_ARRAY_SIZE] OF WORD;
VAR exponent, i, j, k, numeral : WORD;
    bin_Count : ARRAY [0..9] OF WORD;
    bins : bin_matrix;
BEGIN
    IF NData = 0 THEN EXIT
    ELSE IF NData > MAX_SORT_ARRAY_SIZE THEN
        NData := MAX_SORT_ARRAY_SIZE;
    exponent := 1;
    FOR numeral := 1 TO Digits DO BEGIN
        IF numeral > 1 THEN exponent := 10 * exponent;
        FOR i := 0 TO 9 DO bin_Count[i] := 0; { reset the bin counters }
        FOR i := 1 TO NData DO BEGIN
            k := Numbers[i];
            j := (k div exponent) MOD 10; { j is in 0..9 }
            INC(bin_Count[j]);
            bins[j, bin_Count[j]] := k; { store number in the bin }
        END; { FOR i }
        { reorder integers in original array }
        i := 0;
        FOR j := 0 TO 9 DO
            IF bin_Count[j] > 0 THEN
                FOR k := 1 TO bin_Count[j] DO BEGIN
                    INC(i);
                    { copy from bin to numeric array }
                    Numbers[i] := bins[j,k]
                END; { IF }
    END; { FOR numeral }
END; { IntRadixSort }

{---------------------------------------------- Reverse_Array_Order ------}

PROCEDURE Reverse_Array_Order(VAR Data : SortRec { in/out });
VAR first, last, tempo : WORD;
BEGIN
    WITH Data DO BEGIN
        IF NumData = 0 THEN EXIT
        ELSE IF NumData > MAX_SORT_ARRAY_SIZE THEN
                NumData := MAX_SORT_ARRAY_SIZE;
        first := 1;
        last := NumData;
        WHILE first < last DO  BEGIN
            tempo := SortIndex[first];
            SortIndex[first] := SortIndex[last];
```

```
        SortIndex[last] := tempo;
        INC(first);
        DEC(last);
      END; { WHILE }
    END; { WITH Data }
END; { Reverse_Array_Order }
END.
```

Listing 6.4. Source code for the USE_SORT.PAS application program.

```
PROGRAM Use_Sort;
{================================================================

                       Program USE_SORT.PAS
Version 1.0                                    Date 10/21/87
            Copyright (c) 1988, Namir Clement Shammas
This program reads a text file and sorts it according to the portion
of the lines specified by the user.


=================================================================}
{
    library name              type of import


}
Uses CRT,           { screen & cursor control routines }
     DOS,           { needed by other libraries        }
     DataLib0,      { string types                     }
     EditLine,      { using the one-line editor        }
     ComnLib0,      { centering text on the screen     }
     ComnStr0,      { extracting substrings            }
     NumInput,      { controlled integer input         }
     Sort;          { sorting data                     }

{$V-}

TYPE Line_Array = ARRAY [1..MAX_SORT_ARRAY_SIZE] OF STRING90;
VAR First, Last, High : INTEGER;
    Num_Lines : WORD;
    InFilename, OutFilename : STRING80;
    Line : Line_Array;
    SortLine : SortRec;

{-------------------------------------------------------------- Warn ——}
```

```
PROCEDURE Warn;
{- - - - - - - - - - - - - - - - - - - - - - - - - - - - - - - - - - - - -

ROUTINE PURPOSE: routine that informs the user the he/she typed a bad
filename or pathname.
PARAMETERS: None.
                         ROUTINE DEPENDENCIES
                         --------------------

          Identifier Name            Identifier Type        Source Library
          ---------------            ---------------        --------------

            HighVideo                   procedure               CRT
            GotoXY                      procedure               CRT
            NormVideo                   procedure               CRT

- - - - - - - - - - - - - - - - - - - - - - - - - - - - - - - - - - - - }

BEGIN
    HighVideo;
    GotoXY(5,22);
    WRITE(^G'Error: Bad pathname or filename');
    NormVideo;
END; { Warn }

{-------------------------------------------------------- Get_Lines ----}

FUNCTION Get_Lines(    Filename : STRING80;    { input  }
                   VAR Line     : Line_Array; { output }
                   VAR NData    : WORD        { output }) : BOOLEAN;
{- - - - - - - - - - - - - - - - - - - - - - - - - - - - - - - - - - - -

ROUTINE PURPOSE: function that reads lines from a text file.
PARAMETERS:
  INPUT: Filename - text filename containing the source lines.
  OUTPUT: Line - array of lines read from the text file.
          NData - actual number of lines read.
FUNCTION VALUE: if the filename is valid and the text file exits,
the function returns a TRUE value, otherwise it yields FALSE.
HANDLING BAD ARGUMENTS: the routine will read to the end of the file
or a maximum of MAX_SORT_ARRAY_SIZE lines. Longer files are partially
read.

                         ROUTINE DEPENDENCIES
                         --------------------

          Identifier Name            Identifier Type        Source Library
          ---------------            ---------------        --------------

            ClrEol                      procedure               CRT
            GotoXY                      procedure               CRT
            HighVideo                   procedure               CRT
            NormVideo                   procedure               CRT
            MAX_SORT_ARRAY_SIZE         constant                Sort
            Warn                        procedure               local

- - - - - - - - - - - - - - - - - - - - - - - - - - - - - - - - - - - - }
```

```
VAR ok : BOOLEAN;
    filevar : TEXT;
BEGIN
    Assign(filevar, Filename);
    {$I-} Reset(filevar); {$I+}
    ok := IOResult = 0;
    IF ok THEN BEGIN
        GotoXY(5,22); ClrEol;
        WRITE('Reading ...');
        NData := 0;
        WHILE (NOT Eof(filevar)) AND
              (NData <= MAX_SORT_ARRAY_SIZE) DO BEGIN
            INC(NData);
            READLN(filevar, Line[NData])
        END; { WHILE }
        Close(filevar);
        GotoXY(5,22); ClrEol;
    END
    ELSE Warn;
    Get_Lines := ok { return the function value }
END; { Get_Lines }


{------------------------------------------------------- Put_Lines ----}

FUNCTION Put_Lines(     Filename : STRING80;   { input  }
                    VAR Line     : Line_Array; { input  }
                        NData    : WORD        { input  }) : BOOLEAN;
{- - - - - - - - - - - - - - - - - - - - - - - - - - - - - - - - - - -
```

ROUTINE PURPOSE: function that writes lines to a text file.
PARAMETERS:
  INPUT: Filename - text filename receiving the source lines.
         Line - array of lines written to the text file.
         NData - number of lines written.
FUNCTION VALUE: if the filename is valid the function returns a
TRUE value, otherwise it yields FALSE.
HANDLING BAD ARGUMENTS: if the filename is a null string, the function
aborts and returns a FALSE logical value.

ROUTINE DEPENDENCIES

Identifier Name	Identifier Type	Source Library
ClrEol	procedure	CRT
GotoXY	procedure	CRT
SortRec	record	Sort
Warn	procedure	local

```
- - - - - - - - - - - - - - - - - - - - - - - - - - - - - - - - - - - }
```

```
VAR ok : BOOLEAN;
    i, j : WORD;
    filevar : TEXT;
BEGIN
    IF Filename = '' THEN BEGIN
        Put_Lines := FALSE;
        Warn;
        EXIT
    END; { IF }
    Assign(filevar, Filename);
    {$I-} Rewrite(filevar); {$I+}
    ok := IOResult = 0;
    IF ok THEN BEGIN
        GotoXY(5,22); ClrEol;
        WRITE('Writing ...');
        FOR i := 1 TO NData DO BEGIN
            j := SortLine.SortIndex[i];
            WRITELN(filevar, Line[j]);
        END; { FOR  }
        Close(filevar);
        GotoXY(5,22); ClrEol;
    END
    ELSE Warn;
    Put_Lines := ok { return the function value }
END; { Put_Lines }

{-------------------------------------------------------- GoodBye ──}


PROCEDURE GoodBye;
{- - - - - - - - - - - - - - - - - - - - - - - - - - - - - - - - - -

ROUTINE PURPOSE: signs off and halts the program execution.
PARAMETERS: None.
                      ROUTINE DEPENDENCIES
                      --------------------

        Identifier Name        Identifier Type      Source Library
        ---------------        ---------------      --------------

          ClrScr               procedure            CRT
          Write_Blanks         procedure            ComnLib0

- - - - - - - - - - - - - - - - - - - - - - - - - - - - - - - - - - }


BEGIN
    ClrScr;
    WRITELN('End of program');
    Write_Blanks(3);
    HALT;
END; { GoodBye }

{-------------------------------------------------------- Build_Keys ──}
```

```
PROCEDURE Build_Keys;
{- - - - - - - - - - - - - - - - - - - - - - - - - - - - - - - - -


ROUTINE PURPOSE: builds the sort keys by extracting substrings from the
text line array.
PARAMETERS: None.
HANDLING BAD ARGUMENTS: the routine compares the length of each text
line with the user-assigned first and last character positions. The
routine handles three cases:
    1) A text line is shorter than the first character position: in this
       case, a null string is assigned to the sort key.
    2) A text line is shorter than the last character position: in this
       case, the routine extracts what it can and assigns it to the sort
       key.
    3) The length of a text line is adequate: substring extraction
       proceeds as specified by the user.

                        ROUTINE DEPENDENCIES
                        --------------------

        Identifier Name          Identifier Type       Source Library
        ---------------          ---------------       --------------
        PosMidStr                function              ComnStr0
        SortRec                  record                Sort

- - - - - - - - - - - - - - - - - - - - - - - - - - - - - - - - - - }
VAR strlen : BYTE;
    i : WORD;
BEGIN
    FOR i := 1 TO Num_Lines DO BEGIN
        strlen := Length(Line[i]);
        IF First > strlen THEN
            SortLine.DataArray[i].Key := ''
        ELSE IF Last > strlen THEN
            SortLine.DataArray[i].Key :=
                PosMidStr(Line[i], First, strlen)
        ELSE
            SortLine.DataArray[i].Key :=
                PosMidStr(Line[i], First, Last);
    END; { FOR }
END; { Build_Keys }


{*********************************************************************}
{*************************** M A I N ***************************}
{*********************************************************************}


BEGIN

{- - - - - - - - - - - - - - - - - - - - - - - - - - - - - - - - -


                        ROUTINE DEPENDENCIES
                        --------------------
```

```
       Identifier Name              Identifier Type         Source Library
       ---------------              ---------------         --------------
          Build_Keys                  procedure               local
          Center                      procedure               ComnLib0
          ClrEol                      procedure               CRT
          Get_Input                   function                EditLine
          Get_Lines                   function                local
          GoodBye                     procedure               local
          GotoXY                      procedure               CRT
          HighVideo                   procedure               CRT
          NormVideo                   procedure               CRT
          Put_Lines                   function                local
          ShellSort                   procedure               Sort
- - - - - - - - - - - - - - - - - - - - - - - - - - - - - - - - - - - - - }

REPEAT { use a repeat loop to simulate an open loop }
    Center('PROGRAM TO SORT A TEXT FILE',-1,TRUE,0); { from ComnLib0 }
    GotoXY(5,20); HighVideo;
    WRITE('Press the [Enter] key to exit the program now');
    NormVideo;
    GotoXY(5,7);
    WRITE('INPUT FILENAME              : ');
    GotoXY(5,9);
    WRITE('LOCATION OF FIRST CHARACTER : ');
    GotoXY(5,11);
    WRITE('LOCATION OF LAST  CHARACTER : ');
    GotoXY(5,13);
    WRITE('OUTPUT FILENAME             : ');
    REPEAT
        GotoXY(35,7);
        InFilename := Get_Input(40);
        IF InFilename = '' THEN Goodbye;
    UNTIL Get_Lines(InFilename, Line, Num_Lines);
    GotoXY(5,20); ClrEol;
    GotoXY(35,9); Read_Int_Limit(First,1,80);
    IF (First + 19) > 80 THEN High := 80
                         ELSE High := First + 19;
    GotoXY(35,11); Read_Int_Limit(Last,First,High);
    GotoXY(5,22); WRITE('Sorting ...');
    Build_Keys; { construct the sort keys }
    ShellSort(SortLine);   { sort keys }
    GotoXY(5,22); ClrEol;
    REPEAT
        GotoXY(35,13);
        OutFilename := Get_Input(40);
    UNTIL Put_Lines(OutFilename, Line, Num_Lines);
UNTIL FALSE; { end of simulated open loop }
END.
```

C H A P T E R
7

Internal Searching

This chapter presents a library containing routines for various types of searching. Searching and sorting are two important related tasks which have received wide attention. Sorting data paves the way for more efficient searching, since an exhaustive lookup is replaced with a smarter one that scans only a portion of the data.

The SEARCH.PAS library unit, shown in Listing 7.1, contains routines that support the following search methods:

1. Heuristic search in an unsorted array
2. Binary search in an ordered array
3. Searching through an ordered array with the help of an indexed table
4. Hash-based searching

Searching through an unsorted array is an inefficient way of looking for a datum. Assuming that the data in the array have the same probability of being sought, the average search typically scans half of the array. In many cases there is no reason why the array cannot be put into better order. However, for those applications where arrays of data are not sorted, you can apply a heuristic search scheme. This simple method works by sequentially examining the array members until (hopefully) a match is found. If the search is successful, and the matching element is not the first in the array, the matching member is swapped with the previous array neighbor. This causes the elements most frequently sought to bubble towards lower array indices. Assuming that (at least over a significant period of time) there are some array members in greater demand than others, this method reduces search time. What is actually occurring is that the array elements are being dynamically sorted according to their recall frequency. As the preference for a certain set of array members changes, the new sought set bubbles to the beginning of the array. During the transition period the search efficiency drops.

There are two library routines that tackle heuristic searching. The first is used to initialize the array, while the second performs the heuristic search. The routines are as follows:

```
PROCEDURE Init_Heuristic_Search(VAR Data : SortRec { in/out });
```

Initializes the indices of the unsorted array. The **SortRec** record type is imported from the **Sort** library unit. Recall that the imported record structure has the following definition:

```
SortRec = RECORD
    NumData    : WORD;
    DataArray : DataRecArray;
    SortIndex : SortIndexArray
END;
```

The initialization is carried out by assigning to each member of array **SortIndex** the value of its index (that is, each index points to its accompanying **DataArray** element).

```
FUNCTION Heuristic_Search(VAR Data        : SortRec; { in/out }
                          Search_Key  : SortStr; { input  }
                          Occurrence  : WORD;    { input  }
                      VAR ActualOccur : WORD     { output })
                                         : WORD;
```

performs the heuristic search using the indices to avoid actually moving the data records. The routine handles duplicate keys and is able to search for a certain key occurring for a specific number of times.

Binary searching is the second type of searching methods implemented in the SEARCH.PAS library. It works with perfectly sorted arrays and utilizes a form of bisection strategy. The basic algorithm is as follows:

1. Select the median of the array and compare it with the search key.
2. If the search key matches the median, the search stops and the index of the median is returned.
3. If the search key is greater than the median, the left subarray is searched as a separate array. Resume at step (1). If there are no elements beyond the current median, the search halts returning a zero value.
4. If the search key is less than the median, the right subarray is searched as a separate array. Resume at step (1). If there are no elements beyond the current median, the search halts returning a zero value.

The above steps are performed by the following function:

```
FUNCTION Binary_Search(VAR Data        : SortRec; { input  }
                           Search_Key  : SortStr  { input  })
                                          : WORD;
```

Binary search methods blindly start searching at the median element. While this may be adequate for many applications, other methods are available to enhance the search efficiency. The table indexed search method uses an additional table to speed up searching. The index table itself contains a subset of the ordered array elements. Searching begins in the table to bypass unmatching elements quickly. Once a match is found in a table entry, the search resumes in the sorted array itself. Using the information in the table, the routines are much better informed on where to start and stop searching. Figure 7.1 shows a diagram for the indexed search table.

The SEARCH.PAS library declares the following constants and data types to build structures for indexed search tables:

```
CONST MAX_TABLE_SIZE = 52;

TYPE TableInfoRec = RECORD
        TableIndex   : WORD;
        TableKey     : SortStr;
     END;
     TableArrayType = ARRAY [1..MAX_TABLE_SIZE] OF TableInfoRec;
     TableRec = RECORD
        TableArray : TableArrayType;
        Table_Size : WORD;
     END;
```

The **MAX_TABLE_SIZE** declares the size of the indexed table. The **TableInfoRec** record type defines the basic record for the table's building block: the **TableIndex** that stores the array index containing the value in **TableKey**. The **TableArrayType** defines the array of table entries that is incorporated in the **TableRec** record. The latter also contains the **Table_Size** field to keep count of the actual number of entries in the indexed table.

There are two routines in this library to manage indexed searching. They are as follows:

```
PROCEDURE Init_Index_Search(VAR Data  : SortRec;  { input  }
                            VAR Table : TableRec; { output }
                            VAR Done  : BOOLEAN   { output });
```

initializes the indexed search table by selecting entries from the ordered array. The entries are selected as equidistant neighbors, regardless of the first few characters of each key. This routine must be recalled after the array it maps has been modified and resorted.

```
PROCEDURE Index_Search(VAR Data       : SortRec;  { input  }
                       VAR Table       : TableRec; { input  }
                           Search_Key : SortStr;  { input  }
                       VAR Location    : WORD      { output });
```

Figure 7.1. Indexed search table.

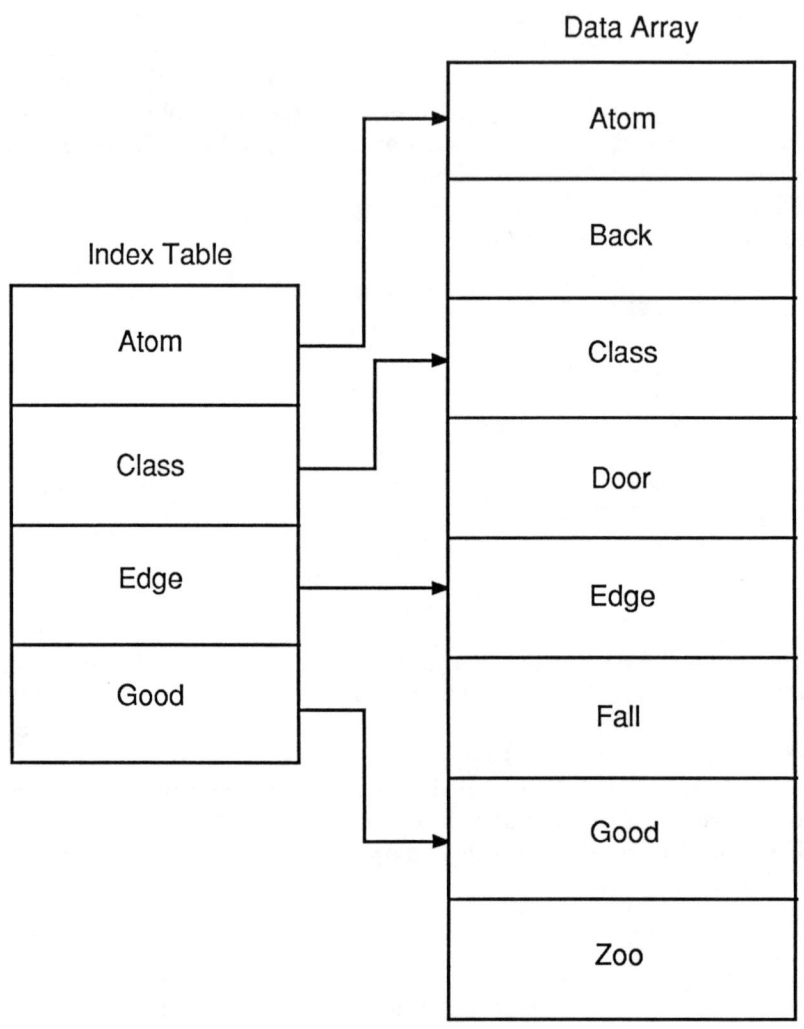

The routine performs indexed searching on an ordered array. Thus, the two prerequisites for this procedure to work are (1) the array has been sorted and no new data has been added since, and (2) the routine for the table initialization has been called.

The indexed searching technique provides an improvement over binary searching. However, for some applications requiring very fast searching, these methods may not meet the desired speed. In this case, hash-based methods can provide the required speed. The basic idea of hash-based searching is simple.

First, think of how easy it is to access an array element: using an integer index you are able to access it directly without scrolling through other elements. The hash-based search is very similar: you take the search key (normally represented by a string type) and convert it into a unique integer address. The unique address is used to zoom quickly in on the storage location for the data at hand.

Unfortunately, the above description of hash-based searching makes it sound too good to be true as a perfect method. Hash-based methods work very well in most cases, but there is a price to pay. The latter has something to do with fine tuning the parameters used in the algorithms.

The first issue in designing a hash-based search is the hashing function itself. In the majority of cases, the hashing function translates the string-typed key into a unique random address. The key word here is RANDOM. Thus, hashing functions are as good as the random number generators they utilize. There are various methods and techniques to implement hashing functions. The library functions **Hash0** and **Hash1** present two methods that use the modulo operator, as suggested by Donald Knuth.

An important question is raised concerning the unique random addresses generated by the hashing functions, "How random and unique are the generated values?" The answer reveals some of the problems with hash-based searches. First, the fact that hashing functions invariably generate duplicate addresses for different keys. This weakens the uniqueness requirement. Second, there is a limitation on the amount of memory and storage locations. Consequently, the number of random addresses generated must fall within a certain range of values. The above two factors cause the collision of different keys that, for either or both reasons, end up being translated onto the same address.

There are various methods for dealing with data collision during hashing. The method used here employs a linked list for each address (you can also replace the linked list structure with a binary tree). Thus, an array-based table of pointers is used to maintain a hash-based search system. Figure 7.2 shows a diagram for the hash table search that employs linked lists to resolve collision. The SEARCH.PAS library declares the following constant and data types for the hash table:

```
CONST MAX_HASH_TABLE_SIZE = 100;
TYPE HashPtr = ^HashInfoRec;
     HashInfoRec = RECORD
         HashKey     : SortStr;
         NextHashPtr : HashPtr;
         { other fields here }
     END;
     HashArray = ARRAY [0..MAX_HASH_TABLE_SIZE] OF HashPtr;
```

The constant **MAX_HASH_TABLE_SIZE** specifies the size of the hash table. The **HashInfoRec** record structure contains at least two fields: one to store the hashing key; the other, a pointer to link up with the linked-list.

The library contains the following routines to manage hash-based searching:

Figure 7.2. Hash table with linked lists.

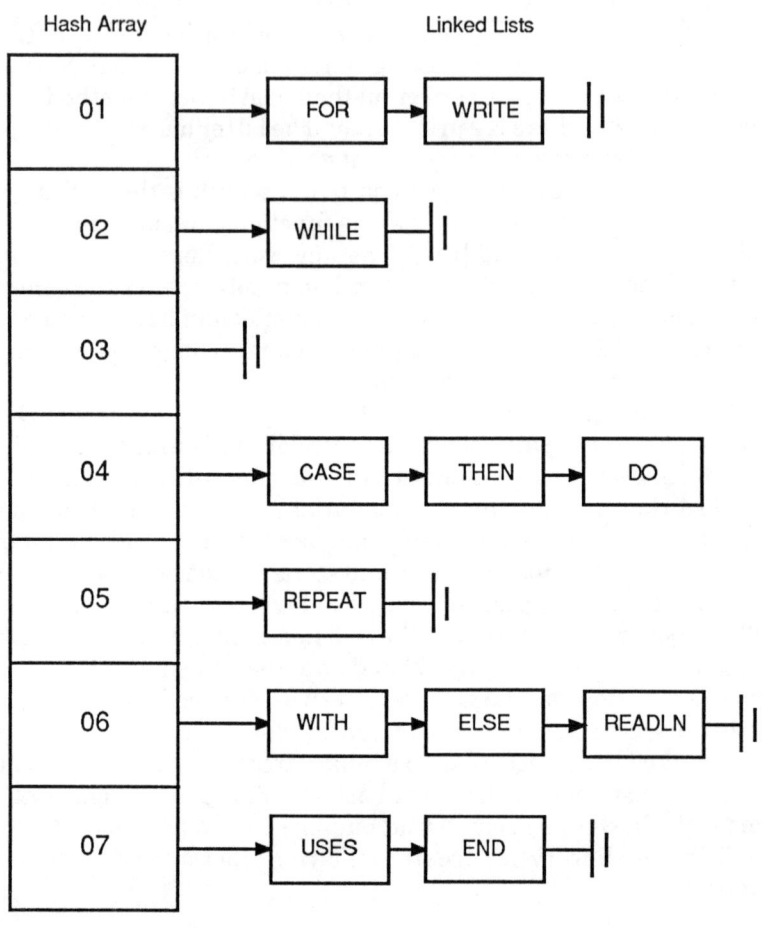

FUNCTION Hash0(Strng : SortStr { input }) : WORD;

is the first hashing function. It is simpler and shorter than function **Hash1**. The probability of collision is greater than that of **Hash1**.

FUNCTION Hash1(Strng : SortStr { input }) : WORD;

is the second, more elaborate, hashing function. It is slower than function **Hash0**, but results in less collision between data.

```
PROCEDURE Init_Hash_Table(VAR HashTable : HashArray { output });
```

initializes the hash table pointers by assigning NILs to each one. This routine must be called before utilizing the next two procedures.

```
PROCEDURE Insert_Hash_Table(VAR HashTable : HashArray; { in/out }
                                Item      : SortStr   { input });
```

inserts a new datum in the hash table. This routine needs to be called several times to build up the hash table.

```
PROCEDURE Search_Hash_Table(VAR HashTable : HashArray; { input  }
                                Item      : SortStr;  { input  }
                                Ptr       : HashPtr   { output });
```

searches the hash table for a match with the 'Item' key. The 'Ptr' pointer-type parameter returns the pointer to the matching item, or NIL if no match occurs. This enables you to access any component of the records stored.

SEARCH APPLICATIONS

I wrote the same application in two versions, for the sake of demonstration. The first employs the indexed search table, while the second version resorts to hash-based searching. The application itself is a simple, expert, inorganic chemistry system. It accepts the name of a simple inorganic compound and displays its chemical formula. As with any expert system, a knowledge database must be consulted by the application to verify the correctness of your input. The name of the chemical compound that you enter consists of two parts, delimited by a space: the cation and the anion. Cations are atoms or radicals (this is a group of atoms that have a strong bond such that they behave like an ionized element) that contribute some of their electrons to the chemical bonds and thus are characterized by a positive charge. By contrast, anions are atoms or radicals that receive electrons and have a negative charge. The simple compound which the expert system tackles must consist of the name of a cation followed by that of an anion. Reversing their order or using two ions of the same type is considered an erroneous input by the expert system.

The limited chemistry knowledge database is stored on two separate text files: ANION.DAT for anions and CATION.DAT for cations. Both files store data using the same structure which consists of lines of text, each containing the following information:

```
<name of ion> <chemical symbol>  <valence>  <atom status>
```

The name of the ion is the search key used in sorting and establishing the search table. What you type is compared with the ion names. The chemical symbol is what the application displays in the case of entering a correct compound name. The valence is a signed integer in the range of -4 to 7. It counts the number of electrons each ion shares in a chemical bond. Cations have positive valences, and anions have negative ones. A compound may consist of multiple cations and anions. The atom status indicates whether or not the ion is a charged atom or a radical. The letter **A** is used to indicate an atom, and the letter **R** signals a radical. Figures 7.3 and 7.4 show the contents of the ANION.DAT and CATION.DAT files.

The two versions of the expert system require that the string type **SortStr** and the record **InfoRec** in the SORT.PAS library be defined as follows:

```
SortStr = STRING[40];
InfoRec = RECORD
    { Info : any data type }
    Symbol : STRING[5];
    Valence : SHORTINT;
    IsAtom : BOOLEAN;
    Key : SortStr;
END;
```

The above customization is needed to accommodate the application.

Listing 7.2 shows the source code for application EXPERT1.PAS. The program contains the following three routines:

1. Procedure **Parse_Line**: parses a string starting at a specified character location to extract the next substring. The space character is the delimiter between extracted substrings. This routine enables you to delimit substrings with multiple spaces.

2. Procedure **Read_Data**: is the routine that reads each data file and parses each line into the various fields. The names of ions are converted into upper case.

3. Procedure **Show_Formula**: is used to display a balanced chemical formula. By "balanced" I mean that the number of cations times their valence, plus the number of anions times their valence, is zero.

The program first reads the data files. If they are not located on the same directory or if you renamed them, you are asked to enter the new name of the new directory path (and the filenames). The data files are read into two **SortRec** records. Each record is sorted and an index is created. The program then prompts you to enter a compound name. The names of the cation and anions are first parsed and then upper-case copies are made. The upper-case strings are used in the indexed search. If both the cation and anion names match database entries, the program displays the chemical formula. Otherwise, it informs you of your error. Table 7.1 shows a sample input and output data you may want to use to test the program. Figure 7.5 shows the software bus schedule for EXPERT1.PAS and the interrelated calls between some of the libraries.

The second version of the expert system employs hashing techniques. Listing 7.3 contains the source code for program EXPERT2.PAS. This version is superior to the previous one in the following aspects:

1. The hash table uses dynamically allocated linked lists. Consequently, it overcomes the limitations of a presized array-based index table. The hash table is able to accommodate as much data as the specified heap size.

2. The nature of hashing requires a fast and simple pointer initialization. There is no sorting to be performed, no index table to initialize. Hash-based searching is much more direct than indexed searching.

3. The hash table is able to take new data without the need for resorting and reindexing, as is the case with the indexed search table. Consequently, hash tables are much more practical for handling variant databases with constantly incoming information.

You may use the same suggested sample data to practice with EXPERT2.PAS. Figure 7.6 shows the software bus schedule for this application and the interrelated calls among some of the libraries.

Figure 7.3. Contents of file ANION.DAT.

```
Chloride Cl -1 A
Sulfide S -2 A
Sulfate SO4 -2 R
Sulfite SO3 -2 R
Phosphate PO4 -3 R
Chlorate ClO3 -1 R
Chlorite ClO2 -1 R
Hypochloride OCl -1 R
Perchlorate ClO4 -1 R
Carbide C -4 A
Oxide O -2 A
Hydride H -1 A
Nitride N -3 A
Hydroxide OH -1 R
Carbonate CO3 -2 R
Bicarbonate HCO3 -1 R
Nitrate NO3 -1 R
Nitrite NO2 -1 R
Bromide Br -1 A
Iodide I -1 A
Iodate IO3 -1 R
Chromate CrO4 -2 R
```

Figure 7.4. Contents of file CATION.DAT.

```
Hydrogen H 1 A
Ammonium NH4 1 R
Sodium Na 1 A
Potassium K 1 A
Calcium Ca 2 A
Ferric Fe 3 A
Ferrous Fe 2 A
Cupric Cu 2 A
Cuprous Cu 1 A
Cobaltous Co 2 A
Cobalt Co 2 A
Magnesium Mg 2 A
Lithium Li 1 A
Zinc Zn 2 A
Chromium Cr 3 A
Barium Ba 2 A
Nicklous Ni 2 A
Nicklic Ni 3 A
Lead Pb 2 A
Mercurous Hg2 2 A
Mercuric Hg 2 A
Stannous Sn 2 A
Stannic Sn 3 A
Aluminum Al 3 A
Silver Ag 1 A
Gold Au 3 A
Cadmium Cd 2 A
```

Table 7.1. Sample Input and Output Data.

Input Compound Name	Displayed Formula
Sodium Chloride	NaCl
ferric sulfate	Fe2 (SO4) 3
Ammonium nitrate	NH4NO3
Calcium Bicarbonate	Ca (HCO3) 2
magnesium hydroxide	Mg (OH) 2
Cupric Sulfate	CuSO4
Ferrous Sulfide	FeS
Cobalt nitrate	Co (NO3) 2
Potassium nitrate	KNO3
sodium iodide	NaI
Hydrogen oxide	H2O
Ammonium Sulfate	(NH4) SO4

Figure 7.5. Software Bus Schedule for EXPERT1.PAS.

SOFTWARE BUS SCHEDULE

PROJECT: EXPERT1.PAS

MODULE DataLib0

	A	B	C	D	E
		Software Bus Schedule			
OUTPUT					
string STRING20	X				
string STRING40	X				
string STRING80	X				
string STRING255	X				

MODULE   CRT

	A	B	C	D	E
		Software Bus Schedule			
OUTPUT					
proc ClrScr		X			
proc GotoXY		X			
func ReadKey		X			

MODULE ComnStr0

	A	B	C	D	E
		Software Bus Schedule			
OUTPUT					
UpperCaseStr			X		
INTERFACE INPUT					
string STRING255	X				

MODULE Sort

	A	B	C	D	E
		Software Bus Schedule			
OUTPUT					
proc Shell_Sort				X	
record SortRec				X	
string SortStr				X	

MODULE Search

	Software Bus Schedule				
	A	B	C	D	E
OUTPUT					
proc Index_Search					X
proc Init_Index_Search					X
record TableRec					X
INTERFACE INPUT					
record SortRec				X	
string SortStr				X	

MODULE main

	Software Bus Schedule				
	A	B	C	D	E
ROUTINE INPUT					
record SortRec				X	
string STRING20	X				
string STRING40	X				
string STRING80	X				
func UpperCaseStr			X		
INPUT					
proc ClrScr		X			
proc GotoXY		X			
proc Index_Search					X
proc Init_Index_Search					X
func ReadKey		X			
proc Shell_Sort				X	
record SortRec				X	
string SortStr				X	
record TableRec					X
funct UpperCaseStr			X		

Figure 7.6. Software Bus Schedule for EXPERT4.PAS.

```
                            SOFTWARE BUS SCHEDULE
PROJECT: EXPERT2.PAS


MODULE DataLib0
                              Software Bus Schedule
                       A      B      C      D       E

OUTPUT
string STRING20        X
string STRING40        X
string STRING80        X
string STRING255       X



MODULE  CRT
                              Software Bus Schedule
                       A      B      C      D       E

OUTPUT
proc ClrScr                   X
proc GotoXY                   X
func ReadKey                  X



MODULE ComnStr0
                              Software Bus Schedule
                       A      B      C      D       E

OUTPUT
UpperCaseStr                         X

INTERFACE INPUT
string STRING255       X



MODULE Sort
                              Software Bus Schedule
                       A      B      C      D       E

OUTPUT
record SortRec                              X
string SortStr                              X
```

MODULE Search

	A	B	C	D	E
		Software Bus Schedule			

OUTPUT

	A	B	C	D	E
array HashArray				X	
proc Init_Hash_Table				X	
proc Search_Hash_Table				X	

INTERFACE INPUT

	A	B	C	D	E
string SortStr				X	

MODULE main

	A	B	C	D	E
		Software Bus Schedule			

ROUTINE INPUT

	A	B	C	D	E
array HashArray					X
string STRING20	X				
string STRING40	X				
string STRING80	X				
func UpperCaseStr			X		

INPUT

	A	B	C	D	E
proc ClrScr		X			
proc GotoXY		X			
array HashArray					X
proc Init_Hash_Table					X
func ReadKey		X			
proc Search_Hash_Table					X
string SortStr				X	
funct UpperCaseStr			X		

Listing 7.1. Source code for library SEARCH.PAS.

```
UNIT Search;
{==============================================================

        Copyright (c) 1987, 1988    Namir Clement Shammas
    LIBRARY NAME: Search
    VERSION: 1.0                              DATE 8/20/1987
    PURPOSE: implements routines for heuristic, binary, indexed, and
            hashed searching. Works with the Sort library.
    UPDATE HISTORY:


==============================================================}
```

```
{******************************************************************}
{***************************} INTERFACE {**************************}
{******************************************************************}

Uses Sort;
CONST MAX_TABLE_SIZE = 10;
      MAX_HASH_TABLE_SIZE = 100;
TYPE TableInfoRec = RECORD
        TableIndex  : WORD;
        TableKey    : SortStr;
     END;
     TableArrayType = ARRAY [1..MAX_TABLE_SIZE] OF TableInfoRec;
     TableRec = RECORD
        TableArray : TableArrayType;
        Table_Size : WORD;
     END;
     HashPtr = ^HashInfoRec;
     HashInfoRec = RECORD
        Symbol   : STRING[5];
        Valence  : SHORTINT;
        IsAtom   : BOOLEAN;
        HashKey      : SortStr;
        NextHashPtr : HashPtr;
        { other fields here }
     END;
     HashArray = ARRAY [0..MAX_HASH_TABLE_SIZE] OF HashPtr;

PROCEDURE Init_Heuristic_Search(VAR Data : SortRec { in/out });
{- - - - - - - - - - - - - - - - - - - - - - - - - - - - - - - -

ROUTINE PURPOSE: initializes the indices of the unsorted array.
PARAMETERS:
  IN/OUT: Data - initialized unsorted array.

                    ROUTINE DEPENDENCIES
                    --------------------
        Identifier Name          Identifier Type      Source Library
        ---------------          ---------------      --------------
          SortRec                    record               Sort

- - - - - - - - - - - - - - - - - - - - - - - - - - - - - - - - }
FUNCTION Heuristic_Search(VAR Data         : SortRec; { in/out }
                              Search_Key : SortStr; { input  }
                              Occurrence  : WORD;    { input  }
                          VAR ActualOccur : WORD     { output })
                                           : WORD;
{- - - - - - - - - - - - - - - - - - - - - - - - - - - - - - - -

ROUTINE PURPOSE: performs heuristic search in an sorted array.
The parameters specify both the sought data and the specific
occurrence number. The function returns the index of the located
element. If the latter is not the first one in the array, it
swaps one element towards the front.
```

PARAMETERS:
    INPUT: Search_Key — the key of the sought datum.
           Occurrence — the specified occurrence number.
    OUTPUT: ActualOccur — the actual number of times the search
            key has been encountered (<= Occurrence).
    IN/OUT: Data — the searched array of data.
FUNCTION VALUE: returns the)updated) index of the matching
element, or zero if no match occurs.

                    ROUTINE DEPENDENCIES

Identifier Name	Identifier Type	Source Library
SortRec	record	Sort
SortStr	string	Sort

- }
FUNCTION Binary_Search(VAR Data   : SortRec; { input }
                       Search_Key : SortStr { input })
                                             : WORD;
{- -

ROUTINE PURPOSE: performs binary searching on a sorted array.
PARAMETERS:
    INPUT: Search_Key — the search key for the sought datum.
           Data — Array of sorted data that is searched.
FUNCTION VALUE: returns the index of the matching element if
found; otherwise, returns zero.

                    ROUTINE DEPENDENCIES

Identifier Name	Identifier Type	Source Library
SortRec	record	Sort
SortStr	string	Sort

- }
PROCEDURE Init_Index_Search(VAR Data : SortRec; { input }
                            VAR Table : TableRec; { output }
                            VAR Done : BOOLEAN   { output });
{- -

ROUTINE PURPOSE: initializes a table for indexed searching.
PARAMETERS:
    INPUT: Data — the sorted data for which the search table is built.
    OUTPUT: Table — the search table constructed for the sorted data.
            Done — flag to signal the construction of the table.
HANDLING BAD ARGUMENTS: if the integer division of the number of
data by the table size is zero, no table is constructed.

ROUTINE DEPENDENCIES

Identifier Name	Identifier Type	Source Library
SortRec	record	Sort

```
- - - - - - - - - - - - - - - - - - - - - - - - - - - - - - - - - }
PROCEDURE Index_Search(VAR Data       : SortRec;  { input  }
                       VAR Table       : TableRec; { input  }
                           Search_Key  : SortStr;  { input  }
                       VAR Location    : WORD      { output });
{- - - - - - - - - - - - - - - - - - - - - - - - - - - - - - - - -
```

ROUTINE PURPOSE: performs indexed searching. The parameter
'Location' returns the index of the matching array member.
A zero is returned if no match is found.
PARAMETERS:
   INPUT: Data – searched data array.
          Table – indexed search table.
          Search_Key – the key for the sought datum.
   OUTPUT: Location – array index of matching element.

ROUTINE DEPENDENCIES

Identifier Name	Identifier Type	Source Library
SortRec	record	Sort
SortStr	string	Sort

```
- - - - - - - - - - - - - - - - - - - - - - - - - - - - - - - - }
FUNCTION Hash0(Strng : SortStr { input  }) : WORD;
{- - - - - - - - - - - - - - - - - - - - - - - - - - - - - - - -
```

ROUTINE PURPOSE: presents a hashing function that takes a string
typed argument and returns an unsigned integer.
PARAMETERS:
   INPUT: Strng – the string argument that is translated into a
                  numeric address.
FUNCTION VALUE: returns the hashed 'address' of Strng argument.

ROUTINE DEPENDENCIES

Identifier Name	Identifier Type	Source Library
SortStr	string	Sort

```
- - - - - - - - - - - - - - - - - - - - - - - - - - - - - - - - }
FUNCTION Hash1(Strng : SortStr { input  }) : WORD;
{- - - - - - - - - - - - - - - - - - - - - - - - - - - - - - - -
```

ROUTINE PURPOSE: presents a hashing function that takes a string typed argument and returns an unsigned integer.
PARAMETERS:
  INPUT: Strng – the string argument that is translated into a
            numeric address.
FUNCTION VALUE: returns the hashed 'address' of Strng argument.

ROUTINE DEPENDENCIES

Identifier Name	Identifier Type	Source Library
SortStr	string	Sort

```
- - - - - - - - - - - - - - - - - - - - - - - - - - - - - - - - - - }
PROCEDURE Init_Hash_Table(VAR HashTable : HashArray { output });
{- - - - - - - - - - - - - - - - - - - - - - - - - - - - - - - - -
```

ROUTINE PURPOSE: initializes a hash table.
PARAMETERS:
  OUTPUT: HashTable – initialized hash table.

```
- - - - - - - - - - - - - - - - - - - - - - - - - - - - - - - - - }
PROCEDURE Insert_Hash_Table(VAR HashTable : HashArray;  { in/out }
                            Item       : HashInfoRec { input });
{- - - - - - - - - - - - - - - - - - - - - - - - - - - - - - - - -
```

ROUTINE PURPOSE: builds a hash table by inserting a single datum. This routine should be called a number of times to build a complete hash table.
PARAMETERS:
  INPUT: Item – datum inserted in the hash table.
  IN/OUT: HashTable – hash table being built.

ROUTINE DEPENDENCIES

Identifier Name	Identifier Type	Source Library
SortStr	string	Sort

```
- - - - - - - - - - - - - - - - - - - - - - - - - - - - - - - - }
PROCEDURE Search_Hash_Table(VAR HashTable  : HashArray; { input }
                            Search_Key : SortStr;  { input }
                            VAR Ptr        : HashPtr   { output });
{- - - - - - - - - - - - - - - - - - - - - - - - - - - - - - - - -
```

ROUTINE PURPOSE: searches hash table for a specific key. The Ptr parameter returns the pointer to the matching record.
PARAMETERS:
  INPUT: HashTable – hash table used in the search.
           Item – the search key for the sought datum.

```
    OUTPUT: Ptr - pointer to matching record, or NIL if no match
            is found.

                        ROUTINE DEPENDENCIES
                        --------------------

        Identifier Name         Identifier Type      Source Library
        ---------------         ---------------      --------------

          SortStr                   string               Sort

- - - - - - - - - - - - - - - - - - - - - - - - - - - - - - - - - }

{*****************************************************************}
{************************} IMPLEMENTATION {***********************}
{*****************************************************************}

{------------------------------------------ Init_Heuristic_Search ---}

PROCEDURE Init_Heuristic_Search(VAR Data : SortRec { in/out });
VAR i : WORD;
BEGIN
    WITH Data DO BEGIN
        FOR i := 1 TO NumData DO
            SortIndex[i] := i;
    END; { WITH }
END; { Init_Heuristic_Search }

{----------------------------------------------- Heuristic_Search ---}

FUNCTION Heuristic_Search(VAR Data        : SortRec; { in/out }
                              Search_Key   : SortStr; { input  }
                              Occurrence   : WORD;    { input  }
                          VAR ActualOccur  : WORD     { output })
                                                       : WORD;

VAR i, j, result : WORD;
BEGIN
    WITH Data DO BEGIN
        ActualOccur := 0; { initialize count for number of matches }
        result := 0;
        i := 1;
        WHILE (i <= NumData) AND (ActualOccur < Occurrence) DO BEGIN
            IF DataArray[ SortIndex[i] ].Key = Search_Key THEN
                INC(ActualOccur);
            INC(i);
        END; { WHILE }
        DEC(i);
        { swap indices }
        IF ActualOccur = Occurrence THEN
            IF i > 1 THEN BEGIN
                j := SortIndex[i-1];
```

```
                    SortIndex[i-1] := SortIndex[i];
                    SortIndex[i] := j;
                    result := SortIndex[i-1]
                END
                ELSE result := SortIndex[1];
        END; { WITH Data }
        Heuristic_Search := result { return function result }
    END; { Heuristic_Search }


    {-------------------------------------------------- Binary_Search ----}


    FUNCTION Binary_Search(VAR Data        : SortRec; { input  }
                           Search_Key  : SortStr  { input  })
                                                    : WORD;
    VAR low, high, median, result : WORD;
        not_found : BOOLEAN;
    BEGIN
        WITH Data DO BEGIN
            { set lower and upper search limits }
            low := 1;
            high := NumData;
            not_found := TRUE; { initialize search flag }
            WHILE ((low+1) < high) AND not_found DO BEGIN
                { calculate median index }
                median := (low + high) div 2;
                IF Search_Key < DataArray[ SortIndex[median] ].Key THEN
                    high := median
                ELSE IF Search_Key > DataArray[ SortIndex[median] ].Key THEN
                    low := median
                ELSE not_found := FALSE;
            END; { WHILE }
        END; { WITH Data }
        IF not_found THEN result := 0
                     ELSE result := Data.SortIndex[median];
        Binary_Search := result { return function result }
    END; { Binary_Search }


    {------------------------------------------------ Init_Index_Search ----}


    PROCEDURE Init_Index_Search(VAR Data  : SortRec;   { input  }
                                VAR Table : TableRec; { output }
                                VAR Done  : BOOLEAN    { output });

    VAR i, j, skip : WORD;
    BEGIN
        Table.Table_Size := 0; { initialize table size }
        skip := Data.NumData div MAX_TABLE_SIZE;
        IF skip > 0 THEN
            WITH Data, Table DO BEGIN
                i := 1;
                REPEAT
```

```
                INC(Table_Size);
                j := SortIndex[i];
                TableArray[Table_Size].TableIndex := i;
                TableArray[Table_Size].TableKey   := DataArray[j].Key;
                INC(i, skip);
            UNTIL (i >= NumData) OR (Table_Size = MAX_TABLE_SIZE);
        END { WITH Data }
    ELSE Done := FALSE;
END; { Init_Index_Search }


{------------------------------------------------- Index_Search ——}

PROCEDURE Index_Search(VAR Data       : SortRec;  { input  }
                       VAR Table      : TableRec; { input  }
                           Search_Key : SortStr;  { input  }
                       VAR Location   : WORD      { output });

VAR i, j, first, last  : WORD;
    found_entry, no_match : BOOLEAN;
BEGIN
    Location := 0; { initialize with a not-found value }
    WITH Data, Table DO  BEGIN
        { perform a quick check to see if sought element in in the
          range of values stored in the array 'Data'.              }
        IF (Search_Key >= DataArray[ SortIndex[1] ].Key) AND
           (Search_Key <= DataArray[ SortIndex[NumData] ].Key)
           THEN BEGIN
               i := 1;
               found_entry := FALSE; { initialize search flag }
               no_match := TRUE;
               REPEAT
                   IF Search_Key > TableArray[i].TableKey
                       THEN INC(i)
                       ELSE found_entry := TRUE;
               UNTIL (i > Table_Size) OR found_entry;
               If found_entry THEN BEGIN
                   first := TableArray[i-1].TableIndex;
                   IF i < Table_Size THEN
                       last  := TableArray[i].TableIndex
                   ELSE
                       last := NumData;
               END
               ELSE BEGIN
                   first := TableArray[i-1].TableIndex;
                   last  := NumData
               END; { IF }
               i := first;
               WHILE (i <= last) AND no_match DO
                   IF Search_Key <> DataArray[ SortIndex[i] ].Key THEN
                       INC(i)
```

```
                    ELSE
                        no_match := FALSE;
                    IF NOT no_match THEN Location := SortIndex[i];
            END; { IF }
        END; { WITH }
END; { Index_Search }


{-------------------------------------------------------------- Hash0 —}

FUNCTION Hash0(Strng : SortStr { input  }) : WORD;
CONST { Hash function constants: prime numbers }
        HASH_CONST1 = 13;
VAR i, most, sum, shift : WORD;
BEGIN
    shift := Ord('A') - 1;
    most := Length(Strng);
    IF most > 3 THEN most := 3;
    i := 1;
    sum := 0;
    WHILE (i <= most) DO
        sum := sum * 7 + Ord(Strng[i]) - shift;
    { use two modulo operators to keep hash address in range }
    Hash0 := (sum MOD HASH_CONST1) MOD MAX_HASH_TABLE_SIZE;
END; { Hash0 }


{-------------------------------------------------------------- Hash1 —}

FUNCTION Hash1(Strng : SortStr { input  }) : WORD;
CONST { Hash function constants: prime numbers }
        HASH_CONST1 = 11;
        HASH_CONST2 = 17;
VAR sum : REAL;
    i, j, shift, strlen, k1, k2 : WORD;
BEGIN
    shift := Ord('A') - 1;
    sum := 0.0;
    strlen := Length(Strng);
    k1 := 9 * strlen;
    shift := Ord('A') - 1 - SQR(strlen);
    FOR i := 1 TO strlen DO
        sum := sum * k1 + (Ord(Strng[i]) - shift);
    WHILE sum > 65000.0 DO
        sum := sum / MAX_HASH_TABLE_SIZE;
    i := Trunc(sum);
    i := (i MOD HASH_CONST1) * HASH_CONST2 + (i MOD HASH_CONST2);
    Hash1 := i MOD MAX_HASH_TABLE_SIZE; { keep hash address in range }
END; { Hash1 }
```

```
{--------------------------------------------------- Init_Hash_Table ——}

PROCEDURE Init_Hash_Table(VAR HashTable : HashArray { output });
VAR i : WORD;
BEGIN
    FOR i := 1 TO MAX_HASH_TABLE_SIZE DO
        HashTable[i] := NIL;
END; { Init_Hash_Table }


{------------------------------------------------- Insert_Hash_Table ——}

PROCEDURE Insert_Hash_Table(VAR HashTable : HashArray;  { in/out }
                                Item       : HashInfoRec { input  });
VAR hash_address : WORD;
    ptr : HashPtr;
BEGIN
    hash_address := Hash1(Item.HashKey);
    NEW(ptr);
    ptr^ := Item;
    ptr^.NextHashPtr := HashTable[hash_address];
    HashTable[hash_address] := ptr
END; { Insert_Hash_Table }


{------------------------------------------------- Search_Hash_Table ——}

PROCEDURE Search_Hash_Table(VAR HashTable  : HashArray; { input  }
                                Search_Key : SortStr;   { input  }
                            VAR Ptr        : HashPtr    { output });
VAR not_found : BOOLEAN;
    hash_address : WORD;
BEGIN
    hash_address := Hash1(Search_Key);
    Ptr := HashTable[hash_address];
    not_found := TRUE;
    WHILE not_found DO
        IF Ptr = NIL THEN not_found := FALSE
        ELSE IF Ptr^.HashKey = Search_Key THEN not_found := FALSE
        ELSE Ptr := Ptr^.NextHashPtr;
END; { Search_Hash_Table }
END.
```

Listing 7.2. Source code for application EXPERT1.PAS.

```
PROGRAM Expert1;
{================================================================

                    CHEMISTRY EXPERT SYSTEM
version 1.0                                       11/20/87

This program applies the Sort and Search library units to
set up a small chemistry expert system. Two data files are
read containing chemistry information regarding the name,
symbol, and valence of atom-based or radical ions. The system
prompts the user to type a compound name and searches through
the sorted data array for the cation and anion names (the search
is case sensitive). If both cation and anion names are found in
the database, the expert system displays the chemical formula
for the corresponding compound.

================================================================}

{$V-,S+,R+}
Uses CRT, DataLib0, ComnStr0,
     Sort, Search;
CONST ANION_FILE  = 'ANION.DAT'; { filename for anion data }
      CATION_FILE = 'CATION.DAT'; { filename for cation data }
VAR OK : BOOLEAN;
    Answer : CHAR;
    AnionLoc, CationLoc  : WORD;
    SpaceLoc : BYTE;
    AnStr, UpAnStr, CatStr, UpCatStr, Compound : SortStr;
    Anion, { mini-database for anion names }
    Cation { mini-database for cation names } : SortRec;
    AnionTable,  { index table for anions }
    CationTable  { index table for cations } : TableRec;

{------------------------------------------------- Parse_Line ------}

PROCEDURE Parse_Line(     Strng   : STRING40; { input  }
                      VAR CharPos : BYTE;      { input  }
                      VAR SubStr  : STRING40   { output });
{- - - - - - - - - - - - - - - - - - - - - - - - - - - - - - - - - -
```

ROUTINE PURPOSE: extracts a substring from the string Strng
starting at the CharPos character location and continuing until
either the end of the string Strng or the next first space
character. If the CharPos index currently points to a space
character, it is incremented until it finds a non-space character.

PARAMETERS:

   INPUT: Strng – the scanned string.
           CharPos – the character location where the substring
            extraction begins.

   OUTPUT: SubStr – the extracted substring.

HANDLING BAD ARGUMENTS: if the Strng variable is a null string,
a null string is returned.

ROUTINE DEPENDENCIES

Identifier Name	Identifier Type	Source Library
STRING40	string	DataLib0

```
- - - - - - - - - - - - - - - - - - - - - - - - - - - - - - - - - - }
VAR strlen : BYTE;
BEGIN
    SubStr := '';
    IF Strng = '' THEN EXIT;
    strlen := Length(Strng);
    WHILE (Strng[CharPos] = ' ') AND (CharPos <= strlen) DO
        INC(CharPos);
    WHILE (CharPos <= strlen) AND (Strng[CharPos] <> ' ') DO BEGIN
        SubStr := SubStr + Strng[CharPos];
        INC(CharPos)
    END; { WHILE }

END; { Parse_Line }

{-------------------------------------------------- Read_Data ------}

PROCEDURE Read_Data(    Filename : STRING40; { input  }
                    VAR Data     : SortRec  { output });
{- - - - - - - - - - - - - - - - - - - - - - - - - - - - - - - - - -
```

ROUTINE PURPOSE: reads the chemistry related information from
a data file and saves it into the mini–database variable Data.
PARAMETERS:
  INPUT: Filename – filename containing the sought data.
  OUTPUT: Data – the variable containing the array of data records.
HANDLING BAD ARGUMENTS: if the file is not found, the program
prompts the user to enter the correct filename. Since this
application seeks particular files, the error may be generated
if these two files are located in another directory. The remedy
is to enter the filenames preceded by the full directory path
names.

```
COMMENTS:
                          ROUTINE DEPENDENCIES
                          --------------------

          Identifier Name                Identifier Type      Source Library
          ---------------                ---------------      --------------

          Parse_Line                     procedure            local
          SortRec                        record               Sort
          STRING20                       string               DataLib0
          STRING80                       string               DataLib0
          UpperCaseStr                   function             ComnStr0

- - - - - - - - - - - - - - - - - - - - - - - - - - - - - - - - - - - - - }
VAR filevar : TEXT;
    line : STRING80;
    atom_char, valstr : STRING20;
    error_code : WORD;
    char_pos : BYTE;
    done : BOOLEAN;
BEGIN
    REPEAT
        Assign(filevar, Filename);
        {$I-} Reset(filevar); {$I+}
        done := IOResult = 0;
        IF NOT done THEN BEGIN
            WRITELN;
            WRITELN('Cannot open file ',Filename);
            WRITELN('Please enter new filename : ');
            READLN(Filename); WRITELN;
        END; { IF }
    UNTIL Done;
    WITH Data DO BEGIN
        NumData := 0;
        WHILE (NumData < MAX_SORT_ARRAY_SIZE) AND
              (NOT EOF(filevar)) DO BEGIN
            INC(NumData);
            WITH DataArray[NumData] DO BEGIN
                READLN(filevar,line);
                char_pos := 1;
                Parse_Line(line, char_pos, Key);
                Key := UpperCaseStr(Key);
                Parse_Line(line, char_pos, Symbol);
                Parse_Line(line, char_pos, valstr);
                Val(valstr, Valence, error_code);
                Parse_Line(line, char_pos, atom_char);
                IF UpCase(atom_char[1]) = 'A'
                    THEN IsAtom := TRUE
                    ELSE IsAtom := FALSE;
            END; { WITH }
        END; { WHILE }
    END; { WITH }
    Close(filevar);
END; { Read_Data }
```

```
{------------------------------------------------------- Show_Formula ----}

PROCEDURE Show_Formula(CatNum,          { input  }
                       AnNum   : WORD { input  });
{- - - - - - - - - - - - - - - - - - - - - - - - - - - - - - - - - - - -

ROUTINE PURPOSE: displays the mathematical formula of a compound.
PARAMETERS:
  INPUT: CatNum - the Cation array index to select a cation.
         AnNum - the Anion array index to select an anion.
- - - - - - - - - - - - - - - - - - - - - - - - - - - - - - - - - - - - }

VAR ansymb, catsymb : STRING[5];
    anval, catval, anmult, catmult : SHORTINT;
    anatom, catatom : BOOLEAN;
BEGIN
    ansymb := Anion.DataArray[AnNum].Symbol;
    catsymb := Cation.DataArray[CatNum].Symbol;
    anval := Anion.DataArray[AnNum].Valence;
    catval := Cation.DataArray[CatNum].Valence;
    anatom := Anion.DataArray[AnNum].IsAtom;
    catatom := Cation.DataArray[CatNum].IsAtom;
    { are absolute valences equal ? }
    IF catval = ABS(anval) THEN
        WRITE(catsymb,ansymb)
    ELSE BEGIN
        anmult := catval;
        catmult := ABS(anval);
        IF (NOT catatom) AND (catmult > 1) THEN
            WRITE('(',catsymb,')',catmult:1)
        ELSE IF catmult > 1 THEN
            WRITE(catsymb,catmult:1)
        ELSE
            WRITE(catsymb);
        IF (NOT anatom) AND (anmult > 1) THEN
            WRITE('(',ansymb,')',anmult:1)
        ELSE IF anmult > 1 THEN
            WRITE(ansymb,anmult:1)
        ELSE
            WRITE(ansymb);
    END; { IF }
    WRITELN;
END; { Show_Formula }

{- - - - - - - - - - - - - - - - - - - - - - - - - - - - - - - - - - - -
```

```
                        ROUTINE DEPENDENCIES
                        --------------------

      Identifier Name              Identifier Type        Source Library
      ---------------              ---------------        --------------

        ClrScr                       procedure              CRT
        GotoXY                       procedure              CRT
        Index_Search                 procedure              Search
        Init_Index_Search            procedure              Search
        Parse_Line                   procedure              local
        Read_Data                    procedure              local
        ReadKey                      function               CRT
        Shell_Sort                   procedure              Sort
        Show_Formula                 procedure              local
        SortRec                      string                 Sort
        SortStr                      string                 Sort
        TableRec                     record                 Sort
        UpperCaseStr                 function               ComnStr0
```

- }

```
BEGIN
    {------ Read anion and cation data ------}
    Read_Data(ANION_FILE, Anion);
    Read_Data(CATION_FILE, Cation);
    {------- Sort data ---------}
    ShellSort(Anion);
    ShellSort(Cation);
    {------- Initialize indexed search tables ------}
    Init_Index_Search(Anion, AnionTable, OK);
    Init_Index_Search(Cation, CationTable, OK);
    ClrScr;
    WRITELN('CHEMISTRY EXPERT SYSTEM':50);
    GotoXY(1,3);
    REPEAT
        WRITELN; WRITELN;
        WRITE('Enter compound name -> ');
        READLN(Compound);
        { exctract cation and anion name }
        SpaceLoc := 1;
        Parse_Line(Compound, SpaceLoc, CatStr);
        UpCatStr := UpperCaseStr(CatStr);
        Parse_Line(Compound, SpaceLoc, AnStr);
        UpAnStr := UpperCaseStr(AnStr);
        { search for cation in database }
        Index_Search(Cation, CationTable, UpCatStr, CationLoc);
        { found cation in database ? }
        IF CationLoc > 0 THEN BEGIN
            { search for anion in database }
            Index_Search(Anion, AnionTable, UpAnStr, AnionLoc);
            { found anion in database ? }
```

```
                IF AnionLoc > 0 THEN BEGIN
                    WRITE(CatStr,' ',AnStr,' is ');
                    Show_Formula(CationLoc, AnionLoc)
                END
                ELSE BEGIN
                    WRITELN('Cannot find ',AnStr,' in my database!');
                    WRITELN;
                END { IF }
            END
            ELSE BEGIN
                WRITELN('Cannot find ',CatStr,' in my database!');
                WRITELN;
            END;
            REPEAT
                WRITELN;
                WRITE('More formula translation? (Y/N) ');
                Answer := UpCase(ReadKey);
            UNTIL Answer IN ['Y','y','N','n'];
        UNTIL Answer IN ['N','n'];
END.
```

Listing 7.3. Source code for application EXPERT2.PAS.

```
PROGRAM Expert2;
{===============================================================

                    CHEMISTRY EXPERT SYSTEM
version 2.0                                    11/20/87

This program applies the hashing feature of the Search library
unit to set up a small chemistry expert system. Two data
files are read containing chemistry information regarding
the name, symbol, and valence of atom-based or radical ions.
The system prompts the user to type a compound name and
searches through the database for the cation and anion
names (the search is case sensitive). If both cation and anion
names are found in the database, the expert system displays
the chemical formula for the corresponding compound.

===============================================================}

{$V-,S+,R+}
{&M 8912, 8912, 200000}
Uses CRT, DataLib0, ComnStr0,
     Sort, Search;
CONST ANION_FILE  = 'ANION.DAT';  { filename for anion data }
      CATION_FILE = 'CATION.DAT'; { filename for cation data }
```

```
VAR OK : BOOLEAN;
    Answer : CHAR;
    AnPtr, CatPtr : HashPtr;
    SpaceLoc : BYTE;
    AnStr, UpAnStr, CatStr, UpCatStr, Compound : SortStr;
    AnionTable, { hash table for anions }
    CationTable { hash table for cations } : HashArray;

{--------------------------------------------------------- Parse_Line ------}

PROCEDURE Parse_Line(    Strng   : STRING40; { input  }
                     VAR CharPos : BYTE;      { input  }
                     VAR SubStr  : STRING40  { output });
{- - - - - - - - - - - - - - - - - - - - - - - - - - - - - - - - - - - -
```

ROUTINE PURPOSE: extracts a substring from the string Strng
starting at the CharPos character location and continuing until
either the end of the string Strng or the next first space
character. If the CharPos index currently point to a space
character, it is incremented until it finds a non-space character.
PARAMETERS:
  INPUT: Strng - the scanned string.
         CharPos - the character location where the substring
            extraction begins.
  OUTPUT: SubStr - the extracted substring.
HANDLING BAD ARGUMENTS: if the Strng variable is a null string,
a null string is returned.

                    ROUTINE DEPENDENCIES

        Identifier Name   Identifier Type   Source Library
        ---------------   ---------------   --------------
           STRING40   string   DataLib0

- }

```
VAR strlen : BYTE;
BEGIN
    SubStr := '';
    strlen := Length(Strng);
    WHILE (Strng[CharPos] = ' ') AND (CharPos <= strlen) DO
        INC(CharPos);
    WHILE (CharPos <= strlen) AND (Strng[CharPos] <> ' ') DO BEGIN
        SubStr := SubStr + Strng[CharPos];
        INC(CharPos)
    END; { WHILE }
END; { Parse_Line }

{--------------------------------------------------------- Read_Data ------}
```

```
PROCEDURE Read_Data(    Filename : STRING40; { input  }
                    VAR Data     : HashArray { output }); 
{- - - - - - - - - - - - - - - - - - - - - - - - - - - - - - - - - -

ROUTINE PURPOSE: reads the chemistry related information from
a data file and saves it into the mini-database variable Data.
PARAMETERS:
  INPUT: Filename - filename containing the sought data.
  OUTPUT: Data - the variable containing the hashed data records.
HANDLING BAD ARGUMENTS: if the file is not found, the program
prompts the user to enter the correct filename. Since this
application seeks particular files the error may be generated
if these two files are located in another directory. The remedy
is to enter the filenames preceded by the full directory path
names.

COMMENTS:
                        ROUTINE DEPENDENCIES
                        --------------------

        Identifier Name           Identifier Type      Source Library
        ---------------           ---------------      --------------
        Parse_Line                procedure            local
        HashArray                 record               Search
        STRING20                  string               DataLib0
        STRING80                  string               DataLib0
        UpperCaseStr              function             ComnStr0


- - - - - - - - - - - - - - - - - - - - - - - - - - - - - - - - - - - }

VAR hashinfo : HashInfoRec;
    filevar : TEXT;
    line : STRING80;
    atom_char, valstr : STRING[20];
    error_code : WORD;
    char_pos : BYTE;
    done : BOOLEAN;
BEGIN
    REPEAT
        Assign(filevar, Filename);
        {$I-} Reset(filevar); {$I+}
        done := IOResult = 0;
        IF NOT done THEN BEGIN
            WRITELN;
            WRITELN('Cannot open file ',Filename);
            WRITELN('Please enter new filename : ');
            READLN(Filename); WRITELN;
        END; { IF }
    UNTIL Done;
    WITH hashinfo DO BEGIN
        WHILE NOT EOF(filevar) DO BEGIN
```

```
            READLN(filevar,line);
            char_pos := 1;
            Parse_Line(line, char_pos, HashKey);
            HashKey := UpperCaseStr(HashKey);
            Parse_Line(line, char_pos, Symbol);
            Parse_Line(line, char_pos, valstr);
            Val(valstr, Valence, error_code);
            Parse_Line(line, char_pos, atom_char);
            IF UpCase(atom_char[1]) = 'A'
               THEN IsAtom := TRUE
               ELSE IsAtom := FALSE;
            NextHashPtr := NIL;
            Insert_Hash_Table(Data, hashinfo);
         END; { WHILE }
    END; { WITH }
    Close(filevar);
END; { Read_Data }


{----------------------------------------------------- Show_Formula ----}

PROCEDURE Show_Formula(CatPtr,              { input  }
                       AnPtr   : HashPtr { input  });
{- - - - - - - - - - - - - - - - - - - - - - - - - - - - - - - - - - - -

ROUTINE PURPOSE: displays the mathematical formula of a compound.
PARAMETERS:
   INPUT: CatNum - the Cation array index to select a cation.
          AnNum - the Anion array index to select an anion.
- - - - - - - - - - - - - - - - - - - - - - - - - - - - - - - - - - - - }

VAR AnSymb, CatSymb : STRING[5];
    AnVal, CatVal, AnMult, CatMult : SHORTINT;
    AnAtom, CatAtom : BOOLEAN;
BEGIN
    AnSymb := AnPtr^.Symbol;
    CatSymb := CatPtr^.Symbol;
    AnVal := AnPtr^.Valence;
    CatVal := CatPtr^.Valence;
    AnAtom := AnPtr^.IsAtom;
    CatAtom := CatPtr^.IsAtom;
    IF CatVal = ABS(AnVal) THEN
        WRITE(CatSymb,AnSymb)
    ELSE BEGIN
        AnMult := CatVal;
        CatMult := ABS(AnVal);
        IF (NOT CatAtom) AND (CatMult > 1) THEN
            WRITE('(',CatSymb,')',CatMult:1)
        ELSE IF CatMult > 1 THEN
            WRITE(CatSymb,CatMult:1)
        ELSE
```

```
                WRITE(CatSymb);
        IF (NOT AnAtom) AND (AnMult > 1) THEN
            WRITE('(',AnSymb,')',AnMult:1)
        ELSE IF AnMult > 1 THEN
            WRITE(AnSymb,AnMult:1)
        ELSE
            WRITE(AnSymb);
    END; { IF }
    WRITELN;
END; { Show_Formula }


{- - - - - - - - - - - - - - - - - - - - - - - - - - - - - - - - - - - -
                        ROUTINE DEPENDENCIES
                        --------------------

        Identifier Name            Identifier Type       Source Library
        ---------------            ---------------       --------------
        ClrScr                     procedure             CRT
        HashArray                  array                 Search
        GotoXY                     procedure             CRT
        Init_Hash_Table            procedure             Search
        Parse_Line                 procedure             local
        Read_Data                  procedure             local
        ReadKey                    function              CRT
        Search_Hash_Table          procedure             Search
        Show_Formula               procedure             local
        SortStr                    string                Sort
        UpperCaseStr               function              ComnStr0


- - - - - - - - - - - - - - - - - - - - - - - - - - - - - - - - - - - - }


BEGIN
    {------- Initialize indexed search tables -------}
    Init_Hash_Table(AnionTable);
    Init_Hash_Table(CationTable);
    {- Read anion and cation data and build hash table -}
    Read_Data(ANION_FILE, AnionTable);
    Read_Data(CATION_FILE, CationTable);
    ClrScr;
    WRITELN('CHEMISTRY EXPERT SYSTEM VERSION 2':50);
    GotoXY(1,3);
    REPEAT
        WRITELN; WRITELN;
        WRITE('Enter compound name -> ');
        READLN(Compound);
        SpaceLoc := 1;
        Parse_Line(Compound, SpaceLoc, CatStr);
        UpCatStr := UpperCaseStr(CatStr);
        Parse_Line(Compound, SpaceLoc, AnStr);
        UpAnStr := UpperCaseStr(AnStr);
        Search_Hash_Table(CationTable, UpCatStr, CatPtr);
```

```
        IF CatPtr <> NIL THEN BEGIN
            Search_Hash_Table(AnionTable, UpAnStr, AnPtr);
            IF AnPtr <> NIL THEN BEGIN
                WRITE(CatStr,' ',AnStr,' is ');
                Show_Formula(CatPtr, AnPtr)
            END
            ELSE BEGIN
                WRITELN('Cannot find ',AnStr,' in my database!');
                WRITELN;
            END { IF }
        END
        ELSE BEGIN
            WRITELN('Cannot find ',CatStr,' in my database!');
            WRITELN;
        END;
        REPEAT
            WRITELN;
            WRITE('More formula translation? (Y/N) ');
            Answer := UpCase(ReadKey);
        UNTIL Answer IN ['Y','y','N','n'];
    UNTIL Answer IN ['N','n'];
END.
```

8

Stacks

Stacks are very important and powerful data structures. They are used in low-level data manipulation by the computer's CPU. This is invisible to you as a high-level language programmer until you start working in assembly language. There are even stack-oriented languages, such as FORTH, with many zealous programmers who always point out the power of these languages.

The stack used by the CPU works by employing a pointer that accesses memory addresses. This enables the computer to store and later recall data off the stack. This also illustrates the two basic components of a stack: a pointer (or height counter) and an accessibility scheme. In this chapter, I will present two stack implementations: one using arrays, the other using unordered linked lists. I will also discuss the advantages and disadvantages of both implementations.

IMPLEMENTING STACKS USING ARRAYS

Implementing stacks using arrays requires that you dimension the arrays and maintain a stack height counter. Figure 8.1 illustrates an array-based stack, using a static array. The first design choice is to select a static array (that is, declare its complete fixed size) or a dynamic array (that is, utilize Turbo Pascal programming tricks to enable the array to increment its size as needed during run-time). Using static arrays can be more space wasteful, but it is faster since no time is spent in increasing its size. By contrast, dynamic arrays use memory more efficiently, but require additional time to increase their size. The exact time depends on the array size and the frequency of array resizing. Increasing the size by small increments often requires more frequent resizing. The choice between using static or dynamic arrays depends mainly on whether or not you know (or can impose) the maximum size of the stack. I have chosen to write the array-based stack library using a static array. Thus, a constant declaring the maximum array size (and, therefore, the maximum stack size) is used. The value of the constant can easily be changed to fit your needs.

Array-based stacks inherit the ease of access associated with arrays. Knowing the stack height counter, you can directly manipulate any stack element. Thus, operations such as rotating the stack become very easy to code.

Using arrays, either static or dynamic, offers another design choice: the direction of stack growth. The first alternative locates the top of the stack away from the first array member, as shown in Figure 8.1. This makes the first array member contain the oldest stack element. The second array member stores the second oldest stack element, and so on. The stack height counter points to the top of the stack. Pushing and popping items to/from the stack is easily implemented in this scheme. The second alternative always stores the top of the stack at the first element. This means that array elements must be moved every time you push or pop the stack. Using large arrays, this becomes time consuming and not very feasible. Thus, the second arrangement may have some appeal, if any, in a few applications where the stack size is small (say four or five elements). The stack height counter also serves to warn you when you have reached the maximum size limit.

The library STACKARR.PAS, shown in Listing 8.1, contains routines to manipulate array-based stacks having the following features:

1. The stack has a maximum size of 100 elements.

2. The stack pushes real numbers defined by record type **StackData**. The real-type is more of a dummy one and will most likely be redefined in custom applications.

When you create custom versions of this library, you can adjust the value of the constant **MAX_ARRAY_STACK** and specify your own data types. In addition, you will most likely need to redeclare record **StackData**.

The STACKARR.PAS library contains the following routines:

```
PROCEDURE Push_ArStk(
          VAR Stack       : StackArrayRec;  { in/out }
              Item        : StackData;      { input  }
          VAR Stack_Full  : BOOLEAN         { output });
```

pushes a data item onto the stack. A boolean flag, **Stack_Full**, is used to signal that the item was not inserted in the stack since it is already full.

```
PROCEDURE Pop_ArStk(
          VAR Stack        : StackArrayRec; { in/out }
          VAR Item         : StackData;     { output }
          VAR Empty_Stack  : BOOLEAN        { output });
```

pops the top of the stack into identifier **Item**. The **Empty_Stack** boolean is used to indicate that an attempt was made to pop an empty stack.

Figure 8.1. Stack implemented using an array.

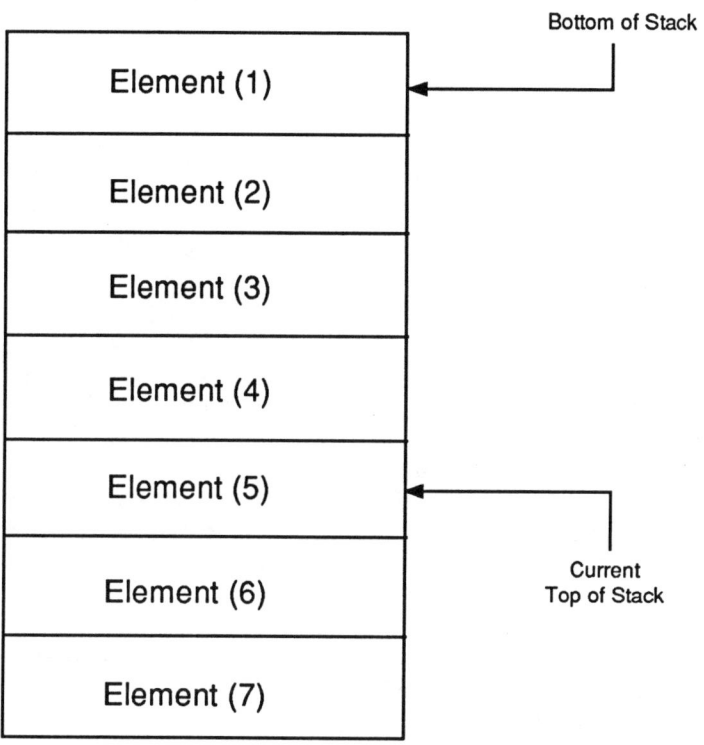

```
PROCEDURE Clear_ArStk(VAR Stack : StackArrayRec { in/out });
```

clears the stack by simply zeroing the stack height counter. The actual data in the array-based stack remains intact. Since Pascal does not formally implement data hiding, you can still access these elements, if need be.

```
PROCEDURE Swap_ArStk(VAR Stack : StackArrayRec { in/out });
```

swaps the two topmost elements in the stack. Your application program should check for swapping when the height counter is less than two.

Large sized array-based stacks can use the array **tail** as a secondary and temporary stack. For example, you may keep a duplicate of the last few entries in the secondary stack. The same strategy can be used in nonnumerical stack manipulation, such as parsing mathematical expressions. Such parsing transforms a mathematical expression into a much simpler stack-based expression known as Reverse Polish Notation (RPN) expression. Scanning a mathematical expression with its multiple parentheses from left to right results in a number of pending operations. These operations are placed at the tail of the array while awaiting the parser to place them back in the correct stack location.

STACKS USING LINKED LISTS

Stacks may also be implemented using unordered linked lists. The dynamically allocated lists offer tailor-fitted stack sizes. As the stacks grow, more memory space is allocated. Similarly, as they shrink, the memory space left behind is recovered. Figure 8.2 shows a list-based stack. Notice that the stack pointer always points to the topmost element. This is very convenient since the topmost element is the first one to be popped out of the stack. This arrangement reduces the time to traverse the linked list. The same diagram also indicates that elements may not be stored in contiguous memory locations (unlike array-based stacks). The spacing between stack elements depends on the number and type of other dynamically allocated objects. However, the above spacing has no effect on the functionality of the stack. Using linked lists to implement stacks relieves you from having to keep a mandatory stack height counter (as is the case with array-based stacks). Each stack element points to the next one, except for the one at the bottom. Its null pointer value indicates that you have reached the bottom of the stack.

The STACKLST.PAS library, shown in Listing 8.2, contains routines that implement a list-based stack. When you create custom versions of this library, you need to redefine the record **StackData** to fit your application. The application program you develop using the library needs to declare a stack pointer and initialize it with NIL. This indicates that the stack is empty.

The routines in library STACKLST.PAS are the following:

```
PROCEDURE Push_LsStk(VAR Top_of_Stack : StackPtr; { in/out }
                         Item          : StackData { input });
```

pushes a data item onto the stack. Since data is dynamically allocated, there is no preset maximum size to guard against exceeding. Extensive use of dynamic allocation in your application perhaps requires a separate routine that monitors the available free memory space.

```
PROCEDURE Pop_LsStk(VAR Top_of_Stack : StackPtr;  { in/out }
                    VAR Item          : StackData; { in/out }
                    VAR Empty_Stack   : BOOLEAN    { output });
```

pops   p of the stack into identifier **Item**. The **Empty_Stack** boolean is used
to in(: that an attempt was made to pop an empty stack.

```
PROCEDURE Clear_LsStk(VAR Top_of_Stack : StackPtr);
```

clears the stack by popping all of the stack elements and recovering their memory space. Unlike the array-based stacks, data in this type of stack is lost.

```
PROCEDURE Swap_LsStk(VAR Top_of_Stack : StackPtr { in/out });
```

swaps the two topmost elements in the stack. Your application program should check for swapping when the height counter is less than two.

APPLICATION: RPN CALCULATOR

Perhaps the most appropriate application for stacks is an RPN calculator. I have chosen to implement such a calculator program to perform math operations on either complex or real numbers. The calculator has the following features:

1. Supports a 100-element stack. However, only the four topmost elements are visible.
2. Allows you to toggle between complex math and real math modes.
3. Accepts real or complex numbers, according to the current mode.
4. Enables you to push, pop, and clear the stack.
5. Permits you to swap the two topmost stack elements.
6. Supports the basic four math operations.

The original program design involved just a complex RPN calculator. I included the real math mode option, since real math operations may be considered subset cases of those in complex math. I chose to develop a small complex math library unit where the code for the four basic math operations reside. Constructing a separate library, CMPLXLIB.PAS, is a good program design practice, because it places a reusable set of functionally related routines in a separate library. The CMPLXLIB.PAS library, shown in Listing 8.3, also serves as a nucleus for a bigger library that you may want to develop. The definition of the complex record type is imported from **DataLib0** as shown below:

```
Complex = RECORD
    Treal,
    Timag  : REAL;
END;
```

I have chosen to declare the complex record in **DataLib0** because I felt that the complex type is a rather **universal** type that can be used by numerous libraries.

The application program RPNCALC.PAS, shown in Listing 8.4, requires the following two customization steps of library STACKARR.PAS:

1. Insert "Use DataLib0" between the INTERFACE and the TYPE keywords.

2. Redeclare the record **StackData** as **Complex**, as shown below:

```
StackData = Complex;
```

The routines in RPNCALC.PAS are as follows:

1. **Procedure VideoDisp:** puts a string on the screen such that its first character is displayed in high-intensity video. The rest of the string is displayed in normal intensity video.

2. **Procedure Init_Screen:** initializes the stack elements and displays the heading, the calculator register names, the list of calculator commands, and the stack elements.

3. **Procedure Update_Regs:** updates the contents of the stack elements. This routine is also responsible for toggling the display for the real and complex math mode. Displaying the stack registers involves accessing the four topmost stack elements. As the stack grows, the top of the stack moves away from the first array element. This means accessing different array elements to store and recall data to the top of the stack.

4. **Procedure Warn:** displays a warning message and then waits for a key to be pressed. The warning message is passed as an argument, enabling the program to display specific diagnostic text.

5. **Procedure Get_Input:** is the main driver of the application program. It is composed of a main REPEAT-UNTIL loop that displays the command prompt and processes your input. The input at the command prompt is merely a character that must match with a highlighted one in the command list. Entering an invalid character causes the program to beep once. The routine also contains code that warns against the following:

    A. Attempting to push a number into a full stack.

    B. Attempting to pop an empty stack.

    C. Attempting to perform a math operation when the stack has less than two elements. The messages displayed are specific to whether the stack is empty or has only one element.

    D. Attempting to swap the two topmost stack elements when the stack has less than two elements.

6. **Procedure Draw_Single_Box**: draws a single line frame.

Procedure Get_Input prompts you for numeric entry following the calculator mode you are in. Looking at its source code, you notice that the procedure is actually using the complex math routines for both modes. This reveals that the real math mode is nothing but the complex mode operating by automatically assigning zeros to the imaginary parts of complex numbers. While this method is slightly wasteful in computing time for the real math mode, its code is smaller.

However, the additional time is not very significant, making this scheme satisfactory.

When the application program runs, it goes into the preset math mode. Currently, this is set to be the real math mode. You can switch the mode to start with the complex mode by setting the constant **DEFAULT_INITIAL_MODE** to TRUE. When the calculator is in real math mode, only one column of real numbers is displayed. In complex mode, the simulated complex stack registers are displayed in two columns. The left one displays the real components of the complex numbers, while the right column shows their imaginary parts. Pressing the [T] key toggles between the real and complex mode, and consequently toggles the visibility of the right column of numbers.

Figure 8.3 shows a screen image of a sample session with application RPNCALC.PAS. The screen shows the names of the four topmost stack registers accompanied by the display of the stack in complex math mode. The list of commands available is also shown, with the hot keys display in high-intensity video. Figure 8.4 contains the software bus schedule for RPNCALC.PAS.

Figure 8.2. Stack implemented using a linked list.

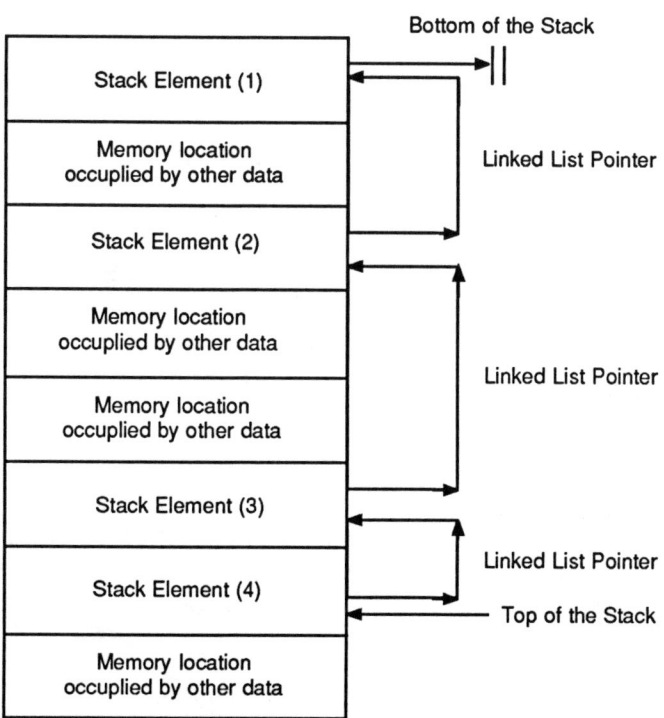

Figure 8.3. Screen image of a sample session with program RPNCALC.PAS.

```
                    RPN CALCULATOR DEMO PROGRAM

    T Register      0.00000000000E+0000   0.00000000000E+0000

    Z Register      3.46000000000E+0001   5.40000000000E+0001

    Y Register      2.10000000000E+0001   6.50000000000E+0001

    X Register      4.20000000000E+0001   1.30000000000E+0002

Math operations -> + - / *
Quit
Clear stack
Push stack
pOp stack
Toggle calculator mode
Enter a number
                        Swap      X      and      Y      registers
Command > e
    Enter real part of complex number : 11
    Enter imaginary part : 21
```

Figure 8.4. Software bus schedule for RPNCALC.PAS.

```
                SOFTWARE BUS SCHEDULE TABLE

PROJECT: RPNCALC.PAS
MODULE DataLib0
                            Software Bus Schedule
                A   B   C   D   E   F   G   H   I   J   K   L   M


OUTPUT
string STRING80     X
record Complex      X



MODULE PCScreen                 Software Bus Schedule
                A   B   C   D   E   F   G   H   I   J   K   L   M


OUTPUT
pointer Screen_Ptr      X
```

MODULE Screen0

```
                            Software Bus Schedule
                        A  B  C  D  E  F  G  H  I  J  K  L  M
```

OUTPUT
proc Disp_Real   X
proc Disp_Str   X

INTERFACE INPUT
pointer Screen_Ptr   X
string STRING80   X

MODULE NumInput

```
                            Software Bus Schedule
                        A  B  C  D  E  F  G  H  I  J  K  L  M
```

OUTPUT
proc Read_Real   X

IMPLEMENTATION INPUT
string STRING80   X

MODULE CmplxLib

```
                            Software Bus Schedule
                        A  B  C  D  E  F  G  H  I  J  K  L  M
```

OUTPUT
proc Add_Complex   X
proc Div_Complex   X
proc Mul_Complex   X
proc Sub_Complex   X

MODULE StackArr

```
                            Software Bus Schedule
                        A  B  C  D  E  F  G  H  I  J  K  L  M
```

OUTPUT
const MAX_COMPLEX_STACK   X
record StackArrayRec   X
proc Clear_ArStk   X
proc Pop_ArStk   X
proc Push_ArStk   X
proc Swap_ArStk   X

INTERFACE INPUT
string STRING80   X
record Complex   X

MODUL main program

			Software Bus Schedule											
	A	B	C	D	E	F	G	H	I	J	K	L	M
INPUT													
const MAX_COMPLEX_STACK						X							
string STRING80	X												
record Complex	X												
record StackArrayRec						X							
proc Add_Complex					X								
proc Clear_ArStk						X							
proc Disp_Real		X											
proc Disp_Str		X											
proc Div_Complex					X								
proc Mul_Complex					X								
proc Pop_ArStk						X							
proc Push_ArStk						X							
proc Read_Real			X										
proc Sub_Complex					X								
proc Swap_ArStk						X							

Listing 8.1. Source code for library STACKARR.PAS.

```pascal
UNIT StackArr;

{=============================================================================


            Copyright (c) 1987, 1988   Namir Clement Shammas
      LIBRARY NAME: StackArr
      VERSION: 1.0                                    DATE 8/27/1987
      PURPOSE: Implement a stack as an array.
      UPDATE HISTORY:


=============================================================================}
{*****************************************************************************}
{************************} INTERFACE {****************************}
{*****************************************************************************}

CONST MAX_ARRAY_STACK = 100; { size of array }
TYPE
     StackData = RECORD
            Stack_Elem : REAL; { or any other fields }
     END;
     StackArray = ARRAY [1..MAX_ARRAY_STACK] OF StackData;
     StackArrayRec = RECORD
        Member : StackArray;
        Height : INTEGER;
     END;
```

```
{--------------------------------------------------------- Push_ArStk ------}

PROCEDURE Push_ArStk(
          VAR Stack       : StackArrayRec; { in/out }
              Item        : StackData;      { input  }
          VAR Stack_Full : BOOLEAN         { output });
{- - - - - - - - - - - - - - - - - - - - - - - - - - - - - - - - - - - - -
```

ROUTINE PURPOSE: pushes Item into an array-based stack.
PARAMETERS:
  INPUT: Item - data pushed onto the top of the stack.
  OUTPUT: Stack_Full - flag used to signal whether or not the stack is
                       full.
  IN/OUT: Stack - the altered stack array.
HANDLING BAD ARGUMENTS: If the stack is already full, the Stack_Full
flag is set to TRUE.

```
- - - - - - - - - - - - - - - - - - - - - - - - - - - - - - - - - - - - }
PROCEDURE Pop_ArStk(
          VAR Stack        : StackArrayRec; { in/out }
          VAR Item         : StackData;      { output }
          VAR Empty_Stack  : BOOLEAN         { output });
{- - - - - - - - - - - - - - - - - - - - - - - - - - - - - - - - - - - - -
```

ROUTINE PURPOSE: routine to return (and remove) the topmost stack
element. If the stack is empty, the boolean Empty_Stack is set to
true. Use this flag to test the status of the stack before attempting
to access the data in argument Item.
PARAMETERS:
  OUTPUT: Item - data popped from the top of the stack.
          Empty-Stack - flag used to indicate whether or not an attempt
          was made to pop an empty stack.
  IN/OUT: Stack - the array-based stack.
          HANDLING BAD ARGUMENTS: If the stack is empty and this routine
is called, the Empty_Stack is set to TRUE.

```
- - - - - - - - - - - - - - - - - - - - - - - - - - - - - - - - - - - - }
PROCEDURE Clear_ArStk(VAR Stack : StackArrayRec { in/out });
{- - - - - - - - - - - - - - - - - - - - - - - - - - - - - - - - - - - - -
```

ROUTINE PURPOSE: clears the stack.
PARAMETERS:
  IN/OUT: Stack - cleared stack.

```
- - - - - - - - - - - - - - - - - - - - - - - - - - - - - - - - - - - - }
PROCEDURE Swap_ArStk(VAR Stack : StackArrayRec { in/out });
{- - - - - - - - - - - - - - - - - - - - - - - - - - - - - - - - - - - - -
```

ROUTINE PURPOSE: swaps the two topmost stack elements.
PARAMETERS:
  IN/OUT: Stack - the array-based stack.

```
- - - - - - - - - - - - - - - - - - - - - - - - - - - - - - - - - - - - }

{*********************************************************************}
{************************} IMPLEMENTATION {************************}
{*********************************************************************}

{------------------------------------------------------ Push_ArStk ------}

PROCEDURE Push_ArStk(
            VAR Stack       : StackArrayRec;  { in/out }
                Item        : StackData;      { input  }
            VAR Stack_Full : BOOLEAN          { output });
BEGIN
    IF Stack.Height < MAX_ARRAY_STACK THEN BEGIN
        WITH Stack DO BEGIN
            INC(Height);
            Member[Height] := Item
        END;
        Stack_Full := FALSE;
    END
    ELSE Stack_Full := TRUE;
END; { Push_ArStk }

{------------------------------------------------------ Pop_ArStk ------}

PROCEDURE Pop_ArStk(
            VAR Stack       : StackArrayRec;  { in/out }
            VAR Item        : StackData;      { output }
            VAR Empty_Stack : BOOLEAN         { output });
BEGIN
    IF Stack.Height > 0 THEN BEGIN
        WITH STack DO BEGIN
            Item := Member[Height];
            DEC(Height);
        END;
        Empty_Stack := FALSE;
    END
    ELSE Empty_Stack := TRUE;
END; { Pop_ArStk }

{------------------------------------------------------ Clear_ArStk ------}

PROCEDURE Clear_ArStk(VAR Stack : StackArrayRec { in/out });
BEGIN
    Stack.Height := 0;
END; { Clear_ArStk }

{------------------------------------------------------ Swap_ArStk ------}

PROCEDURE Swap_ArStk(VAR Stack : StackArrayRec { in/out });
```

```
VAR tempo : StackData;
BEGIN
    WITH Stack DO BEGIN
        tempo := Member[Height];
        Member[Height] := Member[Height-1];
        Member[Height-1] := tempo;
    END; { WITH }
END; { Swap_ArStk }
END.
```

Listing 8.2. Source code for library STACKLST.PAS.

```
UNIT StackLst;
{=====================================================================

           Copyright (c) 1987, 1988    Namir Clement Shammas
    LIBRARY NAME: StackLst
    VERSION: 1.0                                   DATE   8/20/1987
    PURPOSE: Library that implements a stack of complex data using
              a linked list.
    UPDATE HISTORY:

=====================================================================}


{*******************************************************************}
{************************} INTERFACE {*****************************}
{*******************************************************************}

TYPE      StackData = RECORD
               Stack_Element : REAL
          END;
          StackPtr = ^StackRec;
          StackRec = RECORD
              StackData : StackData;
              NextPtr   : StackPtr
          END;
PROCEDURE Push_LsStk(VAR Top_of_Stack : StackPtr; { in/out }
                         Item          : StackData { input });
{- - - - - - - - - - - - - - - - - - - - - - - - - - - - - - - -

ROUTINE PURPOSE: pushes Item in list-based stack.
PARAMETERS:
  INPUT: Item - data pushed onto the top of the stack.
  IN/OUT: Top_of_Stack - the altered stack array.

- - - - - - - - - - - - - - - - - - - - - - - - - - - - - - - }
PROCEDURE Pop_LsStk(VAR Top_of_Stack : StackPtr;   { in/out }
                        VAR Item          : StackData; { in/out }
                        VAR Empty_Stack   : BOOLEAN    { output });
```

```
{- - - - - - - - - - - - - - - - - - - - - - - - - - - - - - - - - -

ROUTINE PURPOSE:  to return (and remove) the topmost stack element.
If the stack is empty, the boolean Empty_Stack is set to true.
Use this flag to test the status of the stack before attempting to
access the data in argument Item.
PARAMETERS:
   OUTPUT: Item - data popped from the top of the stack.
           Empty-Stack - flag used to indicate whether or not an attempt
               was made to pop an empty stack.
   IN/OUT: Top_of_Stack - the list-based stack.
           HANDLING BAD ARGUMENTS:  If the stack is empty and this routine
is
called, the Empty_Stack is set to TRUE.

- - - - - - - - - - - - - - - - - - - - - - - - - - - - - - - - - - }
PROCEDURE Clear_LsStk(VAR Top_of_Stack : StackPtr { in/out });
{- - - - - - - - - - - - - - - - - - - - - - - - - - - - - - - - -

ROUTINE PURPOSE: deletes the list of elements forming the stack.
PARAMETERS:
   IN/OUT: Top_of_Stack - cleared stack.

- - - - - - - - - - - - - - - - - - - - - - - - - - - - - - - - - - }
PROCEDURE Swap_LsStk(VAR Top_of_Stack : StackPtr { in/out });
{- - - - - - - - - - - - - - - - - - - - - - - - - - - - - - - - -

ROUTINE PURPOSE: swaps the two topmost stack elements.
PARAMETERS:
   IN/OUT: Top_of_Stack - the list-based stack.

- - - - - - - - - - - - - - - - - - - - - - - - - - - - - - - - - - }

{*****************************************************************}
{***********************} IMPLEMENTATION {***********************}
{*****************************************************************}

{-------------------------------------------------- Push_LsStk ------}

PROCEDURE Push_LsStk(VAR Top_of_Stack : StackPtr; { in/out }
                         Item          : StackData { input });
VAR ptr : StackPtr;
BEGIN
    NEW(ptr);
    ptr^.StackData := Item;
    ptr^.NextPtr := Top_of_Stack;
    Top_of_Stack := ptr; { point to new element as the top of the stack }
END; { Push_LsStk }
```

```
{----------------------------------------------------- Pop_LsStk -----}

PROCEDURE Pop_LsStk(VAR Top_of_Stack : StackPtr;   { in/out }
                    VAR Item          : StackData; { in/out }
                    VAR Empty_Stack  : BOOLEAN    { output });
VAR ptr : StackPtr;
BEGIN
    IF Top_of_Stack <> NIL THEN BEGIN
        Empty_Stack := FALSE;
        Item := Top_of_Stack^.StackData;
        ptr := Top_of_Stack;
        Top_of_Stack := Top_of_Stack^.NextPtr;
        Dispose(ptr)
    END
    ELSE Empty_Stack := TRUE;
END; { Pop_LsStk }


{------------------------------------------------- Clear_LsStk -----}

PROCEDURE Clear_LsStk(VAR Top_of_Stack : StackPtr { in/out });
VAR done : BOOLEAN;
    dummy : StackData;
BEGIN
    REPEAT
        Pop_LsStk(Top_of_Stack, dummy, done);
    UNTIL done;
END; { Clear_LsStk }


{------------------------------------------------- Swap_LsStk -----}

PROCEDURE Swap_LsStk(VAR Top_of_Stack : StackPtr { in/out });
VAR ptr : StackPtr;
    x, y : StackData;
BEGIN
    { pointer to the second topmost stack element }
    ptr := Top_of_Stack^.NextPtr;
    x := Top_of_Stack^.StackData;
    y := ptr^.StackData;
    Top_of_Stack^.StackData := y;
    ptr^.StackData := x
END; { Swap_LsStk }
END.
```

Listing 8.3. Source code for library CMPLXLIB.PAS.

```
UNIT CmplxLib;
{=====================================================================

            Copyright (c) 1987, 1988   Namir Clement Shammas
      LIBRARY NAME: CmplxLib
      VERSION: 1.0                               DATE 10/19/1987
      PURPOSE: A nucleus library for complex math routines.

      UPDATE HISTORY:

  =====================================================================}

{*********************************************************************}
{***************************} INTERFACE {****************************}
{*********************************************************************}

Uses DataLib0;
PROCEDURE Add_Complex(VAR Result : Complex; { output }
                          First,              { input  }
                          Second : Complex  { input  });
{- - - - - - - - - - - - - - - - - - - - - - - - - - - - - - - -

ROUTINE PURPOSE: adds two complex numbers:
                 Result = First + Second
PARAMETERS:
  INPUT: First - the first complex number.
         Second - the second complex number.
  OUTPUT: Result - the resulting complex number.

                     ROUTINE DEPENDENCIES
                     --------------------

        Identifier Name          Identifier Type      Source Library
        ---------------          ---------------      --------------

          Complex                    record              DataLib0

- - - - - - - - - - - - - - - - - - - - - - - - - - - - - - - - - }
PROCEDURE Sub_Complex(VAR Result : Complex; { output }
                          First,              { input  }
                          Second : Complex  { input  });
{- - - - - - - - - - - - - - - - - - - - - - - - - - - - - - - -

ROUTINE PURPOSE: subtracts two complex numbers:
                 Result = First - Second
PARAMETERS:
  INPUT: First - the first complex number.
         Second - the second complex number.
  OUTPUT: Result - the resulting complex number.
```

```
                    ROUTINE DEPENDENCIES
                    --------------------
      Identifier Name          Identifier Type      Source Library
      ---------------          ---------------      --------------
        Complex                    record             DataLib0

- - - - - - - - - - - - - - - - - - - - - - - - - - - - - - - - }
PROCEDURE Mul_Complex(VAR Result : Complex; { output }
                          First,            { input  }
                          Second : Complex  { input  });
{- - - - - - - - - - - - - - - - - - - - - - - - - - - - - - - -
```

ROUTINE PURPOSE: multiplies divides two complex numbers:
                Result = First * Second
PARAMETERS:
  INPUT: First - the first complex number.
         Second - the second complex number.
  OUTPUT: Result - the resulting complex number.

```
                    ROUTINE DEPENDENCIES
                    --------------------
      Identifier Name          Identifier Type      Source Library
      ---------------          ---------------      --------------
        Complex                    record             DataLib0

- - - - - - - - - - - - - - - - - - - - - - - - - - - - - - - - }
PROCEDURE Div_Complex(VAR Result : Complex; { output }
                          First,            { input  }
                          Second : Complex; { input  }
                          OK     : BOOLEAN  { output });
{- - - - - - - - - - - - - - - - - - - - - - - - - - - - - - - -
```

ROUTINE PURPOSE: divides two complex numbers:
                Result = First / Second
PARAMETERS:
  INPUT: First - the first complex number.
         Second - the second complex number.
  OUTPUT: Result - the resulting complex number.
          OK - flag to signal division-by-zero error.
HANDLING BAD ARGUMENTS: when the Second complex number has both
components equal to zero, the OK flag is set to FALSE.

```
                    ROUTINE DEPENDENCIES
                    --------------------
      Identifier Name          Identifier Type      Source Library
      ---------------          ---------------      --------------
        Complex                    record             DataLib0
```

```
- - - - - - - - - - - - - - - - - - - - - - - - - - - - - - - - - - - - - }

{*******************************************************************}
{***********************} IMPLEMENTATION {*************************}
{*******************************************************************}

{-------------------------------------------------- Add_Complex ------}

PROCEDURE Add_Complex(VAR Result : Complex; { output }
                          First,           { input  }
                          Second : Complex { input  });
BEGIN
    Result.Treal := First.Treal + Second.Treal;
    Result.Timag := First.Timag + Second.Timag
END; { Add_Complex }

{-------------------------------------------------- Sub_Complex ------}

PROCEDURE Sub_Complex(VAR Result : Complex; { output }
                          First,           { input  }
                          Second : Complex { input  });
BEGIN
    Result.Treal := First.Treal - Second.Treal;
    Result.Timag := First.Timag - Second.Timag
END; { Sub_Complex }

{-------------------------------------------------- Mul_Complex ------}

PROCEDURE Mul_Complex(VAR Result : Complex; { output }
                          First,           { input  }
                          Second : Complex { input  });
BEGIN
    Result.Treal := First.Treal * Second.Treal -
                    First.Timag * Second.Timag;
    Result.Timag := First.Treal * Second.Timag +
                    First.Timag * Second.Treal
END; { Mul_Complex }

{-------------------------------------------------- Div_Complex ------}

PROCEDURE Div_Complex(VAR Result : Complex;  { output }
                          First,            { input  }
                          Second : Complex; { input  }
                          OK     : BOOLEAN  { output });
VAR sumsqr : REAL;
BEGIN
    sumsqr := SQR(Second.Treal) + SQR(Second.Timag);
    IF sumsqr > 0.0 THEN BEGIN
        Result.Treal := (First.Treal * Second.Treal +
                         First.Timag * Second.Timag) / sumsqr;
```

```
        Result.Timag := (Second.Treal * First.Timag -
                          First.Treal * Second.Timag) / sumsqr;
        OK := TRUE
      END
      ELSE OK := FALSE;
END; { Div_Complex }
END.
```

Listing 8.4. Source code for application RPNCALC.PAS.

```
PROGRAM RPN_Calculator;

{
    library name              general type of import
    _____               _____

}
Uses CRT,
     DataLib0,      { Complex record structure }
     PCScreen,      { low level screen I/O required by Screen0 }
     Screen0,       { fast screen output of reals and strings }
     StackArr,      { stack manipulation routines }
     CmplxLib,      { basic complex math routines }
     NumInput;      { error-proof numeric input }

{$V-}

{=====================================================================

                    PROGRAM  RPN_Calculator
version 1.0                                              10/19/87
            Copyright (c) 1988,  Namir Clement Shammas

This program demonstrates the use of the stack array library. An RPN
calculator is constructed using the stack library. The calculator
works in both real and complex modes. The user is able to toggle from
one mode to the other. The program supports:
    1) Basic math operations.
    2) Clearing the stack.
    3) Entering real or complex numbers.
    4) Popping the stack.
    5) Pushing the stack.
    6) Swapping the two topmost stack elements.
    7) Toggling between complex and real numeric modes.
Out of the 100 stack registers, only the top four are visible.

======================================================================}
```

```
CONST DEFAULT_INITIAL_MODE = FALSE; { real-mode }
VAR StackReg : StackArrayRec;
    Complex_Mode : BOOLEAN;


{------------------------------------------------- Draw_Single_Box ------}


PROCEDURE Draw_Single_Box(Upper_LeftX,            { input }
                          Upper_LeftY,            { input }
                          Lower_RightX,           { input }
                          Lower_RightY : BYTE { input });


{- - - - - - - - - - - - - - - - - - - - - - - - - - - - - - - - - - - -


ROUTINE PURPOSE: draws a single-line framed rectangular box.
PARAMETERS:
   INPUT: Upper_LeftX  - X coordinate for upper left corner of the box.
          Upper_LeftY  - Y coordinate for upper left corner of the box.
          Lower_RightX - X coordinate for lower right corner of the box.
          Lower_RightX - Y coordinate for lower right corner of the box.

HANDLING BAD ARGUMENTS: for fast display, no checking is done on the
coordinate values.

                        ROUTINE DEPENDENCIES
                        --------------------

         Identifier Name          Identifier Type       Source Library
         ---------------          ---------------       --------------
            DirectVideo               boolean              CRT
            GotoXY                    procedure            CRT

- - - - - - - - - - - - - - - - - - - - - - - - - - - - - - - - - - - - }

VAR i : BYTE;
BEGIN
    DirectVideo := TRUE;
    GotoXY(Upper_LeftX,Upper_LeftY);
    WRITE(CHR(218)); { upper left corner }
    GotoXY(Lower_RightX,Lower_RightY);
    WRITE(CHR(217)); { lower right corner }
    GotoXY(Upper_LeftX,Lower_RightY);
    WRITE(CHR(192)); { lower left corner }
    GotoXY(Lower_RightX,Upper_LeftY);
    WRITE(CHR(191)); { upper right corner }
    { display vertical edges }
    FOR i := Upper_LeftY+1 TO Lower_RightY-1 DO BEGIN
        GotoXY(Upper_LeftX,i); WRITE(CHR(179));
        GotoXY(Lower_RightX,i); WRITE(CHR(179));
    END; { FOR }
    { display horizontal edges }
    FOR i := Upper_LeftX+1 TO Lower_RightX-1 DO BEGIN
```

```
        GotoXY(i, Upper_LeftY); WRITE(CHR(196));
        GotoXY(i, Lower_RightY); WRITE(CHR(196));
    END; { FOR }
END; { Draw_Single_Box }

{------------------------------------------------------ VideoDisp ------}

PROCEDURE VideoDisp(Strng : STRING80 { input  });
{- - - - - - - - - - - - - - - - - - - - - - - - - - - - - - -
```

ROUTINE PURPOSE: displays the first character of the string in high
intensity video and then use normal video intensity to display the rest
of the string.
PARAMETERS:
  INPUT: Strng – string displayed.
HANDLING BAD ARGUMENTS: if string is null, the routine is exited.

                          ROUTINE DEPENDENCIES

Identifier Name	Identifier Type	Source Library
HighVideo	procedure	CRT
NormVideo	procedure	CRT
STRING80	string	DataLib0

```
- - - - - - - - - - - - - - - - - - - - - - - - - - - - - - - }

BEGIN
    IF Strng = '' THEN EXIT;
    HighVideo;
    WRITE(Strng[1]);
    NormVideo;
    Delete(Strng, 1, 1);
    IF Strng <> '' THEN WRITELN(Strng);
END; { VideoDisp }

{---------------------------------------------------- Init_Screen ------}

PROCEDURE Init_Screen;
{- - - - - - - - - - - - - - - - - - - - - - - - - - - - - - -
```

ROUTINE PURPOSE: performs the following initialization processes:
    1) Zeroes the contents of the stack registers.
    2) Displays the registers.
    3) Displays the option menus and input prompt.

```
                         ROUTINE DEPENDENCIES
                         --------------------

         Identifier Name              Identifier Type        Source Library
         ---------------              ---------------        --------------

          ClrScr                        procedure               CRT
          StackArrayRec                 record                  StackArr
          Disp_Real                     procedure               Screen0
          Draw_Single_Box               procedure               local
          GotoXY                        procedure               CRT
          MAX_ARRAY_STACK               constant                StackArr


- - - - - - - - - - - - - - - - - - - - - - - - - - - - - - - - - - - - }
CONST HEADING = 'RPN CALCULATOR DEMO PROGRAM';
VAR i : INTEGER;
BEGIN
    ClrScr;
    Draw_Single_Box(1,1,80,20);
    i := 40 - Length(HEADING) div 2;
    GotoXY(i,2); WRITE(HEADING);
    { initialize array-based stack }
    FOR i := 1 TO MAX_ARRAY_STACK DO BEGIN
        StackReg.Member[i].Treal := 0.0;
        StackReg.Member[i].Timag := 0.0;
    END; { FOR }
    GotoXY(5,4); WRITE('T Register');
    GotoXY(5,6); WRITE('Z Register');
    GotoXY(5,8); WRITE('Y Register');
    GotoXY(5,10); WRITE('X Register');
    FOR i := 1 TO 4 DO BEGIN
        Disp_Real(0.0, 20, (2 + 2*i), 20);
        IF Complex_Mode THEN Disp_Real(0.0, 20, (2 + 2*i), 50);
    END; { FOR }
    GotoXY(5,12);
    WRITE('Math operations -> ');
    HighVideo; WRITE('+ - / *'); NormVideo;
    GotoXY(5,13); VideoDisp('Quit');
    GotoXY(5,14); VideoDisp('Clear stack');
    GotoXY(5,15); VideoDisp('Push stack');
    GotoXY(5,16); WRITE('p'); VideoDisp('Op stack');
    GotoXY(5,17); VideoDisp('Toggle calculator mode ');
    GotoXY(5,18); VideoDisp('Enter a number');
    GotoXY(5,19); VideoDisp('Swap X and Y registers');
END; { Init_Screen }


{------------------------------------------------------- Update_Regs ----}

PROCEDURE Update_Regs;
{- - - - - - - - - - - - - - - - - - - - - - - - - - - - - - - - - - - -

ROUTINE PURPOSE: updates the displayed stack register of the calculator.
```

```
                    ROUTINE DEPENDENCIES
                    --------------------

       Identifier Name          Identifier Type      Source Library
       ---------------          ---------------      --------------
         ClrScr                    procedure           CRT
         GotoXY                    procedure           CRT
         MAX_ARRAY_STACK           constant            StackArr
         StackArrayRec             record              StackArr
         Disp_Real                 procedure           Screen0
         Disp_Str                  procedure           Screen0

- - - - - - - - - - - - - - - - - - - - - - - - - - - - - - - - - - - }

CONST BLANK_STR = `
VAR i, j, high, low : INTEGER;
BEGIN
  WITH StackReg DO BEGIN
    IF Height > 0 THEN BEGIN
      high := Height;
      IF high > 4 THEN low := high - 3
                  ELSE low := 1;
      j := 10;
      IF Complex_Mode THEN BEGIN
        FOR i := high DOWNTO low DO BEGIN
            Disp_Real(Member[i].Treal, 20, j, 20);
            Disp_Real(Member[i].Timag, 20, j, 50);
            DEC(j,2);
        END; { FOR }
        IF high < 4 THEN
            FOR i := 4 - high DOWNTO 1 DO BEGIN
                Disp_Real(0.0, 20, j, 20);
                Disp_Real(0.0, 20, j, 50);
                DEC(j,2);
            END { FOR }
      END
      ELSE BEGIN
        FOR i := high DOWNTO low DO BEGIN
            Disp_Real(Member[i].Treal, 20, j, 20);
            Disp_Str(BLANK_STR, j, 50);
            DEC(j,2);
        END; { FOR }
        IF high < 4 THEN
            FOR i := 4 - high DOWNTO 1 DO BEGIN
                Disp_Real(0.0, 20, j, 20);
                Disp_Str(BLANK_STR, j, 50);
                DEC(j,2);
            END { FOR }
      END { IF Complex_Mode }
    END
```

```
    ELSE BEGIN { Height = 0 }
        j := 4;
        FOR i := 1 TO 4 DO BEGIN
            Disp_Real(0.0, 20, j, 20);
            IF Complex_Mode THEN Disp_Real(0.0, 20, j, 50)
                            ELSE Disp_Str(BLANK_STR, j, 50);
            INC(j,2)
        END; { FOR }
    END; { IF Height > 0 }
 END; { WITH }
END; { Update_Regs }
```

```
{------------------------------------------------------------- Warn ---}

PROCEDURE Warn(Strng : STRING80 { input });
{- - - - - - - - - - - - - - - - - - - - - - - - - - - - - - - - - -
```

ROUTINE PURPOSE: displays a warning message and waits for a key to be
pressed.
PARAMETERS:
  INPUT: Strng - string containing a warning message.
HANDLING BAD ARGUMENTS: the routine aborts if the warning message
is a null string.

ROUTINE DEPENDENCIES

Identifier Name	Identifier Type	Source Library
GotoXY	procedure	CRT
ClrEol	procedure	CRT
ReadKey	function	CRT
STRING80	string	DataLib0

```
- - - - - - - - - - - - - - - - - - - - - - - - - - - - - - - - - - }

VAR akey : CHAR;
BEGIN
    IF Strng = '' THEN EXIT;
    WRITE(^G^G); { three beeps }
    GotoXY(5,24); WRITE(Strng);
    WRITE('.  press any key to continue');
    akey := ReadKey; GotoXY(5,24); ClrEol;
END; { Warn }
```

```
{------------------------------------------------------------- Get_Input ---}

PROCEDURE Get_Input;
{- - - - - - - - - - - - - - - - - - - - - - - - - - - - - - - - - -
```

ROUTINE PURPOSE: to be the main driver for the RPN calculator.

```
                    ROUTINE DEPENDENCIES
                    --------------------

        Identifier Name            Identifier Type        Source Library
        ---------------            ---------------        --------------
            Add_Complex                procedure             CmplxLib
            ClrEol                     procedure             CRT
            Complex                    record                DataLib0
            StackArrayRec              record                StackArr
            Div_Complex                procedure             CmplxLib
            GotoXY                     procedure             CRT
            MAX_ARRAY_STACK            constant              StackArr
            Mul_Complex                procedure             CmplxLib
            Pop_ArStk                  procedure             StackArr
            Push_ArStk                 procedure             StackArr
            ReadKey                    function              CRT
            Read_Real                  procedure             NumInput
            Sub_Complex                procedure             CmplxLib
            Swap_ArStk                 procedure             StackArr
            Update_Regs                procedure             local
            Warn                       procedure             local

- - - - - - - - - - - - - - - - - - - - - - - - - - - - - - - - }


VAR stop, ok, is_full, is_empty : BOOLEAN;
    akey, opchar : CHAR;
    i : INTEGER;
    xnum, ynum, result : Complex;
BEGIN
    stop := FALSE;
    REPEAT
        GotoXY(5,21); ClrEol;
        GotoXY(5,21); WRITE('Command >');
        opchar := ReadKey; WRITE(opchar);
        opchar := Upcase(opchar);
        CASE opchar OF
            'Q' : BEGIN { Quit }
                    REPEAT
                      GotoXY(5,22); ClrEol;
                      WRITE('Are you sure you want to exit ? (Y/N) ');
                      akey := Upcase(ReadKey);
                    UNTIL akey IN ['Y','N'];
                    IF akey = 'Y' THEN stop := TRUE;
                    GotoXY(5,22); ClrEol;
                  END;
            'C' : BEGIN { Clear stack }
                    WITH StackReg DO BEGIN
                      FOR i := 1 TO MAX_ARRAY_STACK DO BEGIN
                        Member[i].Treal := 0.0;
                        Member[i].Timag := 0.0;
                      END; { FOR }
```

```pascal
                  Height := 0;
               END; { WITH }
            END;
   'P' : BEGIN { Push stack }
            WITH StackReg DO
               Push_ArStk(StackReg, Member[Height], is_full);
            IF is_full THEN Warn('WARNING! STACK IS FULL');
         END;
   'O' : BEGIN { Pop stack }
            Pop_ArStk(StackReg, xnum, is_empty);
            { note: xnum is not examined }
            IF is_empty THEN Warn('WARNING! STACK IS EMPTY');
         END;
   'T' : Complex_Mode := NOT Complex_Mode; {toggle mode }
   'S' : BEGIN { Swap X and Y registers }
            IF StackReg.Height > 1
               THEN Swap_ArStk(StackReg)
               ELSE Warn('WARNING! CANNOT SWAP STACK ELEMENTS');
         END;
   'E' : BEGIN { Enter a number }
            GotoXY(5,22);
            IF Complex_Mode THEN BEGIN
               WRITE('Enter real part of complex number : ');
               Read_Real(xnum.Treal);
               GotoXY(5,23);
               WRITE('Enter imaginary part : ');
               Read_Real(xnum.Timag);
               GotoXY(5,23); ClrEol;
            END
            ELSE BEGIN
               WRITE('Enter a number : ');
               Read_Real(xnum.Treal);
               xnum.Timag := 0.0;
            END; { IF }
            Push_ArStk(StackReg, xnum, is_full);
            IF is_full THEN BEGIN
               WRITE(^G^G^G); { three beeps }
               GotoXY(5,24); WRITE('WARNING! STACK IS FULL.');
               WRITE('press any key to continue');
               akey := ReadKey;
               GotoXY(5,24); ClrEol;
            END; { IF }
            GotoXY(5,22); ClrEol;
         END;
   '+' : BEGIN
            Pop_ArStk(StackReg, xnum, is_empty);
            IF NOT is_Empty THEN BEGIN
              Pop_ArStk(StackReg, ynum, is_empty);
              IF NOT is_Empty THEN BEGIN
                Add_Complex(result, ynum, xnum);
```

```
                  Push_ArStk(StackReg, result, is_full);
                END
              ELSE BEGIN { restore popped x register }
                Push_ArStk(StackReg, xnum, is_full);
                Warn('WARNING! STACK HAS 1 ELEMENT');
              END { IF }
            END
            ELSE Warn('WARNING! STACK IS EMPTY');;
          END; { IF }
    '-' : BEGIN
            Pop_ArStk(StackReg, xnum, is_empty);
            IF NOT is_Empty THEN BEGIN
              Pop_ArStk(StackReg, ynum, is_empty);
              IF NOT is_Empty THEN BEGIN
                Sub_Complex(result, ynum, xnum);
                Push_ArStk(StackReg, result, is_full);
              END
              ELSE BEGIN { restore popped x register }
                Push_ArStk(StackReg, xnum, is_full);
                Warn('WARNING! STACK HAS 1 ELEMENT');
              END { IF }
            END
            ELSE Warn('WARNING! STACK IS EMPTY');;
          END;
    '*' : BEGIN
            Pop_ArStk(StackReg, xnum, is_empty);
            IF NOT is_Empty THEN BEGIN
              Pop_ArStk(StackReg, ynum, is_empty);
              IF NOT is_Empty THEN BEGIN
                Mul_Complex(result, ynum, xnum);
                Push_ArStk(StackReg, result, is_full);
              END
              ELSE BEGIN { restore popped x register }
                Push_ArStk(StackReg, xnum, is_full);
                Warn('WARNING! STACK HAS 1 ELEMENT');
              END { IF }
            END
            ELSE Warn('WARNING! STACK IS EMPTY');;
          END;
    '/' : BEGIN
            Pop_ArStk(StackReg, xnum, is_empty);
            IF NOT is_Empty THEN BEGIN
              Pop_ArStk(StackReg, ynum, is_empty);
              IF NOT is_Empty THEN BEGIN
                Div_Complex(result, ynum, xnum, ok);
                IF ok THEN
                  Push_ArStk(StackReg, result, is_full);
              END
              ELSE BEGIN { restore popped x register }
                Push_ArStk(StackReg, xnum, is_full);
```

```
                          Warn('WARNING! STACK HAS 1 ELEMENT');
                    END { IF }
                  END
                  ELSE Warn('WARNING! STACK IS EMPTY');;
                END;
            ELSE WRITE(^G) { beep };
        END; { CASE }
        IF NOT stop THEN Update_Regs;
     UNTIL stop;
     ClrScr;
END; { Get_Input }

BEGIN {─────────── M A I N ───────────}

{- - - - - - - - - - - - - - - - - - - - - - - - - - - - - - -

                    ROUTINE DEPENDENCIES
                    --------------------

        Identifier Name            Identifier Type      Source Library
        ---------------            ---------------      --------------
        Clear_ArStk                procedure            StackArr
        StackArrayRec              record               StackArr
        Get_Input                  procedure            local
        Init_Screen                procedure            local

- - - - - - - - - - - - - - - - - - - - - - - - - - - - - - - - - - - }

     { calculator wakes up in real-mode }
     Complex_Mode := DEFAULT_INITIAL_MODE;
     Clear_ArStk(StackReg);
     Init_Screen;
     Get_Input;
END.
```

9

Linked Lists

In this chapter, I will present libraries for singly-linked, doubly-linked, circular, clustered, and LISP-like lists. Three libraries are offered to implement these list structures; they are as follows:

1. Library LIST.PAS offers routines to manage lists with either single or double links. It also offers a routine to search through a singly-linked list while treating it as a circular list.

2. Library CLIST.PAS supports a special type of linked list, called Clustered Lists. They enhance the search performed on an ordinary list.

3. Library LISPLIST.PAS offers routines that support a two-way conversion between string images of LISP expressions and their repٖ esenta-tion by linked lists.

LIBRARY LISP.PAS

Lists are very important data structures. The other data structure closest to a list is the array. While arrays can be used to implement lists, dynamically allocated records are building blocks used most of the time. The list structure consists of data elements linked by pointers. Lists are basically singly- or doubly-linked. A singly-linked list has each data element employ one pointer to link up with the **next** neighbor (see Figure 9.1a). A doubly linked list has each data element utilize two pointers to link with the **previous** and the **next** neighbors (see Figure 9.1b). Consequently, you can traverse a singly-linked list from the front end to the tail end only. By contrast, a doubly-linked list offers superior flexibility in navigating through the list: you not only can traverse the list from either end, you can also reverse your traversal direction as many times as needed.

A popular variation of the singly-linked list is the circular list. The main characteristic of a circular list is the ability to **wrap-around** the list once you reach the tail end.

Library LISP.PAS, shown in Listing 9.1, contains the routines for the singly-linked, doubly-linked, and circular lists. The library contains routines to maintain ordered and unordered singly-linked and doubly-linked lists. Ordered lists are more efficient in searching, since you do not have to look up every list element. However, some applications need to maintain list elements in chrono-logical entry order.

The list structures declared in this library are as follows:

```
CONST MAX_ARRAY_LIST = 100;
TYPE ListKeyStr = STRING[80];
     { record used by singly-linked and doubly-linked lists }
     ListInfoRec = RECORD
         ListKey : ListKeyStr
         { other fields here }
     END;
     { singly-linked lists data types }
     SListPtr = ^SListRec;
     SListRec = RECORD
         ListInfo    : ListInfoRec;
         NextListPtr : SListPtr
     END;
     { doubly-linked lists data types }
     DListPtr = ^DListRec;
     DListRec = RECORD
         ListInfo    : ListInfoRec;
         NextListPtr,
         PrevListPtr : DListPtr
     END;
     ListArrayType = ARRAY [1..MAX_ARRAY_LIST] OF ListInfoRec;
```

Each type of list structure uses the **ListInfo** record type to store various types of linked data. The minimum component for **ListInfo** is the key field. I have chosen to make the key field a string, but you may change it to any other simple data type. The **ListArrayType** is used for a two-way conversion between linked lists and arrays.

The LIST.PAS performs a number of list-related tasks. They may be classified into three categories, depending on the type of list tackled. I will focus on the algorithms involved in list manipulation, since they are not obvious to many.

The library routines for singly-linked lists are as follows:

```
PROCEDURE Init_SList(VAR Head : SListPtr { output });
```

initializes the head of the list pointer of any new singly-linked list. The pointer is merely assigned a NIL value.

Figure 9.1a. Singly-linked list.

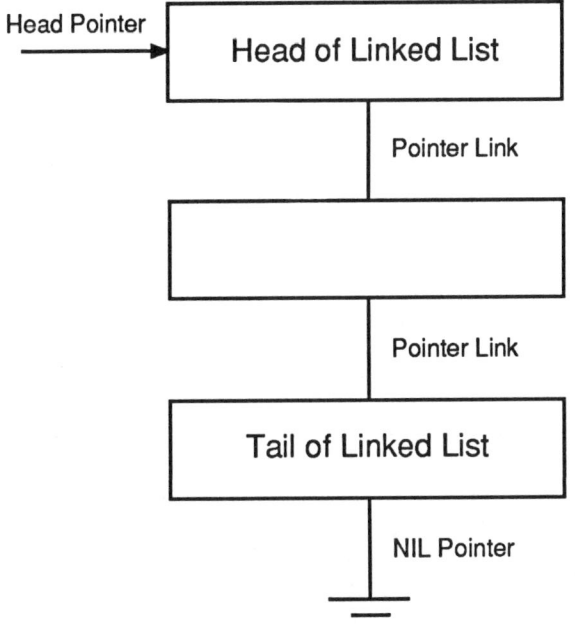

Figure 9.1b. Doubly-linked list.

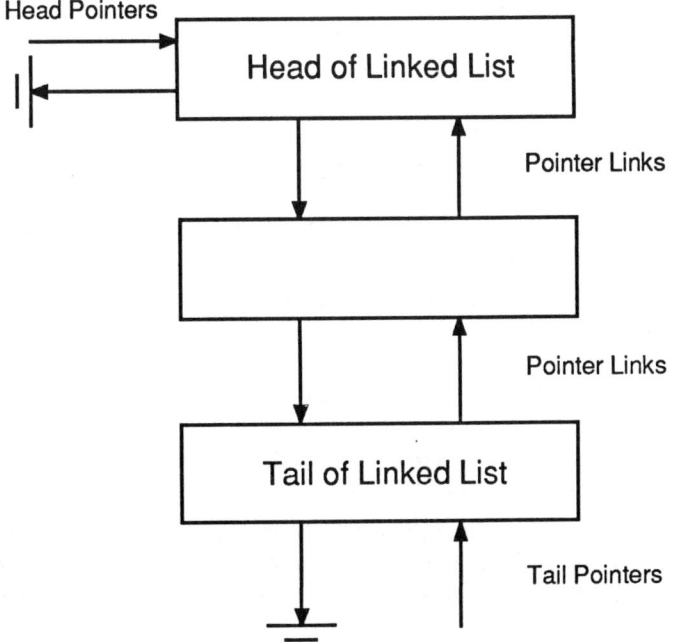

```
PROCEDURE Clear_SList(VAR Head : SListPtr { in/out });
```

clears any existing singly-linked list by dynamically deallocating the memory space of each list element.

```
PROCEDURE Search_SList(VAR Head,                      { input  }
                           ThisPtr,                   { output }
                           LastPtr    : SListPtr;      { output }
                           Search_Key : ListKeyStr;    { input  }
                           Found      : BOOLEAN        { output });
```

searches for **Search_Key** in the unordered list with **Head** as the pointer to its head. The current and previous pointers are also returned in the argument list. The basic search algorithm is as follows:

1. Initialize the **LastPtr** with NIL, **ThisPtr** with the head of the list pointer, and the search-success flag with FALSE.

2. Loop as long as **ThisPtr** points to a meaningful address, and as long as the search has not succeeded. Within the loop, compare the search key with the key field of the list element pointed to by **ThisPtr**. If the comparison is successful, set the search-success flag to TRUE. Otherwise, first copy **ThisPtr** onto **LastPtr**, and then assign **ThisPtr** the pointer of the next list element.

```
PROCEDURE Search_Sorted_SList(
             VAR Head,                      { input  }
                 ThisPtr,                   { output }
                 LastPtr    : SListPtr;      { output }
                 Search_Key : ListKeyStr;    { input  }
                 Found      : BOOLEAN        { output });
```

searches for **Search_Key** in the sorted list with **Head** as the pointer to its head. The current and previous pointers are returned in the argument lists. The basic search algorithm is as follows:

1. Initialize the **LastPtr** with NIL, **ThisPtr** with the head of the list pointer, and the search-success flag with FALSE.

2. Loop as long as **ThisPtr** points to a meaningful address, and as long as the search has not succeeded. Within the loop, test to determine if the search key is greater than the key field of the list element pointed to by **ThisPtr**. If the test is successful, set the search-success flag to TRUE (this actually means that the sought element may be in the list); otherwise, first copy **ThisPtr** onto **LastPtr**, and then assign **ThisPtr** the pointer of the next list element.

3. Outside the above loop, test whether or not search key actually equals the key field of the element pointed by **ThisPtr**. This test should be carried out only if the search-success flag has a TRUE value.

```
PROCEDURE Insert_SList(VAR Head : SListPtr;    { in/out }
                           Item : ListInfoRec { input  });
```

performs a simple list insertion where the added datum is appended at the end. The task of inserting a new element is divided into three steps: pointer initialization, list traversal, and dynamically allocating memory space for the inserted element. The following schematic shows the pointer values during each step. Remember that assignments for the **LastPtr** are made before those for **ThisPtr**:

Action	LastPtr	ThisPtr
initialization	NIL	Head
list traversal	ThisPtr	ThisPtr^.Next
(while ThisPtr <> NIL)		
new element creation	not changed	not changed
	->Next = ThisPtr	->Next = NIL

(Note: the -> indicates a pointer reference to a field.)

```
PROCEDURE Insert_Sorted_SList(VAR Head : SListPtr;    { in/out }
                                  Item : ListInfoRec { input  });
```

performs ordered list insertion. The insertion of different elements with the same keys is prohibited. The steps involved are different from those of an unordered list. The first step involves searching for the location where the new datum is inserted. The outcome of the search may indicate that you are inserting the first list element, or merely adding a new member.

When the first element is inserted, the following schema is used:

Action	LastPtr	ThisPtr	DummyPtr	Head
create	unchanged	unchanged	use with NEW()	unchanged
set	unchanged	unchanged	->Next = Head	DummyPtr
pointers				

When other elements are inserted, the following schema is used:

Action	LastPtr	ThisPtr	DummyPtr
create	unchanged	unchanged	use with NEW()
set	unchanged	unchanged	->Next = LastPtr^.Next
pointers	->Next = DummyPtr	unchanged	unchanged

(Note: the -> indicates a pointer reference to a field.)

```
PROCEDURE Delete_SList (VAR Head       : SListPtr;    { in/out }
                            Search_Key : ListKeyStr;  { input  }
                        VAR Done       : BOOLEAN      { output });
```

attempts to delete an item from an unordered list. The boolean parameter **Done** confirms the deletion process. The first step involved is to search for the deleted element in the list. If the search is successful, the deletion proceeds. Special attention is paid to deleting the head of the list pointer.

```
         Action                    LastPtr          Head
         ------                    -------          ----
store pointer to 2nd element    Head^.Next       unchanged
dispose of head and reset       unchanged        LastPtr


         Action                    LastPtr          ThisPtr
         ------                    -------          -------
store pointer of next element   ThisPtr^.Next    unchanged
dispose of element              unchanged
```

(Note: the -> indicates a pointer reference to a field.)

```
PROCEDURE Delete_Sorted_SList (
          VAR Head : SListPtr;           { in/out }
              Search_Key : ListKeyStr;   { input  }
          VAR Done : BOOLEAN             { output });
```

attempts to delete an item from an ordered list. The boolean parameter **Done** confirms the deletion process. The steps involved are very similar to those for deleting from an unordered list. The only difference is that the routine for searching in an ordered list is invoked.

```
FUNCTION SList_Length (Head : SListPtr { input }) : WORD;
```

returns the size of any singly-linked list. This routine works for both ordered and unordered lists. The function simply traverses the list while keeping count of the number of elements encountered.

```
PROCEDURE SList_to_Array (    Head   : SListPtr;       { input  }
                          VAR XArray : ListArrayType;  { output }
                          VAR NData  : WORD            { output });
```

copies list members to an array. If the list items are kept in an ascending sorted order, the array returned would be in the same order. If there are more list elements than the array's capacity, the extra list elements are ignored.

```
PROCEDURE Array_to_SList (VAR Head   : SListPtr;      { output }
                          VAR XArray : ListArrayType; { input  }
                              NData  : WORD;           { input  }
                              Sorted : BOOLEAN         { input  });
```

copies array members into a list. While the array members need not be sorted,
the list produced can have its elements in ascending sorted order. The **Sorted**
parameter is used to indicate if an ordered array is desired.

The library routines for doubly-linked lists are as follows:

```
PROCEDURE Init_DList (VAR Head, Tail : DListPtr { output });
```

initializes a doubly-linked list. The head and tail pointers are set to NIL.

```
PROCEDURE Clear_DList (VAR Head, Tail : DListPtr { in/out });
```

clears any existing doubly-linked lists. This includes deallocating the dynamic
memory occupied by a list.

```
PROCEDURE Search_DList (VAR Head,                     { input  }
                            ThisPtr    : DListPtr;    { output }
                            Search_Key : ListKeyStr;  { input  }
                            Found      : BOOLEAN      { output });
```

searches for **Search_Key** in the unordered list with **Head** as pointer to the head
of the list. The current pointer is also returned in the argument list. The
algorithm used is identical to that for a singly-linked list. The difference lies in
the fact that a **LastPtr** is not needed, since an element of a doubly-linked list
can refer to its previous neighbor.

```
PROCEDURE Search_Sorted_DList (VAR Head,                     { input  }
                                   ThisPtr    : DListPtr;    { output }
                                   Search_Key : ListKeyStr;  { input  }
                               VAR Found      : BOOLEAN      { output });
```

searches for **Search_Key** in the sorted list with **Head** as the pointer to its head.
The current pointer is returned in the argument list. The algorithm used is very
similar to that for a singly-linked list. The difference lies in the fact that a
LastPtr is not needed, since an element of a doubly-linked list can refer to its
previous neighbor.

```
PROCEDURE Insert_DList (VAR Tail : DListPtr;    { in/out }
                            Item : ListInfoRec { input  });
```

performs simple list insertion. Inserting at the tail of an unordered doubly-
linked list is extremely easy, thanks to the **Tail** pointer. The following pointer
assignment schema is used:

```
          Action                     ThisPtr              Tail
          ------                     -------              ----
set double links               ->Next = NIL          unchanged
                               ->Prev = Tail         unchanged
link last node to new node  Tail->Next = ThisPtr
reset Tail pointer             unchanged             ThisPtr
```

(Note: the -> indicates a pointer reference to a field.)

```
PROCEDURE Insert_Sorted_DList(VAR Head,           { in/out }
                                 Tail : DListPtr;  { in/out }
                                 Item : ListInfoRec { input }));
```

performs ordered list insertion. The insertion of different elements with the same keys is prohibited. This process is more complex than inserting in unordered lists. The new item may be inserted at the new head, at the tail, or anywhere inside the list. In all cases, the routine starts with a list search.

```
    Search_DList(Head, thisptr, Item.ListKey, match);
```

When the new datum is inserted at the tail, the following pointer assignment schema is used:

```
          Action                     ThisPtr              Tail
          ------                     -------              ----
set double links               ->Next = NIL          unchanged
                               ->Prev = Tail         unchanged
link last node to new node  Tail->Next = ThisPtr
reset Tail pointer             unchanged             ThisPtr
```

When the new datum is inserted at the new head, the following pointer assignment schema is used:

```
          Action                     Ptr                  Head
          ------                     ---                  ----
set double links               ->Next = Head         unchanged
                               ->Prev = NIL          unchanged
reset Head pointer             unchanged             Ptr
```

And, when the new datum is inserted inside the list:

```
          Action                     Ptr                  ThisPtr
          ------                     ---                  -------
set double links               ->Next = ThisPtr      unchanged
                               ->Prev = ThisPtr^.Prev unchanged
set Next pointer of            unchanged             ->Prev^.Next = Ptr
  previous neighbor
set Prev pointer of            unchanged             ->Prev = Ptr
  new next neighbor
```

(Note: the -> indicates a pointer reference to a field.)

```
PROCEDURE Delete_DList(VAR Head,                    { in/out }
                           Tail      : DListPtr;    { in/out }
                           Search_Key : ListKeyStr; { input  }
                       VAR Done      : BOOLEAN      { output });
```

attempts to delete an item from an unordered list. The boolean parameter **Done** confirms the deletion process.

```
PROCEDURE Delete_Sorted_DList(VAR Head,                    { in/out }
                                  Tail      : DListPtr;    { in/out }
                                  Search_Key : ListKeyStr; { input  }
                              VAR Done      : BOOLEAN      { output });
```

attempts to delete an item from an ordered list. The boolean parameter **Done** confirms the deletion process. This routine begins by searching the list for the sought element. A successful search is followed by the deletion step. The element removed may be the head, tail, or any element in the list.

When the tail element is deleted, the following pointer assignment schema is used:

```
Action                 Ptr              ThisPtr         Tail
------                 ---              -------         ----
set Ptr links          ThisPtr^.Prev    unchanged       unchanged
                       ->Next = NIL
after disposing
  the Tail element     unchanged        unchanged       Ptr
```

When the head element is deleted, the following pointer assignment schema is used:

```
Action                 Ptr              ThisPtr         Head
------                 ---              -------         ----
set Ptr links          ThisPtr^.Next    unchanged       unchanged
                       ->Prev = NIL
after disposing
  the Head element     unchanged        unchanged       Ptr
```

When any other list element is removed, the links of its previous and next neighbors must first be adjusted, using the following:

```
Action                          ThisPtr
------                          -------
link left and right neighbors
before the element is deleted   ->Prev^.Next = ->Next
                                ->Next^.Prev = ->Prev
```

(Note: the -> indicates a pointer reference to a field.)

```
FUNCTION DList_Length(Head : DListPtr { input }) : WORD;
```

returns the size of any doubly-linked list. This routine works for both ordered and unordered lists. The function simply traverses the list while keeping count of the number of elements encountered.

```
PROCEDURE DList_to_Array(   Head,
                            Tail    : DListPtr;        { input  }
                        VAR XArray  : ListArrayType;   { output }
                        VAR NData   : WORD;            { output }
                            Ascend  : BOOLEAN          { input  });
```

copies list members to an array. If the list items are kept in sorted order, the array returned would also be in order. Since a doubly-linked list may be traversed in either direction, ascending or descending lists may be created. This is indicated using the parameter **Ascend**. If there are more list elements than the array capacity, the extra list elements are ignored.

```
PROCEDURE Array_to_DList(VAR Head,                     { output }
                             Tail    : DListPtr;       { output }
                         VAR XArray  : ListArrayType;  { input  }
                             NData   : WORD;           { input  }
                             Sorted  : BOOLEAN         { input  });
```

copies array members into a list. While the array members need not be sorted, the list produced can have its elements in ascending sorted order. The **Sorted** parameter is used to indicate if an ordered array is desired.

```
PROCEDURE Search_CircList(VAR Head,                    { input  }
                              StartPtr,                { input  }
                              ThisPtr,                 { output }
                              LastPtr     : SListPtr;  { output }
                              Search_Key  : ListKeyStr;{ input  }
                          VAR Found       : BOOLEAN    { output });
```

Searches through an unordered singly-linked list, treating it as a circular list. The search begins at the list element pointed to by **StartPtr**. The last and current list element pointers are returned along with a boolean value for the search outcome.

APPLICATION FOR LIST

I wrote the application EDIR.PAS (see Listing 9.2) that uses singly-linked lists to display files of a DOS directory. The EDIR program is an extended version of the standard DOS DIR command, allowing up to ten filename wildcards. Thus, typing "EDIR *.PAS *.TPU" lists all the files with PAS and

TPU extension names. Similarly, typing "EDIR LI*.PAS ST*.* COMN*.PAS" lists three groups of files: all .PAS with **LI** as the first two letters, all files starting with the letters **ST**, and all .PAS files that start with **COMN**. The output listing of EDIR has the following features:

1. The file directory is listed alphabetically.

2. The size, date, and time stamps of the files are also displayed.

3. Duplicate filenames are detected. Only the first occurrence is included. This may arise from specifying files in different directories.

4. The directory listing is automatically paged.

5. Using EDIR requires that you type in at least one filename wildcard specification; otherwise, simply use the DIR command.

To develop the EDIR.PAS program, I had to make a major design choice in adapting the LIST.PAS library for this application. Handling the file information requires importing the **SearchRec** from the DOS unit. The filename field in the **SearchRec** structure is used as the key for insertion in the list. There are two choices for modifying the **ListInfoRec**:

1. Append a **SearchRec** typed field, as in:

```
ListInfoRec = RECORD
    ListKey : ListKeyStr;
    DirInfo : SearchRec;
END;
```

The above definition causes the filename to be stored twice in the **ListInfoRec**: once as the key field **ListKey,** and the other as a subfield of **DirInfo**.

2. Simply redefine record **ListInfoRec** as **SearchRec,** as shown below:

```
ListInfoRec = SearchRec;
```

The above space-saving definition requires that the **ListKey** identifier be replaced with the **Name** field identified (in record structure **SearchRec**).

I chose to go along with the second design choice. A customized and compact library version, DIRLIST.PAS, is presented in Listing 9.3. This is the version of the linked list library unit used by program EDIR.PAS. Figure 9.2 shows a sample screen image while invoking EDIR from DOS with the "*.PAS *.TPU" command line arguments. The EDIR program writes directly to the video screen to flash the pages of the directory. Figure 9.3 shows the software bus schedule for program EDIR.PAS.

Figure 9.2. Sample screen image of a session with program EDIR.PAS.

Filename	Size	Date	Time
BASECONV.PAS	7915	1987/02/05	20:11:54
CLIST.PAS	10387	1987/02/12	14:32:58
CLIST.TPU	2336	1987/02/12	14:33:02
CMPLXLIB.PAS	5694	1987/02/03	19:26:50
CMPLXLIB.TPU	2432	1987/02/03	19:27:52
COMNLIB0.PAS	2277	1987/02/04	21:57:14
COMNLIB0.TPU	1568	1987/02/05	15:16:12
COMNSTR0.PAS	38554	1987/02/06	18:12:02
COMNSTR0.TPU	7760	1987/02/05	15:16:14
DATALIB0.PAS	1286	1987/02/04	21:05:34
DATALIB0.TPU	768	1987/02/12	14:27:08
DIRLIST.PAS	5645	1987/02/12	11:46:48
DIRLIST.TPU	1328	1987/02/12	14:13:12
DYNSORT1.PAS	3302	1987/02/05	04:38:00
DYNSORT2.PAS	3284	1987/02/05	04:39:42
EDIR.PAS	5186	1987/02/12	14:51:08
EDIR2.PAS	3964	1987/02/12	14:50:38
EDITLINE.PAS	13228	1987/02/04	23:56:36
EDITLINE.TPU	2432	1987/02/05	15:16:10
LISPLIST.PAS	8033	1987/02/10	18:07:54
LISPLIST.TPU	2368	1987/02/10	18:07:58

```
press any key to continue
```

Figure 9.3. The software bus schedule for the EDIR.PAS program.

```
                         SOFTWARE BUS SCHEDULE
PROJECT: EDIR.PAS
MODULE DataLib0
```

	A	Software Bus Schedule B	C	D
OUTPUT				
string STRING20	X			

```
MODULE CRT
```

	A	Software Bus Schedule B	C	D
OUTPUT				
proc ClrScr		X		
boolean DirecVideo		X		
func ReadKey		X		

MODULE DOS

	Software Bus Schedule			
	A	B	C	D
OUTPUT				
record DateTime			X	
integer DosError			X	
proc FindFirst			X	
proc FindNext			X	
record SearchRec			X	
poc UnPackTime			X	

MODULE DirList

	Software Bus Schedule			
	A	B	C	D
OUTPUT				
proc Init_SList				X
proc Insert_Sorted_SList				X
pointer SListPtr				X
INTERFACE INPUT				
record SearchRec		X		

MODULE   main

	Software Bus Schedule			
	A	B	C	D
INPUT				
proc Clear_SList				X
proc ClrScr		X		
record DateTime			X	
boolean DirectVideo		X		
integer DosError			X	
proc FindFirst			X	
proc FindNext			X	
proc Init_SList				X
proc Insert_Sorted_SList				X
func ReadKey		X		
record SearchRec			X	
pointer SListPtr				X
string STRING20	X			
proc UnPackTime			X	

LIBRARY CLIST.PAS

Searching through lists, in general, is a rather slow process. The worst case is an unordered list, since the entire list must be examined. Maintaining sorted lists enables you to determine when to stop, because searching further will certainly not locate the sought element. However, even with a sorted list the search has to **scroll** through the front end of the list. The solution to this problem is perhaps the following: design a list structure (call it the clustered list) where a divide-and-conquer strategy can be applied. Clustered lists are modeled after the fast and slow lanes of a highway. When you are far from your exit, you drive in the faster lane. As you get closer to your exit, you switch over to a slower highway lane. Thus, a clustered list is really a list-of-lists: one main linked list with each element being the head of a secondary level list (see Figure 9.4). Thus, to accelerate the search in the list, two sets of pointers are used: each is equivalent to a highway lane. The first set of pointers, call them the high tracks, enables you to progress quickly in the search by visiting the elements of the main list. As you approach the sought key, the search follows the second set of pointers, call them the low-track pointers. These pointers make the search resume in a secondary level list.

The method proposed above sounds fine, but may leave you asking an important question, "How do we know how **close** we are to a potential target?" Indeed, this technique is rather unusual for classical search algorithms. The answer lies in the fact that we use part or all of the characters in both the search keys and the list element keys to create search values. The difference in the value between the search key and a list element key is compared with a preset constant, the Critical Difference Value (CDV). If the absolute value of the calculated difference is greater than the CDV, the search continues to use the high-track pointers (that is, the search key is still far from its target). By contrast, if the absolute difference is less than the CDV, the lower track pointers are used to search in a secondary list. The value of the CDV is preset by the programmer. A small CDV value results in maintaining data in **higher resolution**. This is equivalent to drawing statistical data using histograms with small widths. The CDV value can be zero, resulting in data stored with maximum resolution.

When the keys of the lists are numeric, they simultaneously become the search values. However, when the keys are string typed, one or more leading characters must be extracted and used to create a search value. For example, using the leading character to create a search value, you may use the following:

```
Search Value := Ord(Strng[1]) - Ord('A');
```

Using the first two leading characters, you may employ the following:

```
Search Value := (Ord(Strng[1]) - Ord('A')) * 100 +
                (Ord(Strng[2]) - Ord('A'))
```

To attain a higher range of values, the LONGINT or REAL types may be used.

The CLIST.PAS library (see Listing 9.4) contains three exported routines to search and insert elements into a list. The third routine converts the ordered clustered list into a sorted array.

The data types declared in this library are as follows:

```
TYPE KeyArray = ARRAY [1..MAX_LIST] OF STRING255;
     CListPtr = ^CListNode;
     CListInfo = RECORD
                    Key : STRING255;
                    { other fields may be placed here }
                 END;

     { Clustered List structure }
     CListNode = RECORD
                    CListData : CListInfo;
                    NextPtr, NextHi : CListPtr;
                 END;
```

where **NextPtr** and **NextHi** are the low- and high-track pointers.
The routines of the library are as follows:

```
PROCEDURE Search_Node (VAR Head       : CListPtr;  { input }
                           SearchData  : STRING255; { input }
                       VAR Found       : BOOLEAN;   { output }
                       VAR LastPtr,                 { output }
                           ThisPtr     : CListPtr   { output });
```

searches for **SearchData** in a clustered list. The basic algorithm is as follows:

1. Initialize the search pointers, the search-success flag, and the high-track flag (set to TRUE).

2. Loop while **ThisPtr** points to a meaningful address, and the search key is greater than the list element key.

   2.1. Assign **ThisPtr** to **LastPtr**.

   2.2. If the high-track pointers are used, calculate the difference between the list and search keys. Test to determine if the absolute value of this difference is greater than the CDV. If the test succeeds, use the next high-track pointer; otherwise, use the pointer for the secondary list, and set the high-track flag to FALSE.

   2.3. If the low-track pointers are used, assign the next pointer to **ThisPtr**.

3. If **ThisPtr** is not NIL, test for the equality of the search and list keys.

```
PROCEDURE Insert_CList (VAR Head     : CListPtr;  { in/out }
                            NewData  : STRING255  { input });
```

inserts a new data string into the clustered list. The new element may be inserted either in the main linked list or in one of the secondary lists. The insertion may follow one of many cases, as indicated by the relative complexity of the routine's code.

```
PROCEDURE CList_to_Array(    Head  : CListPtr; { input  }
                         VAR Keys  : KeyArray;  { output }
                         VAR Count : INTEGER    { output });
```

converts the clustered list into a sorted array. This routine employs two local routines to visit the main list and all of the secondary lists attached to it.

APPLICATION FOR CLIST

I modified the singly-linked application program EDIR.PAS to produce EDIR2.PAS, shown in Listing 9.5. The EDIR2 application produces a sorted list of filenames using one to ten wildcard filename specifications. In a sense, EDIR2 resembles the DOS **dir** command with the **/w** flag: only filenames are displayed.

The decision to make EDIR2.PAS display only the DOS filenames results in the ability to use library CLIST.PAS without any modifications. This is due to the fact that both the filenames and the CLIST keys are strings. Figure 9.5 shows a sample screen image while invoking EDIR2 from DOS with the "*.PAS *.TPU" command line arguments. The EDIR2 program writes directly to the video screen to flash the pages of the directory. Figure 9.6 shows the software bus schedule for program EDIR2.PAS.

Figure 9.4 Clustered list structure.

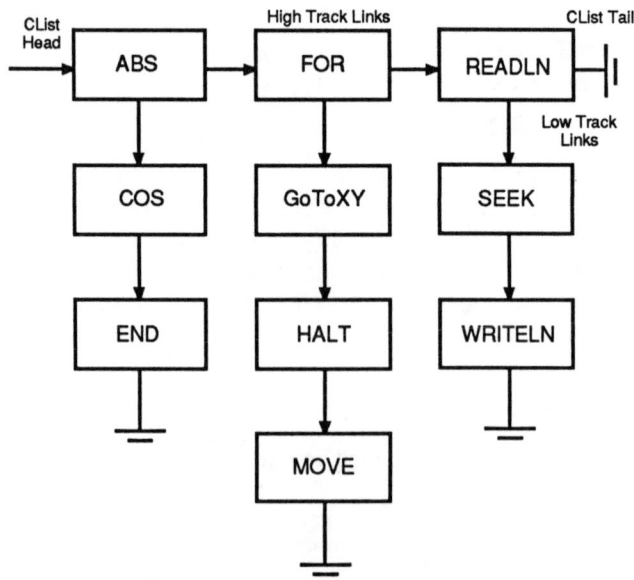

Figure 9.5. Sample screen image of a session with program EDIR2.PAS.

```
BASECONV.PAS CLIST.PAS    CLIST.TPU    CMPLXLIB.PAS CMPLXLIB.TPU
COMNLIB0.PAS COMNLIB0.TPU COMNSTR0.PAS COMNSTR0.TPU DATALIB0.PAS
DATALIB0.TPU DIRLIST.PAS  DIRLIST.TPU  DYNSORT1.PAS DYNSORT2.PAS
EDIR.PAS     EDIR2.PAS    EDITLINE.PAS EDITLINE.TPU LISPLIST.PAS
LISPLIST.TPU LIST.PAS     LIST.TPU     LONGSETS.PAS LONGSETS.TPU
MENUITEM.PAS MENUITEM.TPU MENUPULL.PAS MENUPULL.TPU MINIGREP.PAS
MINIGREP.TPU NONAME.PAS   NUMINPUT.PAS NUMINPUT.TPU PCDOS.PAS
PCINFO.PAS   PCSCREEN.PAS PCSCREEN.TPU RPNCALC.PAS  SCREEN0.PAS
SCREEN0.TPU  SCREEN1.PAS  SCREEN1.TPU  SORT.PAS     SORT.TPU
SPARSMAT.PAS SPARSMAT.TPU STACKARR.PAS STACKARR.TPU STACKLST.PAS
STACKLST.TPU SUPRSTR0.PAS SUPRSTR0.TPU TSTSORT1.PAS TST_LS.PAS
USELISP.PAS  USE_SM.PAS   USE_VM.PAS   VM.PAS       VM.TPU
WORDSTR0.PAS WORDSTR0.TPU

Number of files = 62
```

Figure 9.6. The software bus schedule for the EDIR2.PAS program.

```
                     SOFTWARE BUS SCHEDULE
PROJECT: EDIR2.PAS
MODULE DataLib0
```

	Software Bus Schedule			
	A	B	C	D
OUTPUT				
string STRING20	X			
string STRING255	X			

```
MODULE CRT
```

	Software Bus Schedule			
	A	B	C	D
OUTPUT				
proc ClrScr		X		
boolean DirecVideo		X		
func ReadKey		X		

```
MODULE DOS
```

	Software Bus Schedule			
	A	B	C	D
OUTPUT				
integer DosError			X	
proc FindFirst			X	
proc FindNext			X	
record SearchRec			X	

MODULE CList

		Software Bus Schedule		
	A	B	C	D
OUTPUT				
proc Insert_CList				X
pointer CListPtr				X
INTERFACE INPUT				
string STRING255	X			

MODULE   main

		Software Bus Schedule		
	A	B	C	D
INPUT				
proc ClrScr		X		
boolean DirectVideo		X		
integer DosError			X	
proc FindFirst			X	
proc FindNext			X	
proc Insert_CList				X
func ReadKey		X		
record SearchRec			X	
pointer CListPtr				X
string STRING20	X			

LISPLIST.PAS

LISP is one of the early programming languages and is in the forefront of Artificial Intelligence (AI) languages. The name LISP stands for LISt Processing. As the name suggests, LISP is characterized by its list manipulation features. This includes the ability to tackle deeply nested lists. From a purely data structure standpoint, nested lists are really a misnomer (or an alias, at best), because tree structures are actually used. Lists in LISP are enclosed in parentheses and the individual members are delimited by spaces. For example, (a b c d) is a single-level list with four elements, or atoms, in LISPese. The list (a (b c) d) is a two-level list with three members: the atom **a**, the list (b c), and the atom **d**. A simple graphical representation of the list (a (b c) d) is:

```
a -> d
   |
   b -> c
```

The above representation shows that accessing the nested list (b c) has priority over accessing d. The list ((b c) a d) has the corresponding diagram:

```
a -> d
|
b -> c
```

The list (a d (b c)) is represented by:

```
a -> d -> NIL
         |
         b -> c
```

A more complex example is the list ((a b) c d (e (f g) h) i), which is represented by:

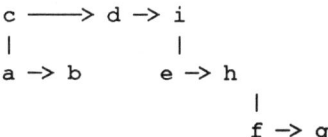

```
c ------> d -> i
|         |
a -> b    e -> h
          |
          f -> g
```

The LISPLIST.PAS library, shown in Listing 9.6, contains only two procedures. They implement a two-way conversion of a LISP expression between a string and a dynamic structure. While implementing a LISP interpreter in Turbo Pascal is possible (especially with version 4.0), the topic requires a separate book.

The data types declared in the LISPLIST.PAS library are as follows:

```
TYPE LispString = STRING[20];

     LispListPtr = ^LispListRec;

     LispListRec = RECORD
         NextListPtr,
         SubListPtr  : LispListPtr;
         AtomName    : LispString
     END;
```

Notice that the **LispListRec** record structure is composed of two pointers and a string-typed field. The first two are used to establish the tree of links between multilevel lists.

The library routines are as follows:

```
PROCEDURE String_to_List(     LStr      : STRING255;   { input  }
                          VAR Head      : LispListPtr; { output }
                          VAR ErrorCode : INTEGER      { output });
```

parses a string to create a LISP list. The names of each element in the list must not exceed the specified limit of 20 characters. The procedure contains a parser for the string **LStr**. The latter is scanned one character at a time. The parser watches for the (,) and space characters. When an open parenthesis is encountered, the current pointer is saved in a stack (implemented using an array) of pointers. Any pending element is saved before scanning proceeds. When a space is encountered the currently scanned element name is saved. To avoid problems with sequences of spaces, a scan-mode flag is used to monitor the state of parsing. The flag indicates whether or not there are any pending elements being scanned. When the close parenthesis is encountered, any pending element name is saved and the pointer from the top of the pointer-stack once more becomes the current pointer.

```
PROCEDURE List_to_String(VAR LStr : STRING255;  { output }
                         VAR Head : LispListPtr { input  });
```

This routine counteracts procedure **String_to_List** . It converts a list structure into a string-based LISP list. The processing of the list structure follows simple guidelines to handle multi-level lists. They are as follows:

1.   If an element has a non-NIL sublist pointer, that pointer is used to access the sublist. The current pointer is pushed onto a stack of pointers.

2.   Accessing the string field of an element occurs when the element has a NIL sublist pointer or has just been popped off the stack of pointers.

Listing 9.7 shows a simple program, USELISP.PAS, that uses the LISPLIST.PAS library. The program simply prompts you to enter a LISP expression, parses it into a network of lists, and then back into a string. The string produced is compared with your input string. Figure 9.7 shows the software bus schedule for the USELISP.PAS program.

Figure 9.7. The software bus schedule for the USELISP.PAS program.

```
                           SOFTWARE  BUS  SCHEDULE
PROJECT: USELISP.PAS


MODULE   DataLib0
                                 Software Bus Schedule
                         A  B  C  D  E  F  G  H  I  J  K  L  M
                         _____
OUTPUT
string STRING255         X
```

```
MODULE LispList
                                    Software Bus Schedule
                          A  B  C  D  E  F  G  H  I  J  K  L  M

OUTPUT                    ───────────────────────────────────
const MAX_LIST_STACK_SIZE    X
pointer LispListPtr          X
record  LispListRec          X
proc String_to_List          X
proc List_to_String          X

INTERFACE INPUT
string STRING255          X


MODULE   CRT
                                    Software Bus Schedule
                          A  B  C  D  E  F  G  H  I  J  K  L  M

OUTPUT                    ───────────────────────────────────
proc ClrScr                  X


MODULE   main
                                    Software Bus Schedule
                          A  B  C  D  E  F  G  H  I  J  K  L  M

INPUT                     ───────────────────────────────────
string STRING255          X
proc ClrScr               X
pointer LispListPtr          X
proc String_to_List          X
proc List_to_String          X
```

Listing 9.1. Source code for library LIST.PAS.

```
UNIT List;
{═══════════════════════════════════════════════════════════════


          Copyright (c) 1987, 1988    Namir Clement Shammas
     LIBRARY NAME: List
     VERSION: 1.0                            DATE 8/21/1987

     PURPOSE: provide routines to handle single and double linked lists.
          Lists may be ordered or unordered. The order/unordered
          lists share a number of routines that are not affected by
          the status of the order.
```

```
    UPDATE HISTORY:


===============================================================}

{*******************************************************************}
{**************************} INTERFACE {****************************}
{*******************************************************************}

CONST MAX_ARRAY_LIST = 100;
TYPE ListKeyStr = STRING[20];
     { record used by singly-linked and doubly-linked lists }
     ListInfoRec = RECORD
         ListKey : ListKeyStr
         { other fields here }
     END;
     { singly-linked lists data types }
     SListPtr = ^SListRec;
     SListRec = RECORD
         ListInfo    : ListInfoRec;
         NextListPtr : SListPtr
     END;
     { doubly-linked lists data types }
     DListPtr = ^DListRec;
     DListRec = RECORD
         ListInfo    : ListInfoRec;
         NextListPtr,
         PrevListPtr : DListPtr
     END;
    ListArrayType = ARRAY [1..MAX_ARRAY_LIST] OF ListInfoRec;


{========================= SINGLY-LINKED LISTS ==================}

PROCEDURE Init_SList(VAR Head : SListPtr { output });
{- - - - - - - - - - - - - - - - - - - - - - - - - - - - - - -

ROUTINE PURPOSE: initializes the head of any new singly-linked list.
PARAMETERS:
  OUTPUT: Head - the pointer to the initialized singly-linked list.

- - - - - - - - - - - - - - - - - - - - - - - - - - - - - - - - }
PROCEDURE Clear_SList(VAR Head : SListPtr { in/out });
{- - - - - - - - - - - - - - - - - - - - - - - - - - - - - - -

ROUTINE PURPOSE: clears any existing singly-linked list.
PARAMETERS:
  IN/OUT: Head - the pointer of cleared singly-linked list.
COMMENTS: Head = NIL when routine ends.

- - - - - - - - - - - - - - - - - - - - - - - - - - - - - - - - }
```

```
PROCEDURE Search_SList(VAR Head,                          { input  }
                           ThisPtr,                       { output }
                           LastPtr    : SListPtr;         { output }
                           Search_Key : ListKeyStr;       { input  }
                       VAR Found      : BOOLEAN           { output });
{- - - - - - - - - - - - - - - - - - - - - - - - - - - - - - - - - -
```

ROUTINE PURPOSE: searches for 'Search_Key' in the unordered list
with 'Head' as the pointer to its head. The current and previous
pointers are also returned in the argument list.
PARAMETERS:
  INPUT: Head - the head of a singly-linked list.
         Search_Key - the sought data element.
  OUTPUT: ThisPtr - the pointer to the sought list element.
          LastPtr - the pointer to the element prior to the sought
               one.
          Found - the logical flag to signal whether or not the search
               is successful.

```
- - - - - - - - - - - - - - - - - - - - - - - - - - - - - - - - - - }
PROCEDURE Search_Sorted_SList(VAR Head,                   { input  }
                                  ThisPtr,                { output }
                                  LastPtr    : SListPtr;  { output }
                                  Search_Key : ListKeyStr; { input  }
                              VAR Found      : BOOLEAN     { output });
{- - - - - - - - - - - - - - - - - - - - - - - - - - - - - - - - - -
```

ROUTINE PURPOSE: searches for 'Search_Key' in the sorted list with
'Head' as the pointer to its head. The current and previous pointers
are returned in the argument lists.
PARAMETERS:
  INPUT: Head - the head of a singly-linked list.
         Search_Key - the sought data element.
  OUTPUT: ThisPtr - the pointer to the sought list element.
          LastPtr - the pointer to the element prior to the sought
               one.
          Found - the logical flag to signal whether or not the search
               is successful.

```
- - - - - - - - - - - - - - - - - - - - - - - - - - - - - - - - - - }
PROCEDURE Insert_SList(VAR Head : SListPtr;    { in/out }
                           Item : ListInfoRec  { input  });

{- - - - - - - - - - - - - - - - - - - - - - - - - - - { - - - - - - -
```

ROUTINE PURPOSE: performs simple list insertion.
PARAMETERS:
  INPUT: Item - the data item in the list.
  IN/OUT: Head - the targeted singly-linked list.

```
- - - - - - - - - - - - - - - - - - - - - - - - - - - - - - - - - - }
```

```
PROCEDURE Insert_Sorted_SList(VAR Head : SListPtr;     { in/out }
                                  Item : ListInfoRec { input  });
{- - - - - - - - - - - - - - - - - - - - - - - - - - - - - - - - - -
```

ROUTINE PURPOSE: performs ordered list insertion.
PARAMETERS:
   INPUT: Item - the data item in the list.
   IN/OUT: Head - the targeted singly-linked list.

ROUTINE DEPENDENCIES

Identifier Name	Identifier Type	Source Library
Search_SList	procedure	local

```
- - - - - - - - - - - - - - - - - - - - - - - - - - - - - - - - - - }
PROCEDURE Delete_SList(VAR Head      : SListPtr;   { in/out }
                           Search_Key : ListKeyStr; { input  }
                           VAR Done   : BOOLEAN     { output });
{- - - - - - - - - - - - - - - - - - - - - - - - - - - - - - - - - -
```

ROUTINE PURPOSE: attempts to delete an item from an unordered list.
The boolean parameter 'Done' confirms the deletion process.
PARAMETERS:
   INPUT: Search_Key - the data element to be deleted from the list.
   OUTPUT: Done - the logical flag returning the success/failure status
           of the deletion process.
   IN/OUT: Head - the targeted singly-linked list.

ROUTINE DEPENDENCIES

Identifier Name	Identifier Type	Source Library
Search_SList	procedure	local

```
- - - - - - - - - - - - - - - - - - - - - - - - - - - - - - - - - - }
PROCEDURE Delete_Sorted_SList(VAR Head : SListPtr;          { in/out }
                                  Search_Key : ListKeyStr; { input  }
                                  VAR Done : BOOLEAN        { output });
{- - - - - - - - - - - - - - - - - - - - - - - - - - - - - - - - - -
```

ROUTINE PURPOSE: attempts to delete an item from an ordered list.
The boolean parameter 'Done' confirms the deletion process.
PARAMETERS:
   INPUT: Search_Key - the data element to be deleted from the list.
   OUTPUT: Done - the logical flag returning the success/failure status
           of the deletion process.
   IN/OUT: Head - the targeted ordered singly-linked list.

ROUTINE DEPENDENCIES

Identifier Name	Identifier Type	Source Library
Search_Sorted_SList	procedure	local

```
- - - - - - - - - - - - - - - - - - - - - - - - - - - - - - - }
FUNCTION SList_Length(Head : SListPtr { input }) : WORD;
{- - - - - - - - - - - - - - - - - - - - - - - - - - - - - - -
```

ROUTINE PURPOSE: returns the size of any singly-linked list.
PARAMETERS:
  INPUT: Head - the head-of-list pointer.
FUNCTION VALUE: the number of elements in a list.

```
- - - - - - - - - - - - - - - - - - - - - - - - - - - - - - - }
PROCEDURE SList_to_Array(    Head   : SListPtr;       { input  }
                         VAR XArray : ListArrayType; { output }
                         VAR NData  : WORD           { output });
{- - - - - - - - - - - - - - - - - - - - - - - - - - - - - - -
```

ROUTINE PURPOSE: copies list members to an array. If the list items
are kept in an ascending sorted order, the array returned would
also be in the same order.
PARAMETERS:
  INPUT: Head - the head-of-list pointer.
  OUTPUT: XArray - the array containing the list members.
          NData - the number of list elements stored in the array.

```
- - - - - - - - - - - - - - - - - - - - - - - - - - - - - - - }
PROCEDURE Array_to_SList(VAR Head   : SListPtr;       { output }
                         VAR XArray : ListArrayType; { input  }
                             NData  : WORD;           { input  }
                             Sorted : BOOLEAN         { input  });
{- - - - - - - - - - - - - - - - - - - - - - - - - - - - - - -
```

ROUTINE PURPOSE: copies array members into a list. While the array
members need not be sorted, the list produced can have its
elements in ascending sorted order.
PARAMETERS:
  INPUT: XArray - the output array.
          NData - the number of elements in the array.
          Sorted - the flag used to signal whether or not the output
          array should be ordered.

  OUTPUT: Head - the head-of-list pointer.

ROUTINE DEPENDENCIES

Identifier Name	Identifier Type	Source Library
Clear_SList	procedure	local
Insert_SList	procedure	local
Insert_Sorted_SList	procedure	local

```
- - - - - - - - - - - - - - - - - - - - - - - - - - - - - - - }
```

`{========================= DOUBLY-LINKED LISTS ==================}`

`PROCEDURE Init_DList(VAR Head, Tail : DListPtr { output });`
```
{- - - - - - - - - - - - - - - - - - - - - - - - - - - - - - -
```

ROUTINE PURPOSE: initializes a doubly-linked list.
PARAMETERS:
  OUTPUT: Head - the pointer for the head-of-list.
          Tail - the pointer for the tail-of-list.

```
- - - - - - - - - - - - - - - - - - - - - - - - - - - - - - - }
```
`PROCEDURE Clear_DList(VAR Head, Tail : DListPtr { in/out });`
```
{- - - - - - - - - - - - - - - - - - - - - - - - - - - - - - -
```

ROUTINE PURPOSE: clears any existing singly-linked list.
PARAMETERS:
  IN/OUT: Head - the head-of-list pointer of cleared doubly-linked
            list.
          Tail - the tail-of-list pointer of cleared doubly-linked
            list.
COMMENTS: The Head and Tail pointers are assigned NIL when the
routine ends.

```
- - - - - - - - - - - - - - - - - - - - - - - - - - - - - - - }
```
```
PROCEDURE Search_DList(VAR Head,                { input  }
                   ThisPtr    : DListPtr;   { output }
                   Search_Key : ListKeyStr; { input  }
              VAR Found       : BOOLEAN     { output });
{- - - - - - - - - - - - - - - - - - - - - - - - - - - - - - -
```

ROUTINE PURPOSE: searches for 'Search_Key' in the unordered list
with 'Head' as the pointer to the head of the list. The current
pointer is also returned in the argument lists.
PARAMETERS:
  INPUT: Head - the head pointer for the doubly-linked list.
         Search_Key - the sought data element.
  OUTPUT: ThisPtr - the pointer to the sought list element.
          Found - the logical flag to signal whether or not the search
            is successful.

```
- - - - - - - - - - - - - - - - - - - - - - - - - - - - - - - }
PROCEDURE Search_Sorted_DList(VAR Head,                { input  }
                              ThisPtr   : DListPtr;   { output }
                              Search_Key : ListKeyStr; { input  }
                              VAR Found   : BOOLEAN     { output });
{- - - - - - - - - - - - - - - - - - - - - - - - - - - - - - -
```

ROUTINE PURPOSE: searches for 'Search_Key' in the sorted list with
'Head' as the pointer to its head. The current pointer is returned
in the argument list.
PARAMETERS:
  INPUT: Head - the head of the singly-linked list.
         Search_Key - the sought data element.
  OUTPUT: ThisPtr - the pointer to the sought list element.
          LastPtr - the pointer to element prior to the sought one.
          Found - the logical flag to signal whether or not the search
                is successful.

```
- - - - - - - - - - - - - - - - - - - - - - - - - - - - - - - }
PROCEDURE Insert_DList(VAR Tail : DListPtr;   { in/out }
                       Item : ListInfoRec { input  });
{- - - - - - - - - - - - - - - - - - - - - - - - - - - - - - -
```

ROUTINE PURPOSE: performs simple list insertion.
PARAMETERS:
  INPUT: Item - the data item in the list.
  IN/OUT: Tail - the tail of the doubly-linked list.

```
- - - - - - - - - - - - - - - - - - - - - - - - - - - - - - - }
PROCEDURE Insert_Sorted_DList(VAR Head,                { in/out }
                              Tail : DListPtr;   { in/out }
                              Item : ListInfoRec { input  });
{- - - - - - - - - - - - - - - - - - - - - - - - - - - - - - -
```

ROUTINE PURPOSE: performs ordered list insertion.
PARAMETERS:
  INPUT: Item - the data item in the list.
  IN/OUT: Head - the head of the doubly-linked list.
          Tail - the tail of the doubly-linked list.

ROUTINE DEPENDENCIES

Identifier Name	Identifier Type	Source Library
Search_DList	procedure	local

```
- - - - - - - - - - - - - - - - - - - - - - - - - - - - - - - }
PROCEDURE Delete_DList(VAR Head,                    { in/out }
                       Tail       : DListPtr;   { in/out }
                       Search_Key : ListKeyStr; { input  }
                       VAR Done   : BOOLEAN     { output });
{- - - - - - - - - - - - - - - - - - - - - - - - - - - - - - -
```

ROUTINE PURPOSE: attempts to delete an item from an unordered list.
The boolean parameter 'Done' confirms the deletion process.
PARAMETERS:
  INPUT: Search_Key - the data element to be deleted from the list.
  OUTPUT: Done - the logical flag returning the success/failure status
          of the deletion process.
  IN/OUT: Head - the head of the doubly-linked list.
        Tail - the tail of the doubly-linked list.

ROUTINE DEPENDENCIES

Identifier Name	Identifier Type	Source Library
Search_DList	procedure	local

```
- - - - - - - - - - - - - - - - - - - - - - - - - - - - - - - - }
PROCEDURE Delete_Sorted_DList (VAR Head,              { in/out }
                                  Tail       : DListPtr;  { in/out }
                                  Search_Key : ListKeyStr; { input  }
                              VAR Done       : BOOLEAN    { output });
{- - - - - - - - - - - - - - - - - - - - - - - - - - - - - - - -
```

ROUTINE PURPOSE: attempts to delete an item from an ordered list.
The boolean parameter 'Done' confirms the deletion process.
PARAMETERS:
  INPUT: Search_Key - the data element to be deleted from the list.
  OUTPUT: Done - the logical flag returning the success/failure status
          of the deletion process.
  IN/OUT: Head - the head of the doubly-linked list.
        Tail - the tail of the doubly-linked list.

ROUTINE DEPENDENCIES

Identifier Name	Identifier Type	Source Library
Search_Sorted_DList	procedure	local

```
- - - - - - - - - - - - - - - - - - - - - - - - - - - - - - }
FUNCTION DList_Length (Head : DListPtr { input }) : WORD;
{- - - - - - - - - - - - - - - - - - - - - - - - - - - - - -
```

ROUTINE PURPOSE: returns the size of any doubly-linked list.
PARAMETERS:
  INPUT: Head - the head-of-list pointer.
FUNCTION VALUE: the number of elements in a list.

```
- - - - - - - - - - - - - - - - - - - - - - - - - - - - - - - - }
PROCEDURE DList_to_Array (    Head,
                             Tail   : DListPtr;    { input  }
                         VAR XArray : ListArrayType; { output }
                         VAR NData  : WORD;         { output }
                             Ascend : BOOLEAN       { input  });
{- - - - - - - - - - - - - - - - - - - - - - - - - - - - - - - -
```

ROUTINE PURPOSE: copies list members to an array. If the list items
are kept in an ascending sorted order, the array returned would
also be in the same order.
PARAMETERS:
  INPUT: Head - the head of the list.
         Tail - the tail of the list.
         Ascend - the flag used to indicate whether or not the array
             is arranged in ascending order.
  OUTPUT: XArray - the array containing the list members.
          NData - the number of list elements stored in the array.

```
- - - - - - - - - - - - - - - - - - - - - - - - - - - - - - - - - - }
PROCEDURE Array_to_DList(VAR Head,                    { output }
                             Tail    : DListPtr;      { output }
                         VAR XArray  : ListArrayType; { input  }
                             NData   : WORD;          { input  }
                             Sorted  : BOOLEAN        { input  });
{- - - - - - - - - - - - - - - - - - - - - - - - - - - - - - - - -
```

ROUTINE PURPOSE: copies array members into a list. While the array
members need not be sorted, the list produced can have its elements
in ascending sorted order.
PARAMETERS:
  INPUT: XArray - the output array.
         NData - the number of elements in the array.
         Sorted - the flag used to signal whether or not the output
             array should be ordered.
  OUTPUT: Head - the head of the list.
          Tail - the tail of the list.

ROUTINE DEPENDENCIES

Identifier Name	Identifier Type	Source Library
Clear_DList	procedure	local
Insert_Sorted_DList	procedure	local

```
- - - - - - - - - - - - - - - - - - - - - - - - - - - - - - - - - - }
PROCEDURE Search_CircList(VAR Head,                   { input  }
                              StartPtr,                { input  }
                              ThisPtr,                 { output }
                              LastPtr    : SListPtr;   { output }
                              Search_Key : ListKeyStr; { input  }
                          VAR Found      : BOOLEAN     { output });
{- - - - - - - - - - - - - - - - - - - - - - - - - - - - - - - - -
```

ROUTINE PURPOSE: searches through an unordered singly-linked list,
treating it as a circular list. The search begins at the list element
pointed to by StartPtr. The last and current list element pointers
are returned along with a boolean search outcome.
PARAMETERS:
  INPUT: Head - the head of the list.
         StartPtr - the starting-point pointer.
         Search_Key - the sought element.

```
    OUTPUT: ThisPtr - the pointer of the matched list element.
            LastPtr - the pointer to the matched element.
            Found - the boolean flag used to indicate success of the
            search.

- - - - - - - - - - - - - - - - - - - - - - - - - - - - - - - - - - - }


{*********************************************************************}
{***********************} IMPLEMENTATION {**************************}
{*********************************************************************}

{-------------------------------------------------- Init_SList -------}

PROCEDURE Init_SList(VAR Head : SListPtr { output });
BEGIN
    Head := NIL
END; { Init_SList }

{-------------------------------------------------- Clear_SList ------}

PROCEDURE Clear_SList(VAR Head : SListPtr { in/out });
VAR Ptr : SListPtr;
BEGIN
    WHILE Head <> NIL DO  BEGIN
        Ptr := Head;
        Head := Head^.NextListPtr;
        Dispose(Ptr)
    END; { WHILE }
END; { Clear_SList }

{-------------------------------------------------- Search_SList -----}

PROCEDURE Search_SList(VAR Head,                     { input  }
                           ThisPtr,                  { output }
                           LastPtr    : SListPtr;    { output }
                           Search_Key : ListKeyStr;  { input  }
                       VAR Found      : BOOLEAN       { output });
BEGIN
    LastPtr := NIL;
    ThisPtr := Head;
    Found := FALSE;
    WHILE (ThisPtr <> NIL) AND (NOT Found) DO
        IF Search_Key <> ThisPtr^.ListInfo.ListKey THEN BEGIN
            LastPtr := ThisPtr;
            ThisPtr := ThisPtr^.NextListPtr
        END
        ELSE Found := TRUE; { found sought element  }
END; { Search_SList }

{-------------------------------------------- Search_Sorted_SList ----}
```

```
PROCEDURE Search_Sorted_SList(VAR Head,                    { input  }
                                  ThisPtr,                 { output }
                                  LastPtr    : SListPtr;   { output }
                                  Search_Key : ListKeyStr; { input  }
                              VAR Found      : BOOLEAN     { output });
BEGIN
    LastPtr := NIL;
    ThisPtr := Head;
    Found := FALSE;
    WHILE (ThisPtr <> NIL) AND (NOT Found) DO
        IF Search_Key > ThisPtr^.ListInfo.ListKey THEN BEGIN
            LastPtr := ThisPtr;
            ThisPtr := ThisPtr^.NextListPtr
        END
        ELSE Found := TRUE; { element might be in the list }
    { confirm suspected match }
    IF Found THEN Found := (Search_Key = ThisPtr^.ListInfo.ListKey);
END; { Search_Sorted_SList }


{---------------------------------------------------- Insert_SList ----}

PROCEDURE Insert_SList(VAR Head : SListPtr;   { in/out }
                           Item : ListInfoRec { input  });
VAR thisptr, lastptr, ptr : SListPtr;
BEGIN
    thisptr := Head;
    lastptr := NIL;
    { traverse to the end of the list }
    WHILE thisptr <> NIL DO BEGIN
        lastptr := thisptr;
        thisptr := thisptr^.NextListPtr
    END;
    NEW(thisptr);
    thisptr^.NextListPtr := NIL; { new node is the new list tail }
    { link back with the 'previous' node }
    lastptr^.NextListPtr := thisptr;
    thisptr^.ListInfo := Item; { assign key and other fields }
END; { Insert_SList }


{---------------------------------------------- Insert_Sorted_SList ----}

PROCEDURE Insert_Sorted_SList(VAR Head : SListPtr;   { in/out }
                                  Item : ListInfoRec { input  });
VAR thisptr, lastptr, ptr : SListPtr;
    match : BOOLEAN;
BEGIN
    Search_Sorted_SList(Head, thisptr, lastptr, Item.ListKey, match);
    { the line below may be commented out to enable multiple
      data items with the same key to be stored in the list }
    IF match THEN EXIT;
```

```
    IF lastptr = NIL THEN BEGIN { new item is the new list head }
        NEW(ptr);
        ptr^.NextListPtr := Head;
        ptr^.ListInfo := Item; { assign key and other fields }
        Head := ptr; { assign new pointer to the head of the list }
    END
    ELSE BEGIN { insert new item inside the list or at its tail }
        NEW(ptr);
        { link ahead with the 'current' node }
        ptr^.NextListPtr := lastptr^.NextListPtr;
        { link back with the 'previous' node }
        lastptr^.NextListPtr := ptr;
        ptr^.ListInfo := Item; { assign key and other fields }
    END;
END; { Insert_Sorted_SList }

{------------------------------------------------- Delete_SList ———}

PROCEDURE Delete_SList(VAR Head       : SListPtr;   { in/out }
                           Search_Key : ListKeyStr; { input  }
                       VAR Done       : BOOLEAN     { output });
VAR thisptr, lastptr : SListPtr;
BEGIN
    { search for item to delete }
    Search_SList(Head, thisptr, lastptr, Search_Key, Done);
    IF Done THEN { found item in list }
        IF lastptr = NIL THEN BEGIN { delete the list head }
            lastptr := Head^.NextListPtr;
            Dispose(Head);
            Head := lastptr;
        END
        ELSE BEGIN
            lastptr^.NextListPtr := thisptr^.NextListPtr;
            Dispose(thisptr);
        END;
END; { Delete_SList }

{---------------------------------------- Delete_Sorted_SList ———}

PROCEDURE Delete_Sorted_SList(VAR Head : SListPtr;       { in/out }
                              Search_Key : ListKeyStr;   { input  }
                              VAR Done : BOOLEAN          { output });
VAR thisptr, lastptr : SListPtr;
BEGIN
    { search for item to delete }
    Search_Sorted_SList(Head, thisptr, lastptr, Search_Key, Done);
    IF Done THEN { found item in list }
        IF lastptr = NIL THEN BEGIN { delete the list head }
            lastptr := Head^.NextListPtr;
            Dispose(Head);
            Head := lastptr;
        END
```

```
              ELSE BEGIN
                  lastptr^.NextListPtr := thisptr^.NextListPtr;
                  Dispose(thisptr);
              END;
END; { Delete_Sorted_SList }


{------------------------------------------------ SList_Length ------}

FUNCTION SList_Length(Head : SListPtr { input }) : WORD;
VAR count : WORD;
BEGIN
    count := 0; { initialize list size }
    WHILE Head <> NIL DO BEGIN
        INC(count);
        Head := Head^.NextListPtr;
    END;
    SList_Length := count { return function value }
END; { SList_Length }


{------------------------------------------------ SList_to_Array ------}

PROCEDURE SList_to_Array(    Head   : SListPtr;       { input  }
                        VAR XArray : ListArrayType; { output }
                        VAR NData  : WORD            { output });
BEGIN
    NData := 0; { initialize the count of returned array members }
    WHILE (Head <> NIL) AND (NData < MAX_ARRAY_LIST) DO BEGIN
        INC(NData);
        XArray[NData] := Head^.ListInfo;
        Head := Head^.NextListPtr
    END; { WHILE }
END; { SList_to_Array }


{------------------------------------------------ Array_to_SList ------}

PROCEDURE Array_to_SList(VAR Head   : SListPtr;       { output }
                        VAR XArray : ListArrayType; { input  }
                            NData  : WORD;           { input  }
                            Sorted : BOOLEAN         { input  });
VAR  i : WORD;
BEGIN
    Clear_SList(Head); { clear list }
    IF Sorted THEN
        FOR i := 1 TO NData DO
            Insert_Sorted_SList(Head, XArray[i])
    ELSE
        FOR i := 1 TO NData DO
            Insert_SList(Head, XArray[i]);
END; { Array_to_SList }
```

```
{========================= DOUBLY-LINKED LISTS =====================}

{----------------------------------------------- Init_DList ———————}

PROCEDURE Init_DList(VAR Head, Tail : DListPtr { output });
BEGIN
    Head := NIL;
    Tail := NIL;
END; { Init_DList }

{----------------------------------------------- Clear_DList ———————}

PROCEDURE Clear_DList(VAR Head, Tail : DListPtr { in/out });
VAR ptr : DListPtr;
BEGIN
    WHILE Head <> NIL DO  BEGIN
        ptr := Head;
        Head := Head^.NextListPtr;
        Dispose(ptr)
    END; { WHILE }

    Tail := NIL; { reset tail pointer }

END; { Clear_DList }

{----------------------------------------------- Search_DList ———————}

PROCEDURE Search_DList(VAR Head,                       { input  }
                       ThisPtr     : DListPtr;  { output }
                       Search_Key  : ListKeyStr; { input  }
                       VAR Found   : BOOLEAN     { output });
BEGIN
    ThisPtr := Head;
    Found := FALSE;
    WHILE (ThisPtr <> NIL) AND (NOT Found) DO
        IF Search_Key <> ThisPtr^.ListInfo.ListKey THEN
            ThisPtr := ThisPtr^.NextListPtr
        ELSE
            Found := TRUE; { element might be in the list }
END; { Search_DList }

{----------------------------------------------- Search_Sorted_DList ———————}

PROCEDURE Search_Sorted_DList(VAR Head,                       { input  }
                              ThisPtr     : DListPtr;  { output }
                              Search_Key  : ListKeyStr; { input  }
                              VAR Found   : BOOLEAN     { output });
BEGIN
    ThisPtr := Head;
    Found := FALSE;

    WHILE (ThisPtr <> NIL) AND (NOT Found) DO
        IF Search_Key > ThisPtr^.ListInfo.ListKey THEN
            ThisPtr := ThisPtr^.NextListPtr
```

```
          ELSE
              Found := TRUE; { element might be in the list }
        { confirm suspected match }
        IF Found THEN Found := (Search_Key = ThisPtr^.ListInfo.ListKey);
END; { Search_Sorted_DList }


{--------------------------------------------------- Insert_DList ------}

PROCEDURE Insert_DList(VAR Tail : DListPtr;    { in/out }
                           Item : ListInfoRec { input  });
VAR ptr : DListPtr;
BEGIN
    { new item inserted at the tail of the list }
    NEW(ptr);
    ptr^.NextListPtr := NIL;
    ptr^.PrevListPtr := Tail;
    Tail^.NextListPtr := ptr;
    ptr^.ListInfo := Item; { assign key and other fields }
    Tail := ptr; { re-assign pointer to new tail }
END; { Insert_DList }


{--------------------------------------------- Insert_Sorted_DList ------}

PROCEDURE Insert_Sorted_DList(VAR Head,              { in/out }
                                  Tail : DListPtr;   { in/out }
                                  Item : ListInfoRec { input  });
VAR thisptr, ptr : DListPtr;
    match : BOOLEAN;
BEGIN
    Search_Sorted_DList(Head, thisptr, Item.ListKey, match);
    { the line below may be commented out to enable multiple
      data items with the same key to be stored in the list }
    IF match THEN EXIT;
    IF thisptr = NIL THEN BEGIN
        { new item inserted at the tail of the list }
        NEW(ptr);
        ptr^.NextListPtr := NIL;
        ptr^.PrevListPtr := Tail;
        Tail^.NextListPtr := ptr;
        ptr^.ListInfo := Item; { assign key and other fields }
        Tail := ptr;
        IF Head = NIL THEN
             Head := ptr;
    END
    ELSE IF thisptr^.PrevListPtr = NIL THEN BEGIN
        { new item is the new list head }
        NEW(ptr);
        ptr^.NextListPtr := Head;
        ptr^.PrevListPtr := NIL;
        Head^.PrevListPtr := ptr;
        ptr^.ListInfo := Item; { assign key and other fields }
        Head := ptr; { assign new pointer to the head of the list }
    END
```

```
    ELSE BEGIN
        { insert new item inside the list or at its tail }
        NEW(ptr);
        { link ahead with the 'current' node }
        ptr^.NextListPtr := thisptr;
        { link back with the 'previous' node }
        ptr^.PrevListPtr := thisptr^.PrevListPtr;
        thisptr^.PrevListPtr^.NextListPtr := ptr;
        thisptr^.PrevListPtr := ptr;
        ptr^.ListInfo := Item; { assign key and other fields }
    END;
END; { Insert_Sorted_DList }

{-------------------------------------------------- Delete_DList ————}

PROCEDURE Delete_DList(VAR Head,                    { in/out }
                           Tail      : DListPtr;    { in/out }
                           Search_Key : ListKeyStr; { input  }
                       VAR Done      : BOOLEAN      { output });
VAR thisptr, ptr : DListPtr;
BEGIN
    { search for item to delete }
    Search_DList(Head, thisptr, Search_Key, Done);
    IF Done THEN { found item in list }
        IF thisptr^.NextListPtr = NIL THEN BEGIN
            { delete the last list member }
            ptr := thisptr^.PrevListPtr;
            ptr^.NextListPtr := NIL;
            Dispose(Tail);
            Tail := ptr; { link tail pointer with new last element }
        END
        ELSE IF thisptr^.PrevListPtr = NIL THEN BEGIN
            { delete the list head }
            ptr := thisptr^.NextListPtr;
            ptr^.PrevListPtr := NIL;
            Dispose(Head);
            Head := ptr; { link head with new first element }
        END
        ELSE BEGIN
            thisptr^.PrevListPtr^.NextListPtr := thisptr^.NextListPtr;
            thisptr^.NextListPtr^.PrevListPtr := thisptr^.PrevListPtr;
            Dispose(thisptr)
        END;
END; { Delete_DList }

{----------------------------------------- Delete_Sorted_DList ————}

PROCEDURE Delete_Sorted_DList(VAR Head,                    { in/out }
                                  Tail      : DListPtr;    { in/out }
                                  Search_Key : ListKeyStr; { input  }
                              VAR Done      : BOOLEAN      { output });
VAR thisptr, ptr : DListPtr;
```

```
BEGIN
    { search for item to delete }
    Search_Sorted_DList(Head, thisptr, Search_Key, Done);
    IF Done THEN { found item in list }
        IF thisptr^.NextListPtr = NIL THEN BEGIN
            { delete the last list member }
            ptr := thisptr^.PrevListPtr;
            ptr^.NextListPtr := NIL;
            Dispose(Tail);
            Tail := ptr; { link tail pointer with new last element }
        END
        ELSE IF thisptr^.PrevListPtr = NIL THEN BEGIN
            { delete the list head }
            ptr := thisptr^.NextListPtr;
            ptr^.PrevListPtr := NIL;
            Dispose(Head);
            Head := ptr; { link head with new first element }
        END
        ELSE BEGIN
            thisptr^.PrevListPtr^.NextListPtr := thisptr^.NextListPtr;
            thisptr^.NextListPtr^.PrevListPtr := thisptr^.PrevListPtr;
            Dispose(thisptr)
        END;
END; { Delete_Sorted_DList }

{------------------------------------------------ DList_Length ------}

FUNCTION DList_Length(Head : DListPtr { input }) : WORD;
VAR count : WORD;
BEGIN
    count := 0; { initialize list size }
    WHILE Head <> NIL DO BEGIN
        INC(count);
        Head := Head^.NextListPtr;
    END;
    DList_Length := count { return function value }
END; { DList_Length }

{------------------------------------------------ DList_to_Array ------}

PROCEDURE DList_to_Array(     Head,
                             Tail   : DListPtr;      { input  }
                         VAR XArray : ListArrayType; { output }
                         VAR NData  : WORD;          { output }
                             Ascend : BOOLEAN        { input  });
BEGIN
    NData := 0; { initialize count returned array members }
    IF Ascend THEN { traverse list from front to back }
        WHILE (Head <> NIL) AND (NData < MAX_ARRAY_LIST) DO BEGIN
            INC(NData);
            XArray[NData] := Head^.ListInfo;
            Head := Head^.NextListPtr
```

```
            END { WHILE }
        ELSE { traverse list backwards }
            WHILE (Tail <> NIL) AND (NData < MAX_ARRAY_LIST) DO BEGIN
                INC(NData);
                XArray[NData] := Tail^.ListInfo;
                Tail := Tail^.PrevListPtr
            END; { WHILE }
END; { DList_to_Array }

{--------------------------------------------------- Array_to_DList ———}

PROCEDURE Array_to_DList(VAR Head,                     { output }
                             Tail   : DListPtr;        { output }
                         VAR XArray : ListArrayType;   { input  }
                             NData  : WORD;            { input  }
                             Sorted : BOOLEAN          { input  });
VAR  I : WORD;
BEGIN
    Clear_DList(Head, Tail); { clear list }
    IF Sorted THEN
        FOR i := 1 TO NData DO
            Insert_Sorted_DList(Head, Tail, XArray[i])
    ELSE
        FOR i := 1 TO NData DO
            Insert_DList(Tail, XArray[i]);
END; { Array_to_DList }

{========================= CIRCULAR LISTS =========================}

{--------------------------------------------------- Search_CircList ———}

PROCEDURE Search_CircList(VAR Head,                     { input  }
                             StartPtr,                  { input  }
                             ThisPtr,                   { output }
                             LastPtr    : SListPtr;     { output }
                             Search_Key : ListKeyStr;   { input  }
                         VAR Found      : BOOLEAN       { output });
BEGIN
    IF Search_Key = StartPtr^.ListInfo.ListKey THEN BEGIN
        Found := TRUE;
        ThisPtr := StartPtr^.NextListPtr;
        LastPtr := StartPtr
    END
    ELSE BEGIN
        LastPtr := StartPtr;
        ThisPtr := StartPtr^.NextListPtr;
        Found := FALSE;
        WHILE (ThisPtr <> StartPtr) AND (NOT Found) DO
            IF Search_Key <> ThisPtr^.ListInfo.ListKey THEN BEGIN
                LastPtr := ThisPtr;
                ThisPtr := ThisPtr^.NextListPtr;
```

```
                IF ThisPtr = NIL THEN { reached the end of the list }
                    ThisPtr := Head; { reset to the head of the list }
            END
            ELSE Found := TRUE; { element might be in the list }
        { confirm suspected match }
        IF Found THEN
            Found := (Search_Key = ThisPtr^.ListInfo.ListKey);
    END; { IF }
END; { Search_CircList }
END.
```

Listing 9.2. Source code for application program EDIR.PAS.

```
Program EDir;
{============================================================


                          PROGRAM EDIR
                Copyright (c) 1988 Namir Clement Shammas
version 1.0                                   Date 11/12/87
This program emulates an extended version of the DOS dir.
It is able to accept up to ten different wildcard specifications.
EXAMPLE:
   >EDIR *.PAS *.TPU
displays, in alphabetized order, all .PAS and .TPU files.
The program is smart enough to detect redundant files, such as those
produced by a command similar to:
   >EDIR *.* *.PAS
since *.PAS specification is a subset of *.*


============================================================}


{$M 8912, 8912, 200000}
Uses CRT, DOS, DataLib0, DirList;
CONST MAX_WILDCARDS = 10;
      DIRS_PER_SCREEN = 21;
VAR Dir_List, Ptr : SListPtr;
    Dir_Data : SearchRec;
    DateTimeVar : DateTime;
    WildCards : ARRAY [1..MAX_WILDCARDS] OF STRING20;
    Ch : CHAR;
    Count, I, N, L, NumDir: WORD;


PROCEDURE PutNum(Symbol : CHAR; { input }
                 N      : WORD { input });
{- - - - - - - - - - - - - - - - - - - - - - - - - - - - - -


ROUTINE PURPOSE: displays a character and a number (in the range of
0 to 99).
```

```
PARAMETERS:
    INPUT: Symbol - the character displayed.
           N - the number displayed. IF N < 10, a '0' character is
               displayed before the number itself.

- - - - - - - - - - - - - - - - - - - - - - - - - - - - - - - - - - - - }


BEGIN
    IF N > 9 THEN WRITE(Symbol, N:2)
            ELSE WRITE(Symbol,'0',N:1);
END;


{- - - - - - - - - - - - - - - - - - - - - - - - - - - - - - - - - - - -


                         ROUTINE DEPENDENCIES
                         --------------------
```

Identifier Name	Identifier Type	Source Library
Clear_SList	procedure	DirList
ClrScr	procedure	CRT
DateTime	record	DOS
DirectVideo	boolean	CRT
DosError	integer	DOS
FindFirst	procedure	DOS
FindNext	procedure	DOS
Init_SList	procedure	DirList
Insert_Sorted_SList	procedure	DirList
ReadKey	function	CRT
SearchRec	record	DOS
SListPtr	pointer	DirList
STRING20	string	DataLib0
UnPackTime	procedure	DOS

```
- - - - - - - - - - - - - - - - - - - - - - - - - - - - - - - - - - - - }


BEGIN
    N := ParamCount;
    IF N < 1 THEN BEGIN
        WildCards[1] := '*.*';
        N := 1
    END
    ELSE BEGIN
        I := 0;
        WHILE (I < N) AND (I < MAX_WILDCARDS) DO BEGIN
            INC(I);
            WildCards[I] := ParamStr(I);
        END;
        N := I;
    END; { IF }
    Init_SList(Dir_List); { initialize directory list }
```

```
FOR I := 1 TO N DO BEGIN
    FindFirst(WildCards[I], Archive, Dir_Data);
    WHILE (DosError = 0) DO BEGIN
        Insert_Sorted_SList(Dir_List, Dir_Data);
        FindNext(Dir_Data);
    END; { WHILE }
END; { FOR }
ClrScr;
Count := 0;
NumDir := 0;
DirectVideo := TRUE;
WRITELN(' Filename     Size     Date        Time');
WRITELN('————— ——— ————  ————');
WHILE Dir_List <> NIL DO BEGIN
    INC(NumDir);
    L := Length(Dir_List^.ListInfo.Name);
    WRITE(Dir_List^.ListInfo.Name);
    WHILE (L <= 12) DO BEGIN
        INC(L);
        WRITE(' ');
    END;
    WRITE(Dir_List^.ListInfo.Size:7);
    WRITE('  ');
    UnPackTime(Dir_List^.ListInfo.Time, DateTimeVar);
    WITH DateTimeVar DO BEGIN
        WRITE(Year:4);
        PutNum('/',Month);
        PutNum('/',Day);
        WRITE('  ');
        PutNum(CHR(0),Hour);
        PutNum(':',Min);
        PutNum(':',Sec);
    END;
    WRITELN;
    INC(Count);
    IF Count >= DIRS_PER_SCREEN THEN BEGIN
        Count := 0;
        WRITELN;
        WRITE('press any key to continue');
        ch := ReadKey;
        IF ch = ^C THEN BEGIN
            Clear_SList(Dir_List);
            Halt
        END
        ELSE ClrScr;
        WRITELN(' Filename     Size     Date        Time');
        WRITELN('————— ——— ————  ————');
    END;
    Dir_List := Dir_List^.NextListPtr; { get next entry }
END;
```

```
    IF Count >= DIRS_PER_SCREEN THEN BEGIN
        WRITELN;
        WRITE('press any key to continue');
        ch := ReadKey;
    END;
    WRITELN;
    WRITELN('Number of files = ',NumDir);
    Clear_SList(Dir_List);
END.
```

Listing 9.3. Source code for application library DIRLIST.PAS.

```
UNIT DirList;


{======================================================================


            Copyright (c) 1987, 1988   Namir Clement Shammas
    LIBRARY NAME: DirList
    VERSION: 1.0                                  DATE 11/12/1987
    PURPOSE: customized version of the List library to handle DOS
             files.       UPDATE HISTORY:


    ====================================================================}


{**********************************************************************}
{************************} INTERFACE {***************************}
{**********************************************************************}

Uses DOS;
TYPE ListKeyStr = STRING[12];
     { record used by singly-linked directory list }
     ListInfoRec = SearchRec; { from unit DOS }
     { singly-linked lists data types }
     SListPtr = ^SListRec;
     SListRec = RECORD
         ListInfo    : ListInfoRec;
         NextListPtr : SListPtr
     END;

PROCEDURE Init_SList(VAR Head : SListPtr { output });
{- - - - - - - - - - - - - - - - - - - - - - - - - - - - - - - -


ROUTINE PURPOSE: initializes the head of any new singly-linked list.
PARAMETERS:
   OUTPUT: Head - the pointer to the initialized singly-linked list.


- - - - - - - - - - - - - - - - - - - - - - - - - - - - - - - - - - }
PROCEDURE Clear_SList(VAR Head : SListPtr { in/out });
```

```
{- - - - - - - - - - - - - - - - - - - - - - - - - - - - - - - - - - - - - - -

ROUTINE PURPOSE: clears any existing singly-linked list.
PARAMETERS:
  IN/OUT: Head - the pointer of cleared singly-linked list.
COMMENTS: Head = NIL when routine ends.

- - - - - - - - - - - - - - - - - - - - - - - - - - - - - - - - - - - - - - }
PROCEDURE Search_Sorted_SList (VAR Head,               { input  }
                                   ThisPtr,            { output }
                                   LastPtr    : SListPtr;  { output }
                                   Search_Key : ListKeyStr; { input  }
                               VAR Found      : BOOLEAN     { output });
{- - - - - - - - - - - - - - - - - - - - - - - - - - - - - - - - - - - - - - -

ROUTINE PURPOSE: searches for 'Search_Key' in the sorted list with
'Head' as the pointer to its head. The current and previous pointers
are returned in the argument lists.
PARAMETERS:
  INPUT: Head - the head of the singly-linked list.
         Search_Key - the sought data element.
  OUTPUT: ThisPtr - the pointer to the sought list element.
          LastPtr - the pointer to element prior to the sought one.
          Found - the logical flag to signal whether or not the search
             is successful.

- - - - - - - - - - - - - - - - - - - - - - - - - - - - - - - - - - - - - - }
PROCEDURE Insert_Sorted_SList (VAR Head : SListPtr;   { in/out }
                                   Item : ListInfoRec { input  });
{- - - - - - - - - - - - - - - - - - - - - - - - - - - - - - - - - - - - - - -

ROUTINE PURPOSE: performs ordered list insertion.
PARAMETERS:
  INPUT: Item - the data item in the list.
  IN/OUT: Head - the targeted singly-linked list.

                    ROUTINE DEPENDENCIES
                    --------------------

     Identifier Name        Identifier Type      Source Library
     ---------------        ---------------      --------------

     Search_SList             procedure              local

- - - - - - - - - - - - - - - - - - - - - - - - - - - - - - - - - - - - - - }

{***********************************************************************}
{**********************} IMPLEMENTATION {*******************************}
{***********************************************************************}

{--------------------------------------------------- Init_SList ------}
```

```
PROCEDURE Init_SList;
BEGIN
    Head := NIL
END; { Init_SList }


{--------------------------------------------------- Clear_SList ———}

PROCEDURE Clear_SList;
VAR Ptr : SListPtr;
BEGIN
    WHILE Head <> NIL DO  BEGIN
        Ptr := Head;
        Head := Head^.NextListPtr;
        Dispose(Ptr)
    END; { WHILE }
END; { Clear_SList }


{----------------------------------------- Search_Sorted_SList ———}

PROCEDURE Search_Sorted_SList;
BEGIN
    LastPtr := NIL;
    ThisPtr := Head;
    Found := FALSE;
    WHILE (ThisPtr <> NIL) AND (NOT Found) DO
        IF Search_Key > ThisPtr^.ListInfo.Name THEN BEGIN
            LastPtr := ThisPtr;
            ThisPtr := ThisPtr^.NextListPtr
        END
        ELSE Found := TRUE; { element might be in the list }
    { confirm suspected match }
    IF Found THEN Found := (Search_Key = ThisPtr^.ListInfo.Name);
END; { Search_Sorted_SList }


{--------------------------------------------- Insert_Sorted_SList ———}

PROCEDURE Insert_Sorted_SList;
VAR thisptr, lastptr, ptr : SListPtr;
    match : BOOLEAN;
BEGIN
    Search_Sorted_SList(Head, thisptr, lastptr, Item.Name, match);
    { exit if the item is in the list already }
    IF match THEN EXIT;
    IF lastptr = NIL THEN BEGIN { new item is the new list head }
        NEW(ptr);
        ptr^.NextListPtr := Head;
        ptr^.ListInfo := Item; { assign key and other fields }
        Head := ptr; { assign the new pointer to the head of the list }
    END
    ELSE BEGIN { insert new item inside the list or at its tail }
```

```
          NEW(ptr);
          { link ahead with the 'current' node }
          ptr^.NextListPtr := lastptr^.NextListPtr;
          { link back with the 'previous' node }
          lastptr^.NextListPtr := ptr;
          ptr^.ListInfo := Item; { assign key and other fields }
      END;
END; { Insert_Sorted_SList }
END.
```

Listing 9.4. Source code for library CLIST.PAS.

```
UNIT CList;
{======================================================================


            Copyright (c) 1987, 1988    Namir Clement Shammas
      LIBRARY NAME: CList
      VERSION: 1.0                                    DATE 6/30/1987
      PURPOSE: presents routines for a special clustered list
               structure.
      UPDATE HISTORY:


======================================================================}
{**********************************************************************}
{**************************} INTERFACE {****************************}
{**********************************************************************}

Uses DataLib0;
CONST
      MAX_LIST = 200;
      CDV = 0; { Critical Difference value }
TYPE KeyArray = ARRAY [1..MAX_LIST] OF STRING255;
     CListInfo = RECORD
                     Key : STRING255;
                     { other fields may be placed here }
          END;
     CListPtr = ^CListNode;
     { Clustered List structure }
     CListNode = RECORD
                     CListData : CListInfo;
                     NextPtr, NextHi : CListPtr;
                 END;

PROCEDURE Search_Node(VAR Head          : CListPtr;  { input  }
                          SearchData     : STRING255; { input  }
                      VAR Found          : BOOLEAN;   { output }
                      VAR LastPtr,                    { output }
                          ThisPtr        : CListPtr   { output });
```

```
{- - - - - - - - - - - - - - - - - - - - - - - - - - - - - - - - -
```

ROUTINE PURPOSE: searches for 'SearchData' in a clustered list.
PARAMETERS:
  INPUT: Head - the head of the clustered list.
        SearchData - the sought data element.
  OUTPUT: Found - the flag to signal whether or not the search was
          successful.
        LastPtr - the pointer to the previous element.
        ThisPtr - the pointer to the matched element.
HANDLING BAD ARGUMENTS: if NewData is a null string, the routine
exits without changing the list.

ROUTINE DEPENDENCIES

Identifier Name	Identifier Type	Source Library
CDV	constant	local
STRING255	string	DataLib0

```
- - - - - - - - - - - - - - - - - - - - - - - - - - - - - - - - - }
PROCEDURE Insert_CList(VAR Head    : CListPtr;  { in/out }
                           NewData : STRING255  { input  });
{- - - - - - - - - - - - - - - - - - - - - - - - - - - - - - - - -
```

ROUTINE PURPOSE: inserts a new data string into a clustered list.
PARAMETERS:
  INPUT: NewData - the datum inserted in the clustered list.
  IN/OUT: Head - the head of the expanded clustered list.
HANDLING BAD ARGUMENTS: If NewData is a null string, the routine
exits without changing the list.

ROUTINE DEPENDENCIES

Identifier Name	Identifier Type	Source Library
CDV	constant	local
STRING255	string	DataLib0

```
- - - - - - - - - - - - - - - - - - - - - - - - - - - - - - - - - }
PROCEDURE CList_to_Array(Head       : CListPtr; { input  }
                         VAR Keys   : KeyArray; { output }
                         VAR Count  : WORD      { output });
{- - - - - - - - - - - - - - - - - - - - - - - - - - - - - - - - -
```

ROUTINE PURPOSE: converts a clustered list into a sorted array.
PARAMETERS:
  INPUT: Head - the head of the clustered list.
  OUTPUT: Keys - the ordered array of list elements.
        Count - the number of elements in the array.

```
                    ROUTINE DEPENDENCIES
                    --------------------

       Identifier Name          Identifier Type      Source Library
       ---------------          ---------------      --------------

        CListPtr                   pointer              local
        visit_hi_node              procedure            nested
        visit_low_node             procedure            nested
```

```
 - - - - - - - - - - - - - - - - - - - - - - - - - - - - - - - - - - }

{*****************************************************************}
{***********************} IMPLEMENTATION {************************}
{*****************************************************************}

{--------------------------------------------- Search_Node -------}

PROCEDURE Search_Node;
VAR high_track : BOOLEAN;
    ord1, diff : INTEGER;
BEGIN
    Found := FALSE;
    high_track := TRUE;
    LastPtr := NIL;
    ThisPtr := Head;
    IF SearchData = '' THEN EXIT;
    ord1 := ORD(SearchData[1]);
    WHILE (ThisPtr <> NIL) AND
          (ThisPtr^.CListData.Key < SearchData) DO BEGIN
        LastPtr := ThisPtr;
        IF high_track THEN BEGIN
            diff := ORD(ThisPtr^.CListData.Key[1]) - ord1;
            IF ABS(diff) > CDV
            THEN
                ThisPtr := ThisPtr^.NextHi
            ELSE BEGIN
                ThisPtr := ThisPtr^.NextPtr;
                high_track := FALSE { switch to low track }
            END; { IF ABS(diff) }
        END
        ELSE
            ThisPtr := ThisPtr^.NextPtr;
        { END IF high_track }
    END; { WHILE }
    IF ThisPtr <> NIL THEN
        Found := (ThisPtr^.CListData.Key = SearchData);
END; { Search_Node }

{--------------------------------------------- Insert_CList ------}
```

```
PROCEDURE Insert_CList;
VAR found : BOOLEAN;
    ord1, diff : INTEGER;
    tempo : STRING255;
    node, lastptr, thisptr : CListPtr;
BEGIN
    IF NewData = '' THEN EXIT;
    ord1 := ORD(NewData[1]); { get ascii code of the first character }
    IF Head = NIL THEN BEGIN { start a new list }
        NEW(Head);
        WITH Head^ DO BEGIN
            NextPtr := NIL;
            NextHi  := NIL;
            CListData.Key := NewData
        END; { WITH }
    END
    ELSE BEGIN { expand list }
        NEW(node);
        WITH node^ DO BEGIN
            CListData.Key := NewData;
            NextPtr := NIL;
            NextHi := NIL
        END; { WITH }
        Search_node(Head,node^.CListData.Key,found,lastptr,thisptr);
        { The following statement may be commented out to enable
          the insertion of duplicates                            }
        IF found THEN EXIT;
        IF lastptr = NIL THEN BEGIN { insert as new list head }
            diff := ORD(Head^.CListData.Key[1]) - ord1;
            IF ABS(DIFF) > CDV THEN
                node^.NextHi := Head
            ELSE
                node^.NextHi  := Head^.NextHi;
                node^.NextPtr := Head;
            { END IF }
            Head := node;
        END
        ELSE BEGIN { insert new data in the middle or at the tail }
            diff := ord1 - ORD(lastptr^.CListData.Key[1]);
            IF diff <= CDV THEN BEGIN
                { insert inside a clustered sublist }
                { LasPtr may be a high or low track node }
                node^.NextPtr := lastptr^.NextPtr;
                lastptr^.NextPtr := node
            END
            ELSE BEGIN
                IF thisptr <> NIL
                THEN BEGIN
                    diff := ord1 - ORD(thisptr^.CListData.Key[1]);
                    IF ABS(diff) > CDV
                    THEN BEGIN {insert between two high track nodes }
```

```
                        node^.NextHi := lastptr^.NextHi;
                        lastptr^.NextHi := node
                    END
                    ELSE BEGIN
                        { swap names in the next high track node }
                        tempo := node^.CListData.Key;
                        node^.CListData.Key := thisptr^.CListData.Key;
                        thisptr^.CListData.Key := tempo;
                        { insert a new swapped first element }
                        { in clustered sublist                }
                        node^.NextPtr := thisptr^.NextPtr;
                        thisptr^.NextPtr := node
                    END; { IF }
                END
                ELSE BEGIN { insert as last high track node }
                    node^.NextHi := lastptr^.NextHi;
                    lastptr^.NextHi := node
                END; { IF }
            END; { IF }
        END; { IF lastptr = NIL }
    END; { IF Head = NIL }
END; { Insert_CList }


{----------------------------------------------- CList_to_Array ------}


PROCEDURE CList_to_Array;


{------------------------------- CList_to_Array : visit_low_node ------}


PROCEDURE visit_low_node(VAR Node : CListPtr { in/out });


{- - - - - - - - - - - - - - - - - - - - - - - - - - - - - - - - - - -
SCOPE: Local.
ROUTINE PURPOSE: recursive routine to visit low tracks of a
clustered list.
PARAMETERS:
  IN/OUT: Node - the node visited.
- - - - - - - - - - - - - - - - - - - - - - - - - - - - - - - - - - - }


BEGIN
    IF (Node <> NIL) AND (Count < MAX_LIST) THEN BEGIN
        INC(Count);
        Keys[Count] := Node^.CListData.Key;
        { WRITE(' ',Keys[Count]:10); }
        visit_low_node(Node^.NextPtr);
    END
END; { visit_low_node }


{------------------------------- CList_to_Array : visit_hi_node ------}


PROCEDURE visit_hi_node(VAR Node : CListPtr { in/out });
```

```
{- - - - - - - - - - - - - - - - - - - - - - - - - - - - - - -
SCOPE: Local.

ROUTINE PURPOSE: recursive routine to visit high tracks of a
clustered list.
PARAMETERS:
  IN/OUT: Node - the node visited.

- - - - - - - - - - - - - - - - - - - - - - - - - - - - - - - - }
BEGIN
    IF (Node <> NIL) AND (Count < MAX_LIST) THEN BEGIN
        INC(Count);
        Keys[Count] := Node^.CListData.Key;
        { WRITE(Keys[Count]:10); }
        visit_low_node(Node^.NextPtr);
        visit_hi_node(Node^.NextHi);
    END;
END; { visit_hi_node }
BEGIN
    IF Head <> NIL THEN BEGIN
        Count := 0;
        visit_hi_node(Head);
    END
    ELSE
        Count := 0;
    { END IF }
END; { CList_to_Array }
END.
```

Listing 9.5. Source code for application program EDIR2.PAS.

```
Program EDir2;
{=================================================================

                        PROGRAM EDIR2
            Copyright (c) 1988 Namir Clement Shammas
version 1.0                                   Date 11/12/87

This program emulates an extended version of the DOS dir /w.
It is able to accept up to ten different wildcard specifications.
EXAMPLE:
    >EDIR2 *.PAS *.TPU
displays, in alphabetized order, all .PAS and .TPU files.
The program is smart enough to detect redundant files, such as those
produced by a command similar to:
    >EDIR2 *.* *.PAS
since *.PAS specification is a subset of *.*.

The total number of files is limited by the size of the 'KeyArray'
declared in unit CLIST.
```

```
=============================================================}

{$M 8912, 8912, 200000}
Uses CRT, DOS, DataLib0, CList;
CONST MAX_WILDCARDS = 10;
      DIRS_PER_LINE = 5;
      DIRS_PER_SCREEN = 21;
VAR Dir_List : CListPtr;
    Dir_Data : SearchRec;
    Files : KeyArray;
    WildCards : ARRAY [1..MAX_WILDCARDS] OF STRING20;
    Ch : CHAR;
    Count, SeqCount, I, N, L, NumDir: WORD;


{- - - - - - - - - - - - - - - - - - - - - - - - - - - - - - - - -

                    ROUTINE DEPENDENCIES
                    --------------------

        Identifier Name          Identifier Type      Source Library
        ---------------          ---------------      --------------

        CListPtr                    pointer              CList
        CList_to_Array              procedure            CLIST
        ClrScr                      procedure            CRT
        DirectVideo                 boolean              CRT
        DosError                    integer              DOS
        FindFirst                   procedure            DOS
        FindNext                    procedure            DOS
        Insert_CList                procedure            CList
        KeyArray                    array                CLIST
        ReadKey                     function             CRT
        SearchRec                   record               DOS
        STRING20                    string               DataLib0

- - - - - - - - - - - - - - - - - - - - - - - - - - - - - - - - - - }

BEGIN
    N := ParamCount;
    IF N < 1 THEN BEGIN
        WildCards[1] := '*.*';
        N := 1
    END
    ELSE BEGIN
        I := 0;
        WHILE (I < N) AND (I < MAX_WILDCARDS) DO BEGIN
            INC(I);
            WildCards[I] := ParamStr(I);
        END;
        N := I;
```

```
        END; { IF }
        Dir_List := NIL; { initialize directory list }
        { search directory }
        FOR I := 1 TO N DO BEGIN
            FindFirst(WildCards[I], Archive, Dir_Data);
            WHILE (DosError = 0) DO BEGIN
                Insert_CList(Dir_List, Dir_Data.Name);
                FindNext(Dir_Data);
            END; { WHILE }
        END; { FOR }
        { convert CList to array }
        CList_to_Array(Dir_List, Files, NumDir);
        ClrScr;
        Count := 0;
        SeqCount := 0;
        DirectVideo := TRUE;
        FOR I := 1 TO NumDir DO BEGIN
            L := Length(Files[I]);
            WRITE(Files[I]);
            WHILE (L <= 12) DO BEGIN
                INC(L);
                WRITE(' ');
            END;
            WRITE('  ');
            INC(SeqCount);
            IF (SeqCount >= DIRS_PER_LINE) THEN BEGIN
                SeqCount := 0;
                INC(Count);
                WRITELN;
            END;
            IF Count >= DIRS_PER_SCREEN THEN BEGIN
                Count := 0;
                WRITELN;
                WRITE('press any key to continue');
                ch := ReadKey;
                IF ch = ^C THEN Halt
                            ELSE ClrScr;
            END;
        END; { FOR }
        IF Count >= DIRS_PER_SCREEN THEN BEGIN
            WRITELN;
            WRITE('press any key to continue');
            ch := ReadKey;
        END;
        WRITELN; WRITELN;
        WRITELN('Number of files = ',NumDir);
END.
```

Listing 9.6. Source code for library LISPLIST.PAS.

```
UNIT LispList;
{==================================================================


          Copyright (c) 1987, 1988   Namir Clement Shammas
     LIBRARY NAME: LispList
     VERSION: 1.0                              DATE 8/24/1987
     PURPOSE: implements routines for a two-way conversion between
              LISP expressions stored as strings and as lists.
     UPDATE HISTORY:


==================================================================}

{*****************************************************************}
{*************************} INTERFACE {***************************}
{*****************************************************************}

Uses DataLib0;
CONST MAX_LIST_STACK_SIZE = 20;
TYPE LispString = STRING[20];
     LispListPtr = ^LispListRec;
     LispListRec = RECORD
         NextListPtr,
         SubListPtr    : LispListPtr;
         AtomName      : LispString
     END;

PROCEDURE String_to_List(    LStr      : STRING255;   { input  }
                         VAR Head      : LispListPtr; { output }
                         VAR ErrorCode : BYTE         { output });
{- - - - - - - - - - - - - - - - - - - - - - - - - - - - - - - - -

ROUTINE PURPOSE: passes a string to create a LISP-like list (actually
a tree).
PARAMETERS:
  INPUT: LStr - the input string.
  OUTPUT: Head - the head of the list created.
          ErrorCode - the character position of error-generating text
              (assigned zero if no error occurs).
```

ROUTINE DEPENDENCIES

Identifier Name	Identifier Type	Source Library
MAX_LIST_STACK_SIZE	constant	local
LispListPtr	pointer	local
LispString	string	local
SaveAtom	procedure	nested
STRING255	string	DataLib0

```
- - - - - - - - - - - - - - - - - - - - - - - - - - - - - - - - - }
PROCEDURE List_to_String(VAR LStr     : STRING255;  { output }
                         VAR Head     : LispListPtr { input  });
{- - - - - - - - - - - - - - - - - - - - - - - - - - - - - - - -
```

ROUTINE PURPOSE: converts a LISP-like linked list into a string form.
PARAMETERS:
  INPUT: Head - the head of a LISP-like list.
  OUTPUT: LStr - the output string.

                         ROUTINE DEPENDENCIES

Identifier Name	Identifier Type	Source Library
MAX_LIST_STACK_SIZE	constant	local
LispListPtr	pointer	local
LispString	string	local
STRING255	string	DataLib0

```
- - - - - - - - - - - - - - - - - - - - - - - - - - - - - - - }
```

```
{*******************************************************************}
{***********************} IMPLEMENTATION {*************************}
{*******************************************************************}
```

```
{$V-}
```

```
{-------------------------------------------------- String_to_List ------}
```

```
PROCEDURE String_to_List;
VAR ok, scan_mode : BOOLEAN;
    ch : CHAR;
    charpos, index1, level, strlen : BYTE;
    num_open   : SHORTINT;
    atom_str : LispString;
    ptr, ptr2 : LispListPtr;
    list_stack : ARRAY [1..MAX_LIST_STACK_SIZE] OF LispListPtr;
```

```
{------------------------------------- String_to_List : Save_Atom ------}
```

```
PROCEDURE Save_Atom;
{ local procedure to save a pending atom }
VAR i : BYTE;
BEGIN
    { extract atom string }
    atom_str := '';
    FOR i := index1 TO (charpos - 1) DO
        atom_str := atom_str + LStr[i];
    ptr^.AtomName := atom_str;
    scan_mode := FALSE;
```

```
END; { Save_Atom }
BEGIN
    strlen := Length(LStr);
    ErrorCode := 0; { optimistic default value }
    { balance parentheses }
    num_open := 0;
    ok := (LStr[1] = '(') AND (LStr[strlen] = ')');
    IF NOT ok THEN BEGIN
        ErrorCode := 1;
        EXIT
    END;
    charpos := 2; { start at second character }
    WHILE (charpos < strlen) AND ok DO BEGIN
        ch := LStr[charpos];
        CASE ch OF
            '(' : INC(num_open);
            ')' : DEC(num_open);
            ELSE { just keep on scanning } ;
        END;
        IF num_open >= 0 THEN INC(charpos)
                        ELSE ok := FALSE;
    END;
    IF ok AND (num_open > 0) THEN ok := FALSE;
    IF NOT ok THEN BEGIN
        ErrorCode := charpos;
        EXIT
    END;
    charpos := 2;
    level := 1;
    scan_mode := FALSE;
    NEW(Head);
    WITH Head^ DO  BEGIN
        NextListPtr := NIL;
        SubListPtr := NIL;
        AtomName := '';
    END; { WITH }
    ptr := Head;
    WHILE (charpos <= strlen) AND ok DO BEGIN
        ch := LStr[charpos];
        CASE ch OF
            '(' : BEGIN
                    IF scan_mode THEN Save_Atom;
                    list_stack[level] := ptr;
                    INC(level);
                    NEW(ptr2);
                    WITH ptr2^ DO  BEGIN
                        NextListPtr := NIL;
                        SubListPtr := NIL;
                        AtomName := '';
```

```
                              END; { WITH }
                              ptr^.SubListPtr := ptr2;
                              ptr := ptr2
                           END;
                  ')' : BEGIN
                           IF scan_mode THEN Save_Atom;
                           DEC(level);
                           IF level > 0 THEN
                               ptr := list_stack[level]
                           ELSE
                               ok := FALSE;
                        END;
                  ` ` : BEGIN
                           IF scan_mode THEN Save_Atom;
                           NEW(ptr2);
                           WITH ptr2^ DO  BEGIN
                               NextListPtr := NIL;
                               SubListPtr := NIL;
                               AtomName := `';
                           END; { WITH }
                           ptr^.NextListPtr := ptr2;
                           ptr := ptr2
                        END;
                  ELSE BEGIN
                           IF NOT scan_mode THEN BEGIN
                               scan_mode := TRUE;
                               index1 := charpos
                             END;
                        END;
             END; { CASE }
             IF ok THEN charpos := charpos + 1 { scan next character }
         END; { WHILE }
         IF (NOT ok) AND (level > 0) THEN ErrorCode := charpos;
    END; { String_to_List }


    {----------------------------------------------- List_to_String ——}

    PROCEDURE List_to_String;
    VAR level, num_paren : BYTE;
        atom_str : LispString;
        ptr : LispListPtr;
        list_stack : ARRAY [1..MAX_LIST_STACK_SIZE] OF LispListPtr;
    BEGIN
        level := 1;
        num_paren := 1;
        ptr := Head;
        LStr := `(';
        WHILE (level > 0) DO BEGIN
            IF ptr = NIL THEN BEGIN
                WHILE num_paren > 0 DO BEGIN
```

```
                    LStr := LStr + ')';
                    DEC(num_paren)
                END;
                EXIT
            END; { IF }
            IF ptr^.SubListPtr <> NIL THEN BEGIN { process sublist }
                list_stack[level] := ptr^.NextListPtr;
                INC(level);
                ptr := ptr^.SubListPtr;
                LStr := LStr + '(';
                INC(num_paren)
            END
            ELSE BEGIN
                atom_str := ptr^.AtomName;
                IF atom_str <> '' THEN LStr := LStr + atom_str + ' ';
                ptr := ptr^.NextListPtr;
                IF ptr = NIL THEN BEGIN { end of (sub)list }
                    Delete(LStr, Length(LStr), 1);
                    LStr := LStr + ') ';
                    DEC(num_paren);
                    DEC(level);
                    IF level > 0 THEN ptr := list_stack[level]
                END; { IF }
            END; { IF }
        END; { WHILE }
    END; { List_to_String }
END.
```

Listing 9.7. Source code for application program USELISP.PAS.

```
Program Use_LispList;
{===============================================================

                    Program Use_LispList
            Copyright (c) 1988 Namir Clement Shammas

A program that takes a LISP expression in string form, converts
it first into linked lists and then back into string form.

===============================================================}

{$M 8192, 8192, 200000}
{$R+}
{$S+}
Uses CRT, DataLib0, LispList;
VAR List_Head : LispListPtr;
    LeStr, LeStr0 : STRING255;
    ErrorCode : BYTE;
```

```
{- - - - - - - - - - - - - - - - - - - - - - - - - - - - - - - - - - - -
                          ROUTINE DEPENDENCIES
                          --------------------

        Identifier Name              Identifier Type      Source Library
        ---------------              ---------------      --------------

        ClrScr                       procedure            CRT
        List_to_String               procedure            LispList
        STRING255                    string               DataLib0
        String_to_List               procedure            LispList


- - - - - - - - - - - - - - - - - - - - - - - - - - - - - - - - - - - }


BEGIN
    ClrScr;
    REPEAT
        WRITE('Enter LISP expression -> ');
        READLN(LeStr0);
        IF LeStr0 <> '' THEN BEGIN
            LeStr := LeStr0;
            String_to_List(LeStr, List_Head, ErrorCode);
            IF ErrorCode = 0 THEN BEGIN
                List_to_String(LeStr, List_Head);
                WRITELN(LeStr0,' ?=?  ',LeStr)
            END
            ELSE BEGIN
                WRITELN('Error at');
                WRITELN(LeStr);
                WRITELN('^':ErrorCode)
            END; { IF }
        END; { IF }
        WRITELN; WRITELN;
    UNTIL LeStr0 = '';
END.
```

10

Binary and AVL Trees

In an earlier chapter I discussed linked lists that are typically characterized by having each node link up with two other nodes. In this chapter I will look at the more advanced linked structures: binary trees. In general, trees (as the name suggests) have an element linked to multiple elements. This results in a faster traversal of a tree structure, compared with linked lists.

Typically, binary trees have each node link up with three other nodes: the parent node as well as the left and right children nodes. In addition, each node has a key field and an optional collection of data. The binary tree structure is normally implemented as a dynamic structure. Figure 10.1 shows a binary tree with its root node, and left and right branches (i.e., subtrees). The root node is the first node accessed when manipulating a binary tree. The **terminal** nodes are known as the leaf nodes. Each node is also regarded as the root of the subtree beneath it. Thus, a binary tree is a structure that easily lends itself to recursive insertion, deletion, and search.

The most important binary tree operation is perhaps the tree searching. It is used for looking up a particular tree node, node insertion, and node deletion. The search in a binary tree starts at the root node and follows these steps:

1. The search key is compared with the key of the root node.
2. If the keys are equal, the search stops with a successful find.
3. If the search key is greater than the root key, the search resumes at the right child node. The right node is treated like the root node and you resume at step (1). If the root has no right child node, the search halts with a negative find.
4. If the search key is less than the root key, the search resumes at the left child node. The left node is treated like the root node and you resume at step (1). If the root has no left child node, the search halts with a negative find.

Figure 10.1. Typical binary tree.

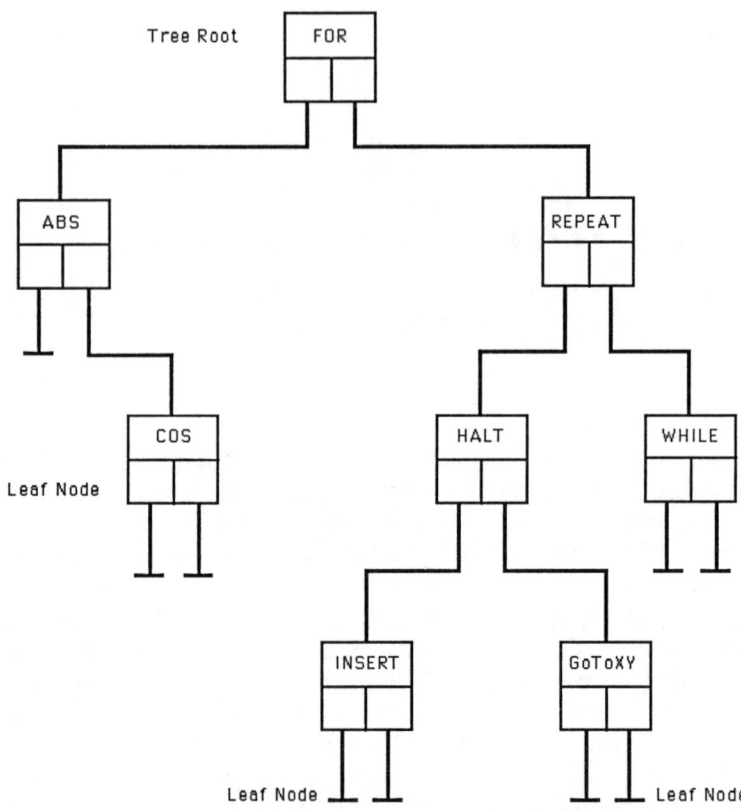

Inserting a new node in a binary tree easily builds on the above node search task. A design decision must be made regarding duplicate keys. If you allow duplicate keys, then modify the above search steps by (a) removing step (2), and (b) making step (3) use the logical >= test. By contrast, if you do not allow duplicate keys, then a successful search should result in exiting the insertion routine without adding a duplicate node.

Traversing binary trees is accomplished in any one of three recursive methods: preorder, inorder, or postorder. With the preorder traversal you visit and/or access a node, its left child node, and its right child node, in that order. Using the inorder traversal you first visit the left child node, then the node itself, and finally the right child node. The inorder traversal permits you to access the node keys of the binary trees in ascending sorted order. The postorder traversal first visits the left child node, then the right child node, and finally the node itself. In implementing a routine to traverse a binary tree, I employ the inorder traversal. Converting the code to implement the other traversal modes is a simple matter of rearranging Pascal statements.

Deleting a node from a binary tree is more elaborate than the insertion. These are the following possible node deletion cases:

1. Deleting a leaf node. This is the simplest case, since the removed node has no descendants. Purging the node from the binary tree is very straightforward.

2. Deleting a node with one empty subtree. This is the case where the deleted node has either a left or right subtree, but not both. The steps involve linking the root of the subtree with the parent node of the removed node.

3. Deleting a node with nonempty subtrees. This case is handled by one of two methods that are **mirror images** of each other. The first technique promotes the left subtree and links the right subtree with a proper node in the promoted left subtree. The second performs essentially the same task, but switching the role of the left and right subtrees.

LIBRARY BINTREE.PAS

I wrote a library for binary tree manipulations, shown in Listing 10.1. The library exports the following constants and data types:

```
{ constant is significant only in rebalancing binary tree }
CONST MAX_TREE_NODES = 100; TYPE BinTreeStr = STRING[40];
TreeDataRec = RECORD
          Key : BinTreeStr;
          { ***** put other fields here ****** }
     END;        TreePtr = ^Binary_Tree_Rec;
Binary_Tree_Rec = RECORD
          TreeData : TreeDataRec;
          Left, Right : TreePtr;
     END;
     TreeRecArray = ARRAY [1..MAX_TREE_NODES] OF TreeDataRec;
```

The most important structure is the record **Binary_Tree_Rec**. It defines the basic structure for the binary tree node. The **TreeDataRec** record is used to define at least the key of the node. To create your custom version of the BINTREE.PAS library, you will most likely add other fields to this record.

The **TreeRecArray** is used to copy the visited tree nodes into an array. The resulting array contains data sorted, by the values of the node keys, in ascending order.

The exported routines in the library are as follows:

```
PROCEDURE Insert_BinTree(VAR Root : TreePtr;      { in/out }
                             X    : TreeDataRec { input  });
```

inserts a new data item in a binary tree. The implementation of this routine is a recursive one.

```
FUNCTION Search_BinTree(
              VAR Root           : TreePtr;       { in/out }
                  X              : TreeDataRec;   { input  }
                  Occurrence_Num : WORD           { input  }) : WORD;
```

searches for a certain occurrence number of a key in a binary tree. This is based on the assumption that the binary tree allows for duplicate keys. If no match is found, the function returns a zero. If the sought datum is encountered fewer times than desired, then the function's value reports that actual number. A successful search should return the same specified occurrence number.

```
PROCEDURE Sort_to_Array(VAR Root  : TreePtr;       { input  }
                        VAR SortX : TreeRecArray;  { output }
                        VAR Count : WORD           { output });
```

visits the nodes of the binary trees and copies them onto an array. This operation supplies you with an ascending ordered array. This empowers you to access the tree data in either ascending or descending order and to traverse the ordered data back and forth very efficiently. This routine employs another recursive procedure, **traverse_tree**, that is not exported by the library. The procedure **Sort_to_Array** serves only to initialize the counter for the array size and launch the first call to the recursive **traverse_tree**.

If there are more nodes in the binary tree than the storage capacity of the array, the surplus nodes are not included in the array. You can detect this when the returned **Count** parameter exceeds the value of the constant **MAX_TREE_NODES**. The difference between **Count** and **MAX_TREE_NODES** gives you the number of surplus nodes.

```
FUNCTION Delete_BinTree(
              VAR Root  : TreePtr;     { input }
                  X     : TreeDataRec  { input }
                  Occur : WORD         { input }) : BOOLEAN;
```

deletes a node specified by the supplied key and the occurrence number. The function returns TRUE if the supplied key found a match, and the deletion is successful. Otherwise, a FALSE boolean value is obtained. This function uses function **find_node** to return the pointer to the sought element.

```
FUNCTION Remove_Tree(VAR Root : TreePtr { input }) : BOOLEAN;
```

This recursive function may be used to remove an entire binary tree and regain the memory space occupied by the tree nodes. The logical value returned by this function has no meaning to the calling program. Instead, it is used during the recursive function calls.

```
PROCEDURE Rebalance_Tree(VAR Root  : TreePtr { in/out });
```

rebalances a skewed binary tree. The nodes of the binary tree are copied onto a sorted array, its nodes deleted, and then the data in the sorted array is appropriately inserted in a new binary tree. This routine should be called when you suspect that extensive tree skewness has occurred. The latter decreases the efficiency of the search operation. This routine invokes a local recursive routine **rebalance** to perform the creation of the more balanced binary tree.

THE AVL-TREE

Despite being versatile data structures, binary trees are plagued by their vulnerability towards becoming unbalanced. This situation is characterized by having some of the subtrees considerably more extended than others. Consequently, this decreases the efficiency of searching in a binary tree. Consider the extreme case of building a binary tree using perfectly ordered data. The result is one very long linked list (that is, a root node with one large straight-linked left or right subtree). This case is not really far-fetched: consider the situation that involves reading the previously sorted files from a DOS directory into a binary tree. The algorithms used in inserting and deleting nodes from binary trees make no provision regarding the state of balance in the tree. This does not make binary trees completely useless, since binary trees do work well with random (or nearly so) inserted data.

In the early sixties two Russian mathematicians, G. M. Ade'lson–Vel'skii and E. M. Landis, came out with an important enhancement for binary trees. They suggested a new set of algorithms for the node insertion and deletion that also maintain a state of near balance in the binary tree. This superior type of binary trees is called an AVL-Tree in their honor. An AVL-Tree is a binary tree that follows these rules:

1.   The difference in the height of the main left and right subtrees is not greater than one level.

2.   Every node in the tree is also an AVL-Tree.

The above definition of AVL-Trees states that a perfect or near-perfect (that is, not exceeding a height difference of one level) balance must be observed throughout the AVL-Tree. Figure 10.2 shows various AVL-Trees. While AVL-Trees are not necessarily perfectly balanced trees, they control and indeed limit the amount of skewness in any subtree. The overhead performed in maintaining the state of near balance is a worthwhile cure for the binary tree's imbalance problem.

Nodes of AVL-Trees have an additional field to keep track of the state of balance in their left and right subtrees. Three states exists: balance, left tilt, and right tilt. This may be represented by integers in the range of [-1..1] or by using an enumerated data type, such as (left, balance, right).

Inserting a new node in an AVL-Tree starts out in a manner similar to binary trees. The new node is compared with the AVL-Tree nodes until it finds the appropriate leaf node to link up with. The path created by the AVL-Tree

---

Figure 10.2. Typical AVL-Tree with pointers and balance indicators.

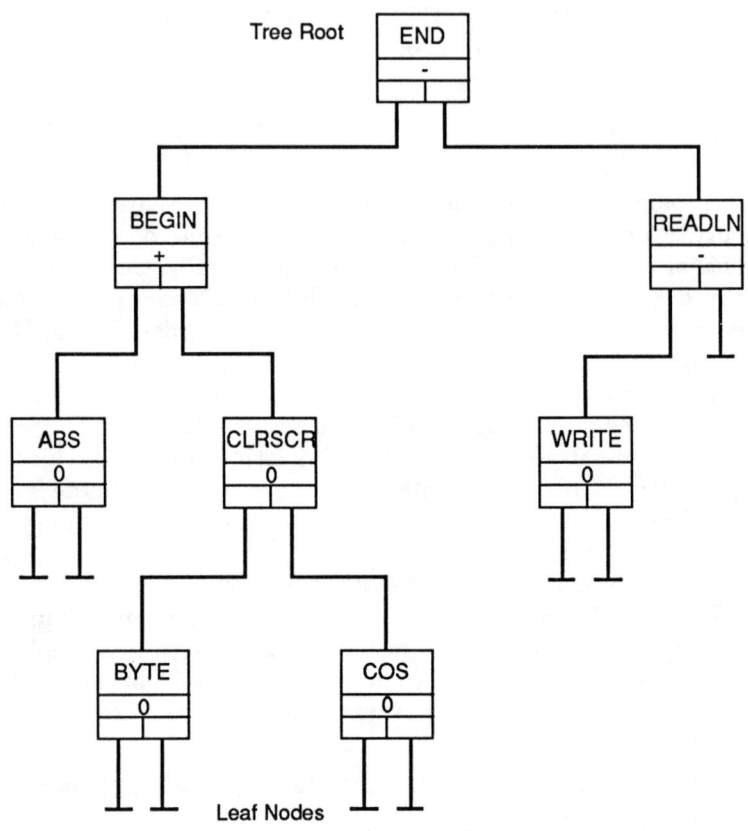

nodes compared with the new node is called the search path. After the new node is inserted, the AVL-Tree algorithms backtracks on the search path to find the closest AVL-Tree node with a left or right tilt status. The sought node is called the pivot node. There are three possible outcomes:

1. No pivot node is found, because every node on the search path has a balanced status assigned to it. This simple case is tackled by adjusting the balance status of the AVL-Tree nodes on the search path. The inserted node is assigned a balanced status which applies to nodes with either truly balanced subtrees or newly inserted leaf nodes.

2. A pivot node is found and the subtree to which the new node is added is the shorter one. This type of node insertion spontaneously serves to add more balance to the AVL-Tree. The balance status for each node on the search path is balanced, beginning with the pivot node.

3. A pivot node is found and the subtree to which the new node is added is the longer one. The status quo of the extended subtree now violates the basic rules for AVL-Trees. Either a single or double rotation is performed to restore the balance (or near- balance) of the AVL-Tree.

LIBRARY AVLTREE.PAS

I wrote a separate library to implement data structures and routines for the AVL-Tree (see Listing 10.2). The library is very similar to the BINTREE.PAS, except you do not need separate routines to rebalance the AVL-Tree. The AVLTREE.PAS library exports the following constants and data types:

```
CONST MAX_TREE_NODES = 100;
TYPE AVLTreeStr = STRING[40];
     BalanceSet = (left_tilt, neutral, right_tilt);
     AVLDataRec = RECORD
         Key : AVLTreeStr;
         { ***** put other fields here ****** }
     END;
     AVLPtr = ^AVL_Tree_Rec;
     AVL_Tree_Rec = RECORD
         TreeData : AVLDataRec;
         Balance  : BalanceSet;
         Left, Right : AVLPtr;
     END;

     TreeRecArray = ARRAY [1..MAX_TREE_NODES] OF AVLDataRec;
```

Notice that I am declaring the enumerated type **BalanceSet** to monitor the tilt in each AVL subtree. The **AVL_Tree_Rec** is composed of four basic fields: the data stored by an AVL-Tree node, the status of balance for the attached subtrees, and the left and right node pointers. The **AVLDataRec** is the record structure that contains at least the key field that enables the AVL-Tree nodes to be placed in order. When you customize the AVLTREE.PAS library you insert new fields or modify the record itself. The array of tree records serves the same purpose as with the BINTREE.PAS: to copy the nodes of the AVL-Tree onto an ordered array.

The routines of the AVLTREE.PAS library are as follows:

```
PROCEDURE Insert_AVLTree(VAR Root : AVLPtr;    { in/out }
                             X    : AVLDataRec { input });
```

inserts a new node into the AVL-Tree and maintains the status of near-balance in the AVL-Tree. While the declaration and use of this routine look very similar to that of the binary tree implementation, the similarity ends there. The code for the AVL-Tree version is more involved?: it invokes the routines **rotate_left** and

rotate_right that are local to the implementation section. These routines monitor the balance of the AVL-Tree.

```
FUNCTION Search_AVLTree(
            VAR Root           : AVLPtr;       { input }
                X              : AVLDataRec;   { input }
                Occurrence_Num : WORD          { input }) : WORD;
```

searches for a certain occurrence number of a given key in the AVL-Tree. The function returns one of the following values:

1. A zero if key **X** is not found in the AVL-Tree.

2. The value of **Occurrence_Num** if **X** is present in the tree that many times.

3. A positive value less than **Occurrence_Num** reports the actual count of **X** in the AVL-Tree.

This function assumes that duplicate keys are allowed in the tree. If the library implementation (or any of its customized versions) is edited to guard against duplicate keys, the argument for **Occurrence_Num** should always be one.

```
PROCEDURE AVLSort_to_Array(VAR Root  : AVLPtr;        { input  }
                           VAR SortX : TreeRecArray;  { output }
                           VAR Count : WORD           { output });
```

Returns the data in the AVL-Tree as a sorted array. If there are more nodes in the AVL-Tree than the storage capacity of the array, the surplus nodes are not included in the array. You can detect this when the returned **Count** parameter exceeds the value of the constant **MAX_TREE_NODES**. The difference between **Count** and **MAX_TREE_NODES** is the number of surplus nodes.

```
FUNCTION Find_AVLNode(VAR Root  : AVLPtr;      { input }
                          X      : AVLDataRec  { input }) : AVLPtr;
```

returns the pointer of a sought AVL-Tree node or the next element if the sought one is not found.

```
PROCEDURE Delete_AVLTree(VAR Root  : AVLPtr;      { in/out }
                             X      : AVLDataRec; { input  }
                         VAR DelOK  : BOOLEAN     { in/out });
```

deletes the key of X if it is present in the AVL-Tree. This routine implements one of the most elaborate basic operations for an AVL-Tree. It uses the routines **balance_left**, **balance_right**, and **delete_both_children** to perform the delicate deletion/rebalancing of an AVL-Tree.

APPLICATION FOR AN AVL-TREE

In the last chapter, I demonstrated the use of the list libraries in implementing an extended version of the internal DOS **dir** command. The application program handled multiple wildcard requests, allowing you, for example, to display your EXE and COM files. The use of an AVL-Tree structure is more appealing than lists in such applications, for two main reasons:

1. The AVL-Tree structure enjoys the efficiency of the insertion sorting characteristics of a binary tree.

2. The AVL-Tree maintains a state of near-balanced tree, making it invulnerable towards processing a set of files previously sorted. Such order can be established by special utilities that arrange the file allocation tables of DOS.

Instead of using the AVLTREE.PAS library in its current form, I will create a customized version AVLDIR.PAS, shown in Listing 10.3. My reasons are the same as they were for creating the customized DIRLIST.PAS library in the last chapter. The customized version only contains the objects required for the directory handling task. There are only two exported routines: **Insert_AVLTree** from the parent library, and the new procedure **Show_Dir** to display the directory.

The changes in the inherited code are as follows:

1. The record structure **AVLDataRec** is equivalent to the record **SearchRec** exported by library DOS. The new key field is field **Name** that stores the complete filename.

2. The customized version of procedure **Insert_AVLTree** guards against duplicate entries. If an attempt is made to insert a duplicate filename, the routine exits without inserting the duplicate.

The procedure **Show_Dir** is a highly specialized version of the AVL-Tree traversal routine. The procedure uses the routines **putnum** and **traverse_tree**. The processes of visiting the AVL-Tree nodes and displaying the directory data are handled internally by **Show_Dir**.

The AVLDIR.PAS library is employed by the application program TDIR.PAS, shown in Listing 10.4. The TDIR program takes up to ten wildcard file specifications. When no arguments are supplied TDIR acts like **dir** *.*. The purpose for TDIR is the collective display of files selected using different wildcards. You can even include subdirectories in the wildcard specifications. Since the routine **Insert_AVLTree** in the AVLTREE.PAS library guards against duplicate entries, TDIR does not display the same filenames selected by various wildcards.

The code for program TDIR.PAS is very short, since the procedure **Show_Dir** in the AVLDIR.PAS library handles the code for displaying the file entries. Figure 10.3 shows the software bus schedule table for the TDIR.PAS program.

The general syntax for using compiled file TDIR.EXE is as follows:

```
> TDIR [<wildcard1> <wildcard2>...<wildcard10>]
```

Figure 10.4 shows a screen image for using TDIR with the "*.EXE *.COM" wildcards on my Turbo Pascal directory.

Figure 10.3. Software bus schedule for application TDIR.PAS.

SOFTWARE BUS SCHEDULE

PROJECT: TDIR.PAS
MODULE DataLib0

	Software Bus Schedule			
A	B	C	D	E

OUTPUT

	A	B	C	D	E
string STRING20	X				

MODULE CRT

	Software Bus Schedule			
A	B	C	D	E

OUTPUT

	A	B	C	D	E
proc ClrScr		X			
boolean DirectVideo		X			
func ReadKey		X			

MODULE DOS

	Software Bus Schedule			
A	B	C	D	E

OUTPUT

	A	B	C	D	E
record DateTime			X		
integer DosError			X		
proc FindNext			X		
proc FindFirst			X		
record SearchRec			X		

MODULE AVLDir

	Software Bus Schedule			
A	B	C	D	E

OUTPUT

	A	B	C	D	E
pointer AVLPtr				X	
proc Insert_AVLTree				X	
proc Show_Dir				X	

```
INTERFACE INPUT
record SearchRec                        X


IMPLEMENTATION INPUT
proc ClrScr                   X
record DateTime                         X
boolean DirectVideo           X
func ReadKey                  X



MODULE main
                                Software Bus Schedule
                      A       B       C       D       E
                      ─────────────────────────────────
INPUT
pointer AVLPtr                                  X
integer DosError                      X
proc FindNext                         X
proc FindFirst                        X
proc Insert_AVLTree                            X
record SearchRec                      X
proc Show_Dir                                  X
string STRING20       X
```

Figure 10.4. Screen image resulting from typing "TDIR *.EXE *.COM" at the DOS prompt.

```
Filename        Size    Date          Time
────────        ────    ────          ────

BINOBJ.EXE      10578   1987/11/02    04:00:00
GREP.COM         5930   1987/11/02    04:00:00
MAKE.EXE        18950   1987/11/02    04:00:00
NONAME.EXE       3392   1987/02/16    04:43:44
TDIR.EXE         9696   1987/12/02    11:55:10
TINST.EXE       63456   1987/11/02    04:00:00
TOUCH.COM        3992   1987/11/02    04:00:00
TPC.EXE         41790   1987/11/02    04:00:00
TPCONFIG.EXE    13670   1987/11/02    04:00:00
TPMAP.EXE       10688   1987/11/02    04:00:00
TPUMOVER.EXE    47232   1987/11/02    04:00:00
TURBO.EXE      115272   1987/11/02    04:00:00
UPGRADE.EXE     42224   1987/11/02    04:00:00

Number of files = 13
```

Listing 10.1 Source code for library BINTREE.PAS.

```
UNIT BinTree;
{==================================================================

          Copyright (c) 1987, 1988   Namir Clement Shammas
     LIBRARY NAME: BinTree
     VERSION: 1.0                                DATE 8/19/1987
     PURPOSE: implements a routine to manipulate binary trees.
     UPDATE HISTORY:

     ============================================================}
{*****************************************************************}
{************************} INTERFACE {****************************}
{*****************************************************************}

{ constant is significant only in rebalancing binary tree }
CONST MAX_TREE_NODES = 100;
TYPE BinTreeStr = STRING[40];
     TreeDataRec = RECORD
         Key : BinTreeStr;
         { ***** put other fields here ****** }
     END;
     TreePtr = ^Binary_Tree_Rec;
     Binary_Tree_Rec = RECORD
         TreeData : TreeDataRec;
         Left, Right : TreePtr;
     END;
     TreeRecArray = ARRAY [1..MAX_TREE_NODES] OF TreeDataRec;
PROCEDURE Insert_BinTree(VAR Root : TreePtr;     { in/out }
                             X    : TreeDataRec { input });

{- - - - - - - - - - - - - - - - - - - - - - - - - - - - - - - -

ROUTINE PURPOSE: inserts new data item X in the binary tree with root
node Root.
PARAMETERS:
   INPUT: X - data item inserted in the binary tree.
   IN/OUT: Root - pointer to the root of the binary tree.
COMMENTS: This routine is recursive.

- - - - - - - - - - - - - - - - - - - - - - - - - - - - - - - - }
FUNCTION Search_BinTree(
          VAR Root         : TreePtr;     { in/out }
              X            : TreeDataRec; { input  }
              Occurrence_Num : WORD       { input }) : WORD;
{- - - - - - - - - - - - - - - - - - - - - - - - - - - - - - - -

ROUTINE PURPOSE: searches for a certain occurrence number of key
X in the binary tree. This is based on the assumption that the
binary tree allows for duplicate keys.
```

PARAMETERS:
    INPUT: X — data item sought in the binary tree.
          Occurrence_Num — the n'th occurrence of a key.
    IN/OUT: Root — pointer to the root of the binary tree.
FUNCTION VALUE: returns one of the following values:
+ A zero if key X is not found in the binary tree.
+ The value of Occurrence_Num if X is present in the tree that
    many times.
+ A positive value less than Occurrence_Num reports the actual
    count of X in the binary tree.

- }
PROCEDURE Sort_to_Array(VAR Root   : TreePtr;   { input }
                        VAR SortX : TreeRecArray; { output }
                        VAR Count : WORD   { output });
{- -

ROUTINE PURPOSE: returns the data in the tree in a sorted array.
PARAMETERS:
    INPUT: Root — pointer to the root of the binary tree.
    OUTPUT: SortX — array of sorted data elements.
            Count — the number of elements in SortX.

                        ROUTINE DEPENDENCIES

        Identifier Name   Identifier Type   Source Library
        ---------------   ---------------   --------------

        traverse_tree   procedure   local nested

- }
FUNCTION Delete_BinTree(
            VAR Root : TreePtr;   { in/out }
                X   : TreeDataRec { input }
                Occur : WORD   { input }) : BOOLEAN;
{- -

ROUTINE PURPOSE: deletes the key X if present in the binary tree.
The occurrence number is also specified.
PARAMETERS:
    INPUT: X — data sought for deletion.
          Occur — the specified occurrence of X.
    IN/OUT: Root — pointer to the root of the binary tree.
FUNCTION VALUE: if the data is located in a node it is deleted,
and the function returns a TRUE value. Otherwise a FALSE value
is returned.

- }
FUNCTION Remove_Tree(VAR Root : TreePtr { input }) : BOOLEAN;
{- -

ROUTINE PURPOSE: recursive logical function used to remove a tree.
PARAMETERS:
    INPUT: Root — pointer to the root of the binary tree.

FUNCTION VALUE: the value returned by the function is of little
meaning. It is most useful during the recursive calls.

```
- - - - - - - - - - - - - - - - - - - - - - - - - - - - - - - - - }
PROCEDURE Rebalance_Tree(VAR Root  : TreePtr { in/out });

{- - - - - - - - - - - - - - - - - - - - - - - - - - - - - - - - -
ROUTINE PURPOSE: routine to balance the binary tree. The binary tree
is copied onto a sorted array, its nodes deleted, and then the data
in the sorted array is appropriately inserted in a new binary tree.
PARAMETERS:
  IN/OUT: Root - pointer to the root of the binary tree.
```

                          ROUTINE DEPENDENCIES

Identifier Name	Identifier Type	Source Library
Rebalance	procedure	local
Sort_to_Array	procedure	local

```
- - - - - - - - - - - - - - - - - - - - - - - - - - - - - - - - }
{****************************************************************}
{***********************} IMPLEMENTATION {***********************}
{****************************************************************}

{-------------------------------------------- Insert_BinTree ------}
PROCEDURE Insert_BinTree(VAR Root : TreePtr;    { in/out }
                             X     : TreeDataRec { input });
BEGIN
    IF Root <> NIL THEN
{ The following code may be uncommented to enable this routine
  to avoid inserting duplicate keys.                          }
{*************************************************************
      IF X.Key = Root^.TreeData.Key THEN EXIT;
*************************************************************}
      { recursive insertion calls to either left or right branches }
      IF X.Key > Root^.TreeData.Key
          THEN Insert_BinTree(Root^.Right, X)
          ELSE Insert_BinTree(Root^.Left, X)
    ELSE BEGIN { insert new node }
      NEW(Root); { create a new tree leaf node }
      { assign key value and other possible fields }
      Root^.TreeData := X;
      Root^.Left  := NIL;
      Root^.Right := NIL;
    END; { IF }
END; { Insert_BinTree }

{-------------------------------------------- Search_BinTree ------}
FUNCTION Search_BinTree(
          VAR Root       : TreePtr;      { in/out }
              X          : TreeDataRec;  { input  }
              Occurrence_Num : WORD      { input }) : WORD;

VAR count : WORD;
```

```
BEGIN
    count := 0; { initialize count for actual occurance of X }
    WHILE (Root <> NIL) AND (count < Occurrence_Num) DO
      IF X.Key > Root^.TreeData.Key THEN Root := Root^.Right
      ELSE IF X.Key < Root^.TreeData.Key THEN Root := Root^.Left
      ELSE BEGIN { match is found }
          INC(count);
          Root := Root^.Left
      END; { IF }
    Search_BinTree := count { return result }
END; { Search_BinTree }

{--------------------------------------------------- traverse_tree ------}
PROCEDURE traverse_tree(VAR Root  : TreePtr;      { input }
                        VAR SortX : TreeRecArray; { output }
                        VAR Count : WORD          { output });

{- - - - - - - - - - - - - - - - - - - - - - - - - - - - - - - - - - -
SCOPE: Local.

ROUTINE PURPOSE: local recursive procedure used to traverse the
binary tree.
PARAMETERS:
  INPUT: Root - pointer to the root of the binary tree.
  OUTPUT: SortX - array of sorted data elements.
          Count - number of elements in SortX.

- - - - - - - - - - - - - - - - - - - - - - - - - - - - - - - - - - - }
BEGIN
    IF Root <> NIL THEN BEGIN
        traverse_tree(Root^.Left, SortX, Count);
        INC(Count);
        IF Count <= MAX_TREE_NODES THEN
            SortX[Count].Key := Root^.TreeData.Key;
        traverse_tree(Root^.Right, SortX, Count);
    END;
END; { traverse_tree }

{--------------------------------------------------- Sort_to_Array ------}
PROCEDURE Sort_to_Array(VAR Root  : TreePtr;      { input  }
                        VAR SortX : TreeRecArray; { output }
                        VAR Count : WORD          { output });
BEGIN
    { initialize the number of array members }
    Count := 0; { initialize the number of array members }
    { initiate the recursive traveral procedure }
    traverse_tree(Root, SortX, Count);
END; { Sort_to_Array }

{--------------------------------------------------------- find_node ------}
FUNCTION find_node(VAR Root : TreePtr;     { input }
                       X    : TreeDataRec; { input }
                       Occur : WORD        { input }) : TreePtr;
```

```
{- - - - - - - - - - - - - - - - - - - - - - - - - - - - - - - - -
SCOPE: Local.

ROUTINE PURPOSE: attempts to find the pointer to the node with a
certain key element, occurring a specified number of times.
PARAMETERS:
  INPUT: Root - pointer to the root of the binary tree.
         X - sought data item.
         Occur - the specified occurrence of X.
FUNCTION VALUE: returns the pointer to the node with matching X
and at the sought occurrence. If this fails, a NIL pointer is
returned.

- - - - - - - - - - - - - - - - - - - - - - - - - - - - - - - - - }
VAR no_match : BOOLEAN;
BEGIN
    no_match := TRUE;
    WHILE (Root <> NIL) AND no_match DO
      IF X.Key > Root^.TreeData.Key THEN Root := Root^.Right
      ELSE IF X.Key < Root^.TreeData.Key THEN Root := Root^.Left
      ELSE BEGIN
             DEC(Occur);
             IF Occur = 0 THEN no_match := FALSE
                          ELSE Root := Root^.Left;
      END; { IF }
    find_node := Root;
END; { find_node }

{----------------------------------------------- Delete_BinTree ------}
FUNCTION Delete_BinTree(
            VAR Root : TreePtr;     { in/out }
                X    : TreeDataRec { input  }
                Occur : WORD       { input  }) : BOOLEAN;
VAR found : BOOLEAN;
    copy_root : TreePtr;
BEGIN
    { search for X appearing Occur number of
      times in the binary tree.              }
    found := find_node(Root, X, Occur) <> NIL;
IF found THEN
        IF Root^.Right = NIL THEN BEGIN
            copy_root := Root;
            Root := Root^.Left;
            DISPOSE(copy_root)
        END
        ELSE IF Root^.Left = NIL THEN BEGIN
            copy_root := Root;
            Root := Root^.Right;
            DISPOSE(copy_root)
        END
        ELSE BEGIN
            copy_root := Root^.Left;
```

```
              WHILE copy_root^.Right <> NIL DO
                  copy_root := copy_root^.Right;
              copy_root^.Right := Root^.Right;
              copy_root := Root;
              Root := Root^.Left;
              DISPOSE(copy_root);
          END; { IF }
      Delete_BinTree := found { return function result }
END; { Delete_BinTree }

{-------------------------------------------------- Remove_Tree ------}
FUNCTION Remove_Tree(VAR Root : TreePtr { input  }) : BOOLEAN;
VAR delete_this_node : BOOLEAN;
BEGIN
      delete_this_node := FALSE;
      IF (Root^.Left = NIL) AND (Root^.Right = NIL)
        THEN delete_this_node := TRUE { remove leaf node with no links }
        ELSE BEGIN
          IF Root^.Left <> NIL THEN { has left branch }
              IF Remove_Tree(Root^.Left) THEN BEGIN
                  Dispose(Root^.Left);
                  Root^.Left := NIL
              END; { IF }
          IF Root^.Right <> NIL THEN { has right branch }
              IF Remove_Tree(Root^.Right) THEN BEGIN
                  Dispose(Root^.Right);
                  Root^.Right := NIL
              END; { IF }
          IF (Root^.Left = NIL) AND (Root^.Right = NIL) THEN
              delete_this_node := TRUE;
      END; { IF }
      Remove_Tree := delete_this_node;
END; { Remove_Tree }

{-------------------------------------------------- rebalance ------}
PROCEDURE rebalance(VAR Root    : TreePtr;        { input  }
                    VAR SortX  : TreeRecArray; { input  }
                        First,                  { input  }
                        Last,                   { input  }
                        Median : WORD           { input  });

{- - - - - - - - - - - - - - - - - - - - - - - - - - - - - - - - - - - -
SCOPE : Local recursive.
ROUTINE PURPOSE: recursive local routine to rebalance the binary
tree using a sorted array.
PARAMETERS:
  INPUT: Root - pointer to the root of the binary tree.
         SortX - array of sorted tree node elements.
         First, Last, Median - indices of the array used
             in building a rebalanced tree.

- - - - - - - - - - - - - - - - - - - - - - - - - - - - - - - - - - - - }
```

```
VAR left_median,
    right_median : WORD;
BEGIN
    IF Root = NIL THEN BEGIN
        NEW(Root);
        Root^.TreeData  := SortX[Median];
        Root^.Left  := NIL;
        Root^.Right := NIL;
    END; { IF }
    IF First < Last THEN BEGIN
        IF First <= (Median-1) THEN BEGIN
            left_median := (First + Median - 1) div 2;
            rebalance(Root^.Left, SortX, First, Median-1, left_median)
        END; { IF }
        IF (Median+1) <= Last THEN BEGIN
            right_median := (Median + 1 + Last) div 2;
            rebalance(Root^.Right, SortX, Median+1, Last, right_median)
        END; { IF }
    END; { IF First < Last }
END; { rebalance }

{-------------------------------------------------- Rebalance_Tree ---------}
PROCEDURE Rebalance_Tree(VAR Root  : TreePtr { in/out  });
VAR  sortx  : TreeRecArray;
     count  : WORD;
BEGIN
    { obtain sorted array }
    Sort_to_Array(Root, sortx, count);
    { delete binary tree }
    IF Remove_Tree(Root) THEN Dispose(Root); { remove root node }
    { rebalance the binary tree }
    rebalance(Root, sortx, 1, count, (1 + count) div 2);
END; { Rebalance_Tree }
END.
```

Listing 10.2. Source code for library AVLTREE.PAS.

```
UNIT AVLTree;
{=====================================================================

        Copyright (c) 1987, 1988   Namir Clement Shammas
    LIBRARY NAME: AVLTree
    VERSION: 1.0                            DATE 8/20/1987
    PURPOSE: implements a structure and routines to manipulate the
             well-balanced AVL-tree.
    UPDATE HISTORY:


=====================================================================}


{*********************************************************************}
{************************} INTERFACE {*******************************}
{*********************************************************************}
```

```
{ constant significant only if an ordered array
  of the AVL-tree nodes is desired.               }
CONST MAX_TREE_NODES = 100;
TYPE AVLTreeStr = STRING[40];
     BalanceSet = (left_tilt, neutral, right_tilt);
     AVLDataRec = RECORD
          Key : AVLTreeStr;
          { ***** put other fields here ****** }
     END;
     AVLPtr = ^AVL_Tree_Rec;
     AVL_Tree_Rec = RECORD
          TreeData : AVLDataRec;
          Balance  : BalanceSet;
          Left, Right : AVLPtr;
     END;
     TreeRecArray = ARRAY [1..MAX_TREE_NODES] OF AVLDataRec;

PROCEDURE Insert_AVLTree(VAR Root : AVLPtr;     { in/out }
                             X    : AVLDataRec { input  });
{- - - - - - - - - - - - - - - - - - - - - - - - - - - - - - - - -

ROUTINE PURPOSE: inserts a datum into the AVL-Tree.
PARAMETERS:
  INPUT: X - data item inserted in the AVL-tree.
  IN/OUT: Root - pointer to the root of the AVL-tree.
                    ROUTINE DEPENDENCIES
                    --------------------

          Identifier Name          Identifier Type        Source Library
          ---------------          ---------------        --------------
          insert_AVL                  procedure               local

- - - - - - - - - - - - - - - - - - - - - - - - - - - - - - - - - - }
FUNCTION Search_AVLTree(
          VAR Root         : AVLPtr;      { input }
              X            : AVLDataRec; { input }
              Occurrence_Num : WORD        { input }) : WORD;
{- - - - - - - - - - - - - - - - - - - - - - - - - - - - - - - - -
```

ROUTINE PURPOSE: searches for a certain occurrence number of key X
in the AVL-Tree. The function returns one of the following values:
+ A zero if key X is not found in the AVL-tree.
+ The value of Occurrence_Num if X is present in the tree that
  many times.
+ A positive value less than Occurrence_Num reports the actual
  count of X in the AVL-tree.
This function assumes that duplicate keys are allowed in the tree.
PARAMETERS:
  INPUT: Root - pointer to the root of the AVL-Tree being searched.
         X - key for the sought element.
         Occurrence_Num - occurrence number for the sought element.
FUNCTION VALUE: returns the highest occurrence number
(<= Occurrence_Num) encountered. A zero indicates that the
sought key has no match in the tree. A successful search should
return the value Occurrence_Num.

```
- - - - - - - - - - - - - - - - - - - - - - - - - - - - - - - }
PROCEDURE AVLSort_to_Array(VAR Root   : AVLPtr;        { input }
                           VAR SortX  : TreeRecArray; { output }
                           VAR Count  : WORD          { output });
{- - - - - - - - - - - - - - - - - - - - - - - - - - - - - -
```

ROUTINE PURPOSE: returns the data in the AVL-tree as a sorted array.
PARAMETERS:
  INPUT: Root - pointer to the root of the AVL-tree.
  OUTPUT: SortX - sorted array of AVL tree nodes.
          Count - number of elements in array SortX.

```
- - - - - - - - - - - - - - - - - - - - - - - - - - - - - - }
FUNCTION Find_AVLNode(VAR Root  : AVLPtr;     { input }
                          X      : AVLDataRec { input }) : AVLPtr;
{- - - - - - - - - - - - - - - - - - - - - - - - - - - - - -
```

ROUTINE PURPOSE: returns the pointer of a sought AVL-tree node OR
the next element if the sought one is not found.
PARAMETERS:
  INPUT: Root - pointer to the root of the AVL-tree.
         X - sought node.
FUNCTION VALUE: returns the pointer to the matching element (if found),
or the one after it if not found.

```
- - - - - - - - - - - - - - - - - - - - - - - - - - - - - - }
PROCEDURE Delete_AVLTree(VAR Root  : AVLPtr;    { in/out }
                             X      : AVLDataRec; { input  }
                         VAR DelOK  : BOOLEAN     { in/out });
{- - - - - - - - - - - - - - - - - - - - - - - - - - - - - -
```

ROUTINE PURPOSE: deletes the key of X if it is present in the AVL-Tree.
PARAMETERS:
  INPUT: X - key to a node that is a candidate for deletion.
  OUTPUT: DelOK - flag signals whether or not deletion was carried out.
  IN/OUT: Root - pointer to the root of the AVL-Tree.

                        ROUTINE DEPENDENCIES

Identifier Name	Identifier Type	Source Library
delete_AVL	procedure	local

```
- - - - - - - - - - - - - - - - - - - - - - - - - - - - - - }

{*********************************************************************}
{***********************} IMPLEMENTATION {***************************}
{*********************************************************************}

{————————————— rotate_right ———}

PROCEDURE rotate_right(VAR Root : AVLPtr { in/out });
{- - - - - - - - - - - - - - - - - - - - - - - - - - - - - -
```

```
SCOPE : Local.
ROUTINE PURPOSE: rearranges the tree nodes by rotating them to the
right.
PARAMETERS:
  IN/OUT: Root - pointer to the root of the AVL-tree.

- - - - - - - - - - - - - - - - - - - - - - - - - - - - - - - - - - }

VAR ptr2, ptr3 : AVLPtr;
BEGIN
    ptr2 := Root^.Right;
    IF ptr2^.Balance = right_tilt THEN BEGIN { rotate once }
        Root^.Right := ptr2^.Left;
        ptr2^.Left := Root;
        Root^.Balance := neutral;
        Root := ptr2
    END
    ELSE BEGIN { rotate twice }
        ptr3 := ptr2^.Left;
        ptr2^.Left := ptr3^.Right;
        ptr3^.Right := ptr2;
        Root^.Right := ptr3^.Left;
        ptr3^.Left := Root;
        IF ptr3^.Balance = left_tilt
            THEN ptr2^.Balance := right_tilt
            ELSE ptr2^.Balance := neutral;
        IF ptr3^.Balance = right_tilt
            THEN Root^.Balance := left_tilt
            ELSE Root^.Balance := neutral;
        Root := ptr3
    END; { IF }
    Root^.Balance := neutral
END; { rotate_right }

{-------------------------------------------------- rotate_left ------}

PROCEDURE rotate_left(VAR Root : AVLPtr { in/out });
{- - - - - - - - - - - - - - - - - - - - - - - - - - - - - - - - - -

SCOPE : Local.
ROUTINE PURPOSE: rearranges the tree nodes by rotating them to the
left.
PARAMETERS:
  IN/OUT: Root - pointer to the root of the AVL-tree.

- - - - - - - - - - - - - - - - - - - - - - - - - - - - - - - - - - }
VAR ptr2, ptr3 : AVLPtr;
BEGIN
    ptr2 := Root^.Left;
    IF ptr2^.Balance = left_tilt THEN BEGIN { rotate once }
        Root^.Left := ptr2^.Right;
        ptr2^.Right := Root;
        Root^.Balance := neutral;
```

```
            Root := ptr2
        END
        ELSE BEGIN { rotate twice }
            ptr3 := ptr2^.Right;
            ptr2^.Right := ptr3^.Left;
            ptr3^.Left := ptr2;
            Root^.Left := ptr3^.Right;
            ptr3^.Right := Root;
            IF ptr3^.Balance = right_tilt
                THEN ptr2^.Balance := left_tilt
                ELSE ptr2^.Balance := neutral;
            IF ptr3^.Balance = left_tilt
                THEN Root^.Balance := right_tilt
                ELSE Root^.Balance := neutral;
            Root := ptr3
        END; { IF }
        Root^.Balance := neutral
END; { rotate_left }


{-------------------------------------------------- insert_AVL ------}

PROCEDURE insert_AVL(VAR Root       : AVLPtr;      { in/out }
                         X          : AVLDataRec; { input  }
                     VAR InsertedOK : BOOLEAN      { in/out });
{- - - - - - - - - - - - - - - - - - - - - - - - - - - - - - - - - -

SCOPE : Local recursive.
ROUTINE PURPOSE: workhorse recursive routine to perform node insertion
in an AVL-Tree.
PARAMETERS:
  INPUT: X - data item inserted in the AVL-tree.
  IN/OUT: Root - pointer to the root of the AVL-tree.
          InsertedOK - flag used to signal whether or not the
             insertion was done.


- - - - - - - - - - - - - - - - - - - - - - - - - - - - - - - - - - }


BEGIN
    IF Root = NIL THEN BEGIN
        NEW(Root); { create new memory space }
        WITH Root^ DO BEGIN
            TreeData := X;
            Left := NIL;
            Right := NIL;
            Balance := neutral
        END;
        InsertedOK := TRUE
    END
{ The following commented ELSE IF clause is used to guard
  against duplicate keys. Uncomment to use it. }
{************************************************************
    ELSE IF X.Key = Root^.TreeData.Key THEN BEGIN
```

```
            InsertedOK := FALSE;
            EXIT
      END
************************************************************}
      ELSE IF X.Key <= Root^.TreeData.Key THEN BEGIN
              insert_AVL(Root^.Left, X, InsertedOK);
              IF InsertedOK THEN
                  CASE Root^.Balance OF
                      left_tilt  : BEGIN
                                        rotate_left(Root);
                                        InsertedOK := FALSE
                                   END;
                      neutral    : Root^.Balance := left_tilt;
                      right_tilt : BEGIN
                                        Root^.Balance := neutral;
                                        InsertedOK := FALSE
                                   END;
                  END; { CASE }
          END
          ELSE BEGIN
              insert_AVL(Root^.Right, X, InsertedOK);
              IF InsertedOK THEN
                  CASE Root^.Balance OF
                      left_tilt  : BEGIN
                                        Root^.Balance := neutral;
                                        InsertedOK := FALSE
                                   END;
                      neutral    : Root^.Balance := right_tilt;
                      right_tilt : BEGIN
                                        rotate_right(Root);
                                        InsertedOK := FALSE
                                   END;
                  END; { CASE }
          END; { IF }
END; { insert_AVL }

{--------------------------------------------------- Insert_AVLTree ———}

PROCEDURE Insert_AVLTree(VAR Root : AVLPtr;     { in/out }
                             X    : AVLDataRec { input });

VAR inserted_ok : BOOLEAN;
BEGIN
    inserted_ok := FALSE;
    insert_AVL(Root, X, inserted_ok)
END; { Insert_AVLTree }

{--------------------------------------------------- Search_AVLTree ———}

FUNCTION Search_AVLTree(
            VAR Root         : AVLPtr;      { input }
                X            : AVLDataRec;  { input }
                Occurrence_Num : WORD        { input }) : WORD;
VAR count : WORD;
```

```
BEGIN
    count := 0; { initialize count for actual occurance of X }
    WHILE (Root <> NIL) AND (count < Occurrence_Num) DO
      IF X.Key > Root^.TreeData.Key THEN Root := Root^.Right
      ELSE IF X.Key < Root^.TreeData.Key THEN Root := Root^.Left
      ELSE BEGIN { match is found }
          INC(count);
          Root := Root^.Left
      END; { IF }
      Search_AVLTree := count { return result }
END; { Search_AVLTree }

{-------------------------------------------------- traverse_tree ----}

PROCEDURE traverse_tree(VAR Root  : AVLPtr;        { input }
                        VAR SortX : TreeRecArray; { output }
                        VAR Count : WORD          { output });
{- - - - - - - - - - - - - - - - - - - - - - - - - - - - - - - - - -
```

SCOPE : Local Recursive.
ROUTINE PURPOSE: local recursive routine used to traverse the AVL-tree.
PARAMETERS:
  INPUT: Root - pointer to the root of the AVL-tree.
  OUTPUT: SortX - sorted array of AVL tree nodes.
          Count - number of elements in array SortX.

```
- - - - - - - - - - - - - - - - - - - - - - - - - - - - - - - - - - }
BEGIN
    IF Root <> NIL THEN BEGIN
        traverse_tree(Root^.Left, SortX, Count);
        INC(Count);
        IF Count <= MAX_TREE_NODES THEN
            SortX[Count].Key := Root^.TreeData.Key;
        traverse_tree(Root^.Right, SortX, Count);
    END;
END; { traverse_tree }

{---------------------------------------------- AVLSort_to_Array ----}
PROCEDURE AVLSort_to_Array(VAR Root  : AVLPtr;        { input }
                          VAR SortX : TreeRecArray; { output }
                          VAR Count : WORD          { output });
BEGIN
    { initialize the number of array members }
    Count := 0; { initialize the number of array members }
    { initiate the recursive traveral procedure }
    traverse_tree(Root, SortX, Count);
END; { AVLSort_to_Array }

{---------------------------------------------------- Find_AVLNode ----}
FUNCTION Find_AVLNode;
VAR no_match : BOOLEAN;
BEGIN
    no_match := TRUE;
```

```
        WHILE (Root <> NIL) AND no_match DO
          IF X.Key > Root^.TreeData.Key THEN Root := Root^.Right
          ELSE IF X.Key < Root^.TreeData.Key THEN Root := Root^.Left
          ELSE no_match := FALSE;
        Find_AVLNode := Root;
END; { Find_AVLNode }

{--------------------------------------------------- balance_right ------}
PROCEDURE balance_right(VAR Root  : AVLPtr; { in/out }
                        VAR DelOK : BOOLEAN { in/out });
{- - - - - - - - - - - - - - - - - - - - - - - - - - - - - - - - - - - -
SCOPE: Local.

ROUTINE PURPOSE: restores the balanced or near-balanced state of an
AVL-Tree by rebalancing a right subtree.
PARAMETERS:
  IN/OUT: Root - pointer to the root of the AVL subtree.
          DelOK - boolean flag used in verifying the deletion.

- - - - - - - - - - - - - - - - - - - - - - - - - - - - - - - - - - - - }
VAR ptr2, ptr3 : AVLPtr;
    balnc2, balnc3 : BalanceSet;
BEGIN
    CASE Root^.Balance OF
        left_tilt  : Root^.Balance := neutral;
        neutral    : BEGIN
                        Root^.Balance := right_tilt;
                        DelOK := FALSE
                     END;
        right_tilt : BEGIN
                        ptr2 := Root^.Right;
                        balnc2 := ptr2^.Balance;
                        IF NOT (balnc2 = left_tilt) THEN BEGIN
                          Root^.Right := ptr2^.Left;
                          ptr2^.Left := Root;
                          IF balnc2 = neutral THEN BEGIN
                              Root^.Balance := right_tilt;
                              ptr2^.Balance := left_tilt;
                              DelOK := FALSE
                          END
                          ELSE BEGIN
                              Root^.Balance := neutral;
                              ptr2^.Balance := neutral;
                          END; { IF }
                          Root := ptr2
                        END
                        ELSE BEGIN
                            ptr3 := ptr2^.Left;
                            balnc3 := ptr3^.Balance;
                            ptr2^.Left := ptr3^.Right;
                            ptr3^.Right := ptr2;
                            Root^.Right := ptr3^.Left;
                            ptr3^.Left := Root;
                            IF balnc3 = left_tilt THEN
```

```
                                ptr2^.Balance := right_tilt
                        ELSE
                                ptr2^.Balance := neutral;
                        IF balnc3 = right_tilt THEN
                                Root^.Balance := left_tilt
                        ELSE
                                Root^.Balance := neutral;
                        Root := ptr3;
                        ptr3^.Balance := neutral;
                    END; { IF }
                END;
    END; { CASE }
END; { balance_right }

{--------------------------------------------------- balance_left ------}
PROCEDURE balance_left(VAR Root  : AVLPtr; { in/out }
                       VAR DelOK : BOOLEAN { in/out });
{- - - - - - - - - - - - - - - - - - - - - - - - - - - - - - - - - - - -

SCOPE: Local.
ROUTINE PURPOSE: restores the balanced or near-balanced state of an
AVL-Tree by rebalancing a left subtree.
PARAMETERS:
   IN/OUT: Root - pointer to the root of the AVL subtree.
           DelOK - boolean flag used in verifying the deletion.

- - - - - - - - - - - - - - - - - - - - - - - - - - - - - - - - - - - - }
VAR ptr2, ptr3 : AVLPtr;
    balnc2, balnc3 : BalanceSet;
BEGIN
    CASE Root^.Balance OF
        left_tilt  : Root^.Balance := neutral;
        neutral    : BEGIN
                        Root^.Balance := left_tilt;
                        DelOK := FALSE
                     END;
        right_tilt : BEGIN
                        ptr2 := Root^.Left;
                        balnc2 := ptr2^.Balance;
                        IF NOT (balnc2 = right_tilt) THEN BEGIN
                            Root^.Left := ptr2^.Right;
                            ptr2^.Right := Root;
                            IF balnc2 = neutral THEN BEGIN
                                Root^.Balance := left_tilt;
                                ptr2^.Balance := right_tilt;
                                DelOK := FALSE
                            END
                            ELSE BEGIN
                                Root^.Balance := neutral;
                                ptr2^.Balance := neutral;
                            END; { IF }
                            Root := ptr2
                        END
```

```
                    ELSE BEGIN
                        ptr3 := ptr2^.Right;
                        balnc3 := ptr3^.Balance;
                        ptr2^.Right := ptr3^.Left;
                        ptr3^.Left := ptr2;
                        Root^.Left := ptr3^.Right;
                        ptr3^.Right := Root;
                        IF balnc3 = right_tilt THEN
                            ptr2^.Balance := left_tilt
                        ELSE
                            ptr2^.Balance := neutral;
                        IF balnc3 = left_tilt THEN
                            Root^.Balance := right_tilt
                        ELSE
                            Root^.Balance := neutral;
                        Root := ptr3;
                        ptr3^.Balance := neutral;
                    END; { IF }
                END;
    END; { CASE }
END; { balance_left }

{-------------------------------------- delete_both_children ------}
PROCEDURE delete_both_children(VAR Root,            { in/out }
                                  Ptr   : AVLPtr; { in/out }
                              VAR DelOK : BOOLEAN { in/out });
{- - - - - - - - - - - - - - - - - - - - - - - - - - - - - - - - - -

 SCOPE: Local.
 ROUTINE PURPOSE: routine used to delete a node with two empty subtrees.
 PARAMETERS:
   IN/OUT: Root - pointer to the root of the AVL subtree.
           Ptr - shared pointer.
           DelOK - boolean flag used in verifying the deletion.
                        ROUTINE DEPENDENCIES
                        --------------------
```

Identifier Name	Identifier Type	Source Library
balance_left	procedure	local

```
- - - - - - - - - - - - - - - - - - - - - - - - - - - - - - - - - - }
BEGIN
    IF Ptr^.Right = NIL THEN BEGIN
        Root^.TreeData := Ptr^.TreeData;
        Ptr := Ptr^.Left;
        DelOK := TRUE
    END
    ELSE BEGIN
        delete_both_children(Root, Ptr^.Right, DelOK);
        IF DelOK THEN balance_left(Ptr, DelOK);
    END; { IF }
END; { delete_both_children }
```

```
{————————————— delete_AVL ———}

PROCEDURE delete_AVL(VAR Root  : AVLPtr;      { in/out }
                         X      : AVLDataRec; { input }
                     VAR DelOK  : BOOLEAN     { in/out });
{- - - - - - - - - - - - - - - - - - - - - - - - - - - - - - - -
```

SCOPE: Local Recursive.
ROUTINE PURPOSE: recursive local routine to perform node deletion.
The balance of the AVL-Tree is also monitored and adjusted, if need be.
PARAMETERS:
    INPUT: X - key to a node that is a candidate for deletion.
    OUTPUT: DelOK - flag that signals whether or not deletion was carried
                    out.
    IN/OUT: Root - pointer to the root of the AVL-Tree.

                    ROUTINE DEPENDENCIES

Identifier Name	Identifier Type	Source Library
balance_left	procedure	local
balance_right	procedure	local
delete_both_children	procedure	local

```
- - - - - - - - - - - - - - - - - - - - - - - - - - - - - - - - }
VAR ptr : AVLPtr;
BEGIN
    IF Root = NIL THEN
        DelOK := FALSE
    ELSE
        IF X.Key < Root^.TreeData.Key THEN BEGIN
            delete_AVL(Root^.Left, X, DelOK);
            IF DelOK THEN balance_right(Root, DelOK);
        END
        ELSE
            IF X.Key > Root^.TreeData.Key THEN BEGIN
                delete_AVL(Root^.Right, X, DelOK);
                IF DelOK THEN balance_left(Root, DelOK);
            END
            ELSE BEGIN
                ptr := Root;
                IF Root^.Right = NIL THEN BEGIN
                    Root := Root^.Left;
                    DelOK := TRUE
                END
                ELSE BEGIN
                    delete_both_children(Root, Root^.Left, DelOK);
                    IF DelOK THEN balance_right(Root, DelOK);
                END; { IF }
            END; { IF }
            Dispose(ptr)
END;{ delete_AVL }
```

```
{------------------------------------------------ Delete_AVLTree ------}

PROCEDURE Delete_AVLTree(VAR Root  : AVLPtr;      { input }
                             X      : AVLDataRec; { input }
                         VAR DelOK  : BOOLEAN     { in/out });
BEGIN
    DelOK := FALSE;
    delete_AVL(Root, X, DelOK)
END; { Delete_AVLTree }
END.
```

Listing 10.3. Source code for application library AVLDIR.PAS.

```
UNIT AVLDir;
{=======================================================================

            Copyright (c) 1987, 1988   Namir Clement Shammas
        LIBRARY NAME: AVLDir
        VERSION: 1.0                                DATE 11/30/1987
        PURPOSE: A customized AVL-Tree structure and routines to handle
                 DOS directories.
        UPDATE HISTORY:


========================================================================}

{**********************************************************************}
{*************************} INTERFACE {*******************************}
{**********************************************************************}

Uses CRT, DOS;
TYPE AVLTreeStr = STRING[40];
     BalanceSet = (left_tilt, neutral, right_tilt);
     AVLDataRec = SearchRec; { from unit DOS }
     AVLPtr = ^AVL_Tree_Rec;
     AVL_Tree_Rec = RECORD
         TreeData : AVLDataRec;
         Balance  : BalanceSet;
         Left, Right : AVLPtr;
     END;

PROCEDURE Insert_AVLTree(VAR Root : AVLPtr;      { in/out }
                             X     : AVLDataRec { input });
{- - - - - - - - - - - - - - - - - - - - - - - - - - - - - - - - - - -

ROUTINE PURPOSE: inserts a new directory entry in an AVL-Tree that
stores the set of files.
PARAMETERS:
  INPUT: X - inserted directory entry.
  IN/OUT: Root - pointer to the root of the AVL-Tree storing the
               directory of files.
HANDLING BAD ARGUMENTS: the procedure guards against duplicate
entries.
```

```
                          ROUTINE DEPENDENCIES
                          --------------------

        Identifier Name            Identifier Type       Source Library
        ---------------            ---------------       --------------

        insert_AVL                 procedure             local

- - - - - - - - - - - - - - - - - - - - - - - - - - - - - - - - - - - }
PROCEDURE Show_Dir(VAR Root  : AVLPtr { input });
{- - - - - - - - - - - - - - - - - - - - - - - - - - - - - - - - - - -
```

ROUTINE PURPOSE: routine used to display the directory by visiting
the nodes of the AVL-Tree storing the file entries.
PARAMETERS:
    INPUT: Root - pointer to the root of the AVL-tree.

```
                          ROUTINE DEPENDENCIES
                          --------------------

          Identifier Name          Identifier Type       Source Library
          ---------------          ---------------       --------------

          Count                    word                  local
          ClrScr                   procedure             CRT
          DirectVideo              boolean               CRT
          NumDir                   word                  local
          ReadKey                  function              CRT
          traverse_dir             procedure             local
- - - - - - - - - - - - - - - - - - - - - - - - - - - - - - - - - - }
```

```
{******************************************************************}
{***********************} IMPLEMENTATION {*************************}
{******************************************************************}
```

CONST DIRS_PER_SCREEN = 21;

```
VAR Count, { counts number of lines displayed }
    NumDir { counts number of files } : WORD;
{------------------------------------------------- rotate_right ------}
PROCEDURE rotate_right(VAR Root : AVLPtr { in/out });
{- - - - - - - - - - - - - - - - - - - - - - - - - - - - - - - - - -
```

SCOPE : Local.
ROUTINE PURPOSE: rearranges the tree nodes by rotating them to the
right.
PARAMETERS:
    IN/OUT: Root - pointer to the root of the AVL-tree.

```
- - - - - - - - - - - - - - - - - - - - - - - - - - - - - - - - - - }
VAR ptr2, ptr3 : AVLPtr;
BEGIN
    ptr2 := Root^.Right;
    IF ptr2^.Balance = right_tilt THEN BEGIN { rotate once }
        Root^.Right := ptr2^.Left;
        ptr2^.Left := Root;
        Root^.Balance := neutral;
        Root := ptr2
```

```
      END
      ELSE BEGIN { rotate twice }
          ptr3 := ptr2^.Left;
          ptr2^.Left := ptr3^.Right;
          ptr3^.Right := ptr2;
          Root^.Right := ptr3^.Left;
          ptr3^.Left := Root;
          IF ptr3^.Balance = left_tilt
              THEN ptr2^.Balance := right_tilt
              ELSE ptr2^.Balance := neutral;
          IF ptr3^.Balance = right_tilt
              THEN Root^.Balance := left_tilt
              ELSE Root^.Balance := neutral;
          Root := ptr3
      END; { IF }
      Root^.Balance := neutral
END; { rotate_right }

{------------------------------------------------- rotate_left ------}

PROCEDURE rotate_left(VAR Root : AVLPtr { in/out });
{- - - - - - - - - - - - - - - - - - - - - - - - - - - - - - - - - -

SCOPE : Local.
ROUTINE PURPOSE: rearranges the tree nodes by rotating them to the
left.
PARAMETERS:
  IN/OUT: Root - pointer to the root of the AVL-tree.

- - - - - - - - - - - - - - - - - - - - - - - - - - - - - - - - - - }
VAR ptr2, ptr3 : AVLPtr;
BEGIN
    ptr2 := Root^.Left;
    IF ptr2^.Balance = left_tilt THEN BEGIN { rotate once }
        Root^.Left := ptr2^.Right;
        ptr2^.Right := Root;
        Root^.Balance := neutral;
        Root := ptr2
    END
    ELSE BEGIN { rotate twice }
        ptr3 := ptr2^.Right;
        ptr2^.Right := ptr3^.Left;
        ptr3^.Left := ptr2;
        Root^.Left := ptr3^.Right;
        ptr3^.Right := Root;
        IF ptr3^.Balance = right_tilt
            THEN ptr2^.Balance := left_tilt
            ELSE ptr2^.Balance := neutral;
        IF ptr3^.Balance = left_tilt
            THEN Root^.Balance := right_tilt
            ELSE Root^.Balance := neutral;
        Root := ptr3
```

```
      END; { IF }
      Root^.Balance := neutral
END; { rotate_left }

{----------------------------------------------------- insert_AVL ------}
PROCEDURE insert_AVL(VAR Root      : AVLPtr;     { in/out }
                         X          : AVLDataRec; { input  }
                     VAR InsertedOK : BOOLEAN     { in/out });
{- - - - - - - - - - - - - - - - - - - - - - - - - - - - - - - - - -

SCOPE : Local recursive.
ROUTINE PURPOSE: workhorse recursive routine to perform node insertion
in an AVL-Tree.
PARAMETERS:
  INPUT: X - data item inserted in the AVL-tree.
  IN/OUT: Root - pointer to the root of the AVL-tree.
          InsertedOK - flag used to signal whether or not the
          insertion was done.

- - - - - - - - - - - - - - - - - - - - - - - - - - - - - - - - - - }
BEGIN
    IF Root = NIL THEN BEGIN
        NEW(Root); { create new memory space }
        WITH Root^ DO BEGIN
            TreeData := X;
            Left := NIL;
            Right := NIL;
            Balance := neutral
        END;
        InsertedOK := TRUE
    END
    ELSE IF X.Name = Root^.TreeData.Name THEN BEGIN
        InsertedOK := FALSE;
        EXIT
    END
    ELSE
        IF X.Name < Root^.TreeData.Name THEN BEGIN
            insert_AVL(Root^.Left, X, InsertedOK);
            IF InsertedOK THEN
                CASE Root^.Balance OF
                    left_tilt  : BEGIN
                                     rotate_left(Root);
                                     InsertedOK := FALSE
                                 END;
                    neutral    : Root^.Balance := left_tilt;
                    right_tilt : BEGIN
                                     Root^.Balance := neutral;
                                     InsertedOK := FALSE
                                 END;
                END; { CASE }
        END
        ELSE BEGIN
            insert_AVL(Root^.Right, X, InsertedOK);
```

```
              IF InsertedOK THEN
                  CASE Root^.Balance OF
                      left_tilt  : BEGIN
                                      Root^.Balance := neutral;
                                      InsertedOK := FALSE
                                   END;
                      neutral    : Root^.Balance := right_tilt;
                      right_tilt : BEGIN
                                      rotate_right(Root);
                                      InsertedOK := FALSE
                                   END;
                  END; { CASE }
          END; { IF }

END; { insert_AVL }

{----------------------------------------------- Insert_AVLTree ------}

PROCEDURE Insert_AVLTree(VAR Root : AVLPtr;    { in/out }
                             X    : AVLDataRec { input  });
VAR inserted_ok : BOOLEAN;
BEGIN
    inserted_ok := FALSE;
    insert_AVL(Root, X, inserted_ok)
END; { Insert_AVLTree }

{------------------------------------------------------ putnum ------}

PROCEDURE putnum(Symbol : CHAR; { input  }
                 N      : WORD  { input  });
{- - - - - - - - - - - - - - - - - - - - - - - - - - - - - - - - - -

ROUTINE PURPOSE: displays a character and a number (in the range of
0 to 99).
PARAMETERS:
  INPUT: Symbol - character displayed.
         N - number displayed. IF N < 10, a '0' character is
             displayed before the number itself.
- - - - - - - - - - - - - - - - - - - - - - - - - - - - - - - - - - }

BEGIN
    IF N > 9 THEN WRITE(Symbol, N:2)
            ELSE WRITE(Symbol,'0',N:1);
END;

{---------------------------------------------------- traverse_dir ------}

PROCEDURE traverse_dir(VAR Root : AVLPtr { input  });
{- - - - - - - - - - - - - - - - - - - - - - - - - - - - - - - - - -

SCOPE: Local.
```

ROUTINE PURPOSE: local recursive routine that displays the directory
entries according to the specified wildcards. This routine is
dedicated to the TDIR.PAS utility.
PARAMETERS:
    INPUT: Root - pointer to the root or a node in the AVL-Tree.

                        ROUTINE DEPENDENCIES

         Identifier Name   Identifier Type   Source Library
         ---------------   ---------------   --------------
            Count   word   local
            ClrScr   procedure   CRT
            DateTime   record   DOS
            NumDir   word   local
            putnum   procedure   local
            ReadKey   function   CRT


```
- - - - - - - - - - - - - - - - - - - - - - - - - - - - - - - - - - - }
VAR strlen : BYTE;
    ch : CHAR;
    date_time_var : DateTime;
BEGIN
    IF Root <> NIL THEN BEGIN
        traverse_dir(Root^.Left);
        INC(NumDir);
        strlen := Length(Root^.TreeData.Name);
        WRITE(Root^.TreeData.Name);
        WHILE (strlen <= 12) DO BEGIN
            INC(strlen);
            WRITE(' ');
        END;
        WRITE(Root^.TreeData.Size:7);
        WRITE('  ');
        UnPackTime(Root^.TreeData.Time, date_time_var);
        WITH date_time_var DO BEGIN
            WRITE(Year:4);
            putnum('/',Month);
            putnum('/',Day);
            WRITE('   ');
            putnum(CHR(0),Hour);
            putnum(':',Min);
            putnum(':',Sec);
        END;
        WRITELN;
        INC(Count);
        IF Count >= DIRS_PER_SCREEN THEN BEGIN
            Count := 0;
            WRITELN;
            WRITE('press any key to continue');
            ch := ReadKey;
            IF ch = ^C THEN Halt
                    ELSE ClrScr;
```

```
            WRITELN('  Filename      Size     Date          Time');
            WRITELN('————  ——  ———    ——');
        END;
        traverse_dir(Root^.Right);
    END;
END; { traverse_dir }


{----------------------------------------------------------- Show_Dir —}

PROCEDURE Show_Dir(VAR Root  : AVLPtr { input });
VAR ch : CHAR;
BEGIN
    ClrScr;
    Count := 0;
    NumDir := 0;
    DirectVideo := TRUE;
    WRITELN('  Filename      Size     Date          Time');
    WRITELN('————  ——  ———    ——');
    traverse_dir(Root);
    IF Count >= DIRS_PER_SCREEN THEN BEGIN
        WRITELN;
        WRITE('press any key to continue');
        ch := ReadKey;
    END;
    WRITELN;
    WRITELN('Number of files = ',NumDir)
END;
END.
```

Listing 10.4. Source code for library TDIR.PAS.

```
Program TDir;
{=================================================================


                        PROGRAM TDIR
            Copyright (c) 1988 Namir Clement Shammas
version 1.0                              Date 11/30/87


This program emulates an extended version of the DOS dir.
It is able to accept up to ten different wildcard specifications.
EXAMPLE:
   >TDIR *.PAS *.TPU
displays, in alphabetized order, all .PAS and .TPU files.


The program is smart enough to detect redundant files, such as those
produced by a command similar to:
   >TDIR *.* *.PAS
since *.PAS specification is a subset of *.*


=================================================================}
```

```
{$M 8912, 8912, 200000}
Uses CRT, DOS, DataLib0, AVLDir;
CONST MAX_WILDCARDS = 10;
VAR Root : AVLPtr;
    Dir_Data : SearchRec;
    WildCards : ARRAY [1..MAX_WILDCARDS] OF STRING20;
    Ch : CHAR;
    I, N : WORD;


{- - - - - - - - - - - - - - - - - - - - - - - - - - - - - - - -


                        ROUTINE DEPENDENCIES
                        --------------------

          Identifier Name            Identifier Type      Source Library
          ---------------            ---------------      --------------

            AVLPtr                      pointer            AVLDir
            DosError                    integer            DOS
            FindNext                    procedure          DOS
            FindFirst                   procedure          DOS
            Insert_AVLTree              procedure          AVLDir
            SearchRec                   record             DOS
            Show_Dir                    procedure          AVLDir
            STRING20                    string             DataLib0

- - - - - - - - - - - - - - - - - - - - - - - - - - - - - - - - - - - - }
BEGIN
    N := ParamCount;
    IF N < 1 THEN BEGIN
        WildCards[1] := '*.*';
        N := 1
    END
    ELSE BEGIN
        I := 0;
        WHILE (I < N) AND (I < MAX_WILDCARDS) DO BEGIN
            INC(I);
            WildCards[I] := ParamStr(I);
        END;
        N := I;
    END; { IF }
    Root := NIL; { Initialize root of AVL-tree }
    FOR I := 1 TO N DO BEGIN
        FindFirst(WildCards[I], Archive, Dir_Data);
        WHILE (DosError = 0) DO BEGIN
            Insert_AVLTree(Root, Dir_Data);
            FindNext(Dir_Data)
        END; { WHILE }
    END; { FOR }
    Show_Dir(Root);
END.
```

ARTICLE REFERENCES

Shammas, N. "Sparse Matrices: Byting Off More Than You Can Chew?" *Turbo Tech Report Newsletter*, Vol. 2, No. 2. Redwood City: M&T Publishing, March/April 1987.

Shammas, N. "Virtual Memory: Getting Away with False Addresses." *Turbo Tech Report Newsletter*, Vol. 2, No. 2. Redwood City: M&T Publishing, March/April 1987.

Shammas, N. "Fast Screen Management." *Turbo Tech Report Newsletter*, Vol. 2. No. 3. Redwood City: M&T Publishing, May/June 1987.

Shammas, N. "V.I.P., Clustered Binary Trees and Clustered List Data Structures." *Dr. Dobb's Journal*, No. 131. Redwood City: M&T Publishing, Sept. 1987.

Shammas, N. "Data Hiding and Its Variations." *Dr. Dobb's Journal*, Vol. 12, No. 10. No. 132. Redwood City: M&T Publishing, October 1987.

Shammas, N., "Sorting Large Sequential Text Files," *Turbo, Tech Report Newsletter*, Vol. 2, No. 5. Redwood City: M&T Publishing, Sept./Oct. 1987.

BOOK REFERENCES

Aho, A., J. E. Hopcroft, and J. D. Ullman. *Data Structures and Algorithms*. Reading: Addison-Wesley, 1983.

Amsbury, W. *Data Structures from Arrays to Priority Queues*. Belmont: Wadworth, 1985.

Gineet, G. H. *Handbook of Algorithms and Data Structures*. Reading, : Addison-Wesley, 1984.

Hale, G. J. and R. J. Easton. *Applied Data Structures Using Pascal*. Lexington: D. C. Heath, 1987.

Horowitz, E. and S. Sahni. *Fundamentals of Data Structures in Pascal*. Second Edition. Rockville: Computer Science Press, 1987.

Korsh, J. F. *Data Structures, Algorithms, and Program Style*. Boston: PWS Computer Science, 1986.

Kruse, R. L. *Data Structures and Program Design*. Second Edition. Englewood Cliffs: Prentice Hall, 1987.

Miller, L. H. *Advanced Programming Design and Structure Using Pascal*. Reading: Addison-Wesley, 1986.

Reynolds, C. W. *Program Design and Data Structures in Pascal*. Belmont: Wadworth, 1986.

Sincovec, R. F. and R. S. Wiener. *Data Structures Using Modula-2*. New York: John Wiley, 1986.

Stubbs D. F. and N. W. Webre. *Data Structures with Abstract Data Types and Pascal*. Monterey: Brooks/Cole, 1985.

Tenenbaum, A. M. and M. J. Augenstein. *Data Structures Using Pascal*. Englewood Cliffs: Prentice Hall, 1981.

Wiener, R. S. and R. F. Sincovec. *Software Engineering with Modula-2 and Ada*. New York: John Wiley, 1984.

Wirth, N. *Algorithms + Data Structures = Programs*. Englewood Cliffs: Prentice Hall, 1976.

Index

If you hate typing, read this!

Many programmers dislike typing source code that is already available in electronic form. They find it a complete waste of time to key in listings and spend even more time hunting for typos.

This offer provides you instant access to the code in this book. It enables you to begin utilizing the book's libraries in your own custom programs, or use the sample applications. You may select one of three disk formats made available for your convenience: two 5.25" DSDD, one 5.25" HD, or one 3.5" DSDD disk.

Send your order to:

     Namir C. Shammas
     P.O. Box 1297
     Glen Allen, VA 23060

     Attn: Turbo Pascal Disk Offer

- -

Please send me _____ copies of the TURBO PASCAL DISK. Enclosed is a check or money order for $24.95 (shipping and handling included).

Disk format available:

       5.25" DSDD _____(default choice)

       3.50" DSDD _____(need 3.5" drive)

       5.25" HD   _____ (need AT drive)

Please type or print the information below:

Name _____

Company (for business addresses) _____

Address _____

City _____State _____Zip Code _____

Daytime Phone (_____) _____ - _____